Endorsements

Carolyn Figlioli fully lives out the title of her powerful book: Reckless Love, Crazy Faith. She is a courageous, tenacious woman who lives passionately committed to following Jesus wherever He asks her to go—even to a warzone. Our Iris teams serving in the most desperate places of the world are my biggest heroes. It is my great honor to endorse this book and champion Carolyn, a cherished member of our Iris family. This book shares her inspiring, and at times heart-wrenching, journey in South Sudan where a group of children and youth won her heart forever. She and the children prayed their way through years of living in escalating conflict with violence and ever-present death threats. God used them to transform lives with His supernatural power in prisons, hospitals, villages, refugee camps, and even amongst the army. Their own faith became so deep as Holy Spirit met them with glory-encounters in worship, preserved their lives, and used them to begin to change a nation. I will never forget praying with Carolyn through some of the tensest moments, standing in faith with her for God to make a way for them to get safely to Uganda. God never failed them, and He will never fail you either. As you read, let Father God expand your heart to believe for more glory, power and love in your own story with Him. We can all "stop for the one" with God's love whether it is in a warzone or in our local coffee shop. Ask yourself whose life He is calling you to touch today.

Heidi G. Baker PhD, Co-founder and Chairman Iris Global

Reckless Love, Crazy Faith is a story that lives up to its name. It is a modern day "Moses leading the children out of the wilderness" struggle. Just when you think the path is leading to freedom, there is a curve in the road. As you ride this adventure with Carolyn and the children, you will be on the edge of your seat and after you come to the end of their struggle, you will undoubtedly examine your own faith and wonder if you could have made this journey. I believe their story is so important that it is featured in our television and digital release docudrama series titled Walk With Me. This story is that powerful and that life-changing. It will stay with you long after you put the book down.

Sondra Martin Hicks
Founder and CEO
HeartStone Pictures

Printed in the United States of America
First Printing, 2019
ISBN 978-1-7341010-0-3

Carolyn Figlioli Ministries Publishing
410 Spyglass
McQueeney, TX 78123

www.irisminsudan.org

Although this story is true, all names have been changed to fictitious names in order to protect the identity of the innocent and those who wish not to be known. In no way do the fictitious names hint at the real identity of the characters in this story. The only names that are real are the two opposing leaders of the current civil war in South Sudan.

RECKLESS LOVE CRAZY FAITH

A Miraculous Journey of Faith

C. M. Figlioli

Introduction

As I began to write this story, our story, thinking of a title was the last thing on my mind. It had taken me three years to decide to even write it. I was still trying to process everything that had happened to us and everything we had gone through together. And now that I have decided it was time to tell the story, its unfolding has been likened to a late blooming rose awakening from a long winter's sleep, a slow starter carrying the most beautiful fragrance. I now feel a desperation to get the story out there, to those who need to hear it, to those who are in the struggle of their lives, so that you may be encouraged by our story, to encourage you that nothing really is impossible to those who believe.

Nothing in our lives can prepare us for the impossible. Nothing can prepare you for the doctor's diagnosis that you only have months to live. Nothing can prepare you for the day that you come home and find that your daughter is missing. Nothing can prepare you for the day that soldiers and mortars and war came to your door. How do you work through this? How do you walk this one out? Is God really in it with me? All the way?

I also have a deep desire to tell this story so that my children will never forget their heritage and how their lives were spared through the hand of God. Everyone has a story to tell. Some stories never get told and are soon forgotten after the main character is long dead and forgotten. I need for this story to be kept alive, to bring hope where there is no hope and to remind my children to never take this life for granted.

When the time came to bring a name to this story, I thought about everything we had been through together and I knew that I could not tell the story without the theme of love and faith weaving and binding throughout. My children, my team and I really do have crazy faith. We will believe anything that God tells us and do anything he tells us to do. And I really do have a reckless love for these children who have become such a part of who I am now.

The word "reckless" is defined as heedless of danger or the consequences of one's actions. Remaining in the midst of a war zone for the sake of these children when everyone around us is running to safety might be considered reckless by some. Preaching to an army while being protected by machine guns as I stand in an open field might be considered reckless. Voluntarily bringing food and water to soldiers who have put our very lives in danger is a bit reckless. Even more reckless is doing the same for their enemies. God has poured into me a reckless love for these children and for the Sudanese people whom I am now grafted into and it runs deeper than the underground water which is pumped through our compound borehole.

But, this story really began years ago in the middle of a garbage dump in Mozambique. I visited Iris Ministries in Pemba, Mozambique in 2007. I experienced the power and presence of God in a way I never thought possible. One year later I again traveled to Pemba and I also visited the Iris base in Maputo, Mozambique. My life would never be the same.
I encountered the love of Jesus in such a way that it would forever carve my destiny. I found myself standing in a garbage dump in Maputo, Mozambique. As far as the eye could see there were layers upon layers upon layers of trash, compacted and dozed and piled, year after year.

As I climbed to the top and looked around I was overwhelmed by what I saw and I thought to myself, “What am I doing here? What am I supposed to do with this? I am just one person. What could I possibly offer these people?” There were so many people digging through trash trying to find something to eat amidst columns of smoke which were billowing up across the great expanse. There were large vulture-like birds swooping in and out of the dump. There were also beautiful white birds that glided over the dump as if skimming the waves on the ocean. Up on the surface of the dump the flies were as thick as moths beating a flame and as persistent.

We spent an hour up on top praying for people and somehow found words to encourage them. Toward the end of our visit to the dump I noticed a small crowd of people off to my right who seemed distressed. A bulldozer had been pushing trash around in neat little piles. The people just stood in front of the dozer refusing to let it pass. I asked my interpreter what he thought the problem was. He hesitantly informed me that there was a dead baby buried in the trash! My heart stopped for one beat and my eyes opened wide as if someone had turned off the lights while I desperately needed to see! "We have to do something," I cried!

I practically ran over to the place where the baby was buried and dropped to my knees, digging in the trash, my fingers raking through the slop of someone's dinner, shoving aside wads of cardboard and paper in desperation, when all of a sudden, I saw a tiny foot. I gently removed more filth until I saw the torso, the tiny head, eyes closed, mouth closed as if in sleep. He was so still. I ever so gently wiped his little face, caressing him and wanting him to live.

Silent tears rolled down my face because he was so perfect and his umbilical cord was still attached. He hadn't been dead long as his little body was still supple and he still felt somewhat warm. He was soft and pliable and I remember thinking, "God, what do I do with this? Why are You showing me this?" I didn't know how to even pray. If I prayed for life, what kind of life would he really have?

The people around us began to grow agitated and my interpreter gently informed me that we needed to leave. I stood up, the baby cradled in my arms, as if to take him with me so that I could give him a proper burial at least. My interpreter looked at me sadly, shaking his head and told me that I must leave the baby here. I looked at him in disbelief and sobbed, "I can't do this." He told me that these people would be angry if I took him. I asked him to find me a piece of cloth at least to bury him in if I had to put him back in this horrible place.

The hardest thing I have ever had to do was to put that precious baby back in the trash. My shoulders shook as I sobbed over his little life that was not lived. As I stood up I heard the Lord speak to my spirit, "This is the human condition. Many people come and help but they leave the people right where they found them. I'm calling you to more. If you say yes, if you go for Me, this baby's death will not be in vain. I will give you many children." I stood up and my interpreter, who was a pastor, saw something happening in me and putting his hand upon my heart, he began to pray for me.

As I stood there with tears streaming down my face I said yes to God. I said yes to forever. Little did I know then what forever would look like or what it would cost me.

Chapter One

South Sudan is nestled in the heart of Africa, cradled by Ethiopia, Kenya, Uganda, the Democratic Republic of Congo, and the Central African Republic. On the northern border she is capped by Sudan. This was not always the case. South Sudan gained its independence from Sudan on July 9, 2011 after both nations signed the 2005 Naivasha Agreement, a peace accord, which put an end to the longest-running civil war in the history of Africa. In due course a new nation was born, South Sudan.

Within two years the country was once again thrown into turmoil due to disagreements between the top leaders of this new nation, President Salva Kiir Mayardit and Vice President Riek Machar, both from the Sudanese People's Liberation Movement (SPLM) Party under the leadership of the late John Garang de Mabior.

South Sudan, comprised of ten states in 2011, is one of the most diverse countries in Africa, with over 60 different ethnic groups, the Dinka and Nuer being the two groups involved in the latest clashes, and contained two completely different topographies, one being sub Saharan and the other revealing the lush tropical climate typical of Uganda.

The predominant religions of South Sudan are Christianity and Islam. These religious groups coexist peacefully with no religious clashes occurring at any time, even though one of the reasons for the split from northern Sudan was due to the threat of Sharia law being imposed upon all people. Over the course of the following years of civil war, the Christian Church and the Muslim leadership would work together for peace, united in purpose to see an end to civil war in this new nation.

Our incredible story begins its unfolding with my arrival in Sudan in the fall of 2009. I had never paid attention to Africa or its politics and I really had no idea about the civil war in Sudan. I did read about the Darfur Genocide online and have since learned that there is still a problem in that region.

By the time I arrived in South Sudan the peace treaty was firmly in place with only the formality of signing the papers remaining. The desire of the people to be free from tyranny was no longer a dream. It was a reality. I arrived in Yei in August, directly from the Harvest Missions School in Pemba, Mozambique, where I had completed almost three months of training and ministry. The graduates from this school were encouraged to include a ten to twenty day extended outreach to a nation that we had a heart for. I knew I was called to Sudan and I chose Sudan for my extended outreach.

Two weeks before I completed my training in Mozambique, the leadership approached me and asked me if I would like to lead the small group of two on the outreach. I was tasked to care for the two missionaries who were to travel with me, encourage them throughout our extended outreach and ensure that they boarded the plane back to their respective countries.

The rest of the trip was in the hands of the missionaries on the ground in Sudan. That should have told me that I was already being groomed for leadership. I had been a leader for most of my Naval career and I was also a Navy Reserve Officer Training Corps Instructor at a high school in Texas. I was already leadership material but, the Lord had spoken to me about being a follower first. When I entered in to full-time missions I wasn't aspiring to lead anyone. I just wanted to learn how to follow again, to sit and watch and learn. And now, already I was being put in a leadership position.

As the small twin-engine plane glided over the green vegetation of this vast terrain, interrupted sporadically by dirt trails and narrow compacted dirt roads, I wondered where the cities were. As we approached the city of Yei the outline of a city began to appear. From 2,000 feet the only visible roads were dirt strips with tall, leafy mango trees on either side. From the air, tin roofed single-story block buildings and shanties ran along in orderly rows with intersecting dirt roads forming city blocks.

As we landed amidst mango and palm trees, a herd of goats scattering at the approach of our aircraft on the dirt runway, dust kicking up from the spinning wheels, I saw a beauty here that would become home to me. As soon as my foot touched the red brown dirt I stood in wonder and said to myself, "This is home". This vast land, dotted randomly with mud huts and grass thatch roofs was home.

Within our first week in country we met some of the people from Samaritan's Purse (SP) in Yei, which is an organization that was founded by Franklin Graham. The director of SP was very interested in employing me because I had experience in finance. He approached me right away and asked if I would join SP in Sudan as their finance specialist as they were desperate to fill the position.

He asked me to pray about it even after I told him that I didn't want the position. He insisted that I should at least pray about it. I said I would. I wanted to be with Iris Ministries in Sudan and nowhere else. Two days before our mission trip came to an end this young man again approached me and asked if I had prayed about his offer. I told him, "Honestly, no I didn't". He asked me if I would seriously pray about it and this time I told him that I would and meant it.

Upon praying I received a clear word from the Lord that I was to join SP for one year. I was not very happy about this and I drug my feet, halfheartedly filling out the online application. I have learned in my walk with the Lord that obedience is necessary to the Lord but even more necessary if we are to come into the fullness of our callings. He always has a reason for delays and answering prayers in a way different than we would expect.

Because of my military experience, I knew that there would be places that I didn't want to go yet knew I must. I have also found that once I came into agreement with God, promotion would eventually come. Good followers become good leaders. Within two days I received a call from SP headquarters in North Carolina asking for a resume. I replied that I did not have a resume as it was locked up in storage and I was in Africa. After spending some minutes with me on the phone while I stood outside an airport in Mozambique, I was hired right there. This was just another confirmation for me that I had heard the Lord.

I couldn't understand why God wanted me at Samaritan's Purse. I didn't want to be there, although I did do a very good job. I was very involved in ministry along with my financial duties. One could always find me praying for the men and women who came to my office for pay or travel funds. Six months into my assignment, Samaritan's Purse moved their entire operation north to Akuem, which is at the northern edge of South Sudan. It was then that I discovered why the Lord wanted me at SP and specifically Akuem.

Regarding the topography and culture of Akuem, Akuem is the exact opposite of Yei. Where Yei was green and lush, the soil a rich moist brown, rich for agriculture, Akuem was extremely hot and dry, reaching 130 degrees Fahrenheit, not a blade of grass anywhere during the dry season, and the soil was hard clay that was unable to soak up the rain when it came. This caused severe flooding which created miles wide lakes where the indigenous people made use of crude hand carved wooden canoes in order to paddle to town from the small huts which were built upon raised mounds of hard packed dirt.

Every Sunday after church, two Kenyan brothers and myself drove in to the town of Aweil on a thirty mile stretch of murum covered road. Murum is a hard, rocklike dirt used to make dirt roads more firm which helps when the rains come. We ministered together as we preached at several churches and discipled our neighbors.

Aweil is the closest big city which is a 45-minute drive away. It was on one of our trips to Aweil that I met the street kids of Aweil who soon stole a piece of my heart. Every Sunday afternoon was spent engaging them in play or handing out bread or buying them shoes. Six months later my year at SP was finished and I knew that it was my time to go to Iris Ministries in Yei where the Lord would give me the vision for the street children of Aweil. I didn't yet know what He wanted me to do for these children.

As I waited for the timing of things, I volunteered at the Iris Yei Children's Center. It was a fairly new center with no missionary housing. I lived in a tent for my first six months there which a typical camping tent that you could not stand up in yet it was big enough to at least put a single bed inside so I wasn't sleeping on the floor.

The people of Yei are a relational people who take time to visit even at the expense of being hours late for a previous engagement. The nights are cool and the sky lights up with a billion stars. On nights where there is a full moon a flashlight is not necessary. The mornings come with the squawk of the Namungoona bird, the African Pied Crow. The rainy season comes twice a year as the rains fall hard in the spring and then again in late summer, lasting until the end of fall. The seasons of Africa are reversed from America or Europe. In reference to temperature Africa's summertime is in December and their winter is in June.

The Children's Center was organized on fifty acres of rich farmland, the living area only about one quarter of this. The Center also ran a Primary School for the Center's children and included many of the local village children, for a total of just over 600 children. Eight structures were built for classroom use which were comprised of brick overlaid with concrete, the walls chest high. Beyond this point it was left open to facilitate a breeze on hot days.

When the heavy rains came, the children huddled on the opposite side of the classroom in which the rain might be blowing in. Each structure was topped with an iron sheet roof. The floors were of hardpacked dirt and each classroom contained very small wooden benches with no desks. This school, although a bit rugged, was the most affordable primary school in town on purpose. Iris believes that all children should be educated so they only charged fees that were enough to pay the teacher's modest salary. The average class size was eighty students, some classrooms spilling students into the aisles and out the door, therefore leaving no room to walk around.

I loved the children right from the beginning. One would always know where to find me, sitting with the mamas on colorful woven mats shucking maize of peanuts, or with the children playing stick ball or football (soccer) or the African form of hopscotch. I learned to dig in the fields and to plant and harvest crops, recognizing the different plants and calling them by name. I also learned to cook some of the local food such as posho, an African staple made from ground maize corn. I also began to learn the language, an abbreviated form of Arabic called Juba Arabic, after the capital city of South Sudan. The people of Yei also spoke Kakwa, a tribal language. I also bought two goats and started a goat herd which eventually grew to thirty.

I loved ministering to the children because they were little sponges, so hungry to learn everything that I poured into them. I met with the teenaged girls, twenty-six at that time, every Wednesday night and eventually included the boys when I took over as director in 2013. I also took all 110 children every Friday night and we walked to our church off compound to worship and pray until late in the night.

I spent every waking hour with this new family, all the while waiting for the vision and the timing of my Aweil dream. After almost two years at the Yei Children's Center I finally received the vision and the "go" from the Lord to start the Aweil ministry. Saying goodbye to the children of Yei was extremely difficult for both the children and myself. We cried as my car pulled away, loaded with everything I owned. I told them that I would come and visit as often as I could.

Aweil is the capital city of Northern Bahr El Ghazal and is home to the Muonyjan, the Dinka tribe. It is a peaceful region with no tribal violence or cattle raiding problems, which is generally the case in other regions of South Sudan. Bahr El Ghazal is not the only area of South Sudan whose home belongs to the Dinka tribe. They are also found in Lakes State, Upper Nile, Equatoria and many of the other states.

The climate in Bahr El Ghazal is sub-Saharan and is not amenable to agriculture to any great extent. Most of the region's food and supplies are brought in from Khartoum, Sudan to the north, or from Uganda which across the border far to the south. The people are generally poor and many children cannot afford to attend school. The street children, I was soon to learn, are mostly young boys looking to earn money to go to school. My ministry focused on these boys and my mission was to settle them back into their family homes and into school and off of the streets of Aweil.

Chapter Two

I had been on the mission field in South Sudan now for four years and living in Aweil was the most difficult. Our small compound was robbed three times in as many months. Fencing material, chain link, metal poles, all of these things were not available in Aweil. Our fence was made up of straw thatch and wooden fence posts, very easy to break into. It was just a physical deterrent that kept people from wandering in unseen. There were two water sources available to us just outside of our fence. One was a borehole and another was a hand dug well. The hand dug well water was not drinkable in my eyes yet the village people still drank from it. We used it for laundry and house cleaning.

Many times I found the village children standing on the brick wall encasing the well and I would find plastic bottles or shoes and any assortment of debris floating inside. I really couldn't understand why people drank from this when the borehole was so close. A borehole is a hand pump water system that is drilled by a large drilling rig. When it is completed it has a nice concrete drainage system and a sturdy metal handle used for pumping water up from depths of about 80 meters.

The people of Aweil welcomed my team and I and they were excited that white people were moving into their town. I think we were the only white people who lived in the town. I never saw any other whites the entire time I was there, unless they came in from Samaritan's Purse in Akuem or further north from Wanjok. Samaritan's Purse was still in Akuem and would drive into town once in a while. Every day as we drove or walked through the streets people would call out greetings to us. It is really a friendly town. I became very close to my neighbor and she was a Godsend to me when I became very sick once, taking care of me, bringing food and doing my laundry as if I was one of her family.

The temperatures could reach as high as 130 degrees Fahrenheit in the noon day sun and would only drop to 100 degrees at night. I never seemed to be able to drink enough water to quench my never-ending thirst, sometimes dreaming of having water IV's in my arms. On still, hot nights I would pull my simple cot, made of roughcut poles and crisscrossed twine for the bedsprings, outside at night to make it more bearable for sleeping, falling asleep with a wet towel draped across my midsection and fanning myself with a piece of cardboard until I fell asleep

I had never experienced such heat. It seriously felt as if I lived in a clothes dryer that never shut off. When I was with Samaritan's Purse I had to live in a safari style tent made of heavy canvas with thickly screened windows and a zippered tent flap for my door. The zipper was broken leaving the flaps hanging open for the six months I lived there. In order to dress and undress I had to hang a piece of material across the front, exposing my calves and feet below and my head above. Almost daily I found dead scorpions or spiders or lizards in or near my tent. Needless to say, I always checked my shoes in the morning.

Within the first month in Aweil, when I was still with SP, I contracted Typhoid. I really thought that I was going to die. Trying to lie down in a tent under a blazing hot sun in 130-degree temperatures was like putting myself on an oven rack and closing the door and setting the knob to bake. The winds were so strong during the dry season that open fields carried winds across them that looked like mini tornadoes and any clothes left hanging on the line could end up at a friend's house half a kilometer away.

Typhoid is not caught but comes upon a person when they touch something that is contaminated, such as a bathroom door handle or a water pump handle, anything another human touches when they haven't washed their hands after using the toilet. I had fever, chills, diarrhea, and vomiting and I would lie on the concrete floor of my office, desperate to find relief through the barely cool cement floor.

I trudged back and forth across the hot, dusty compound feeling like my sandals were melting under my tired feet, not a blade of grass in evidence, making my way to a pit latrine where a thousand flies fought over the right to hover over the hole in the ground, and myself trying not to vomit from the nausea that all of this produced.

One night an incredible storm blew in bringing heavy rains and gusty high winds, the first storm that I had experienced here. It was already dark and the wind had come up suddenly. Since the zipper was broken on my tent so I could not close the flaps. I remember thinking that I needed to go to the latrine because once the rain started I wouldn't be able to come out of my tent without being drenched in the downpour.

I ran to the latrine, my tent flap flapping like a hummingbird's wings, and as I reached the latrine and grabbed the door, the wind yanked the door from my grasp just as I entered in, leaving me to fight with the door unaware of the critter that entered in with me. Once I secured the door, I squatted down and right at that moment a bat flew out of the latrine hole, bouncing off the walls and my head trying to find its way out! I screamed and almost ran out with my pants around my knees! It was my first experience with Sudanese bats. I later learned that they are harmless and really try to avoid human contact.

I ran back to my tent, never having relieved myself, and wondered how I was going to keep my tent from being soaked or worse, from blowing away. At this point the rain was a deluge and the winds grew stronger. I stood at my tent door fighting with the flaps as if I was trying to catch a caged bird and finally managed to hold the flaps shut through the entire storm, almost 45 minutes! As soon as the storm abated we ventured out to investigate the damage and found that one of the tents had flown into our back fence causing it to fall as the tent continued its tumble over the fence.

Two other tents had also torn loose from their moorings, all the contents drenched and strewn about. After that storm we learned to pull our vehicles up to the tents and tied the tents to the vehicles with tie down straps.

Upon my return to Aweil at the end of January 2013 I hired a truck to bring my supplies up from Yei by road. I had flown up two weeks earlier to look at compounds and signed a lease for one. My pastor, who is Sudanese, was with the truck and stayed with me in Aweil for two days before heading back to Yei. When he was ready to leave he told me that I was a true missionary to be able to live in this heat and dust. I laughed and told him that I'm sure I will complain at some point.

There was a fence around the compound but it was sorely in need of repair. My Aweil pastor and I set to work digging holes for posts, running barbed wire along the top and shoring up the grass thatch. My hands looked almost like ground beef full of blisters and cuts from the barbed wire. I then had to climb up on the hot tin rooves to install solar panels as I was the only one on my team of four who knew how to manage it. We also ran wire through the three structures of our compound and dug small trenches for the underground lines to connect the three houses. We then set about painting our small rooms.

In order to fetch our water, we carried 20-liter jericans from our borehole to our compound which was about one hundred yards away. Jericans are plastic jugs that look something like a 4-wheeler Jeep's gasoline can. Outside of the town center of Aweil there was no running water or any type of plumbing system. We hauled water using a wheelbarrow and our backs which is very labor intensive for us foreigners who were not raised to do this.

Our compound had an outdoor pit latrine which was nothing more than a grass thatch structure about six feet high with an opening on the side for a door, whereby one had to start talking to the grass thatch or grunt a noise as they came upon the latrine so as not to walk in on someone. It was set up on a small mound for some odd reason, leaving our upper bodies poking up over our fence line. I felt very-self-conscious knowing that everyone knew what I was doing whenever my head popped up. Small children would run by calling my name.

One night as I was using the latrine I heard a noise, a rustling, just on the other side of the grass thatch fence. I shined my flashlight over the fence and there were three teenaged girls squatting to urinate. We were all startled, they because my flashlight illuminated them, and me because I was shocked that they were doing this along my fence line. I soon learned that the ground in Bahr El Ghazal was so hard that many could not dig pit latrines and would allot entire fields for the purpose of relieving themselves of bodily waste. I actually named one such field on the edge of town "Squatter's Field" because one would see many people dotting the landscape taking care of business out in the open. That night I learned that our field was a squatter's field, a place of defecating. One could smell the stench when the heat and wind were right, the heat being intense yet we pressed on.

When we finally finished with the renovation of our compound and set out to investigate our town we managed to find the street boys little by little with the help of our pastor and some of the street boys I had met from my previous stay in Akuem. During the day they usually found a place to sleep to escape the heat of the day and were somewhat hidden unless one knows where to look. The children don't speak much Arabic, mostly Mwonyjan, the local Dinka language. I soon learned how to speak basic phrases and words so that I could at least communicate on an elementary level. We found that there were about 250 boys living on the streets. The boys who lived on the streets of Aweil suffered even more than I could ever imagine. There were no pit latrines, only filthy, muddy public alleyways which were often used by men to make a short call, if you know what I mean. There were a few fields, no houses to sleep in, only abandoned market stalls flooded with debris and human waste in the rainy season, or closed up shop sidewalks to lay their heads on to sleep at night, or an abandoned railroad car, always with the fear of being attacked or robbed of what little they had.

I found a few boys feverish with malaria literally curled up on the side of the road, people stepping over and around them as they went about the business of the day, the boys nothing more than an obstacle to bypass like a plastic bottle or some rubbish left out, oblivious to their sufferings. Many children had gaping wounds on their legs with the smell of rotting, putrefied flesh, hundreds of flies fighting for the right to pick and eat at their rotting wounds. I believe the wounds were due to a lack of any type of fruit, a vitamin C deficiency, or even a lack of protein. These wounds could only be treated with antibiotic creams and bandages, knowing that the next day the wound would be soiled again. This is the reality of living on the street with no bathing facilities or available water.

These ones God had not forgotten, the ones that He loved, the ones that He called me to. Each day my team would feed these boys, and a few girls, as one of us tended to their wounds and sicknesses, after we discipled them and ended each day with a game of football. In the Dinka culture girls are never allowed to wander the streets. Girls bring high bride prices and are considered a commodity when it comes to marriage. Educated girls could bring the highest bride price. The few girls that joined our group were homeless yet actually had parents or a parent also living on the street with them. The parents of these girls were either alcoholics or mentally incapacitated or both. My intentions for these street children was not geared toward building a permanent home for them. I learned that many of these children did in fact have families who lived in the surrounding villages, although some of the boys came from villages as far away as 100 kilometers.

When I asked the children why they lived on the streets many told me that they came to the city to earn money for school fees. In many African countries school is not attainable because of the cost of school fees. South Sudan was no different. These children came from poor families, although most of the country was considered poor. Because of poor soil quality the land was not very conducive to agriculture, therefore, they could not grow much of their own food to sustain their families or even to sell in the market. The children ventured to the cities looking for and expecting to work in order to earn enough to pay for their schooling or to help their families. This never produced any good result, leaving these children begging on the street to survive, too ashamed or deflated to go back home. Once on the street it was only a matter of time before they were entangled in the street life, sniffing super glue, sucking on gasoline-soaked rags to stem their hunger pangs and drinking homemade moonshine, which was so toxic that it made people crazy as it killed off their brain cells.

Our living compound was about two miles outside of the town center from where our ministry took place and we were not in possession of an enclosed vehicle to carry our supplies back and forth to the ministry site. Instead, we had two motorcycles and another three wheeled motorcycle with a large wagon attached. Each day at 7:30 in the morning we loaded our commercial grade cooking cauldrons, plastic dishes, empty jericans for water, lentils for cooking along with onions and oil and large sacks of flat bread, the local staple. We were given a large compound on the edge of the market for our ministry. The governor offered us this site without charging us rent because he wanted these children off the street as much as we did. He actually invited us to dinner at his house twice and we accepted. Later, when the war began, we learned that he was to be the top military commander of the Sudanese People's Liberation Army (SPLA).

Each day we found the children waiting for us and as we rounded the corner they would yell, "Carolina, Carolina!" My heart swelled with so much love for this ragtag bunch of beautiful boys. The ministry compound had strong exterior walls, thereby keeping everyone out that we didn't want inside. The interior opened up to a large open area for a good football game. We built two grass thatch shelters in order to give us shade for cooking and ministry. Next to this compound was an elementary school which contained the largest hand dug well I have ever seen. Its circumference was about twelve foot across and approximately eighty meters deep, the first twenty or so feet being solid rock as are most water holes. In order to draw water, we tied a rope to a jerican handle with the top partially cut off, hauling the water up, hand over hand, in order to fill our ten to fifteen jericans each morning. It was hard work and the older boys never minded helping us. So much water was needed because we had to cook food, wash the dishes, and tend to the many wounds including scabies, which required a full bath.

We eventually chose our youth leaders from the older street boys who helped us to manage everything we did. If there is one thing that I have learned about older street children it is that they want to be needed. They live in an environment which is not conducive to growing in and learning good leadership practices, although there is a leadership hierarchy on the streets, usually instilling fear in the followers. When these children are given any type of responsibility they rise to the task and always do very well. I also assigned the young boys, ten to twelve years old, to be my guards as I shopped in the market because rival gangs would try to steal food if you weren't watching. I told them that they were protecting their own food and supplies so it became their responsibility to protect it. They took their roles seriously and even the street police were amazed at the change in these children who used to be the thieves they were protecting us from.

With the help of my Sudanese staff we began to learn the family history and situation of the boys and also what village they were from. Within the eight months that we worked with these children (150 children enrolled) we managed to rescue eighty eight of them off of the streets, bringing them back home to their families, paying their school fees and giving desperately hungry families food to get them through the dry season. The traders in the marketplace always beat the street boys with a stick whenever too many of them steered close to a vendor's stall because they were found stealing merchandise in order to eat. Within two months, the traders asked me what we were doing with these children as they were no longer stealing in the market! I told them that we were teaching them about the love of God and we fed them. When a child knows who they are, who's they are, and their stomachs are full, it is much easier to teach them morals and values. It's a lot more effective than beating them with a stick which never changed a thing. To God be the glory because they were learning that He was their provision. They grew to love God and trust Him and us.

Many of the boys arrived at our gate with empty soda or water bottles containing small rocks. I didn't understand why they collected these small rocks until my pastor explained it to me. The boys squeezed super glue onto the rocks inside the bottom of the plastic bottle and then shook the bottle and inhaled the fumes which gave them a sense of euphoria. Many of the boys also smoked and carried lighters, all ages, even as young as ten years old. I tried to ban them from coming inside with these implements but they would leave without eating or without ministry or wound care. I was desperate to see them living a better life so I came up with a new plan. We allowed them to bring these implements inside our gate but they had to leave them near the gate in a designated area and collect them as they left after our program was finished for the day. It worked, they stayed. We soon began to notice that some of the boys quit bringing these things, being convicted in their hearts and leaving these things permanently. We never told them that they were bad only that their habits and actions could harm them physically.

Many of the boys had ring worms so terrible that they needed to bathe in a special medicine from head to toe. Each day the children, about half of them teenagers, would come inside and gather for church. After church we fed them and after eating we provided medical attention and medication and they played football (soccer). Doctors Without Borders was another ministry which we heavily relied upon. They treated women and children for free!

Hallelujah! At first the doctors were not happy that we were bringing so many street children in for treatment but they began to see how effective our program was and soon welcomed our children. At one point as I was bringing in a child for wound care the doctor brought me to a street boy that the UN had picked up off the street after his head was almost crushed by a car. The city of Aweil, nor any city in South Sudan for that matter, had no place for these children to go to so the doctor asked me if I could make sure that this boy took his medication and would I change the dressing. It was a great partnership of building trust when the doctor asks you to take up the aftercare for a sick child.

One of the little girls in our program was very shy and never spoke. She smiled but remained reserved. I thought that maybe she was just a bit afraid of our skin, as is the case many times. I heard it said once that an African boy was stunned when he saw his first white man. He was actually afraid. He thought the man had turned his skin inside out! But the white man showed the boy that his skin was right side out by letting him feel his skin to see for himself. I'm sure that it was only a story. Quite often when a small baby first sees me the baby screams in terror, trying to climb up their mama's shirtfront as if she were a tree and I a lion. I've learned to approach babies with my mouth closed and a gentle smile and a piece of candy in hand. Bribery works every time, well almost every time.

This small reserved girl began to make steps toward coming closer to us. I had a small team of three who were white and I had a team of eight who were Sudanese. The little girl began to draw close by helping us to wash dishes and put the supplies into the wagon at the end of the day. I noticed that she never wanted to be near the boys. Maybe they were too rough, I don't know. About two weeks before we were due to leave Aweil as our program was terminating, we heard some very disturbing things concerning this girl. From our best guesstimate we figured her to be about eight years old. We learned that one of the older boys in our program was selling this little girl to other boys for sexual play. I was so grieved that I wanted to take this boy and turn him over to the authorities. I consulted with the social services office and they told me that they could do nothing without proof.

I then asked if I could take this little girl to live with me at our Yei Children's Center in two weeks. He told me that he first needed to do an assessment of her situation and find her parents or family. We went through the quick process of getting her mother's permission after assessing that she was indeed an at-risk child. Her mother was mentally challenged and also an alcoholic, living under a tree in the place where all the homeless adults lived. The papers were filed and finished within two weeks time. We brought this little girl with us to Yei. She was filled with joy and so much peace. She never showed any regret or fear of the unknown. She just knew that her life was better by leaps and bounds. She was safe at last.

We bought three new outfits of clothes for her to wear. Every day for a week she changed her clothes three times a day so that she could wear all of her clothes every day. She was enthralled with the idea of having clothes as all she ever had was what she happened to be wearing on her slight frame, her clothes usually filthy and hanging in tatters. We showed her the bed she would sleep in and when I tucked her in that first night she just rolled all over and her smile lit up the room. The other girls giggled with delight. She told me that she had never slept in a bed in her short life and now she had her own. Every meal was like a buffet feast for her, having had only garbage food left over from others. Upon finishing each meal our children took their plates to the kitchen to be washed. This beautiful little girl would follow those plates and eat what the other children did not finish. I tried to stop her from doing this and told her to go and get fresh food, that she could have as much as she wanted. It took some months for her to trust and know that we would never run out of food.

Chapter Three

It was right before this time that we were preparing to leave Aweil for good as our budget had dried up with not enough funds coming in to keep it going. I was really praying about whether I wanted to continue my ministry in Aweil, South Sudan. I didn't have a strong team to help me continue the work and I was tired and there was no one to take it over or to even help raise funds for the work. I was a bit disheartened by what I had seen on the mission field in the last three years also. I didn't see the full-on commitment that I expected to see. Some were committed fully to the mission they were called to but I also saw others who were rarely willing to do the hard things that needed to be accomplished and they worked as if they were putting in the required time. I wasn't seeing the heart in it. Previously, I had had two great ministries in America and a job working with children that I loved. I seriously thought about going back to that because at least I didn't need to push people to do what God had called them to do. I was tired of doing much of the work alone or with only one other and having to ask people to pull their load.

In the seventh month of my time in Aweil, I received an email from Rolland Baker, the co-founder of Iris Global, asking me to take over the Yei Children's Village in Yei, South Sudan. Something had happened to cause the government officials to force all of the missionaries at the Children's Village to leave. Although the Yei team knew of the trouble well before hand they were somewhat surprised when it came and had no choice in the matter but to leave the country. The base founder and director decided to also quit at this time so there wasn't anyone left in the country except for me. There were many innocent victims in this troubling time. This is the way it is in third world countries where the government is so new that laws aren't put into place yet in order to fight against injustice. When Rolland asked me to be the one to step up, I really struggled with it because I did love those children but I never wanted to run an orphanage.

The last thing I wanted was an orphanage, it was too much for me. From my point of view this was a lifetime commitment and I wasn't ready for this. I needed some time to pray and to think about what I really wanted to do and more importantly, what God wanted from me. When Rolland asked me to go to Yei my immediate heart response was a no. I remember looking up to heaven and reminding God, "I don't want this. I really need a break, maybe doing something else that is not in such a difficult place. I need a sabbatical or something." I told Rolland that I would pray about it. After a week of praying and thinking and praying some more and thinking even more, I responded with a sincere yes, although still a bit halfheartedly. I felt that God was asking me to do this and I wanted to be obedient to Him but my heart wasn't in it, yet. I couldn't just leave these children that I had known for two years before I came to Aweil, abandoned and without hope.

In my heart it was a temporary fix and I told Rolland that I would only do it for a year. I told God that I couldn't raise the money it takes to cover all the costs of running this center and that He would have to assure me that He would take care of that part. I mean, I couldn't even raise enough to keep my current program going. How did I think I would be able to do this? This is why I really had to hear from the Lord, because if He asked me to do this then He would provide the resources for it. Even today, as I write this, I still tell the Lord that if He doesn't provide for us then I can't do this on my own. I don't know enough people with money to help us. He does. Obviously, this was the greatest test of my faith up to this point. I was now responsible for the well-being of over one hundred children who had nowhere else to go. We would sink or swim and God was in charge of it all.

Chapter Four

I closed down my ministry in Aweil, juggling two bases for almost a month, flying back and forth twice, closing down one and starting up another. When I arrived in Yei on that first trip back I came face to face with 111 children who were traumatized and scared and didn't trust anyone. They had been abandoned, left, with no explanation, even the one that they called mama had left them. Why on earth would they trust anyone now? They knew me and were glad to see me but they didn't even trust me at that time. They had really been hurt. It would take a long time to heal and even longer to trust. I arrived permanently in Yei in September of 2013. There was no money in the bank and very little food left in the coffers. I had no idea of how to manage a children's home and didn't even know where to start.

I spent the first weeks connecting with the children again, praying with them, worshipping together, and sitting with my staff, deciding how to move forward with what we had. I told the children right away that my primary focus in the beginning was to help them to be spiritually and mentally well. We would worry about all the other things as they came. God would take care of it all. I'm sure they doubted this but they had no choice but to move forward with me. They had nowhere else to go. The first months were really difficult. The children constantly fought with each other, talked back to me, snuck out at night, skipped school, and refused to do their assigned chores. I was the only missionary at the base and felt pretty much alone in the night after all the staff went home except for a handful of Sudanese mamas. Praise God for the mamas! After three months with no days off and full on ministry, by December I was exhausted and a bit overwhelmed. And then the unthinkable happened.

Civil war broke out in South Sudan. In the summer of 2013, Salva Kiir Myardit fired his cabinet and his Vice President. I was still in Aweil at that time and I remember thinking, "He just fired the Vice President! This is definitely going to bring a revolt. Something is going to happen and that something will not be good." When I left Aweil I had to leave all of my belongings there. I had furniture, clothes, kitchen supplies, two motorcycles, a three-wheel cycle with a trailer, solar equipment and so many other things. The truck that I had hired was on its way to Yei when they reached a bridge that had been washed out by heavy rains. This was the only safe route to Yei and now it was blocked. The truck turned back and left all of my belongings in Aweil. After the war started in December all of the roads going north were either closed or taken over by the South Sudan Army or the rebels. I lost everything and only had the clothes I was wearing and a few things that fit into a small carry-on suitcase.

In the two months previous to my departure from Aweil the Lord began to speak to me about trusting Him. I kept hearing over and over, "Do you trust Me?" I always answered, "Yes Lord, I trust You." I also started to hear Him tell me, "Don't hold tightly to the things of this world." I asked Him why He was telling me this because I had given up everything to follow Him. Why was He now telling me to not hold onto these things? I was a bit confused but I responded positively to His words. When I left Aweil on an airplane, expecting my things to arrive in two days, I flew on to Juba.

The next day I learned about the truck turning back. I was sitting on the floor of my hotel room and I was a bit frustrated because I was tired and it seemed things were already going wrong. I then prayed to the Lord, "God, it's all Yours. Everything I have is Yours. All of these things in Aweil are Yours God." It was then that I realized He had been telling me beforehand not to hold tightly to the things of this world. Now that I had lost everything, down to my underwear, literally, I wasn't sad or upset. I was in total peace after praying my prayer. I never once fretted about losing everything after that prayer. I knew that God would give me everything I needed because I trusted Him. I had no money to buy new things. I was in the same predicament as the children. We were in this together and God would care for us.

The deadly conflict that began on December 15, 2013 caused thousands of deaths and over one million people to be displaced in Internally Displaced People's (IDP) Camps. The conflict erupted in the capital city of Juba. Although it was publicized as a political war, all who lived in the country knew that it was a tribal war. There were many, many stories being told by the locals of relatives and friends being killed or tortured because of their ethnicity. In our city we could hear sporadic gunfire at night as soldiers moved from house to house, killing anyone who was from a different tribe than their own. The children at our Home came from six different tribes, the tribe in question not being one of them, so we felt somewhat safe for a while. The children were afraid of being taken captive and the boys forced to be child soldiers. The girls were afraid of being taken captive and forced to be wives to the rebels. We had to constantly remind them how big God is and how He would care for all of us.

Our children were familiar with the children of war. The United Nations (UN) brought children to us when they were able to rescue them from Joseph Kony, the leader of the Lord's Resistance Army (LRA). Kony would travel at night with his men and boys, high on drugs, and invade small villages, capturing children and massacring the adults, even forcing the children to kill their own parents, leaving a trail of bloodshed everywhere he went. These children would come to us traumatized by what they had been through and by the things they saw and were forced to do. This was the fear that invaded our home and threatened our children. Would this new war bring these atrocities to us? We slept on the floor at night to avoid any bullets that might be come in through the windows. I allowed no one to leave their houses at night, even to go to the latrine. No lights were on. We lived in darkness. The daylight hours remained somewhat calm in our area. Further north, the battles were intense and entire villages and towns were burnt to the ground.

A friend of Iris Ministries had an orphanage in Juba where some of our girls originated from. These children were rescued from the streets of Juba and the girls were street wise and street tough. When the conflict erupted in Juba my friend asked if she could send her girls to stay with us for a time until things quieted down in the city. Two days later we received 36 children from Juba. And a monkey. They arrived in two large custom vans with their belongings load up top. It was a miracle that they were able to drive all the way from Juba without being ambushed and everything taken. God's protection remained on them.

This was just two days before Christmas and I found myself with 147 children and I still had no permanent missionaries to help me. I had a Sudanese staff of eighteen people but much of my staff went home to their own families each night. We did have a visiting team from Mozambique, four of them, to help for two weeks. I had been working non-stop every day and late into the night and I was up early every morning. This was my daily routine for months. I had had no days off in the months since September and I was tired, so tired. And now this, a war.

With the arrival of 36 new children, a myriad of shuffling these children needed to happen. The boys were living in three houses and now had to be condensed into two. The 36 girls that had just arrived were packed into the now vacant house and were also dispersed among the other girl's houses at our center. We encountered many problems with this new mix into our already unstable family. The "Juba" girls were from the mean streets of the capital city. They were also of a different tribe than the predominant one at our center in Yei, which was Kakwa, who were known as agricultural people.

Most of the Juba girls were either Dinka or Mandari, a people known as the cattle keepers. The girls were street tough and solved every problem with arguing and fighting, the fighting sometimes becoming violent. Every single day there was an argument amongst the girls and arguing back and forth between the girls and the staff mamas. Each house had a local Sudanese widow who carried the title of "mama". The girls were supposed to respect the mamas and obey them. They did not.

The Juba girls were unaccustomed to routine or peaceful negotiation. Their instinct was to yell and to be heard and to fight for what they deemed as their rights, whether right or wrong. Trying to calm the girls down usually resulted in me yelling to be heard amidst all of their yelling to be heard. It was chaos, pandemonium and I had reached a breaking point.

I had a melt down after one particularly rough day of screaming and arguing amongst the girls. One of the Juba girls had threatened to run away. She was a big girl, sixteen years old. I ran after her and as she reached the compound gate I caught up to her and tried to hold her back by standing between her and the gate. When I saw that she refused to be stopped, I tried to stop her hands and arms from constantly fighting against me by holding them.

We found ourselves wrestling so as to release my hold on her and we fell to the ground together. At this point all I could think to do was to hold her tightly there on the ground, my arms and legs wrapped securely around her, trying to calm her down enough to hear me, talking to her in a calm, loving voice. She just kept crying and wriggling to get away. I knew her personality and knew she would not calm down. I told her that I really did love her. If I let her go then she would have to promise not to run and I would leave her be, no punishment. She relented. I released her and told the other girls to talk to her as she wouldn't talk to me yet. The children still did not trust anyone so it added to the problem.

Within minutes she had taken hold of one of the mama's medication and was threatening to swallow all of it. I immediately called some girls and a mama to help me wrestle the medication away from her. She ran crying back into her house. I stood there shaking. I remember thinking about the Bible and how the priests would tear their clothes and throw dirt on themselves when they were horribly upset about someone sinning against God.

The camel's back had broken and the next thing I knew, I threw myself on the ground and began to throw dirt on myself, crying out, "This can't be my life!" The mamas ran over to comfort me and the children just stared in shock. Everything got really quiet. I was sobbing. I was exhausted. I couldn't take anymore fighting. I hate conflict. I hate when people yell. It makes me shake inside. And here I was right in the middle of a war! I knew I had to get it together or the children would be afraid and they needed me to be the sane, calm one here. I got up and dusted myself off and went into my house, still shaking. It was also during this time that I became very sick physically.

A few days later I awoke feeling very nauseous. I managed to make it through our church service and preached the message before racing to my house and vomiting my guts out, living on the latrine for the next three days. Nothing would stay down. Antibiotics didn't help. My staff was worried about me because I had become so thin, dropping from a healthy 155 pounds to 125. I am a tall person and carry 155 pounds well. I now looked anorexic. On Saturday morning at 3:00 a.m. I caught a glimpse of myself in the mirror as I made my way once again to the latrine. I knew then that I needed medical help.

Every doctor and foreign aid agency had left Yei because of the conflict so there was no help in the city for me and I didn't know what was wrong with me. There were still two girls left from the Iris Mozambique team. They had volunteered to stay on an extra month just to help me even though a war had just erupted. One of them suggested that I go to Uganda to seek medical help which would require me to leave the country for three to four days.

I managed to reserve a seat on the plane that flew in twice a week from Uganda, which was a miracle because people were leaving the country in droves. Upon arriving at the hospital in Kampala the doctors ran a battery of tests and found nothing wrong with me except that I was severely dehydrated and suffering from exhaustion. I had literally been working too hard for too long added with not eating or drinking enough. I had also come to a place where something had to change or I would die, physically and even spiritually.

I had thrown myself into caring for all of these children and for the staff whom I loved, trying to make everything fit and run like a well-oiled machine, and I neglected my own well-being in the process. I spent the next week in Kampala, Uganda resting and eating. I remember eating a lot of food. I was ravenous. I did manage to gain back ten pounds over the next few weeks after returning to South Sudan.

I had also thrown myself on the altar of the Lord, no turning back and had come to a point where I needed to see more of the power and reality of God in my life. I needed to know what He meant by working from a place of rest. I really needed wisdom. I didn't have a user's guide or "how-to" manual on raising 146 children in a third world country in the midst of a war zone. I stayed in bed for those three days in Kampala and gave myself over to God and asked Holy Spirit to change me, to change my mode of business and always doing and to give me an unwavering heart for these children who never asked for any of this.

I wanted to be in such unity with Jesus that I would not be shaken or rattled from running into the fire with Him if necessary. I was ready for a baptism of fire, a sacrifice that would bring an intimacy with Him that could never be broken. In this world there will always be something competing for His affection. I thought that I had already offered Him everything. I lost everything in Aweil, I had been through such a fire in ministry just living there. What then was now competing for His affection in me?

I remember sitting on the hotel room bed on day two of my recovery in Uganda watching the local Christian television station. The music video, "The Motions" by Matthew West came on and I just started weeping. This was the song that had taken me over the edge into full time missions before I came to Africa. When I heard it, no matter what I was doing or where I was, my eyes would tear up because I felt like I had been going through the motions, afraid to step out in full radical faith. This song was my call to give my life for Jesus. Matthew West's words, "I don't want to spend my whole life asking, what if I had given everything?" resonated within me, urging me to give my all for Jesus.

I was now faced with releasing everything to Him. South Sudan was on the verge of all out civil war. The last Americans were being taken out of Juba. I was one of two Americans still left in Yei, living in a violent country with no medical care, no food coming in, all roads closed to the border, and asking myself if I was still willing to stay for these children, the ones that the Father loves? The story started to spread in America among my friends and church family that I refused to leave the children. While in Uganda, I found myself sitting in a hotel room having a Skype interview with a Fox News affiliate in my hometown of San Antonio, Texas, Fox News Channel 29. The story ran on New Year's Day and went viral. I started to receive phone calls from the CNN International desk, emails from the Navy Times Magazine, and Facebook friend requests from people all over the world who were picking up my story on You Tube.

God was orchestrating greater and more inconceivable things in my life than ever before. I was astounded by His faithfulness. Here I was hanging on the last thread of a thin rope, the devil's foot on my neck, and God pulled out all the stops to show me that the greatest provision yet and an outpouring of love and wild abundance than I could ever imagine was coming like a flood into the ministry. He had asked me to trust Him and I decided this was the best thing for me to do.

When I arrived home from my five days in Uganda I was still a bit weak and thin but all I wanted to do was to dance with my children before the Lord with all my heart and soul. I knew what God wanted of me and I was so ready to give it to Him, completely, letting go of all control and trusting Him to care for us. This was the beginning of a great adventure I had no idea was coming.

God was now asking for more. He wanted my ministry and I spent hours every morning at the feet of Jesus letting Him fill me again with His desire for me and the ease of ministry I had forgotten. He was teaching me that I had to operate from this position of rest or everything I did would eventually fall apart. When I came back into South Sudan I was a walking revival. As soon as I reached our compound we set up the sound system and the generator and the new keyboard I had bought for the kids while in Uganda and we danced and sang until we were exhausted, or at least I was.

Chapter Five

Later in the night I was chatting with one of my older girls as we listened to worship music and talked about the goodness of the Lord. After everyone had gone to bed, at midnight gunfire made its way into the town of Yei. This went on for three hours, moving along the bush in the darkness, men shouting, people crying, and more shooting. I went with our watchmen and two visiting missionaries and some of our older boys and we put all of the houses on lockdown, with all lights out and told everyone to remain quiet and to not be afraid, trust God. Locked in our houses we all began to seek the Lord with all our hearts from a place of peace and rest.

In the short time that I had been home, I had begun to teach the children about rest. It was no accident that I found myself at the end of myself when I did. We needed to learn this in order to make it through the coming years with war constantly at our door. It was also at this time that the Lord gave a scripture to one of my older boys during a time of soaking and prayer.

"So, you shall serve the Lord your God, and He will bless your bread and your water. And I will take sickness away from the midst of you. No one shall suffer miscarriage or be barren in your land; I will fulfill the number of your days. I will send My fear before you, I will cause confusion among all the people to whom you come, and will make all your enemies turn their backs to you." (Exodus 23:25-27)

Sandy and Rebecca, the two visiting missionaries, told me that they were amazed at how peaceful I was through it all. We could hear the gunfire throughout the next three hours coming closer, moving away, coming closer again, never once fearing for our lives. We heard the rata-tat-tat of sporadic gunfire as the SPLA soldiers, we later learned, were searching houses for rebel soldiers. I somehow knew that we were not in danger because this was a tribal war and we were obviously not a part of the rebel tribe. This night we were deep into the presence of the Father's heart and His love for us. I called one of the Iris Leaders from America to update her on our position and to ask her to pray for us and to tell others to keep praying. We declared the Word of God and prayed His Word and it seemed as if we just had a Holy Ghost party!

I remember crawling around on my hands and knees, keeping low and out of the path of bullets. I crawled down the hallway to my bedroom to the safe and gathered all of our money and crawled back to the living room and grabbed first aid supplies and backpacks in case we needed to run. I had three backpacks in case we needed to split up into three groups. The Iris leader was still on speaker phone and I was laughing, uncontrollable laughing, all the while trying to pack the three backpacks. I thought, "Am I losing my mind? Why am I laughing? This is serious stuff!" Nehemiah 8:10 came to mind, "The joy of the Lord is my strength." Another scripture that kept coming to my remembrance is:

"My brethren, count it all joy when you fall into various trials, knowing that the testing of your faith produces patience." (James 1:2)

I have learned that one will not see revival unless you offer the sacrifice of praise under fire. We were praising God under fire. We were living sacrifices on the altar of fire and the more we worshipped our Lord the higher He took us away from the enemy camp. When a fire is set and the flames burn hot the heat causes things to rise. The atmosphere above the fire causes things to rise. I felt like we were in this place of offering ourselves as a sacrifice and the hotter the flame became the higher we rose. Seriously, and oddly enough, I was never once afraid. We even managed to sleep for a few hours on the floor. I did finally manage to pack an emergency bag of passports, money, medications and other necessities. All of my military training automatically kicked in so I didn't really need to think, reacting from instinct.

At 5:00 a.m. I heard the rattling of pots in the kitchen and found that our cook had gotten up to light the cook fire in the kitchen. All of our food is cooked over an open fire, using charcoal made locally or wood cut from trees for firewood. As smoke wafted from the kitchen, I walked out onto the compound and told the two missionaries to cover my cook Yalina and I in prayer while we prepared breakfast. I made coffee for my staff that were there, telling the children to stay inside for now. Then at 8:00 a.m. the gunfire erupted again. Yalina and our handful of mamas and I ran for cover! Finally, at 10:00 a.m. we were able to bring the children their breakfast while they were told to stay inside the houses, with me running back and forth across the compound to deliver cups of tea and plates of bread. My children still tell me that they remember this so clearly as if it were yesterday.

At 11:30 a.m. things had been quiet for a few hours and I felt it was safe so I brought all of the children together under the mango trees to worship and we gave thanks to the Lord for protecting us and prayed for each other. The older children, myself and our two visitors then ministered to the children and the staff, speaking the word of life and destiny over each one there under the mango tree, a gentle breeze blowing across our faces and warm sunshine caressing our tired bodies. Again, we felt the Holy Spirit outpouring as He ministered to each one, all fear erased, peace remaining.

The remainder of the day continued on in relative peace and quiet, an eerie stillness across the land. The children played quietly and we didn't allow them to leave the compound, although our compound wasn't even fenced in at this time, so I did random checks to ensure that my older boys wouldn't get too curious and go looking for trouble. We ate our meals outside as usual although we remained alert. We found out later through local sources that the two feuding tribes pursued each other all across the country, including Yei where we thought it could never happen. Our peaceful city of refuge was no more.

One group of soldiers went house to house to find the other and shoot them down in cold blood. We heard spurts of machine gun fire (AK47) and knew that they had found another family of the opposite tribe to kill. It was very distressing to us who thought that every life was valuable. Our children also wondered if any of their friends were victims during the dark of night shooting. Not knowing what is happening is the hardest part of this. With no television or radio able to report the truth, one just never really knew what was going on unless we used the telephone network of friends and family to gather information that we knew was truth.

As night began to fall, just before darkness settled in, we worshipped and prayed again with all of the children and peace surrounded us as we locked in for the night, turning off lights and closing windows and doors. After everyone was safely tucked in for the night, I could touch the silence, it was so tangible. There was an unnatural stillness in the land, as if even the animals locked themselves away, not knowing what was to come. The moon was full and illuminated everything as I walked out to the watchman's shelter to make sure they were okay and had everything they needed and told them to stay inside the shelter because their bodies would not stop a bullet.

The watchmen were drinking coffee, warming their hands over a small fire and talking about the things that were coming with the war. Two of my older boys sat with them and it gave me peace to know that our watchmen were still there, even though they had no weapons. My watchmen only carried bow and arrows because I didn't like guns around the children. As I walked back to my house one of the watchmen escorted me. He didn't like that I was walking alone. We walked back to my house on this warm night, having no need of a flashlight because of the brightness of the moon, passing our goats lying in the middle of the dirt trail sleeping as if nothing was amiss. I listened to worship music before turning in for the night and reminded myself that my God reigned and all of my days were numbered by Him. I needed to make plans to evacuate in case things grew worse. These were my thoughts as I drifted off to sleep this night, praying for a quiet night.

Chapter Six

Although our town is not as large as Juba, it covers a wider area beyond the city borders, branching out into smaller sub-villages. In the city center a two-story hotel looms above the smaller market kiosks, along with a hospital and a nurse's training school. Our town also has three or four well known banks. There is a good-sized market, covering about four city blocks, where one can buy vegetables and meat, fish and dry goods, and plenty of fruit, clothes, electronics and solar equipment. These are our shopping malls African style and all of these items are imported from Uganda on large container trucks. The British call these trucks lorries. There are no paved roads, instead all are hardpacked dirt and are lined with any number and type of trees and greenery. Even though we are considered a major city, the first major city with a customs office this side of our country's border, we still do not have paved roads. After living here and learning about our town, this surprised me.

After this week's gunfire and civil unrest, I decided to talk with the commissioner of Yei. He is a very nice man who has helped us in the past and I went to ask him for permission to travel to Uganda with the children because one cannot just take a country's children, even if there is an active war in the area. There is always a process, even in a land where these processes aren't in place yet. I wanted to avoid running in the night with all of the children down dark bush trails while rebels laid in wait because we are under fire. I needed to have a plan to leave before it got worse. I have never lived in a war zone before so I had no idea what to expect or what plans needed to be formulated but all of my military training told me to have an escape plan. The commissioner was sympathetic to our plight and asked us to wait a day or two to see what happens. I liked him and respected him and in honoring his request I believed that even more doors would be opened for us later on. I didn't feel a sense of urgency yet so we waited in stillness and in peace, knowing that God is always in full control.

This afternoon I made some phone calls and sent emails and began to reach out to a few Ugandan non-governmental organizations (NGO's). Although it was still somewhat peaceful in Yei, the underlying tension all over the country and the fighting that is still active just north of us has caused the food supply from Uganda to dwindle rapidly. The merchants are still afraid to cross the border into South Sudan for fear of being attacked and robbed by rebel soldiers or bandits who have been hijacking their trucks and produce. Because of the lack of food on the shelves, the exchange rate of Sudanese pounds to United States dollars has dropped drastically, affecting the local trade market.

Foreigners in South Sudan deal in US dollars so the exchange rate is critical for us. The drop caused market prices to rise severely in order for traders to earn a profit. This was also something which caused me great concern and became a factor when deciding whether we would stay and ride out the storm or go and take refuge in Uganda. Uganda is the only country that brings in South Sudan's fuel and food. Now that the roads are closed the market is running out of everything. I have been told that when this trouble came during the last war, the one in 2006 with the north, the soldiers were positioned every 500 meters along the roadways to keep the roads open and safe for traders to come. This has not been the case this time. Another night has passed quietly allowing us to sleep well.

Today I went into town and fifty percent of the shops are already closed and boarded up, the traders having left town for a safer place across the border. The market has always been a loud and busy place, a relational place with people laughing and talking, a place where every other store has concert speakers blaring music, vendors calling out to shoppers to come and buy, mamas and grandmas laughing about last night's village story, and the rata-tap-tap of men playing dominoes or Ludo, another favorite game here. As I drove through town I was one of only three vehicles on the road. The market shelves were looking thin with not much produce and even then, the fresh produce was days old and wilted. It reminded me of my time living in Aweil where it took days for trucks to make it there and when they did arrive, the produce wasn't in very good shape.

The market was as quiet as an early Sunday morning when most people are in church. You could almost hear a pin drop in the dust as I made my way through the vegetable and fish market as we were still here and my children still required food. The vendors who remained were very subdued and quiet. There was no banter and chatter between the women and I, or the cooing of their babies as I tickled them, nor the conversations about produce that we had with each other. There were no children running about and no men playing cards or dominoes. The atmosphere was serious and tense, as if the traders just wanted to make their day's profit and leave quickly before anything happened. Soldiers were walking on the streets with AK-47's and some were even carrying RPG's. There were always military trucks on the road loaded with soldiers.

A few days have passed since I spoke to the commissioner so I returned to see him. Again, he asked me to wait. "Things are getting better", he said. I also heard from the Lord as I prayed that morning and was reminded that even Moses had to get the Pharaoh's permission to take the Israelites out to the desert to worship Him. If Moses had to wait then I too could wait for this. I had also received an email from my spiritual mom who reminded me of a word that the Lord had given me when I was initially called to Sudan. Sudan was never on my radar and I didn't pray to come here. At that time the Lord impressed upon me to "Get out of your country, away from your family and from your father's house, to a land that I will show you." (Genesis 12:1)

He also impressed upon me that He would show me as I went and not before. The word that my spiritual mom sent to me was the same scripture but with the second part, Genesis 12:2, "I will make you a great nation; I will bless you and make your name great; And you shall be a blessing." God always reminds His people to bless other people, even their enemies, because this is His forever nature. Sometimes He will allow His people to remain in the midst of chaos, suffering and turmoil in order to dislodge the enemy in that land. That's why so many missionaries go to these dark places. This really ministered to me because I knew I had an assignment not yet finished here.

We continued to wait upon and hear from the Lord. I have been so amazingly blessed to still have Rebecca and Sandy with me. The original four that came to visit for the Christmas holidays were such a relief for me during this crisis. They have been absolutely amazing with the children and with our many outreaches to the community. Our compound was transformed because of their help and the time that they spent with our children. I sometimes think that they were angels in disguise sent to care for the children while I tackled the administrative hurdles of this season.

A few days later we received the news that there was a group of refugees in our city from Bor which is in the north and they were seeking refuge here in Yei. They have set up camp and are living under tarps on the abandoned United Nations Mission (UNMIS) compound. There aren't any NGO's left in our town at this time, everyone having evacuated on the first flights out as soon as the conflict started. There were no humanitarian aid projects available to supply the refugees with food or shelter. To make matters worse these particular refugees were considered the enemy by some of the fighting soldiers as they were from one of the tribes who caused the crisis. These refugees had to be desperate in order to consider seeking refuge in our neck of the woods.

My Iris pastor is also the pastor of a local church alliance group in Yei which Iris Ministries formed called Partners in Harvest, which brings together various churches from other denominations for the purpose of bringing unity to our church community and to share at conferences, training, and to pray together. The leaders immediately called for all available churches to mobilize food, clothing and bedding for these refugees. I had just gone into town to buy supplies in order to stockpile whatever dry goods I could find and afford. I wanted to have enough food to last us at least one month until things calmed down and the Uganda-Yei road opened again. I had purchased many fifty-kilogram sacks of beans, maize flour and rice, and cooking oil, and powdered milk for the children and other dry goods which we needed.

When my pastor came to me to ask if Iris could help, I told him, "Well, I could give 10% of what we have. The Lord will bless it because it is like giving the tithe." Immediately, the Lord really spoke to my heart and said, "Why don't you give 90% and live off of My 10% and see what I will do?" I stood there looking at my pastor, not saying anything, and in my mind, I am thinking, "Are You sure Lord?" I hesitated for less than a minute and immediately gathered the children to help me load the food and pray for multiplication over this food for the refugees and for us. My pastor didn't even bat an eye when we loaded most of our food into the truck because he knows me, that I don't hesitate to obey the Lord. We gave 90% of our reserve stock to the refugees and kept only 10% for ourselves!

This might seem like a crazy thing to do when one is responsible for the lives of so many children. But I decided that I would rather look crazy and trust God and give the more than the little, giving out of our widow's mite, so that we could truly bless those with nothing, giving our best to them and seeing an explosion of love and blessing in return so that we could give even more. I knew that God would cover my mistake if I truly missed it and didn't hear Him correctly. No one can out give God, no one. God has blessed us to be a blessing. In Genesis chapter 26, verses 1-3, the Lord told Abraham to stay where he was, in a land of great famine, and Abraham would never lack, so I claimed this same blessing for us at Iris South Sudan. As I write this book, some six years later, I can tell you that we have never lacked for anything in all these years. The Lord has always been extravagant and He will forever be to those who open their hands to give and their eyes to see it.

Chapter Seven

During that first year, the Lord showed us how extravagant He was. We had a small herd of goats, about 20, and the females usually had one baby at a time. After we gave 90% of our food away our goats began to have twins and one even had triplets where it had never happened before! Some of our staff commented to me that these goods are especially fruitful because it is not normal to have so many twins and triplets. Another testimony concerns our borehole which is located in the center of our compound and requires semiannual maintenance to keep it working properly.

Water is a commodity in Africa and I prohibited the local community from coming into our compound to take water from our borehole after hearing about boreholes drying up during the dry season. I could not take that chance with so many children in my care. The maintenance man came to check our borehole equipment on a regular visit and when he finished he handed me the bill and was actually somewhat stern with me as he said, "You need to use more water. You have too much water!" I was shocked! Too much water in the dry season? How can this be? Only God could do this!

After this I flung wide our gates and invited the village women to come in every day and to partake of our rich water source! The scripture in Exodus 23:25-27 immediately came to mind. We had prayed this in! This is what the blessing of God looks like. It is the law of the kingdom of God that what one sows, that is what one will reap.

"But this I say: He who sows sparingly will also reap sparingly, and he who sows bountifully will also reap bountifully. So, let each one give as he purposes in his heart, not grudgingly or of necessity; for God loves a cheerful giver. And God is able to make all grace abound toward you, that you, always having all sufficiency in all things, may have an abundance for every good work." (2 Corinthians 9:6-8)

God is not slack. He always keeps His promises to us. All He needs from us is our faith to mix with His promise. Faith is the ingredient that begins the flow. There were so many examples in the Word of God where Jesus told people that it was their faith that did things, that healed them, that caused their sins to be forgiven. Faith is the foundation of our belief. It was a step of faith that we took to become believers. In Hebrew's 11:6 Paul tells us that without faith it is impossible to please God. Jesus told his disciples in Luke 18:8, "When the Son of Man returns will He really find faith on the earth?" This very week I began my women's ministry, meeting every Friday morning with the women from the village who came to drink from our well, discipling them and praying with them, becoming their friend. Little did we know at this time how much we would need each other. God did.

During all of the conflict happening in our country, we have continued to minister to our neighbors. Our visiting missionaries, our pastor and a handful of our older children set off today to minister at the town prison and at the hospital. We visit these places at least monthly and the children are so desperate to go that they actually argue about who went last time and who would get to go this time because everyone wants to go every time. Our children do not fear persecution, are not intimidated and are not ashamed of the gospel. They have lived their lives in the midst of terrible suffering and they know the seriousness continuing to keep running our race, bringing the Kingdom of God and His righteousness to as many as possible. I had been teaching them about revival and holy desperation because we noticed a spiritual famine in our land as we witnessed people running from their homes and villages. We knew that without God people would die, some because they didn't know God and others because they didn't know how to pray. We were desperate to help them in any way that we could.

The harvest is rich and plentiful and just because we are in the midst of a broken land we could not cower in our tents and houses and around our cozy fires having wonderful fellowship and separating ourselves from the world. This is the perfect time for kingdom advancement! A few days ago, we went to a small nearby village and they were so surprised to see us there. What? People were still doing outreach during these terrible times? Those were the looks on the faces of the people we encountered. Also, there was relief, someone to pray for them and emphasize with them in this struggle. Upon receiving the gospel message their faces radiated joy because they were so encouraged by the Word of God and by the prayers of the faithful. Everywhere we traveled, along deserted roadways, approaching long abandoned homes, people tentatively came out of hiding to meet with us. We and the people in the villages were always on high alert, furtively looking around for danger in the bush, as we carried on with our daily lives.

There were many downhearted and suffering men and women in the prison today where no one had visited since Christmas. They were also encouraged by our prayers and fellowship with them. The prison compound is nothing more than one long and empty dormitory style building, containing no beds, only mats on the floor if they had one. At Christmas we took fifty blankets to the prison because they had none and we could only hope that the prisoners were allotted their blankets and prayed that they were not sold in the market the next day by the prison staff. Corruption runs deep in this country. There are many articles concerning this online. In the Yei prison men and women were housed together along with children if they were in this place. The serious criminals were chained at the ankles to prevent them from trying to run away. The perimeter fence was nothing more than a piece of chain link fence with no barbed wire. If someone tried to run they were shot, which was a serious deterrent.

We continued visiting the hospitals where the wounded and sick lay waiting for the few doctors that were still available to see them, many of the patients going days without treatment. In the hospitals of South Sudan, a family member must bring food or the patient will not eat and the family member must also bathe and care for the patient if needed. The nurses only check vitals and give medicine. If there is no one to feed and bathe the patient, they are not admitted. The person who stays with the family member usually sleeps on the floor on a mat. When visitors come to visit other patients, people sit on the unrelated sick person's bed, the visitors might make a lot of noise with everyone talking, there is just an assortment of chaos that breathes inside of a hospital dormitory which does not allow for rest.

Last night we took a seriously ill man to the hospital who was convulsing and there was no doctor available until morning so we were told to just leave him on a bed and someone would get to him in the morning. This is the normal way of life in a third world country where human life is expendable. We ended up transporting this man to another hospital that could care for him right away, praise God. I remember some years ago a school student had drowned in a pond just outside of our front gate without anyone's knowledge. When one of the missionaries went to try and revive her with CPR it didn't help so we loaded her body in our tipper truck and took her to the morgue. The hospital was angry with us because we didn't go to the police. The police were angry with us because we disturbed her body to try and save her. I was stunned by it all. This is when I learned that if someone has had an automobile accident and is seriously injured, even barely hanging onto life, it is illegal to move that person or take them to a hospital until police can come and investigate. I told my team, "If I ever get seriously hurt, take me to the hospital and I'll get you out of prison after I get patched up!" I could go on forever concerning the insanity of some of the laws.

Anyway, we continued to reach out to the marketplace shoppers and vendors, as empty as it was, setting up our generator, if we had fuel, and preached the gospel. There were still those few vendors who stood strong and sold food to those of us who desperately needed it. As soon as we returned home from an outreach the children immediately began to practice their singing and reading the Bible and praying to prepare to go to another village, prison or hospital to reach those in need. The harvest is so rich and we want the storehouses full for the glory of God so we continue to go!

Tonight, as we gathered at our church just outside of our compound, knowing that soldiers were likely to be in the bush, we chased after revival in prayer for our land. Fires were burning all around us as it was the season for clearing the land to prepare it for planting. The farmers set fire to the dry grass on the perimeter of their fields on purpose to save the time and energy required for digging up all the old growth and clearing the debris. It is just easier to burn it all. As you can imagine, there were many fires each night. The fires could not be set during the day because of strong winds. At night the winds died down. While we were praying in the church with our children, I asked them, "Do you want to see revival in South Sudan or are you just as comfortable if you don't? Do we just sit comfortably while friends are literally dying in this war and hope that it doesn't come near us, or do we cry out for revival to come so that we can live in a place where we are all truly dying daily to ourselves and living for Jesus?"

We prayed and we danced and we worshipped until late into the night. We gave it everything we had, crying out for revival in our land, the fire in our hearts as strong as the fires all around us. The next morning, we awoke as if we were hung over, our voices raspy, our eyes tired, but our hearts were fully alive and burning for Jesus. The children asked me, "Can we do this again tonight?" When will we reach the point where we are tired of wars and rumors of wars? When will we cry out for revival or die? That is where my older kids and I were, and still are, in these last days. We thirst and hunger to see a move of God that will change a nation. Otherwise we die.

Are we comfortable in our comfortableness or are we willing to face death to see revival? All of the great revivals came out of sacrifice and fire. I have learned that revival does not come to those who wait or even cry out. Revival comes to those who expect it and are willing to give everything, not counting the cost, to see it come, those who are starving and hungry and desperate. Desperate people do desperate things. I pray for holy desperation to hit us all, in every country, to see revival come upon the earth because my heart refuses to take the pain of death and suffering forever. My heart cries for revival. We need to become desperate for our nations, for the nations of the world, the body of Christ, one in Spirit, for His glory!

Chapter Eight

Isaiah, one of my older boys, has become very ill. He is a healthy fifteen-year old and has had the flu but within days he began to complain of pain in his lungs and that he was having trouble breathing and gasping for breath. There are no doctors in Yei who were available give us a diagnosis. Yesterday my first full-time missionary, Dorinda, arrived and she happens to be a nurse. Sandy and Rebecca are now gone, having traveled back to their countries, leaving me on my own to care for the children along with my Sudanese staff. Today is Dorinda's first day in country. This was God's perfect timing for my sick child. I immediately led her to him and asked her if she could diagnose him and tell us how to treat him. Dorinda listened to his lungs and exclaimed with concern that Isaiah's left lung has collapsed. She heard no movement or breathing from it. She insisted that we needed to get Isaiah to a doctor, to a hospital. I told her that there were no hospitals operating nor doctors. We were at war. The NGO's were gone. I could see her face fill with disbelief, as if she was thinking, "Are you kidding here!" She then exclaimed, "What are we supposed to do now?" "Pray", I said.

All we could do was pray. I called my spirit-filled older children together and we set up five prayer teams of five children each and I instructed them to lay hands on Isaiah and to pray for him for half an hour each shift throughout the morning, switching teams every half hour. We were also treating him medically as best we could, having no medical background ourselves except for this missionary nurse. Our only other option was to send him to Uganda with one of my staff, which I couldn't do because we didn't have the funding and the roads were too dangerous to try and drive across the border. God seriously had to show up and help Isaiah or he could die.

After the prayer teams had been praying for two hours, we reassessed him and found that his lung had fully inflated and he was breathing normally! Just hours earlier we had to fight fear and frustration, really fight it, and we needed a plan from heaven. That plan was five children, five teams, every half hour prayer, laying on of hands, with children leading the teams, not adults. This is what I heard from the Lord. All I could do was to obey Him in this. I have learned not to question what I am hearing. I have learned that God loves unrelenting, not a grain of doubt, faith in Him. It is such a struggle sometimes. Even me, as I have seen much, I have to fight my emotions in order to stay focused on God and what I know to be true. Isaiah is still experiencing some pain after his lung began to work again but he is breathing normally. We will continue to give him medication for the pain and inflammation and we thank God for what He has done. It is truly a miracle in a time of crisis. Once again, God is faithful.

Our family continues to meet daily to worship God and to pray. It seems that the more we step up our worship the more the enemy attacks. This is often the case when one is serious about the things of God. Satan hates it that we worship what he feels to be his place of rulership. He will do anything to kill, or at least destroy us and our faith in God. We need breakthrough for all of our children suffering illness in this place of war and having medical treatment available except what we had to offer in our limited knowledge, so we continue daily to press on and press in, living from the secret place, waiting for wisdom in all of this.

One morning, very early, I was in my house worshipping the Lord. I always open my front door, leaving just the screened door closed. Almost every day an African Pied Wagtail bird appears at my screen door and chirps away without a care in the world. It's the strangest thing. This small white bird with black stripes and a broken right foot even sits on the clothes line as I hang my clothes to dry. I would talk to him and he would sit there and chirp.

This particular morning, as I sat in my chair with my eyes closed, praying to God and enjoying the worship music, I felt a presence in my house and when I opened my eyes there were three of my children who had slipped in to join me. Within the hour, more had come, so serious about hearing from God for our lives. They were hungry for more of Him. It was such an amazing time. We waited expecting, no longer coming to beg and plead for revival, we just came expecting. These mornings would become routine for us, another way of spending time with the Father of this family. There will be attacks, sometimes big ones, when you set yourself up to go after revival and to enter into the most intimate place with Jesus. As we gathered for corporate prayer and worship this week, after our young man's miracle, together we engaged to go ever deeper with the Lord.

The position of our hearts will define our position in the battle. I choose to keep my eyes on the King and position myself as close to Him as possible. God has shown me clearly, after a misunderstanding with a team mate, that if I don't love and commune with people here on the earth, do I really expect it to change when I go to heaven? Heaven will not be a cure-all, end-all, spirit and soul make-over. We must learn to do this here and now. I heard His voice in my mental thoughts, "Is the person with whom you are offended going to go to heaven?" I responded, "Of course." The Lord said, "Then what makes you think it will change when you get there to heaven?" I was fully convicted and knew that I must learn to love, above all things, and to love from my heart.

I now live in a culture that fellowships together, eats together, plays together, studies together, cooks together, works together, doing everything together. It is unheard of to be alone or to do things alone here. Even in the work of washing clothes, the children gather together in a group, helping each other, fellowshipping together. I am reminded of Dalton Thomas' book, Unto Death, where he quotes another writer, "the periods and places of quiet are exceptions to the rule and more often reflect the church's willingness to accommodate to its hosts culture." Basically, status quo brings status quo. I want revival, change, renewal. The children also want these things. They are tired of war. They want to do something about it and refuse to sit idly by and wait to see what will happen. I love this. I want to help usher this in with them and with all of the churches here who have this heart. These ones will see the kingdom of heaven here on earth if they keep this course. It is for everyone, all nations, all walks of society, as we unite in one spirit.

A few years ago, before I came to Iris South Sudan, two concrete foundations had been laid for building more missionary dorms on the backside of our property. These foundations have lain dormant for some years, the foliage growing around it, goats basking in the sun there, and children playing upon them. It has been in my heart to make one of these into a "Prayer House" so that the children will have a place to go to dwell with God. I walked out there today and stood upon one of the foundations and looked out over the land. It is on the high point of our land, surrounded by beautiful rows of corn and ground nuts and cassava and all manner of crops that have been planted here. In the distance there were gently rolling hills covered in every shade of green, dotted with small village huts. It was a quiet and serene place where one could meditate and reflect on issues of the heart and I offered it to the Lord as an altar, a foundation of testimony to His faithfulness to us.

Within two months we miraculously received an unexpected donation to build this prayer house and we began to build even though we had other pressing needs. I remembered the story in Haggai where the Lord spoke to the people through His prophet Haggai that have only cared about their lives and had no concern for Him or His temple.

"Thus speaks the Lord of hosts, saying, 'This people says, '"The time has not come, the time that the Lord's house should be built.'" Then the word of the Lord came by Haggai the prophet, saying, '"Is it time for you yourselves to dwell in your paneled houses, and this temple to lie in ruins?'" (Haggai 2:2-3)

"You looked for much, but indeed it came to little; and when you brought it home, I blew it away. Why?", says the Lord of hosts. "Because of My house that is in ruins, while every one of you runs to his own house." (Haggai 2:9)

My spirit sincerely desired to build a house dedicated to prayer and worship for the Lord Most High. I desperately desired to have a place of prayer that was dedicated for only this. Upon completion of this house of prayer we danced and celebrated the Lord and His faithfulness to us. Every Friday night found us there. Every Wednesday and Friday morning found us there. And every day you would find someone praying there. It truly was a house of prayer.

Chapter Nine

Soon after the refugees arrived in Yei we visited their camp with their permission and brought our church to them! There were about 300 people living here with only tarp structures for their shelters. They had no blankets or beds, only plastic mats on dirt floors. There is no one in Yei to help care for their needs and they are fearful to leave the compound for fear of being beaten or shot by the opposing tribe. There were two UN guards and an SPLA soldier assigned to their front gate and they were happy to see us, raising their hands in thanks as we drove through with a tipper truck full of our children, our sound equipment, and everyone singing as we came to bring the Good News.

We learned that there was a great mix of religions in this place. This Sunday service boasted no religion, only the love of God. At the end of our service, most of the people raised their arms to rededicate their trust in Him in these critical days, also receiving a fresh baptism of the Holy Spirit with the gift of tongues after a short teaching. I felt that the people were very encouraged and we promised to return in a few days for a time of discipling and to play with the children.

As I looked at these tall, warrior-like men, with their tribal markings etched into the skin of their faces, I still thought about how afraid they must have been to run here from so far north, straight into the territory of their enemies, looking for refuge. I told them that we have declared Yei a city of refuge and that God will not forsake them here. This is a bold statement but I felt that the Lord wanted the people to hear this. My heart burst with love for them. I looked and saw our children sitting among them and began to count the tribes represented here. There were Bor Dinka, Bahr Al Ghazal Dinka, Nuer, Mundari, Kakwa, Congo, and Ugandan. I am reminded of the scripture in Philippians where every tribe and every tongue will confess that Jesus Christ is Lord (Philippians 2:10) and I smiled. This is His church, with no walls or barriers of the heart, everyone sitting together under a mango tree worshipping the one true God.

This week found Dorinda and myself running back and forth to a clinic which had resumed business with many of our children who had malaria, an unusually high number all at one time. We were told by the clinic nurse that a very persistent strain of malaria was in our region and could only be treated through a quinine drip (IV) whereas before this latest strain malaria, tablets were prescribed. Always in prayer, Dorinda and I refused to accept so much sickness on our base and we ramped up our prayers. At the same time three of our girls living in the same house had an infection in their bodies that caused their legs to swell and there were no clinics that were able to diagnose it. As I prayed, I was reminded again of the scripture in Exodus 23:25-30 which states:

"So, you shall serve the Lord your God, and He will bless your bread and your water. And I will take sickness away from the midst of you. No one shall suffer miscarriage or be barren in your land; I will fulfill the number of your days. I will send My fear before you, I will cause confusion among all the people to whom you come, and will make all your enemies turn their backs to you."

I held onto His promise that He would take sickness from among us declaring that our compound was a malaria-free zone. I reminded God that we have been worshipping and serving Him each and every day and we believe His word. I wrote this scripture on the whiteboard that hangs in the kitchen so that our children could read it as they stood in line for their meals, teaching them to believe in the power and the promise of the Word of God. I also went into every house on our compound and applied anointing oil on the doors and windows, declaring the Blood of Jesus around all who enter in.

I had been taking anti-malarial medicine for three years since there is no vaccine for malaria. I heard in my spirit, "Do you believe what you are declaring to be true?" Yes, of course I believe it. And then I thought to myself, "I am declaring this yet I am still taking this medicine to prevent me from getting malaria." Now what am I believing? Pastor John Hagee, my pastor in America, always says, "If you're believing for rain, carry an umbrella!" Ouch! I threw my medicine away and have never taken another anti-malarial drug since that day. We were malaria-free for fourteen months, unheard of! Only the Lord can do this because mosquitos are always buzzing around so one cannot escape them.

Tonight, I was pleasantly surprised to find all of our older boys in the Prayer

House first before anyone else. Whenever I visit churches around South Sudan, the majority of the congregants are women and rarely are there many youth boys. This was a first for us as it has been so difficult at times to persuade many of our boys to come for just worship and prayers on youth nights. I would always have to go and round them up, almost forcing them to attend. It moved my heart that they came early and it was also on that night that I decided to anoint those who came early and earlier today I had decided to anoint our children with the Rose of Sharon anointing oil before we worshipped. The Rose of Sharon is the Name of Jesus as the bridegroom, the beautiful One.

Anointing oil is not magical or holy in the sense that the oil itself must be protected. Anointing someone is a prophetic act to remember and declare what God can do. In James 5:13, James tells the church to have the elders anoint the sick with oil and pray for their healing in the name of the Lord. It is a prophetic act that helps to cement what you believe to be true. When you receive the anointing of oil before worship, it is meant to draw you closer to the Lord, thinking of His fragrance. When you receive anointing oil when you are promoted in the church, it is to remind you that it is God who promotes leaders. Anointing someone or something should always point to God. It should never point to man and his ability or holiness.

After our evening of worship, as we walked back to the living area of our compound, we found a pack of wild dogs that were fighting with our dog and chasing our goats. There are many packs of stray dogs in Africa that aren't fed by anyone nor can they find food because food is scarce and people have little enough for themselves, much less animals. Dogs are not loved and pampered here in Africa. They are owned to work at shepherding goats, sheep or cows and as guard dogs for property security. You cannot go to buy dog food at a dog food store and people do not have pets here. There is no concept of having pets, especially having an animal inside your house! It is abhorrent to this culture to have animals in one's house except chickens. I have seen chickens in houses. We are teaching our children to care for our animals and to treat them respectfully. They have grown to love our dog, Rambo.

Stray dogs in our part of Africa are almost always very skinny, their ribs and hip bones jutting out at every angle, although they are not rabid nor do they attack or bite humans. Just last night wild dogs attacked and killed one of our female goats while she was in labor with her twins. In South Sudan the goats are the responsibility of the boys in the family. Ours is no different so all of our boys ran after the dogs with rocks and sticks until they chased them out of our gates. Finally, all was quiet and everyone was able to go to their houses for the night. About an hour later I heard a loud commotion outside at the boy's houses. As I went to investigate, I saw that they had just killed a black mamba snake which our dog had alerted the boys to. After all this commotion tonight, I knew that the devil was so mad about the boys being first to worship and being anointed this night, so he tried to retaliate. Everything that goes wrong in our lives is not always the devil but I felt this night was different.

This morning, I learned that one of our beloved house mamas has died in her village. She has been very sick for a few months and has had health problems all year so I told her to take as much time as she needed to get rest and get well. She traveled to her village in November hasn't been in Yei until last week when she was in the hospital. I loaded our tipper truck with many of our older children who were close to this mama and we drove to the village to spend the day with her and her family. It's very sad really when she probably could have been taken care of better if this war had not happened. There aren't many good hospitals in this country as it is, then to have the few doctors who know enough leave, well, people die as I would later learn when it really hit close to home.

Lately during my morning devotions, the Lord has really been speaking to me about trials and tribulations.

"I will not drive them out from before you in one year, lest the land become desolate and the beasts of the field become too numerous for you. Little by little I will drive them out from before you, until you have increased, and you inherit the land." (Exodus 23:29)

He sometimes drives out our enemies little by little *until* we have increased enough to take possession of that which He has given us. I think of my last five years here in Africa and how each year has been harder than the last and how I asked the Lord even last month, "When will I get rest?" The Lord spoke to me clearly through all of this. He gives most mission minded people, whether in your own neighborhood or across the globe in a foreign country, territories and the anointing for that territory, a position and a calling a little at a time as He prepares us to take possession of the entirety of a thing. He only gives us what we can properly steward and carry each step of the way and He teaches us to do this from a position of rest. I say many times, "I am so glad that God doesn't show me the big picture because it would overwhelm me and I would run the other way!"

Chapter Ten

Everything that we have been through during the first few months of the conflict, the hardships and the miracles, taught us to see and to know the might of our God, to see and to know the faithfulness of our God. God has filled us with so much peace through it all, showing us that even though everything may look like total chaos, there is also an amazing rest as we walk through it because we draw close to Him, abiding in Him in every situation. I find myself drawn ever closer to God, now more than ever, because I have seen that He has every answer that I need and He is the help I need more than any other.

Even when things don't seem to be going well, when the children are sick in droves, when we encounter snakes in the grass, or whether we are jolted when we hear the guns shooting in the night, it is in this place of total dependence and trust in God that one can relate to the idea of a child completely trusting his parent. There is no fear, no anxiety, only trust and being in a restful place. My grandson Solomon is the most trusting little boy I know concerning my relationship with him. I throw him into the air, I flip him around, hang him upside down, swing him around and he is as loose as a noodle, totally and fully trusting that I won't drop him, and laughing uproariously all the while. This is how we should be with our Father who loves us more than I could ever love my grandson and I love him more than anything in this world.

Last night, just a few nights after encountering the black mamba snake near the boy's house I encountered another snake within striking distance. I walked directly in front of it thinking it was a stick because it didn't move, as if dead. I calmly called the watchman to bring a stick to kill it. This morning near our church one of our older girls spotted yet another snake where the children use the latrine and my girls killed it. God continues to show me that His favor is upon us and that it is for His glory. All of us, the body of Christ, we are highly favored of God and He chooses to highlight different people in different seasons to show His glory. During this time of conflict He is pouring out His abundance upon these amazing children, revealing His glory to them and His provision for them. It is wildly wonderful!

There are many people and churches around the world who have been so faithful to us. They are standing together with us in these terrible times. God sets us up by design! He causes amazing things to happen, not by chance, but by design. I have been through many more trials in this last season than I care to recount and I still face trials almost daily. There have been times that I really wanted to quit, throw in the towel, cash in my chips, shut the door. Instead, I kept hearing this little voice inside my head, "When I return will I find faith?" I don't want to be that person who says, or even answers in their heart or mind, "Sorry Jesus, but I didn't think You were going to show up so I picked another plan." Before I came to Africa I used to have plan A, B and C. Here in Africa I am learning every day that Plan Jesus has to be my only plan.

The children and Dorinda and I continue to gather together for worship many nights and mornings each week, seeking God's face with desperation. We had been singing many songs about rain, the sound reverberating in our spirits, so that even as we passed each other on our compound, throughout the day we would say to each other, "I see the cloud is coming! It's gonna rain!" We seriously believed that we would see the rains of revival come to us and to South Sudan. I love their childlike faith so much. Every time we gather for worship they are just as passionate as the last time of gathering for worship. I am so encouraged by this generation and I pray that it would happen all over the world, in churches and in school houses and in communities. It is our most fervent hope that we would see the glory of God cover the earth and not just our little corner of it.

During this season of uncertainty, God has proven to us over and over again that He is steady and reliable and certain of our future. He truly encourages us to understand radical faith and dependence on Him in all things. What I love about these hard and difficult seasons is having to walk through it as if I purposely set out to ask for the impossible, to prove that He is the God of all impossibility. I don't test God, I just don't hesitate to ask for the things that I need and believe that He will give them, no matter how crazy it sounds or looks. He is our Father. Why would our Father purposely set us up to fail? Why would our Father purposely withhold life and liberty from us? Because that is not the character of our Father. I really want to encourage people to "practice" faith, believing for the unseen, for the impossible. The Father's heart is to bless us, to simply bless us, as we follow Him. In Psalm 23, the scriptures declare that goodness and mercy follow us everywhere we go, all of the days of our lives. God radiates goodness and mercy and when we abide in Him, the overflow is our inheritance! How wonderful.

Chapter Eleven

We are now some months into the conflict and we have decided to have an outreach in the city center which is called Freedom Square. Soccer matches, Christian crusades and important government and political gatherings are held here. It is a very large dirt field, surrounded by shops and a few government buildings, and also an iron sheet roofed, bleacher style concrete seating area on the long side of the field. When South Sudan gained its independence and became a nation the ceremony was held that day in this place where thousands came to celebrate.

Today, after sharing the message of hope, we called forth those who desired to receive prayer for healing. A lame man came forward for prayer, dragging one of his legs, actually using his hand to pull at his trouser leg to help his lame leg move forward, as if his leg was an extension of his arm. Our children laid hands on him and prayed for him to be healed. The man was then asked to test his leg by wiggling it or to do something that he couldn't do before the prayer. He hesitantly lifted his leg, bent it at the knee and a broad smile spread across his face like the sunrise of a new day. He then tried walking and was astounded because he was walking as if his leg had never been lame, as if he were just like every other able-bodied man! He jumped up and down shouting excitedly and took off running around the field! He ran around the entire soccer field shouting something in Arabic, waving his hands all the while.

A football match was being played and when this man went running by all of the players and onlookers stopped to watch this crazy man. He had been healed! Everybody in the town knew of this man. Our town is not that big. Everyone knows everyone. The football game stopped and the players and onlookers came over to our small stage to investigate. It was an incredible day for the children to see that God would continue to move on their behalf. Later this week when we went into town many people recognized us and told us that they saw the miracle or heard about it. We are contending for revival in Yei!

This Sunday morning as I was preparing for children's church, two of the older children came running into my house out of breath and told me that there is a big problem. Samuel, one of our five-year old boys, has fallen into the latrine pit! What? My mind could not comprehend a child falling through a small hole in the cement. All I could think of was to grab a long piece of solar cable, about 30 feet long that was lying on a shelf nearby. My thinking was that I could lower myself down to bring him up. The latrine was about one hundred yards from my house and the three of us ran as fast as we could.

When I arrived, there was a circle of children and mamas standing around the latrine. They parted as I came through and I saw that Samuel had already been pulled out of the pit and was being soaped down and washed. He just stood there, his little body covered with soap, rivulets of water running down his face, looking as peaceful as you please. There were no feces on him nor even the smell of it. The children were crying and upset yet Samuel was as calm as you please, not in the least bit traumatized. I looked into the latrine and saw that a large portion of the cement floor had caved in, about three feet in diameter, and had slid into the bottom of the pit, resting in a diagonally just above the waste, which was about 40 feet down.

I was told that Samuel was in the latrine with the door locked and screaming loudly. Our watchmen heard a child screaming from the direction of the latrine and ran to investigate. They then proceeded to rip the door off of its hinges in an effort to get in quickly. When the door finally came loose, the watchmen were amazed at what they saw. There was Samuel on all fours holding onto a large piece of cement so that he wouldn't slip into the abyss. He looked up with big eyes that said, "Please get me out of here"! Nearby was a ladder and the watchman lowered it down into the pit, careful not to disturb the slab of cement that Samuel was clinging to. Samuel gingerly climbed up the large ladder, his tiny seven-year old hands holding on tightly around the large makeshift rungs. As soon as he came up over the lip, the mamas grabbed him and soothing him and cooing over him with concern they checked all of his body parts looking for any injuries. By the time I arrived everything was a bit calmer. That's how fast everything happened.

If the entire floor had caved in Samuel would have been crushed. I believe that either an angel or God Himself stopped that floor from going under and had put that ladder close by. When there is ongoing construction on our compound, the builder will always make a ladder from scrap wood. He then leaves it at the construction site until the job is finished. Our current construction site is on the other side of the compound which means the ladder should not have been where it was. As a matter of fact, just yesterday it was up near my house, over a hundred yards from the latrine. In this world we will have trouble, trials, and persecution but God is faithful to deliver us from them all. Once we knew that Samuel was okay I told the children that we should sing the song, "Thank You Jesus" as it was all we could say. We sang with thanksgiving and we prayed a prayer of thanks. Then we continued with our Sunday morning and went to church and worshipped God with all of our hearts.

This week our town has been quiet, the people hopeful that the conflict is over. I was working at my desk when all of a sudden one of our girls came running in crying, "Amina is hurt bad. Her eyes won't open up and she is just laying there!" I ran up to our school and saw where she was lying on the ground seemingly unconscious. I talked to her and patted her face to try to wake her up. She finally came to and didn't remember anything about the accident so it is a mystery to us. One of our bicycles was lying nearby so we knew she had fallen from the bike. No one saw what had happened and there were no obstacles nearby that she could have hit her head on. Amina had a swollen area on her head and she didn't know who I was, just calling me madam, the name that the children call female teachers, so we rushed her to the clinic. She also wanted to go to sleep.

I was very concerned so I drove our car like an ambulance, very fast, flying over our dirt roads, slamming through potholes, all the while singing and praying at the very top of my voice to keep Amina awake. I was even making a siren sound for the in-town driving. I'm fairly sure that people thought we were mad. I didn't care, I did whatever it took to get my child to the clinic. Amina was not responding to anything we did or said. There are no CT scanning machines here in our town, perhaps even the country. All we could do was pray and wait. Amina's face was now swollen. I had my iPod in my backpack and I turned it on because I had a healing scripture playlist on it. I placed it near her ear and let it play. For the next fifteen hours she did not respond, did not move, did not go to the latrine, did not eat. She just lay there, the iPod playing the scriptures throughout the night. When morning came, Amina sat up like nothing had happened, with no memory of the bike incident, asking, "What am I doing here in the hospital?" It is still a mystery to this day what really happened. We just praise God again and again for His goodness and mercy that follows us all our days.

Chapter Twelve

I went into town today to investigate the situation concerning the conflict and to see if the shops had reopened, or even if the trucks from Uganda were back on the road bringing much needed food and supplies. On the road bordering the marketplace there were some soldiers walking and carrying hand held rocket launchers, fully loaded! I was thinking that one wrong move, one slip of the foot, one enemy bullet, and this thing might shoot off down the main road, killing innocent civilians. I also saw army trucks with fifty-caliber machine guns mounted on the back. These vehicles are called "technicals". I really hated seeing these reminders of war which kept it real. It's feels like we are always on the edge of a cliff, waiting to jump off if something happens or sitting with feet hanging over the edge just waiting. This brings so much stress and tension to our minds and bodies.

I thank God that my children do not see these daily reminders of war, reminding them every day that they have lost their freedom once again. The children have known only four years of peace, then to have it snatched away, it can cause people to lose their hope. We try to keep their days as normal as possible, filling them with activity. I have been feeling the tension lately, the stress of making so many decisions that affect us all. It's a lot for one person to bear. I think everything is catching up to me, like post-traumatic stress syndrome, but it isn't post yet. We are still in it. I have been asking God to help me to hold onto my peace. I am always on edge, feeling wound up in anticipation of something bad happening. I have been asking for people all over the world to pray for us, for God's peace to be a real and tangible thing for us here in South Sudan.

Lately, I have also been thinking a lot about the children's history. I don't want them to forget how far God has brought them in their journey through this life. Last year we found out that there were three teenaged boys in our local prison who had been arrested for trying to break into a gas station. The station is located on the main road and one light remains on all night, illuminating a small office located close to the pumps. The boys were trying to unscrew the lightbulb so that they wouldn't be seen and as they were doing this, one of the boys was shot in the back by a policeman, killed while trying to unscrew a light bulb. This is insanity. This is incompetence. There were no repercussions at all to the policeman who did this. All in a day's work I guess.

The three boys who were not shot were so traumatized that they wouldn't talk to anyone. We found out about the boys at an NGO meeting we were attending a few days after the incident. I immediately told my pastor that we needed to get them out of there before they too were killed. It took us two weeks to persuade the authorities to release them to us. I praise God that we were known and respected by the leaders of the town because it is the only reason that they released them to us, no fine imposed and no sentence to fulfill. Since then, two of them have been so radically transformed by the love of God and by our love for them that it is now difficult for me to remember them as they were. One of the boys never did change and ended up leaving on his own to parts unknown.

Two of these boys have remained with us and five years later they are respectful, loving, helpful and hard-working young men. One boy was elected by his entire school to be the president, or better known as head boy, of the school in Luwero, Uganda! This is complete redemption. These who were once so lost are now found and living like royalty, from the pit to the palace as my pastor always says. I praise God for chances like this to bring lost ones to redemption to those whom the world has forgotten and written off as a wasted case. There is an abundance of treasure to be found in people who have been hiding from God, waiting for the treasure hunters to go and find them. Our lives are much richer when we find them. Many times, I find myself becoming tired and weary from the work of the ministry and I think on these boys and others like them and I praise my God in heaven that He trusts me with His treasures.

Many people pray for the harvest to come and many churches pray for the harvest and for revival. Jesus said to pray for the "laborers". He said that the harvest is here, it is rich, it is ready. We need to pray for the laborers, not the harvest. Jesus redeemed mankind on the cross so the harvest is guaranteed! We are the reason that He came in the flesh, to guarantee the harvest. It is very difficult to find people who are willing to come to the hard places such as South Sudan. Most times it is fear that stops the ones who are called yet resist. Also, many will not step into the mission God has called them to until they see all of the finances sitting in the bank and a roadmap of the plans for everything that needs doing. God is looking for faith in Him, not faith in what people are capable of. If God is calling you to a difficult and maybe even desolate place He will take care of you. If you are truly called by the Lord and go where He says go in the time that He sets, then it would defeat His purpose to have a person die and not complete His mission.

Whenever fear sets in, I remind God that He called me here so why wouldn't He protect me, right? Many are afraid to come because they don't think they could live like this. I can tell you by experience that you can live anywhere in any situation if you allow God's grace to work in and through you. After living here for ten years, I find that I am just as comfortable with little as opposed to having all my needs and wants met and even exceeded. When I had much of everything I found myself trusting in my bank account vice trusting in God. I found myself trusting in great medical care vice trusting in God. In the book of Luke, chapter and verse 18:8, Jesus says to His disciples, "When the Son of Man returns will He really find faith on the earth?" It is time to trust God and do what He has called us to do. He is faithful to complete what He has started in us. We are praying for the laborers to come, here where they are needed. Help us to pray for the laborers.

It is now the end of April 2014, five months since the beginning of the civil war, and the early rains are here. This week the children have been on spring break which allows us more time to spend with each other. Our aspiration is to take them deeper into the things of God and the kingdom of heaven. It is so wonderful because we are not on a time schedule and have the freedom to slow down and digest what is being discussed between us. If Jesus is with us, indwelling us, then we should have tangible evidence of this. Our perspective has changed from even one year ago concerning just how much access we have to throne room encounters.

One of our older boys, who is sixteen, has always been a quiet, serious young man, keeping mostly to himself. He rarely talks or smiles, always very serious. His parents passed on, although he does have siblings who also live with us. His big sister mothers the boys, washing their clothes and cooking special food for them sometimes. She really is such a treasure to them and to us here at Iris. Last night the Lord moved me to pull him into a motherly embrace and to tell him how very proud I am of him, how much I love him and that God sees him when he thinks no one else does. He just started weeping and I was so touched that his shell had opened up a bit. This is why we press in to the Father's heart. He is the one who heals our children. We have no other options. We don't have access to trauma healing and counselors, only Jesus and our love for the children. He is our all in all.

It is not unusual at all to find Dorinda and I on our faces in the middle of the day for three hours in a glory encounter, only to open our eyes and find two, three, even ten youths on the floor with us. I asked Jesus, "Why now, what is it that we or You are doing that has caused You to come at this time?" He answered me, "The children have been ushering this in for three years now, since the days when you first started Friday night worship. This last year they have been seeking Me wholeheartedly. I find them hard to resist. I am bringing My glory to this place to consume all who want to enter in. You are ravishing My heart."

The Father, the Son and the Holy Spirit find it hard to resist youth all over the world who have been seeking Him unrelentingly in the most extreme circumstances, not caring about a comfortable place to worship, not caring that they have the same worship songs week in and week out, not caring that they haven't seen much change in the atmosphere in one, two, even three years, just a world of youth who keep going after God because nothing else satisfies them anymore. They have heard that God is fun and full of love for all people and that encounters are amazing with Him and that they can live from that place.

The youth of this world are looking for the real thing so they are drawn to this place of seeking God and only Him until He manifests Himself to them. So many youth groups try too hard to "entertain" the youth with games and movies and food and light shows. In our home there are none of these things, yet we have been desperate for His presence, more than ever before, because our encounters with Him are full of Holy Spirit and His presence. Our youth nights are for the teenagers but, every week I find our ten to twelve-year old children slipping into our times of encounter on youth nights. I see them and I smile and never chase them away. They have become serious seekers, hands outstretched, rocking back and forth, weeping, soaking in the presence of God. We don't have an amazing youth band or smoke and strobe lights or loud booming speakers or carpeted floors or anything to "draw" the youth. I have an iPod, the knowledge of God and a pretty good small portable speaker for my iPod. It's all I've ever had here. It is more than enough for these young seekers of the living God. They have encountered Him and once you encounter God there is no going back. We were created for encounter.

We are living for eternity from an eternal mindset in the present reality of our nation at war. Our children have seriously been inquiring of me if they can go to the north to share the good news of Jesus Christ, where rebels have entered mosques and hospitals and have been shooting women and children for no reason other than tribe affiliation. "Can we go and tell them about the Father's love for them?", they ask. They are not afraid, they just want the youth in these rebel groups to know what they know, the amazing love of an amazing God, even at the risk of their own lives. How can I tell them no, it is too dangerous? Yet, I must, for now. I have a responsibility to them as a mother, to care for them and to protect them.

Today, once again the leaders of the two armies are meeting in Addis Ababa, Ethiopia to negotiate for peace. All previous meetings have yielded nothing except more distrust and more desire for each to have full power over this one nation. It has become very disheartening and physically and mentally taxing for we the people who have waited so long for freedom, most never knowing anything else but war and turmoil. I have received many requests from people in first world countries who want to come and visit our nation. They have communicated with me that they have heard from God and right now is their time to come, "I am called for such a time as this.", they say. Yet, when another rebel uprising happens, the next email is a cancellation. Missions, or being called by God to go somewhere at a certain time, is what the Acts church did. Trials and tribulations and even persecution comes with it. Can I say that again? Trials and tribulations and even persecution comes with the calling of God.

It upsets me when we as the church preach a message about running into the darkness, even unto death, but when persecution arises, the church puts the brakes on until everything is happy-clappy again. It has happened to us time and again. Individuals have cancelled their trips due to the perceived danger and so have church teams. "Our medical insurance doesn't cover war zones," they say. Or, a safer ministry in another nation has been introduced and all of a sudden, their calling changes.

I really have a desire to see people experience the fullness of their calling, to really see how God is with them, truly with them, despite all the dangers. When you say yes to Jesus, then trust Him to walk with you through that yes. It grieves my heart to see people look back in regret at a lost opportunity. Please trust Jesus when He calls you. He will walk with you and show you great and mighty things about yourself, your spirit and character, that you never realized before.

The present situation should not affect that calling. If one perceives that they have heard from God and it was confirmed again and again, then why are people afraid to trust God? I have on my staff a missionary who is twenty-three years-old who came a month after the conflict began in Yei. Almost everyone in her family questioned her decision, asking her to rethink it, but she knew that she was called by God for this time and she came. This is what the calling of God and the response looks like. It isn't always neat and tidy and wrapped with a bow and covered by medical insurance. None of us have medical insurance and we are full time missionaries. If we die the we go right into glory. It's a win, win situation!

God normal doesn't change His mind when He impresses on our hearts to go. He is the same yesterday, today and forever. When we tell everyone that God told me to go and then cancel because of a little persecution, what does that say about the warrior Christian we are supposed to be and what does that say about our faith? How does it look to my children who live here and still worship God with all their hearts and ask to go to the rebel camp? It doesn't look good when I have to tell them that yet another team cancelled because they were afraid that it was too dangerous for them. If we want people to come to Christ and live a life of victory, we have to be willing to go through the fire to find them. Paul speaks about fear in the book of Romans, in chapter eight, verse fifteen through seventeen:

"For you did not receive the spirit of bondage again to fear, but you received the Spirit of adoption by whom we cry out, 'Abba Father.' The Spirit Himself bears witness with our spirit that we are children of God, and if children, then heirs – heirs of God and joint heirs with Christ, if indeed we suffer with Him, that we also may be glorified together."

The Spirit of adoption is Christ Himself dwelling in us. The word "Spirit" in this verse is capitalized, therefore delineating that it is a person, the person of Christ Jesus. If we are in Christ, we will suffer but we will not fear because He has delivered us from fear. If we preach this, then we must believe this and walk in the fullness of it. Of course, we must use wisdom. God doesn't want us to blindly run into a barrage of bullets to save a soul. Neither would He call us to do this. If God is calling you to do something, even if it looks scary, do it. He either called you or He didn't. You will see an example in a later chapter where I had to face my fear by going into a dangerous place at the risk of my life, because God called me to go there at that time. It was in His timing so I felt His peace to go.

I'm always reminded of the story in Numbers chapter 13 where the leaders, the priests who were charged to have faith in God, they were commissioned by Moses to go into and spy out the land that was promised to them by God. He told them to report back all that they had seen and found. The men came back carrying the largest bunch of grapes that any of them had ever seen, so big that it took two men to carry one bunch on a pole! These men, all except for two, knowing that God promised them this place, could only speak of the giants that they saw and were full of fear. They saw themselves as grasshoppers. When all excuses had been heard and the people were incited to fear, only Joshua and Caleb were allowed to see the promise of God fulfilled in their lifetime because they did not shrink back. They saw the same giants but they saw their God as bigger than the giants and they knew that they were called.

When you read about Joshua and Caleb all through the story of their lives you will find that they spent their time near the tent of meeting and even in the tent. Joshua didn't want to leave. Be encouraged by Christ Jesus and His power in you. Use wisdom, hear His voice, even seeking confirmation. You can only experience this kind of faith when you spend your time in His presence, seeking His faith and His word. God can do far more than we could ever dream of or even imagine but we can only bear witness to these things if we go.

Chapter Thirteen

We are now in the sixth month of the conflict which has been contained in the north of South Sudan, about 200 miles from us near a major city called Bor. Here in Yei it remains fairly quiet with shops opening for trade again. Also, many of the NGO's have returned. Today I was sitting quietly before the Lord reading my Bible when suddenly a thought came into my mind, "Go and preach to the soldiers." I was taken aback! "What? Preach to the soldiers? Preach to what soldiers, where?" I had no desire to preach to the soldiers nor have I ever even contemplated it so I knew this could be from the Lord so I decided to go with it. I asked my pastor if he knew anyone at the SPLA Headquarters in Yei whom we could gain permission from and he told me that he did and proceeded to contact this person.

The next morning, we found ourselves in the Brigadier General's office! "Why do you want to come and speak to my men," he asked. I explained to him how we really wanted to encourage his men to stay focused, strong and healthy and to pray for them to have peace during these difficult times. He was quiet and thoughtful. Finally, he said, "You can come tomorrow."

This was all happening so fast. I didn't have a message prepared but I know that Holy Spirit does. This is a colossal door opener for the gospel of Jesus Christ and I feel in my heart to speak to them about their identities as sons and soldiers. What does this mean to a military man? I have been laboring in prayer all week, feeling as if the heavens were a brass ceiling. Our team is ready to go, Dorinda and I, our pastor and a missionary who is visiting from South Africa. The next morning, Tuesday, we arrived early in the morning and were immediately directed to the Brigadier General's office and my first thought was, "Oh no, he has cancelled," which happens quite often because of current tensions in our nation.

Upon entering his office, the General was sitting behind a humble wooden desk, no pictures on the wall, and nothing fancy in regard to furniture. He invited us to sit on plastic yard chairs, which are popular in South Sudan. I already like this man because he didn't put on airs and didn't carry pride around as in, better than you attitude, which is many times the case with leaders. As he continued to wrap up his work, we sat there in silence feeling a bit uncomfortable to say the least. Finally, after about ten minutes he arose and kindly asked us to follow him. We were led outside to a small gathering of soldiers standing in formation under four large, leafy mango trees, about fifty to sixty men and a handful of women in full camouflage uniforms armed with AK47's and ammunition belts.

Without pretense, he introduced us and my pastor and I began to share our message to encourage the men and women from the Bible and from the Lord. We were informed that we had only fifteen minutes to talk so we talked fast! I immediately shared with them my life as a soldier for thirty years (military career and ROTC instructor combined). I neglected to tell them that I was in the Navy as Uganda has no Navy. As soon as I told them that I was a soldier and I worked hard and played hard, if you know what I mean, and I knew where their minds were and where they were coming from, I had their attention and respect.

After our brief message, the Army Chaplain took over and prayed for the men and dismissed them. Many of them came to greet us, shaking our hands firmly and smiling. It was actually nice to be back in an element that I was a part of for so many years. We visited with the General and some of his men for another thirty minutes or so and right before we were leaving the general asked if it would be possible for us to come back the following week when more of his men would be on the base. I responded with enthusiasm that we would be honored and were so thankful to have such an opportunity. I had been thinking that the reason we were speaking to such a small group and for only a short time was that perhaps he wanted to "try us out" before allowing us to speak to his battalion. We left with the knowledge that we were invited back.

A week has passed and we are returning to the SPLA Base today. We decided that it would be nice to bring these men some packages of biscuits (a type of cookie) and tea and sugar. These are prized possessions for soldiers as they travel well and don't spoil. The General was actually glad to see us and greeted us with a smile and a firm handshake, not having us wait in his office this time. He then led us to a large open field, about fifty yards square, dense bush surrounding us on three sides. There were approximately 200 men and a handful of women assembled in military formation with squads and columns, in full battle gear, gun belts, weapons (AK47), camouflage fatigues, black boots, their faces stern, standing at attention as if sentry's at an armory, awaiting the arrival of the general.

The General's top brass were standing in a smaller formation directly opposite and facing the battalion, their backs to the bush. The bush pressed in, thick, dense grass climbing up to a man's waist, trees heavy laden with limbs and leaves, the fruit in its infant stages of growth, just as everything should look three months into the rainy season. I noticed four gunmen, soldiers who were squatting attentively behind a 50-caliber machine guns which were pointed out into the bush. These weapons were too large for a man to carry and were resting on short two-foot tripods ready to fire when commanded or alerted. There were also soldiers with AK47s intermittently positioned around us, again facing outward, alert and standing at the ready should any sign of danger appear. I learned later that within the governmental rank and file the tension has become increasingly unstable causing all soldiers to be on high alert. I realized that an attack from the opposition could ensue at any time and found myself gazing into the bush every now and then, being just a bit intimidated.

As I preached, I could see myself standing in the field, as if hovering above the scene and peering down from this lofty position thinking that if I died today I would rather step into heaven preaching the gospel rather than running the opposite way, a bullet in my Bible and not in my back. One never knows how one will respond to danger until you find yourself making the choice. I made the choice to stay. This thought spurred me on and encouraged me even more to tell these soldiers about their God given identities as sons of God who are called to be peacemakers and that God blesses the peacemaker.

I have been studying sonship and our identity as sons as seen through the eyes of our Father and also as experienced by young men in the Jewish culture in the time of Jesus upon the earth. I thought about the baptism of Jesus and what it meant at that time but also what the Father said to Jesus, and why then? When a Jewish boy reached an age of maturity his father then announced his sonship to everyone at a formal ceremony, declaring publicly that the son could now make decisions in the father's name as a trusted equal. Sonship was based upon the maturity level of the son rather than the actual age. Jesus did not have a modern-day bar mitzvah because this ceremony wasn't introduced until the early Eastern Europe era. Until that time, a boy was not called a son, but was referred to as a child, as long as he acted immaturely. When a son showed himself mature to his father, it was then that the father proudly announced to the community that his son was now a man and an heir and he was proud of him.

When Jesus was baptized and came up out of the water His Father said, "This is My son! I am well pleased with him." This was His introduction as a Son, no longer a child. I explained this to the men of war standing before me in their battle array, these hardened soldiers, who had killed their brothers in this civil war, that sonship was their inheritance through Christ Jesus, to be presented to the Father as sons, no longer children in the eyes of their Father. When I presented the offer for those who wanted to be presented as sons of God, every single hand went up, every single one, a little over 200 men. The men repented and accepted Jesus as their Savior, as a brother, a joint-heir, a son. I believe God is going to do a good work in them, even in these chaotic times, and one day they will lay down their arms and take up their plough sheers.

Last week when we were here, the chaplain mentioned that they had a Battalion church but it was in poor condition and this was the reason that many of the men quit attending church as they would spend more time having to avoid the rain coming in through large gaping holes in the roof than hearing the message. Before leaving our compound to come here I knew that I wanted to donate some money to help the Battalion Chaplain replace the leaking grass roof on their small church, replacing it with iron sheets, basically a tin roof. He was pleased and couldn't wait to get to work. After we had fellowshipped with the soldiers a bit I asked if we could pray for the General. He was happy to receive us again into his office. When we asked how we could pray for him, he shared with us some of the daily stresses he endured, one being the constant problems to be solved.

I had told his men earlier as we fellowshipped that being a leader in the military in America, the best way to bring unity and victory to the Battalion was to change the way my subordinates approached problems. The General doesn't need more problems, he needs solutions and only Holy Spirit can give them good solutions through His wisdom. I told the men that like Aaron and Hur, it was their responsibility to lift their General up in prayer, not constantly the other way around. The General was so grateful to hear this. We also learned that he is responsible for all of Equatoria State, which is the bottom one third of the country of South Sudan. After we prayed for the General he extended the invitation to us to visit his bases all over his region, encouraging his soldiers and praying for them. Brigadier Generals don't just tell a little old Texas girl to go into all his territory and preach the gospel every day!

I am so humbled by this, that God would allow me to partner with Him. "God, who am I that you would think of me"? He assigns those who are sincere, with hearts full of faith, and who are available, having the desire to do what He commands us to do with no stipulations attached. No more qualification is needed by Him except to walk humbly, be merciful and to love justice. If we walk by people in need and have something to give them, then we have walked by God Himself as we are all created in His image.

I truly believe that everyone has something to offer in the building of the kingdom of God, from small children, special needs persons, housewives and mothers who have one of the hardest jobs, professional careerists, and full-time ministers. Jesus didn't lay down a bunch of rules. All He commanded us to do was to go! Jesus said that if we give even a cup of water to the thirsty then we have given to Him. Water costs us nothing in the west. Here in this country and other third world countries water is very costly. I know that in many places the ladies and children walk for miles to get to a water source then carry a 20-liter water container back home on her head, carrying a baby on her back and another little one in tow. Water is needed for washing clothes, bathing, cooking and even for crops. Can you imagine carrying this much water every single day? It is costly. Yet, when you enter a home in South Sudan the first thing that is offered to you, besides a chair to sit on, is a clean cup of water. At every single home you visit a cup of water is brought first and foremost. This speaks volumes to me.

Many people are overwhelmed by the great need in the world. These days it seems that many people are in need. I look at the things that I "used to" think I needed and I see now that I never really needed them after all. It isn't until you've given everything or lost everything that you realize what is really needed. I used to have a rental storage room in America full of "stuff" and I wondered just how much of that is really needed. Living in a culture of just having the bare necessities really makes one aware of what is really needed in life. My life is very uncluttered here. I still have great need for our children but I just trust God to provide for their needs. Many people ask me when they come for a visit, "What do you need for yourself?" I never realized, until a friend came from my hometown to visit, just how little I actually need. I am content with the little I have, I am uncluttered and unburdened of much. I gave away everything in my storage room in America and turned in the key. Now I really do have nothing there but some clothes hanging in a closet for my annual trips home.

There are many in this world who have great need and we all have something to offer. We have houses and storerooms full of things that we haven't even looked at for years thinking that one day we "might" need them. One shirt given to someone in need is a treasure beyond compare in this part of the world. I see it here when I bring new clothes for our children. They are so delighted to receive used clothes and they wear them proudly, washing them by hand and ironing them, putting them carefully away. One shirt, one dollar, one cup of water is all that is needed by many people in our part of the world. Don't let the "big" picture overwhelm you into doing nothing. Just stop for the one in front of you, the one who needs a cup or bottle of water, a shirt, a meal, a hand up and not a hand out, although sometimes that's all we can do. If each person in this world gave something to another all would have a need met. How simple and yet, how profound. Seriously, we are blessed by God to bless others.

Today I awoke to another typically rainy day as we are in the rainy season now so it comes every day, sometimes like a torrent, a waterfall of rain coming in sheets. I drove to the airstrip on a slippery, muddy, potholed road and this was my second trip this week. The airstrip, if you remember my arrival in South Sudan, is just a small dirt runway and there is one small building made from mud bricks baked in a wood fire. The customs office is nothing more than two men asking you to open your luggage in front of all the other passengers, your luggage on the floor, as you are bent over with your rear in the air. There is no x-ray scanner and if the guys are feeling cordial that day, they just wave you through checking nothing. It would be so easy to come in or go out with weapons in your luggage if you are a "friend" of the right people. That's just how it is.

As I drove, many soldiers were at the road check points due to the increase of bandits and opposition forces lurking around our city in the bush. Most of them recognized as I drove up and instead of stopping me which is protocol, they smiled and waved me through the checkpoint. I was encouraged to realize that I could now call these men friends instead of strangers not to be trusted. They usually stop travelers and ask, "Where you are going? Where are you coming from?" Then they tell you to get out of your car because they want to check all of your luggage even though it was just checked at the airport by their own men. So, you just plop your luggage on the hood of your car for all to see.

Lately, I've been packing my underwear and bras on top because these things are never shown in public, not even on your clotheslines. I can tell you, these men were very quick about asking me to shut my suitcase and move on! The soldiers haven't been paid in months because of the war so I have begun buying mandazi, a large doughnut like bread that we eat for breakfast, and I give this to them as I go through the checkpoints along with a bottle of water.

(Here I am six years later in Uganda and I am still handing out bottles of water to the police checkpoint in our town every time I go through.). I know that I am exactly where God has planted me and I can never say that God changed His mind because it is too dangerous for me to be here.

When you are in the perfect will of God there is no sacrifice too great nor any danger too great for Him to rescue you from. You just know who He is and who you are in Him, that relationship that supersedes all others, that places all things below us where we don't really worry about our situation or the sacrifice as long as He is with us. This is His perfect will for each of us, just to be with Him and to know Him intimately, whatever this looks like and to be in perfect peace about it. I love how Heidi always reminds us that we are all original masterpieces of the Father. She tells the story of her father being an art collector and how he would never buy copies because they are worthless. The original is the only thing of worth. That is how God created us, as originals, created individually, fearfully and wonderfully and our extraordinary worth is found in this alone. No one is any better than the other and no one can be "as good as" another. There is such freedom in this!!

Chapter Fourteen

Today after church the children asked me, "Can we go to the hospital today? We must go and pray for the sick and wounded in the hospital, we just have to!" How could I say no to this? We ate lunch and then departed for the hospital with our children between ten and sixteen-years old. I tell our children that this too is church because God says we are His church when we go and do what He commands us to do. He did command us to heal the sick and visit those in prison so we go and bring church to these people who cannot go to a church building. The next day as I was driving into town I was flagged down by some prisoners who were working by the roadside. It was the hottest day this week and sweat rolled off their backs in rivulets as they dug ditches, their backs bent to the task, sweat rolling off their brows, their skin glistening in the hot sun. They recognized us from all of our visits for prison ministry. In South Sudan prisoners are trusted not to run so they are not chained and are allowed to interact with people who walk by.

It's really amazing how much respect there is both from the prisoner and the police toward each other. Remember, this is a very relational people who don't set aside their culture just because they are imprisoned. I stopped to talk with them, shaking their hands, as is the proper thing to do. I asked them how they were doing and they said, "Mama, we have no water and we are thirsty. Can you give us some small money so we can send a guard to go get water?", they asked. We told them not to worry, that we would bring the water to them. They were so happy when we came back with two cases of water and some biscuits, shaking my hand and blessing me. I of course also prayed for them. These are still our brothers and it is so nice to be able to stop and shake their hands and talk to them, the guards being so very nice about it all.

The scene was so casual, almost as if they weren't prisoners. This day they were able to maintain their dignity in public and this makes al the difference when we go and visit them. Many of them are in the prison waiting for their appointed time with the court for committing adultery. This is serious business in this nation. Imagine how that would fit in with the western culture? Sadly, I think that half of our society would be in jail for this "crime".

Dorinda continues to volunteer at the hospital in town, the one in which we take our children to minister twice a week. This week a lady brought her child in who had such a horrendous infection in her ears that she could no longer hear. The doctor said that her inner ear was eaten away because the infection had been there for so long and there was nothing he could do. Dorinda asked the mother and the doctor if she could pray for the girl because Jesus could fix this. She said a short "simple" prayer because she wanted to honor the doctor's time. The waiting room outside was full of the sick and suffering. After Dorinda said, "Amen", the doctor finished writing the results of the exam in the little girl's book.

Medical books are required in South Sudan, the book being an elementary school small soft back note taking book. There is someone who sits near the waiting room and sells them, making their profit. While the doctor was discussing the daughter's situation with the mother, Dorinda whispered the little girl's name while the girl wasn't looking. The little girl immediately turned to look at Dorinda! Her ears had cleared! The doctor and the mother were stunned. They didn't know what to do. He probably thought, "Well, now what do I write in this book???" Jesus doesn't care how much we know or what we say, He just needs someone who is available and believes enough to pray. He has this!

Tonight, we are on our way for a night of ministry in the community market just outside of the SPLA Barracks where many soldiers go to drink and hang out with the fellows. This is the only market which requires permission before anyone sets up a crusade or ministry. Upon arriving at the small market place, we met with the Chaplain and another church leader and were informed that we had received permission from the SPLA to show the film, so we set up our equipment. The film had just started when a high-ranking soldier came over to tell us that we would need to shut everything down and leave quickly. He said that it was just too dangerous to do these things at night with the rebels so close. I asked him for five minutes on the microphone and I blasted a salvation message, shooting it out like a flaming arrow, because I didn't want people to leave without hearing anything. We then packed it all up and went home. Unfortunately, this marked the end of our night time campaigns in Yei.

We are now preparing to take a team to Terekeka, which is about 60 kilometers north of Juba, the capital city. The cattle keeper Mandari tribe makes their home in this area of South Sudan and we desired to bring the gospel to them. The Mandari are serious cattle people who are known for raiding cattle from other tribes and are also on the receiving end of raids in return. Much of the time the young boys wear no clothes and if they do it is a thick blanket which draped around them and tied over one shoulder with nothing underneath. As young children, for both boys and girls, it is traditional to have horizontal lines carved into their foreheads with their tribal markings.

The Dinka do the same but the markings are different. Skulls have been found with marks cut into them which indicates how deeply the children's foreheads are carved into. Both tribes also extract certain adult teeth which gives each tribe a distinct, yet different, lisping sound while talking. Both of these practices are very painful and the boys must endure it without making a sound. In the rural areas this tradition is still practiced. I feel like I am in a National Geographic story whenever I go and visit them. They are really very nice people, very hospitable.

Chapter Fifteen

We embarked on our six-day journey, staying the first night with one of our pastors who lives in Juba at the base of a small mountain called Dar Jebel, which is what the name means. Our pastor's congregation was anxiously and excitedly awaiting our arrival and cheered us into the compound, ululating and dancing. We promptly unload, pitched tents without delay and immediately presented ourselves to the congregation, who had been singing and dancing the entire time. I felt as if I were late and was expected to catch up. No "prep" time here! I really do love ministering this way as it requires one to follow the Holy Spirit and not lean on our own preplanned agenda. Before anyone even preached we prayed for an older lady who was blind. Immediately she received healing in one of her eyes! The Lord was already moving in power. She was very happy and raised her hands to heaven in thanksgiving. We did too!

The next morning, we drove into the city of Juba and visited St Mary's public cemetery. Homeless people dwell here amongst the gravestones, their small hovels consisting of tarp and plastic, pieces of tin or wood, and whatever else they can find to tie it all together. The flies are a constant nuisance and plague small children with runny eyes and noses and children who don't wear diapers or pants. On this particular day it was raining and sloshy, slippery mud was everywhere which meant that the flies were hibernating in warmer places. It was surreal to walk into this place and see gravestones spread about in no particular order as if they were random stepping stones. They were supposed to lie flush to or flat on the ground, but because of the incessant rain, the stones were partially submerged in the mud, leaving an edge slanting up from the earth. In order to approach the humble homes of these precious people we were compelled to gingerly step around the headstones, many times the headstone lying in the place of the door mat.

We also came upon a small church structure comprised of irregular wooden poles which had been cut from local trees and ceiling beams of crudely cut two by fours strapped together with thin metal strips and an iron sheet roof. The structure had no walls. One of our older boys, who grew up in our Iris Yei Children's Village, is now a man and works at our sister orphanage in Juba, and he built this church structure for these precious people, with the help of the orphanage. We were not expected to visit this day, coming unannounced, but some of the ladies who lived in the cemetery brought chairs for us to sit on, carrying them over their heads in the steady rain.

It was a cold, dreary rainy day yet these beautiful women were soaked to the bone to make sure we were comfortable. I was wearing a raincoat and felt so bad that the ladies were soaked through just to be hospitable that I gave my coat to one of the ladies to keep. The hospitality of the people of South Sudan is so humbling. They place the most importance upon welcoming strangers into their homes no matter where you live or who you are, even when they have nothing themselves. I am always so humbled by this and I pray that I could be even half as hospitable as these are.

A few men were present whom we later learned were the pastor and elders, most of whom were already drinking alcohol at ten in the morning. This was also the case for many of the women. St Mary's is a very sad and dark place, the children running wild, parents drunkenly making their children take a drink, making them dance and do other "cute" things to entertain them in their drunkenness, with many late night secret abuses forced upon the innocents. Regardless of all that I knew, my heart was still touched to see that the people were yearning to know the Lord and to receive prayer for deliverance. They come from all corners of the cemetery to hear the word of God with great expectation.

After a short message, a lady came forward and explained to us that a week ago she had stolen a backpack from someone, finding witchcraft items inside and ever since then her family has been sick and has been attacked by demons in the night. Over the years I have heard many, many stories from so many people who have been attacked in the night by an unseen force which chokes and scratches them. Even my own children have been attacked. The lady then left the church hurriedly and quickly returned, carrying the pack that she had stolen. We lit a small fire right there inside the church on the dirt floor and burned the witchcraft items that were found in the pack. We then prayed for this lady and her two children, all whom knelt before us in repentance, and for them to be set free from the demonic attack in their home. Later that day we handed the pack over to the police, not revealing the source of the pack

We then returned to Dar Jebel and the next morning we packed up our tents and set off for Terekeka, a four hour drive north. After navigating muddy roads with deep trenches, weaving our way through hundreds of long horned cattle on the road, we were welcomed by a small group of people in the village, singing and dancing for us as we arrived. We were immediately led to a small church gathering under a mango tree along the muddy banks of the mighty Nile River. We set up camp, a few of us deciding to wander around the neighborhood to meet the people. I met a young lady in the process of brewing the local gin outside of her small hut and I talked with her for a bit, learning how to make gin out of maize corn. She told me that she brewed it in order to make a living but she didn't drink it herself. She said that it was a good and inexpensive way to make money to support her family.

The more we moved around the village, the more apparent it became that alcohol was a difficult obstruction to a life of freedom here in this village. We saw many, many children who looked as if they had fetal alcohol syndrome, and finding many of the children and adults mentally slow also. We encountered a small baby who had a cleft lip, the mother already intoxicated at this early hour of the day. Next to her was an old grandmother who was lying on a plastic woven African mat in front of her house who appeared to be in quite a bit of pain, her face scrunching up with eyes closed. All we could do was pray for her and afterwards she said that she felt some ease of her pain. There were quite a few children with deformities and mental problems and we noticed a strong odor of alcohol on the breath of at least half of the people we encountered who also appeared to be intoxicated. We sensed such heaviness and sadness in this place.

The following day we walked around the village, going from house to house, and visited people. We met an old man curled up on an old woven twine and wooden bed, his skin draped over his bones as if it were a size too large who had been crippled for twenty-five years. He had been bedridden for the last three years. He wasn't able to talk and his arms were bent at a permanent thirty-degree angle, both his arms and legs so stiff making it impossible for him to even sit up. He couldn't have weighed more than 120 pounds. He was so frail that I was fearful that he might break if he moved at all. He also smelled of urine.

We learned this man's story from his wife. Twenty-five years ago he was a young, strong, healthy and dedicated policeman. There was an altercation between him and an uncle who accused him of stealing a cow. Because the cow was never recovered the uncle paid a witch doctor to put a curse on this old man, who was young at the time. The very next day this man's strength gave out and the doctors could find nothing wrong with him. He has deteriorated over the years to this point of being immobile. We then prayed for him, breaking off curses and witchcraft. I was very nervous about the next step because of his frailty but I felt that I heard God.

I asked the wife if I could sit him up. I felt the Lord impress upon me that this man needed to remember what it felt like to sit up. The family was hesitant but they agreed. We gently moved his legs around and draped them over the side of the bed, gently raising him up to a sitting position, keeping our hands upon him so he wouldn't fall over. After a few minutes we slowly removed our hands and found that he was able to sit on his own! A tear rolled down his cheeks. We asked if he was in pain and he shook his head no. We asked him now if we could stand him up. He nodded his head yes. We helped him to stand up, supporting him firmly on each side. After a minute we slowly let go and he was standing on his own!

The biggest miracle was to see the dignity that was restored to him. When he stood up he set his face like flint, pulling his shoulders back, his head lifted up, his chin jutting out, and he stood like a soldier, like the policeman he was for almost 20 years before he was crippled, tears rolling down his face. Tears were rolling down my face and the other person with me. It was such an amazingly special moment. I told his grown son that they needed to bring him back into the daily life around him. He needed to sit up and to stand and to talk. He needed to live and not just lay there waiting to die.

Other members of our team encountered a demon possessed intoxicated man walking aimlessly along the road who was manifesting demons. He was acting really strange, speaking in a demonic voice and language that clearly wasn't anything South Sudan. The team stopped the man and stood in front of him and rebuked the demons with a word. As they started to pray for the man he fell to his knees and began to weep, sobbing, as tears gushed from his eyes. The team kept praying for him, feeling his anguish and they travailed with him. Soon he began to calm down and as he stood up he embraced the members of the team in gratitude, laughing and smiling, filled with joy, and he exclaimed that he was going home to his family and starting a new life with them.

I would like to interject a quote about demons from a book I am reading, "The Apostle: The Life of Paul (John Pollock Series)":

"Stories of demons and evil spirits '"do not baffle Christians in the less developed world outside of the industrialized nations. Nor will any spiritually sensitive Westerner who has slept unknowingly near the altar to the spirits in a tribal house, or has confronted a witch doctor, be disposed to doubt. The powers of evil may prefer sophisticated forms in the West, but the rest of the world is wary of dismissing evil spirits or demons as figments of the imagination.'" When one has seen the immediate transformation before their very eyes of a person delivered from demons, that one will never doubt again the reality of evil spirits and demons. Also, that one will not fear again about confronting them, knowing the power of Jesus Christ in us and the authority that we carry is stronger than any demon."

We rarely rested in the five days we were here as people kept coming for prayer, for answers, for the Savior. Even when we stopped for gas or food, we would pray for people. There is such a desperation in the people of this nation, such a desperate need for a Savior. The harvest is truly plentiful. We need the laborers. On our last night in this village, we had an evening service but the turnout was small and the people were not very enthused. I have never seen this happen before. Africans are always hungry for the Word of God and those who come to church are enthusiastic. We prayed seriously for these people, for God to come in and deliver them from this heavy oppression.

We left Terekeka with heavy hearts only because we really felt that the people here needed to be discipled on a regular basis. Many times, evangelists come into a village or city and put on a big crusade, the preacher yelling and preaching with gusto and vigor, the people jumping up and down with excitement, and everyone seemingly encouraged. But if you were to check back with these same people in two weeks, you would find them just as they were when the evangelist first came on the scene. Nothing really changes unless the people are discipled. Jesus commanded us to go into all the world and make disciples of all nations. He didn't command us to go into the world and get all people to say the salvation prayer. This is not the goal, the end game, the game point. My heart was beginning to burn with this. I knew that I needed to do outreach different.

Chapter Sixteen

It is now December and the dry season is upon us, the rains having stopped two weeks ago. Everyone's crops have been harvested and the land now rests until the rains begin again in April. There will be a lack of food in many households as many do not have enough land to grow food and then to also store it for the dry season. There has also been a rash of robberies around our town. Here in our third world country, there are no alarm systems, no deadbolt locks, and no doorbell cameras. There are no security cameras or fail proof fences. One can easily climb over any gate. Even NGO compounds are being robbed at gunpoint. We have had to cancel all of our outreaches that take us from our town of Yei because NGO vehicles are being hijacked and robbed on the roads north, most specifically Land Cruisers, leaving the passengers stranded or dead.

I have informed my watchmen not to approach our gates at night, even if they hear someone at the gate. I told them to just remain alert and to pray. If the watchmen were to approach the gate they risk being shot during an armed entrance. Many NGO's hire armed security guards but we don't. It's a personal choice of mine, not wanting guns on our compound or around our children. It's enough to hear them being shot in the night so close by and men carrying guns in our home would bring more fear in our children and I cannot take the chance of having a shootout in the night, stray bullets going amiss and killing someone. We only use bow and arrows as our defense. I have since learned that men are more afraid of bow and arrows than of guns. The guys tell me that an arrow carves a path in the body that can't be repaired easily, especially when one must pull the entire arrow through the wound. And, our guys are really good shots, rarely missing the mark.

We have continued our outreaches here in our town. Last night we went to the police station as the police commissioner personally asked us to come and show the Jesus film to his troops and to minister to them. December is the most difficult month for them because crime is at an all time high. The abundance of Christmas presents in each house is too tempting for criminals so they raid and rob. Just last night one of our employee's house was robbed. The bandits stole all of her clothes and the Christmas presents that she had just bought for her grandchildren this week. I felt so bad for her because she had spent all of her pay on these presents. The policemen were so receptive to us and the film even though they had seen it before. After the movie we laid hands on them and spoke life and destiny into each one as we prayed.

Just as we were preparing to leave, the commissioner commented that he had received a sense of peace and joy for himself and his men and women and he asked us to please come again on Christmas Day, if just to pray for his troops and the prisoners. The SPLA chaplain was also in attendance on this night. Since we had a large team of visitors we were excited to send six of them to share a word at three of his SPLA churches on Sunday morning. One of the churches belonged to the Wounded Warriors, soldiers who had been severely wounded in battle. We agreed to come to their community to bring the healing touch of Jesus to their beaten and battered bodies. In the midst of all this ministry we are still preparing for Christmas while also blessing our neighbors and we are planning a youth conference for this coming week. The holidays and the teams invite much activity, for which we are always thankful.

Four days before Christmas, we went to town and bought candy, enough for a village, and balloons and inexpensive plastic trinkets, such as bracelets, fake watches, bouncy balls and other such things. We gathered some of our children and had them fill all of the bags with a bit of each. We then sent out our Christmas cheer giving team of children, separating them into five groups, and told them to go to all the houses in our area and to give a bag to each child that they could find. The receiving children were so happy, even following our children all the way back to our compound to see if there was something more. Our village children had never encountered a group of people giving things away to them. They were ecstatic that they were receiving all of these amazing things. This was going to be the best Christmas ever for us and we were praying for peace on that day, no shooting of guns, no fear of soldiers in the bush. We seriously wanted peace for Christmas.

Christmas day has come and the joy of all of these children shouting and prancing about like reindeer, expectant and waiting for presents to roll out of my house. The night was peaceful and peace was in the land. Our compound is a humble little place where there is no inside place to gather so we all gathered under our group of mango trees for Christmas. All of the presents, wrapped in blue and white striped plastic bags, were gently laid at the base of a mango tree, no sparkly lights or tinsel, no popcorn strings or angels. It was a humble but beautiful mango tree with tons of love beneath it. We sang some worship songs and we prayed and thanked God for the greatest gift of all, Jesus. And we danced and danced and danced. Finally, we opened presents and everyone received a new pair of clothes and underwear and some candy and plastic trinket toys. And everyone was happy, no complaints that they didn't get the iPad they wanted or the XBox or the Playstation. They were happy with their humble little gifts, running into their houses to try on their new Christmas clothes. They don't know what it is like to receive an abundance of gifts so there was no expectation beyond some new clothes. Our life is simple, yet not.

The nation as a whole enjoyed a peaceful Christmas with no fighting in any part of the country. We are so thankful for this and we really pray that it holds. We also shared Christmas with the refugees just down the road from us on Christmas Eve. The children had no idea that we were coming and they were so excited and full of joy to see us. We managed to work through our pastor and the elders of the tribe in order to find out how many children were living there and what their ages were. We went to the market and bought each child a new set of clothes for Christmas. The only present that most Sudanese families give to each other is a new set of clothes that they wear to church on Christmas morning. We brought toys and food and three Christmas goats to roast! We also brought the candy gift bags to the children here. It was a wonderful day filled with fellowship and love.

Chapter Seventeen

As we enter into the new year of 2015, it has been quiet concerning the internal fighting between tribes. We are praying for it to continue. The teachers are preparing to start another school year and have come to our office to gather the school supplies, which we store for them during the long breaks so that they aren't stolen or vandalized. Our children help to carry the heavy plastic tubs up the little teak tree lined path to the school, which had also grown over with a thick green foliage of elephant grass. We have dispatched our older boys to the football field to cut the grass with our machete-like grass cutters. We call them slashers, long enough to swing to the grass, bent at a forty-five-degree angle at the bottom, and sharpened.

We have been receiving UN notices almost weekly since December concerning the dangers of traveling around the country. There is still a rash of carjacking, the gunmen stopping the car at gunpoint, taking the money, clothes and luggage from the passengers, and the car, and leaving the people alone on isolated stretches of road, sometimes fully exposed with no clothes on. Last week a car coming to Yei from Juba was attacked and six women were raped. There has been a noticeable escalation of violence concerning the assortment of crimes being committed. Foreigners are being told to avoid any unnecessary travel on the roads between villages, mostly Yei to Juba, unless traveling in a convoy.

Some people have asked me why I stay in a place that is like this as a normal way of life. I tell them that I am a mom and unless I can take my children with me, I'm not going anywhere. I find it difficult to understand sometimes how someone could think of leaving a compound full of children to concern themselves only with their own safety. It is inconceivable to me. I am not "holier than thou", just being real here. Leaving never enters my mind and when it does, it is a fleeting thought that is usually out of frustration and weariness but never followed through on.

The economic crisis in the country is hitting everyone hard. Last month the rate of exchange from South Sudanese Pounds to U.S. dollars was 660 SDP to $100 USD. In the last month we have jumped from 660 SDP to 1,000 SDP per $100 USD. Just one year ago the SDP rate was 295 SDP per $100 US dollars. For those who have US dollars, it actually gives us more product for our dollars but for the natives who have never had US dollars and go to the market to buy fish or maize flour it is catastrophic. As the US dollar fluctuates drastically so do market prices and what used to cost 100 SDP now costs almost 200 SDP. Crime has skyrocketed as people become desperate to eat. In the capital city of Juba there is a violent crime or robbery against a foreigner at least once a day in order to get US dollars.

We have never seen so many crimes committed against foreigners in the history of this nation. We have now been without diesel fuel for a week and have no idea when it will come into the country again so, we only drive our vehicle when absolutely necessary, taking motorcycle taxis instead when we need to go into town. Because of this lack of fuel, we have begun to store diesel in barrels that we managed to purchase, buying the fuel on the black market at higher prices, but at least we have fuel. My staff who are Sudanese are also suffering and they can't afford the things they need to feed their families because of the high market prices and I am now considering how much I can afford to raise their pay until this passes, if it passes. People are really suffering and feeling the pinch of war.

This week's security report, which covers a one-week period, mentioned the following situations:

On 19 May two NGO vehicles were robbed on the Yei to Juba road. Also, on the same day, an NGO employee was driving his car when he was stopped by people claiming to be security personnel. These criminals confiscated a very large sum of money from the NGO. The next day, a mutatu (taxi) was driving on the Yei to Juba road when gunmen ran out of the bush and drug the 12 occupants in the vehicle into the bush. One woman escaped and was rescued by an NGO vehicle. No one knows what happened to the other passengers. On 25 May, two cars and a truck were robbed in separate incidents on the Yei to Juba road. The next day, four cars and an NGO vehicle were robbed on the Yei to Juba road.

As for the southwestern part of our country, the security situation in Mundri West County in May is due to ethnic animosity between the town residents and cattle keepers from the Dinka tribe, who's cattle were found grazing on land that belonged to the town's people. Deadly armed confrontations took place between a local vigilante group and some of the cattle keepers. On 21 May, two SPLA soldiers were killed on the road leading to Rumbek. This same day, four fuel tankers were stopped by armed gunmen and were redirected to another location near Maridi town, two tankers were then emptied of their fuel before the gunmen left in a hurry.

The next day, the Mundri West County Commissioner and the Executive Director proceeded to a crime scene where someone was killed. While at the scene a soldier from the armed escort group protecting the officials discharged his weapon, killing the Executive Director. The Commissioner fled for his safety. After this shooting, the SPLA soldiers stationed in the town of Mundri went on a rampage in the town, discharging their weapons in the air and stealing goods from local shops. The local vigilante group known as the "Arrow Boys" then charged into the armory of the Police and Prisons and confiscated weapons. They in turn went after the unruly SPLA soldiers and surrounded the soldiers and forced them at gunpoint into their own barracks to await further instructions.

The next day, fifteen fully loaded World Food Program trucks were dispatched to two internal refugee camps when they were stopped at gunpoint and all of the provisions were then offloaded and taken into the bush by others assisting the gunmen. Two days later, a Wild-Life Officer and his body guards were shot and killed in Mundri. The next day, the town of Malikal was recaptured by the SPLA after battling with the opposition forces over the territory. And on 21 May, the Commissioner of Rumbek North traveling with a border Advisor was killed in an ambush by opposition forces and his advisor was found three days later unharmed.

As you can see, the situation has once again begun to escalate and now four of the ten states in South Sudan are off limits to foreigners. All foreigners have been encouraged to evacuate due to the increase in violence between tribes and between rebel and government forces. Our economy is in the dirt due to the sharp increase in the value of the dollar versus the South Sudanese pound. People are starving for lack of food. A rebel commander has instructed the people of a very large town in the north to leave the town because he is commandeering it and if the people are still there by morning they shall be killed. People are running for their lives by the thousands, carrying nothing, no money, no food, no belongings, in their haste to escape the turmoil. Tribal conflict is also overwhelming the UN IDP camps, where people are refugees and should feel safe. This has now forced the UN to evacuate people even from the camps. Where will this end? When will this end? How will this end?

These are the questions the innocent bystanders are asking.

It is absolute chaos here. Things are escalating quickly and I can't even read the news anymore without imagining things getting any worse, yet they do. Jesus is the only answer for this war, this crisis, this chaos. We still travel the road when necessary and trust that Jesus will guide us and care for us as we go. In the midst of these extreme times, we have received three new team members, Brian, Sandy, and Haley. These three were part of the team that had come to visit at Christmas. They had gone back to their countries and all were impressed to come back and serve God in this place. I am so happy and relieved to have help. It has been a long journey for myself and Dorinda, the only two here for almost two years.

Last night a strange incident occurred at our compound gates. It has been our usual habit to pray for God to encamp His angels around our compound to protect us day and night and we seriously believe that they have been dispatched on our behalf. Sometime after 11:00 pm, three men on a motorcycle stopped at the front gate to our compound. It was a quiet night and no one moves about this late at night, for any reason, other than to do mischief. When the men stood at the gate looking in, our watchmen just stood still, watching them. Per my instructions some months ago, our watchmen did not approach these men. There is nothing worth losing our lives over. Approaching the gate at night puts everyone's life at risk. As long as no one opens the gate then it is that much more difficult for invaders to enter in to our compound.

The three men alighted from the motor bike, all the while quietly staring into our compound, whispering amongst themselves, unaware of our watchmen. After a few minutes, one man unexpectedly and swiftly jumped on the motorcycle and speedily departed. The other two men quietly moved over to the side gate, which was about a hundred yards away near the boy's houses, still unaware of our watchmen, whispering as they went. The entire time our watchmen stood still and observed and listened, remaining quiet, bow and arrows at the ready. When the men arrived at the side gate, one of the men swiftly ran off into the bush as if a lion were chasing him, leaving the other man looking after him in confusion, seemingly not knowing why the man had run.

The last man then proceeded to move to our farthest gate which was about one hundred and fifty yards away near our office building. After arriving there this lone man stopped and looked in, and suddenly, without provocation, this man like the two before him swiftly ran away. Our watchmen were so puzzled. Why did they run from the gates when there was no obvious reason? Our watchmen had not moved from their position as they were able to see everything from their vantage point. Our fence is a chain linked fence making it easy to see. The only explanation that we have is we believe there were angels standing guard at every gate and when the men saw them they ran. We believe the prayers that we pray are heard by God, not using vain repetitions, but praying with purpose, especially in these critical days that we find ourselves living in. God always cares for us and He hears us when we call and protects us. We are so very thankful.

Lately, the Lord has been speaking to me very clearly about getting back to the basics concerning evangelism and most things spiritual. His exact words to me were, "It's time to get back to the basics." It's that simple. Last week when we had had no fuel for a month, I fasted and I casually spoke out that if God wanted me to walk everywhere to do missions then I would walk. We could not let the lack of fuel stop us. This was the time for harvest and people were dying because of this war. If we didn't go then who would reach the ones that we were supposed to reach? There was a desperation in my soul for the lost like never before. I knew that we were being nudged by the Lord to walk and minister to people.

As I reflected upon the differences between today's evangelistic efforts and those of almost 2,000 years ago, the one thing that stood out was that Jesus walked and we drive, yet Jesus reached so many people. Jesus walked. Jesus walking and talking and going to the masses, versus the masses coming because of His program, his sound system set up, His famous guest speakers and free admission. I thought about all the preparation it takes to stage and load all of our equipment to show the Jesus film in the villages, to stage and load cooking utensils, dishes, tents, tarps and fueling vehicles, and sometimes hiring vehicles all for the sake of sharing the gospel. I really wanted to get back to the basics. The disciples were sent out with nothing, not even extra clothes to change into, or money to buy themselves food. We were going to walk for the next outreach! Who needed fuel?

Chapter Eighteen

Four days later I am so excited as we head out early on a Friday morning, just carrying our backpacks with four of our older children, along with our pastor and three of his church leaders, and we walked, Brian, Sandy, Haley and I. We had only walked seven miles out of town but it took us almost five hours! As we walked along the dirt road, a few vehicles flying past leaving a plume of dirt in their wake, we fellowshipped together and talked about Jesus. Our first stop was at a roadside motorcycle repair place where five men were working on a motorcycle. This is a village shop along the roadside so it was mostly under a mango tree next to a small thrown together structure made of wood with a dirt floor that doubled as a restaurant of sorts. Inside were a few white plastic chairs. We greeted the men warmly and asked if we could pray for them. We also asked them if any were sick or if any were suffering a financial crisis or personal relationship crisis. They gathered the chairs for us to sit on, as is the custom here, and as they rearranged the chairs inside of the structure we asked them to sit so that we could pray for them.

We prayed for each man individually, taking our time and listening to Holy Spirit. One man told us that he was sick, suffering from malaria and typhoid. People here are amazingly resilient and can actually function with these sicknesses! Another man told us that he had been robbed of all his life savings a few days ago and now had no money for food. We prayed for these needs, for Jesus to heal the sick man and to restore what was taken from the man who was robbed, and they were so thankful that we had stopped for them and they felt so encouraged. We could see the change in their countenance. Two days later when we were on our way back home, we encountered the sick man and he came up to us full of joy and excitedly told us that he was completely well, no sickness! He was beaming and praising Jesus!

While we were praying for the men by the roadside a young girl of about twelve years was peering around the wooden structure as she listened in on what was happening inside. When we emerged from this little place she timidly came up to us and asked us if we would come to her house to pray for her sister who had a lame leg. I thought about how much this little girl cared for her sister and what boldness it took to approach us to ask us to pray. We followed her, moving away from the roadside down a trodden path deeper into the bush which had grown waist high already. Soon her little compound appeared before us where we found many family members sitting on mats and chairs, children running around and playing, the mother looking at us in surprise, taken aback that all these people would appear on her compound.

We explained to the mother that her little girl had approached us with her request to pray for her sister. Upon our arrival they hurriedly went into their small huts and emerged with all of their stools and chairs, even running to the neighboring hut for more. This is the hospitality of the Sudanese people. I never fail to notice this and I am always so blessed. We shared a gospel message with them before we prayed for them and they reacted as if we had brought church to them. Wait a minute, we are the church! We prayed for the family and encouraged them. The girl was not visibly healed but the family was blessed that we would veer so far off of the road to come and minister to them. Everyone was so happy and I wonder who was happiest, us or them. We too left encouraged.

After we left their compound, hugging the women and shaking hands with the men, we returned to the roadside, following the bushy trail and we stopped to rest in the shade of a bamboo tree when a motorcycle carrying three soldiers approached. Two of the soldiers were armed with AK47s, one of them a Commander or Major as he had two gold stars on his shoulder. They stopped next to us and spoke to us harshly, demanding to know what we were doing.

“Why are you foreigners walking around with backpacks? Don’t you realize that rebels are around?! Maybe you are here to supply the rebels?! We don’t trust the whites because they want to arm the rebels.”, they angrily accused us.

“Further north”, they continued, “white people are shot on sight by rebels because they don’t trust them either, accusing them of supplying food and arms to their enemies.”

There was a “rumored” incident last year where an unnamed UN container was intercepted and “supposedly” contained hundreds of weapons. This “supposed” incident brought about a breach of trust between the Sudanese and the whites. Even though the UN is comprised of many different nations, the Americans are automatically pointed out or referred to. It's almost as if everyone who is white is from America.

After listening to their reprimands, I sincerely apologized for causing them to feel distrustful of us. This seemed to appease them a bit. I then asked them to call the Chaplain at the SPLA Barracks explaining that he was my friend and knew who we were. He then surprised me by actually calling the Chaplain! The Chaplain immediately told them that we were friends of the SPLA and that we had been guests at their church often, ministering to and encouraging the soldiers there. He asked these men to allow us full access to the roads in Yei and for us to have freedom to move where we needed to go as we could be trusted.

The soldier disconnected the call and smiled at me and I felt that we were no longer, "those whites". He told us that we could freely move about but we must still remain alert to the rebels. We assured him that we would and that if we were captured we would preach the gospel even to them. He laughed at this. He said that they will now also keep an eye on us for our safety. This showed tremendous favor with the authorities and I find it amazing that God set all this up last year because we were obedient to go when he asked us to go and minister to the SPLA. We do indeed reap what we sow and obedience is better than sacrifice. Our God always responds to obedience, integrity and faith.

We joyfully continued on our way, excited about having this open door to the nation. As we walked we saw a group of young people up ahead standing in the shade of a heavy-laden mango tree, just full of ripeness and stunningly yellow colored mangoes. We stopped to greet them and as we talked we were able to share the gospel of salvation with them. One of the phrases I like to use is, "What have you got to lose"? If someone is not sure about the gospel message, I usually tell them that Jesus is faithful to make the mystery known to them if they sincerely desire to know the truth. The only thing needed for salvation is a willing heart. There is nothing to lose and everything to gain. It is just a prayer and if the mystery is revealed, hallelujah, a life is changed. If the person isn't serious about the prayer, it still connects them to heaven and one day they will remember it.

Everywhere we go these days, many people are asking for the salvation of Jesus Christ or they are recommitting their lives to Him. When war is at the door, people take a look at their lives and also at the possible outcome. The people were also surprised to see foreigners still walking the dusty roads during these dangerous times and then stopping to sit with them. Maybe they thought that our message was important enough to brave the roads? Or maybe they just thought we were crazy and they were interested in what we were about?

As we moved on we prayed for people all along the road. We finally arrived at a small village and were able to stay with a family who were the caretakers of a small church. The pastor of this church walked with us all day and he had arranged for us to stay with this family on their compound. We set our packs down and wasting no time, we separated into three teams and each team went out to visit the village, hut to hut. We fasted lunch and didn't bother to set up our tents before going, we were so excited.

As we approached a fairly large compound we encountered only women and children. We prayed with them and talked about salvation and the man of the house arrived. He did not look very pleased to see us. We learned that he was the pastor of a local denominational church and he accused us of coming to his village without permission from the headman or chief and that we didn't inform the local churches that we were coming. Our pastor did in fact give notice the week before and received permission and the pastor whom we stayed with did in fact inform those few churches in this small village. We politely informed the man that we had in fact done all these things and that we were so sorry that he was not properly informed. We asked him if he wanted us to leave but he allowed us to stay, although we were almost finished by this time. We prayed a prayer of blessing over him and his family. He was peaceful and even smiling when we left. We were told later by our pastor that there was a hard spirit of religion in this area and that most of the churches did not acknowledge each other or work together on anything, even to the point of telling their congregants not to attend any functions of the other churches.

It grieves my spirit, and I'm sure that it grieves the Holy Spirit, that there is so much division in the body of Christ. At times there seems to be more unity among the unbelievers than the body of Christ, the church. Jesus was about to go to the cross, about to give His life for what He believed in, His creation. His last prayer, according to the Book of John, was that we would be one as He and His Father are one. He didn't pray for the body of Christ to split into twenty different denominations, and then give these denominations a name, and then make all these rules to be in them. He had no rules. Only believe, was His rule. Only believe in your heart and confess with your mouth.

People have asked me why I don't plant churches. I tell them that there are enough churches and if I want to be part of the unified body of Christ then I should come alongside these churches that are already planted and help them, minister to them, honoring their traditions as much as possible and unite with them in one faith. My prayer is always that we may be one as He and His Father are one.

We continued to walk about the village and we encountered a young lady who asked us to pray for her mother. If I could say that there was one encounter that touched me the most it was this one. The mother had been sick in bed for four years. As we entered the dark little mud bricked hut with grass roof, we were struck with empathy for this frail, thin form that lay curled into herself, waiting to die. I don't think she could have walked if her life depended on it. Her face was just a skeleton with skin on. We were told that she hadn't taken any sustenance in two weeks and was no longer aware of her surroundings. Her husband works in Juba which is just over 100 miles away. His brother-in-law summoned him to come and do something about the situation. The husband had arrived just yesterday and he was talking on the phone as we arrived. He was a very large man and appeared somewhat aloof, although he might have had much on his mind.

After we prayed for this frail woman, we gathered outside and sat under the grass thatch roof overhang of the hut, sitting on the "skirt" of the house. The skirt is likened to a two-foot high and two-foot wide baseboard, which runs alongside the length and width of the outside of a hut. The purpose of the skirt is to protect against erosion during heavy rains which cause water to rise and settle against the house. As we sat there, we asked them if they were Christians and were informed that they were but the husband was not. As we were sharing a message from the gospels, the husband remained aloof and did not participate in our conversation, looking as if he didn't want to be there. I told the husband that I believed we were there for him and not so much for his wife. She was ready to meet the Lord, but was he? He was somewhat taken aback by my comment. I asked him if he believed that were true.

He said that if God touches his heart today, or anytime, then he will believe and receive his salvation, but as of yet, God had not touched his heart. This was very evident. As I began to talk with him, one on one, the others continued their conversation without me. One of my older boys sat with me and listened attentively. I learned that this man was a soldier so I told him that I too was once a soldier, for thirty years, and I know what his life has been like. He immediately became alert. I had his attention. He began to respond to me. I told him my testimony and how I am now a much happier person, having more blessings than I can count, and am fully satisfied with my life for the first time. He quietly took it all in. I could see the wheels spinning in his head but I didn't see the drums beat in his heart. I asked him if I could pray for God to touch his heart.

He seemed a bit resistant at first and I reassured him that he wouldn't be forced to do anything or to even respond. All I wanted to do was ask that God would do what He wanted to do in this man's heart, to touch him so he might see the truth. He agreed. I started to pray for him and I started to speak about his destiny, saying the man's name many times to reinforce that the prayer was about hm. I told him that God needed brigadier generals in His army and he was in line for that position should he answer the call. I prayed on and spoke a rich word of destiny over him. When we were finished praying, his face and countenance were bright, completely changed, and he was smiling. I knew that he hadn't cared for his sick wife, even neglecting her, and I knew that he didn't love God, yet I felt such a deep love for this man and I told him so. He was "touched", you could physically see it.

We didn't revisit the subject of salvation with him but my son, who had been sitting with us, told him about the parable of the two sons who were told by their father to go and work in the field. One said no but he went anyway. The other said yes but he never went. My son asked the man, "Which one did God honor"? Even this man knew it was the son who said no but went in the end. This is what we left him with. That evening we learned that within the very hour that we had left, his wife went on to glory. I can only hope that this man reached out to the Lord and received Him as Savior. I guess we won't know until we go home to glory ourselves. At least we left him with much to ponder.

At the next house on our journey we encountered the religious spirit once again and they were not very receptive to our being there nor to the gospel message of salvation. I should explain what a religious spirit is. A religious spirit is a type of demonic spirit that influences a person, or group of people, to replace a genuine relationship with God with works and traditions and the laws of the church instead of the love of God. People that have this spirit believe that their works will earn their salvation. One of our boys preached an amazing word and there was no response from the people, just a dull look. They didn't seem very receptive to us and didn't try to make us welcome. Even for a religious spirit, this was unusual because the Sudanese people are hospitable people. We blessed this house and the people there, shook the dust from our shoes, and moved on.

As we continued down the dusty road, the late afternoon sun hanging low in the sky, a young man from that group ran after us, and a bit out of breath, he said, "I would like to receive salvation. How can I do this?" When we told him that he should probably lift up his hands, as if in surrender to the Lord, he snapped up his arms and bowed his head, as if he was desperate to receive the salvation of the Lord. This young man ran after his salvation, refusing to be one of the dull eyed people in a crowd, praise Jesus! We invited him to join us the next day for discipleship training to teach him how to walk in his new salvation.

At the last house that we went to there were four giant grave monuments in the middle of the compound. Many times, when people in South Sudan are buried, if the family can afford it, the family hires a mason to build a large slab the size of a grave. It is laid out flat and has two or three smaller tiers on top. It almost looks like the top of a coffin, likened to the tombs of the pharaohs of Egypt. The family feels that this is a way to keep their relatives close and in remembrance.

I shared with them about the story of the wedding feast in the Book of Matthew, chapter twenty-two, as they continued to sit on the gravestones. It is a beautiful story of a rich king who invites all of the people to his wedding feast. One by one the people responded that they were too busy on that day and could not come. The king became angry and told his servant to go and invite all of the poor, the beggars, the foreigners, all that are on the highways and bi-ways. These people came to the feast and were joyful, as was the king. The people who were too busy began to have second thoughts and one decided to come to the feast. When the king saw him, he had that man thrown out. He told the people, "Many are called, but few are chosen".

We told the people who were sitting on gravestones that Jesus invites all of us to the feast but we have to respond. Are we now too busy? One man, who had been drinking, was so convicted that he stood up and said, "I am a sinner and I am sorry for how I have lived my life. I want forgiveness, I want to go to this feast and be with Jesus and I want to stop drinking." We prayed for him while everyone looked on. The others who were there seemed unconcerned and unmoved by the message or by the man who came forward. We also invited this man to our discipleship training the next day and the next morning, while we were teaching the new converts and discipling them, this same man came in completely sober, on a Saturday, in a suit, hungry for the living word of God. He was a new man, born again and set free.

What I realized during this walkabout was how many people are passed by when we just drive on by. These are the people who would never attend a Christian gathering. These are the people who "have heard it all before". They haven't had a personal encounter with the lover of their souls. I have learned much from the people of Africa and how they spend their lives, their entire lives, planting and weeding and harvesting. It is literally their life's blood. Their entire being and living and moving revolves around their fields and the harvest. If they don't plant, they don't eat. If they don't weed their land the harvest will be small. If they don't harvest they surely don't eat. They don't wait for someone else to plant and weed and then just take the harvest. They toil under the blazing sun with very little water or food and all by hand and hoe, no machinery employed. How would it change our focus if we looked at the Lord's harvest field that He has given us as our own life's blood, as our food? How would this change the way we approach ministry?

We are each commanded to bear fruit, fruit that lasts, that special fruit that He has created in us to produce. Each person that God has created has a ministry, a field to tend to. There is a great, great need in this world for the kingdom of light. Are we giving rise to a brighter world or are we allowing it to dim? How can we not want to please Him, to make this our life's blood to see His smile as we bring Him fruit each day? I see the lives He affects through our ministry and I am filled with joy to stay in my field and to toil for the harvest.

Chapter Nineteen

As we enter into the year 2016 we have been somewhat relieved over the last few months as the conflict has moved away from our region for now but this too would soon change, drastically. This month we have received two more team members, Rebecca and Katherine. Last month we received word that all banks in South Sudan, whether foreign or domestic, would no longer be allowed to dispense US dollars to the account holders. There has been no official announcement, nor have letters been sent out, nor have public notices been posted. Unfortunately, those in power over these things carry out their plans, whatever feels good at the time with little or no concern as to how it will affect the people at large.

I immediately went to the bank to withdraw all of my money as soon as I heard of the latest law being enforced even by foreign bankers when they denied me my money! All of our funding was wired directly to this account. Without it we don't eat. We were told that if we were to hand carry US dollars into the country then we would be free to do so but, we could not wire it in and then withdraw it in US dollars. We would need to withdraw it in Sudanese pounds at an extremely low exchange rate, losing thousands of dollars in the process.

Since yesterday I have been scrambling to find a way to get all of our US dollars out of the bank. I decided that I would wire it to my bank account that I have in Uganda. When I went to the bank to do this the manager explained to me that I needed a reason for wiring it. I was not allowed to just wire my money. Are you serious? I was incredulous. They were holding my money hostage. The manager was a Kenyan and was somewhat caught in the middle of this. He said that it is a South Sudan foreign investor's policy and not a bank policy. South Sudan can make the rules concerning money coming in and going out so his hands were truly tied. He asked me if I knew anyone in Uganda? He then told me to get an invoice from my friend in Uganda for the amount that I wanted to wire, which was close to $50,000 USD!

I have a contractor who manages all of the solar work on our compound and I knew that he could send me an invoice that would be legit for that amount. I am so thankful that this banker was really trying to help me. I also praise God for His wisdom in all of this because every day I find myself making decisions that could drastically affect our lives. I praise God that I never cancelled my Uganda bank account because I hadn't used it in at least two years. My friend sent the requested invoice without delay and I managed to have the funds wired to my bank in Uganda. I am now traveling to Uganda to withdraw the funds to bring it right back into South Sudan. This is so crazy, seriously. I would now need to travel out to Uganda each and every month to withdraw our monthly funding. I call it my monthly $1,000 ATM run. This covers airfare, taxi's and hotels for a three-day trip as planes only fly twice a week to our little city.

The economic crisis is critical these days. Everyone feels the brunt of it and some are literally dying of starvation. The bank of South Sudan has officially declared that the exchange rate would be at the mercy of the current black-market rate so now there is no longer a set rate. This has created havoc in the marketplace and at fuel stations. People are crying out because prices are floating all over the place, nothing being stable, depending upon the rate of currency exchange for that day! Can you imagine trying to make a budget when prices change daily, even hourly? The situation has become so serious that I have provided 25 Kg bags of maize flour and beans and oil and sugar to the women who are neighbors, and have encouraged them to remain in the peace that only God can give and that we would always try to help where we could. Our hope though, is only in Him.

The prices in the market have already doubled this year, and have doubled again this week. Last week I paid $2 USD per kilogram for meat. This week I paid $4 USD per kilogram. Last week we were able to feed all of our family, 150 people, cabbage for $11 USD. This week that same cabbage is now $40 USD. In Africa we pay by the minute for phone usage, buying airtime cards and loading up our phones. Last week $3 USD worth of airtime lasted me at least two weeks. I loaded my $3 USD's worth of airtime this week and found that in three days time I was already out of airtime. Things are really going south fast. These are the typical problems faced by the innocent people when a country is at war. When other nations see the headlines that a war is waging in a nation, all they see is the actual fighting and shooting. People never see the immediate effects on the people who try to live daily in the midst of it all. The shooting is the least of our worries. Trying to eat to stay alive is of greater concern.

I am so upset with all of this and I shouldn't feel guilty because I can still feed my children three meals a day when the orphanage down the road is down to one meal a day and possibly not even every day. I wake up in the mornings with my heart in turmoil for these people. All of this has prompted me to call a holy fast on our compound for the nation and for those who are suffering and what our role is to be in it.

The children in our family never complain but remain joyous and full of hope for our future. They really trust that God will work out all of these things for our good. The alternative is a place that we don't entertain. I love the genuine faith of the children and I am encouraged by them so many times. Today, New Year's Day, we are observing the holy fast that God has called us to as a family. We set up our sound system in our prayer hut and opened our gates in case our neighbors wanted to join us. For the first time I have closed and locked our kitchen completely. In previous years I left the kitchen open in order for the smaller children to be able to eat. This was to be our first mandatory fast for everyone, young and old. It was a Biblical fast. I restrained the goats and the dogs from eating, locking them inside their pens with no food. We were serious about this. The older children also felt the importance of this fast weighing upon them.

We came together, one large family, and we fasted and we prayed all day. We prayed a prayer of repentance from Nehemiah 9:29-37 for our nation. The children and staff were crying tears as we prayed. Our children were grieved in their hearts for the state of their country. They examined the scriptures and prayed the scriptures. I was amazed by the move of God in their spirits. They were serious about this, serious to see something change, for peace, and they were praying not the peace of man but the peace of God, peace that only He can bring. There was such maturity in these young people. Some have even committed to continuing a fast with me through the month of January, of one meal a day.

At the end of the day the Lord gave me a word for our year. His exact words to me:

"This is going to be a year of great trust and faith. You know the way. You have been down this road many times. I have given you a year of peace, of rest, now there is more to be done. This is the time to take up your shield of faith and sword of the Spirit and follow Me. We have much to do this year. You are ready, you know the way. You have all that you need, you have Me, all of Me. I will withhold nothing if you ask of Me. I know that your motives are as Mine.

I know that your vision is as Mine."

I wondered what could possibly happen that would require such faith and trust. I set this word aside for the time being and we continue on with our lives, although things have been escalating here concerning the war. The world thinks that there is a great peace agreement in place and that it was signed and everything is A-OK. This is so far from the truth. We just received a message from the United Nations that is as follows:

In an official press statement released on December 11, 2015, the government of the Republic of South Sudan threatened to shoot down aircraft engaged in illicit activities or which violate the country's airspace by failing to properly identify themselves. South Sudan also recently deployed a functional radar-guided Strategic Surface-to-Air Missile near Juba.

The South Sudanese government is currently engaged in an armed conflict with opposition forces led by the former vice president Riek Machar, which has led to the displacement of more than two million people. Although the conflict is primarily concentrated in Unity, Jonglei, and Upper Nile states, other areas of the country have experienced periodic fighting. Instability persists across the country due to retaliatory attacks, intercommunal violence and cattle raiding, and economic uncertainty.

Health care in South Sudan is extremely limited and poor. U.S. citizens with medical conditions should not travel to South Sudan, and all travelers should ensure their travel is covered by overseas medical insurance, including medical evacuation.

The government of South Sudan has limited capacity to deter crime or provide security to travelers, particularly outside of Juba. In addition to instability related to the current armed conflict, the risk of violent crime is high in South Sudan. The U.S. Embassy in Juba has imposed a curfew from 10:00 p.m. to 6:00 a.m. and has implemented other measures to protect U.S. government personnel living and working in South Sudan. These include requiring personnel to travel in armored government vehicles and coordinating with the host government for travel outside of Juba.

Due to security concerns, spouses and family members of U.S. government personnel are not permitted to reside in South Sudan. U.S. citizens should consider those restrictions and take measures to mitigate exposure to violent crime and other threats. U.S. citizens currently working on humanitarian relief or development efforts in Juba, or elsewhere in South Sudan, should closely follow the security policies and procedures of the sponsoring organization.

Carjacking and banditry are common in South Sudan. If travel outside of Juba is necessary, it should be undertaken preferably with a minimum of two vehicles with appropriate recovery and medical equipment in case of mechanical failure or other emergency. Additionally, there are widespread fuel shortages across South Sudan, and access to gasoline and or diesel cannot be guaranteed."

We remained undeterred through all of this, continuing with our outreaches with backpacks and tents, with a new determination to reach the lost and suffering. Today we walked to Goja, traveling down a small bush road which eventually turned into a path. We walked for four hours, stopping along the way to pray and minister to the people we met. Once we arrived in Goja we had our Land Cruiser bring our sound equipment so that we could show the Jesus Film as the church has requested it. Afterward, we prayed for the sick and the oppressed. Saturday morning we organized discipleship training for the church. Throughout these two days many have received salvation and many have been healed and set free from addictions.

People who were intoxicated from alcohol yesterday were now sober and attending our discipleship training today. God has touched many lives and we feel that He gained some good ground in Goja. Little did we know at this time that Goja would be destroyed by mortar fire this same year. There is nothing good about war. But God will use the opportunity to gather the harvest because this is the best time for harvest, in the midst of chaos and conflict and the people are desperate for a savior. Much of the world, except for soldiers, would choose to stay home during these times because of fear. There were no more teams coming to visit us, some even cancelling at the last minute, because of their fear of the conflict. We knew that the harvest needed gathering so we chose to go into the field and get to work.

My favorite experience during this particular outreach was when we came to a compound and found an older gentleman sitting by himself. He was about 65 years old and his face just shone so brightly and his smile made one feel as if they were looking at a fresh new morning. Even the atmosphere within this compound felt different, peaceful, joyous. As soon as he saw us entering in he went inside his home and carried out some plastic chairs for us to sit on, again this being normal hospitality here, and his son came from the next compound with his wife and small baby. The entire family was so bright and full of light. We felt as if we had stepped into heaven. We really enjoyed each other's fellowship and we lifted God up in our conversation. It was such an unexpected treat to find this rich presence of God in a simple little compound tucked in the African bush, no mega church around, no electricity or famous orators, just this sweet family and the sweetness of God.

Some time ago, I was sharing with some of our visitors about my thoughts on ministry and I had made the comment, "I love outreach because it's a no-brainer, it's all Holy Ghost." They had asked me if I ever get any time off and I laughed and told them that for the most part, no. Whenever I travel I am ministering somewhere or telling people about what I do. I then commented that I really love outreach because it is like a vacation for me. I experience great joy and great peace and I feel refreshed at the end of an outreach. I commented that I sure wish the administrative part of my ministry could be this way. I think we all do.

I find it so amazing that when we go and sit with the poor in spirit it is there that we encounter the "rest" of God, the wonder of God, the peace of God. We never once read that Jesus then took a small vacation to Hawaii so He could rest and recover after hard ministry. He went off by Himself to sit with His Father yes, but most of His time was spent with the poor in spirit and with His disciples. The only time He appeared a bit agitated was when He had to answer to the church leadership and the religious spirit.

Pertaining to the administrative part of my ministry, I find myself constantly unraveling messes that we make. And then I need to take a vacation to Hawaii to get rest. I am kidding of course, about Hawaii, although I have been there numerous times as I used to live there once upon a time. The longer I live in Africa, the more refreshed I appear to my friends in the U.S. of A. when I disembark from the airplane flight over the sea. They always comment about how good and healthy I look, not some tired, worn out missionary on her last leg.

Once we set off for outreach we slow down to first gear, sometimes neutral, and we take time for people, having true empathy, and we pray as long as they need us to, listening to their stories, as long as it takes, to get to the heart of the matter. To get to the heart of the matter. Some missions are so focused on the numbers that they forget about the heart matters that brought about the bondage in the first place. We all have this pressing "mission" to take Jesus to the people but we must first tend to their heart matters so that the ground of their hearts can be made ready for fresh seed.

One day as I was meditating I wondered about world outreach and lives laid down for outreach. What if our lives were outreach, where we lived everyday as if we were on outreach in the bush? How would that look? How would we care differently about everyone we encountered, even the church? Here in South Sudan, when we go on an outreach, most of our reach is to the already existing church. There are numerous bush churches who are so hungry for more of God and for His Word and I am so passionate and full of fire when I teach and minister in these places because I know they are hungry. Much of our reach is to set people free, to listen to what has bound them, causing them to be stuck.

In the middle of all this musing and meditation the Lord answered me. "The world is My outreach," He impressed upon me. "Every day I am on a mission. I am at rest and full of joy and passion and peace as I reach out to My people, especially in their sufferings because you are My outreach." Affliction either draws a crowd or repels a crowd. If it draws a crowd, we share in their sufferings and we find a unity there that bears the fruit of loving each other. The greatest commandment is at work, and the second like it.

Jesus said, "You shall love the Lord your God with all your heart, with all your soul, and with all your mind. This is the first and greatest commandment. And the second is like it: You shall love your neighbor as yourself. On these two commandments hang all the Law and the Prophets." (Matthew 22:37-40)

This Sunday morning, I shared about the fruit of true outreach. In the midst of every struggle a story is born, even if all looks lost in the beginning. Job lost it all. Yet, today the church is encouraged to love God no matter what because He is good and He loves us and will redeem everything that has been taken by the devil.

Jesus told John the Baptist, "And blessed is he who is not offended because of Me." (Matthew 11:6)

John had asked his friends to ask Jesus if He was really who He said He was. Later in Matthew chapter 11, Jesus told John's friends that John was the greatest man born among women to ever live.

Later Jesus Himself cried out in a loud voice to God, "My God, My God, why have You forsaken Me?" (Mark 15:34)

The scripture in Isaiah 46:10 was my message today, that God knows the end from the beginning and He will do as He pleases to make sure His outreach is successful, His mission accomplished, His family brought home.

The world is His outreach. Are we willing to be a part of it, no matter what? Are we willing to be the sacrifice? God did not go down to the cross and help Jesus sacrifice Himself. Jesus had a mission and He had to sacrifice Himself by Himself, so that the outreach of God would reach to the ends of the earth. Are we willing to sacrifice ourselves, however that may look, in order to complete our outreach that God has given us, an extension of Himself?

Chapter Twenty

Day to day we live for Jesus. We are in the land that He created, a beautiful land with beautiful people who have encountered darkness. In the midst of this beauty, my heart is grieved. This war is killing the innocent, the ones who have no voice in this and there is nothing we can do about it. Yesterday, Dorinda was working at the hospital and was told of a family who had arrived there with a boy that was so malnourished that the doctor was amazed that he was still alive. The mother was also pregnant and in the first stage of labor. The doctors labored over the malnourished boy, giving him oxygen in his little lungs. He was laboring fiercely to breath, gasping for air, his hands grasping for life. In the midst of the scramble to save his little life, while the mother's condition progressed into full blown labor as she writhed on the floor near her dying son in pain, both body and heart.

The baby was sideways in her womb and the mother was taken into surgery for an emergency C-section. In the meantime, the mother's malnourished son, who was fighting for his life, passed on to glory, never to feel the loving touch of his mother with his last breath, nor did she see his little face or lips for a final kiss goodbye. Oh Jesus, oh Jesus. When the doctor asked the father why they had waited so long to bring the boy in he replied, "We were hiding in the bush 50 miles up the road, running from the town of Layna because all the town had gone mad and was in turmoil and soldiers were shooting people. We had to run through the bush all the way to Yei." Oh Jesus, we need you to invade the hearts of these evil men who cause the innocent to die. We need You. Deliver us, oh Lord, deliver us. Our hearts break with this news and so much more like it.

Up north in Aweil, 50% of the town has fled further north into Darfur, Sudan begging for food and shelter from the country that these people had fought to gain their freedom from. The markets are bare and people have no money and children are dying along the road trying to make it north. Jesus, Jesus. We are preparing to go to Aweil in the north, in Bahr El Ghazal, to see what God wants to do through us. I don't have a plan but I do have a purpose, God's outreach is to all people. The days are short and the time draws near to the Lord's coming. How will we help in the end time harvest? Everyone needs to be reached, everywhere, with food, with clothes, with the gospel. The fields are ripe in the earth. Where is our outreach? Do we fear the world or do we have the fear of the Lord in us, to set the captives free?

One of our older boys, Ezra had a very prophetic dream one night. As I write this book, looking back on our journey, I knew that it was the foretelling of what was to come. Ezra dreamt that I went to Uganda and brought back a plane filled with school t-shirts and pastor's collars, the white bands that go on the front of a man's shirt collar, to represent that he is a pastor. Here in South Sudan it is popular in any denomination to wear these collars to easily identify pastors, especially while traveling, and most especially in a war zone. It is a great door and road opener as pastors have so much more access than anyone else. When I travel a long distance in a car I always take my pastor with me because he can get us through so many road blocks and we don't pay corruption fees.

Anyway, in this dream when the children of Iris gathered around to look inside the plane, I began to divide the children into two groups, the older and the younger, because I was to fly off again. The children became upset and asked me why I was preferring one group over the other. So, I told them that they were all coming and let us go! The children began to pile into the mouth of the plane. That was the end of Ezra's dream.

I believed that this was such a prophetic dream as I frequently remind the children that they are marked for the nations of the world, they are missionaries, being that they are saved and discipled so they are no longer the mission field. They are now the missionaries. I speak this over them often. I sensed that the plane represented international travel and the school t-shirts represented the training of the children. I also felt that the collars represented the equipping of the children in ministry and being sent out to the nations. Ezra had given the dream testimony in church this morning so I prayed this prophesy over the children. It is my heart's desire to see this come to pass and the foremost reason that I am here in Africa. My heart focuses on the future of these children and what God will do through the upcoming generation. We are here to equip them and to send them out.

The nation has fallen deeper into its economic crisis. The New York Times and the United Nations (UN) and British Broadcasting Corporation (BBC) have all reported on the situation in South Sudan. I discontinued the posts on our Face Book page, knowing that the people who aren't living in the midst of this, well it seems very far away and not very personal to anyone. I am okay with this. I understand. Our crisis isn't everyone's crisis. I understand and empathize with the different countries as each has its own problems to focus on. I have also ceased my posts as the time is drawing near to full-scale war. I must now take care not to put our lives in danger by speaking anything negative on social media that could come back to haunt us later.

The USA has also imposed economic sanctions on the South Sudan government, banning all exports from the United States from entering into South Sudan. As I perused the Amazon Webpage, trying to order some items for shipment to my U.S. address, my order was refused and I was not allowed to order anything. The website stated, *"Due to export controls and economic sanctions laws and regulations, we are unable to process transactions from your current location."* Wow, I was taken aback. This is really happening. We now needed a secret VPN that showed we were in Atlanta, Georgia or somewhere in the USA, just so we could order something online from here.

The people here feel hopeless and very tired of the power struggle, continuing to labor for life and freedom. Every day we hear of another report of highway banditry, or rebels on the loose, or market prices soaring, or more shooting and fighting. Will this ever end? It's comparable to post-traumatic stress disorder, always ever on the alert for the next thing, except for the fact that we are living in the conditions of PTSD at this present time. It is physically and mentally draining, taking all of our strength to stay focused on God and His plan in all of this. I know that we will be okay and that He will continue to be glorified here. This is food for our souls. We press on and have made up our minds that God is all we want and we are relentless in this. I have such compassion for those who are in the struggle without Jesus, which makes it all the more necessary for us to keep going out, to continue reaching out, as long as we are able.

Last night we received a call from the hospital concerning a three-year old girl who was critically ill and needed whole blood. If she did not receive it soon she would die, it was this perilous. Her hemoglobin level was life-threatening and her fever was spiked high. She needed blood. The hospital does not have the capacity to store whole blood and the little girl's mother wasn't in good health, not enough to give blood, due to malnutrition because of this war. The hospital called me because I have a rare type of blood which makes me a universal donor, O negative, and I was on the call list as a donor. People here do not give blood unless it is for a close family member, and still, many hesitate or refuse. I immediately jumped into the Land Cruiser and went to the hospital.

After the nurse had extracted my blood, filling the bag full, she pulled the needle from my arm, and as I continued to apply pressure to my arm I followed that bag of life to the little girl and I watched as they set the IV into her arm that began the flow that would bring life. I laid my hand gently on her head and prayed while she was receiving my blood. She was in so much pain that I couldn't even touch her, such a delicate little girl. Two days later, her IV's were discontinued and she was moving around cheekily, full of life. I was told a few days later that she was released with a clean bill of health. Praise Jesus for the blood. The life is in the blood and He is the giver of life.

A few days later, another hospital in town held another patient, a lady who was pregnant. She was very pale and her hemoglobin level was so low that the baby was also in danger. Dorinda was visiting a village friend and happened to see this lady. She told Haley, who had that particular blood type, and the two of them went to the clinic to give this lifegiving blood for the lady and her baby. They lived to see another day, to live life. In the West we take it for granted that there will always be blood when we need it, never giving it a second thought. Even after surgery we don't think about the blood that was used to replace ours. We just expect it. Here in Africa, in any third world country, there is no blood bank. If someone in your family does not give blood then you die. Period. Other people will not give their blood for you for fear of dying themselves. Those of us at Iris South Sudan have put ourselves on call to give blood at any time, as often as we can. It is just another way to reach out. Everything we do matters here, everything.

Chapter Twenty-One

It is now May and the situation in South Sudan is still really difficult. Our friends at the hospital told us that so many families are coming in who are malnourished, entire families, because of the extreme economic crisis we are facing. There just isn't any money to cover the extreme cost of things. There are no caps on exchange rates or market prices so everyone is allowed to gouge prices and charge what they like. I really cannot wrap my mind around why there is no government control over these situations. It is as if the leaders who are responsible have washed their hands of the people's problems and are only looking after themselves and since they have all the money, these things don't affect them. The situation is severely detrimental to the people. We have also learned that 90% of the people in the hospitals are sick with malaria, almost as if we are in an epidemic. We have been evermore diligent to ensure that our children are using their mosquito nets at night.

Today we flew to Aweil in Northern Bahr El Ghazal for our last outreach in South Sudan. At that time, we didn't know that it would be our last outreach. My friend Wilfred, another Iris missionary in Pemba, Mozambique, came to join us. Her heart, like ours, burns for the people of South Sudan to be free. I couldn't take any of our children on this outreach because it cost too much and our funds were somewhat low. The team consisted of myself, two of our pastors, Brian, Dorinda, Wilfred and Sandy. Aweil is far to the north and traveling by road was not possible. We needed to fly to get there. We boarded the plane and left Yei behind. It was a small puddle jumper aircraft and we soon landed in Juba twenty minutes later. We would need to stay overnight in Juba in order to catch our early morning flight to Aweil. There are only two flights a week to this remote area. We were filled with anticipation and expectation.

The next morning dawned bright and clear and hot, yet still promised us a nice day to come. Unfortunately, the Juba airport has been dubbed as one of the worst airports in the world. Passengers waiting to go inside are greeted by a mass of humanity, all struggling to get through the door when it opens, most of them not wanting to stand in any lines at all. It is typical for the natives to go directly to the front of the line, squeezing in front of everyone else, having no thought of respect or honor to wait in a line. These people become agitated if the wait is longer than fifteen minutes and they soon begin to complain, shoving their way forward. One must be diligent to hold their ground if they ever want to get their bags checked through. We finally managed to check our bags and had to wait in the immigration line for our passports to be stamped. This is another line that can crush a person because of the impatience of people.

The waiting area is a tarp covered area because of the maintenance and upgrade being done to the existing waiting area. The floor seemed to be constructed of a few large pieces of unstable plywood that bent and wobbled as one walked on them. There were a few places where someone's foot must have broken through resulting in one-foot deep openings in the walkways and nothing has been done to cover them. I watched as a lady literally fell through the floor boards, crying out in pain, people jumping up to help her

I'm fairly sure that there are no safety and health laws observed here. The injured lady limped over to a seat that was broken and leaning forward, as if it was ready to launch a person out of it. No one came to offer her a bandage or any kind of help. I was just stunned. It was extremely hot under the tarp cover and we were all corralled under it like cattle waiting to go through the chutes. There were usually about one hundred people waiting in this area thrown together for about fifty people, with only about forty seats available to sit down on. There were no water fountains or drink machines. If you were thirsty, you would need to go out and buy your drink and go through the security fiasco once again, diligently standing your ground to keep your place in line. It just wasn't worth it.

Finally, we were boarded and seated, fastening our seatbelts, settling in for takeoff. Just over an hour later our plane landed safely in Aweil. The baggage claim in Aweil is other-worldly. We exited the plane and walked to the edge of the landing strip as a beat-up pick-up truck drove past us up to the cargo door of our large plane. The bags were piled high, almost to toppling point, and driven over to us. They pull one bag at a time and checked every bag number, even though you know which bag is yours. They checked every single one before going back for the second load. It was the same for the third load. All the while, the sun is burning down on us as we stand and wait. The waiting area and tarmac were just hard-pressed dirt so once you had your luggage you had to drag it across a wide expanse of dirt and rocks.

By load number three, the plane had already loaded the new passengers and their bags and were lifting off, up into the sky, Juba bound, with our luggage on it. We still hadn't seen our bags and the man was moving very slow. It would be four days before we could hope to see our bags again, as the next flight wasn't until then. There are no shops to buy decent clothes so we knew that we would wear these same clothes each and every day. The only things that any of us had with us were the clothes on our backs, our Bibles, our phones, our money and passports. We did manage to get to the market to buy soap and battery-operated lanterns and a towel. Halelujah for the small things that made us smile.

Our week in Aweil was really incredible! Our main focus was the three-day conference that was held at the church directly across the road from my old compound. It was so good to see my old neighbors again! We fell into each other's arms and laughed and hugged and rejoiced to see each other again. They didn't know that I was coming, so it was a big surprise. The people came from surrounding villages, some walking for three full days under the burning sun in temperatures of 125 degrees to get here to the conference venue. The opening morning of most conferences in South Sudan is always slow and it takes an hour or two for all of the attendees to show up. When the pastors and speakers are also late, the schedule no longer exists. Knowing this, I plan accordingly and usually have one less teaching than scheduled. We just sing and dance and beat the drums until the people come. They even have a song which says that people will come when you beat the drums.

When we arrived at the church early the next morning, the entire church was filled and overflowing with people, singing and dancing! This has never happened to me since coming to South Sudan. I was so surprised and really full of joy. The people were hungry and thirsty for the Living water and they were so happy to be there! The next three days were incredible and everyone was filled to overflowing. If we had stayed another three days, the people would still not be satisfied. Our messages carried the theme of the spirit of perseverance, the spirit of suffering, and the spirit of fire and evangelism. These sound like depressing messages but the people were so excited to be encouraged to lay down their lives for the gospel. The fire most definitely fell in this church.

At the noon hour, we broke into smaller groups of eight men or eight women and ate a meal together. The meal was served on a large round tray piled high with posho, a doughy maize mixture, and a meat sauce and greens. All of the women either squatted around the tray or sat with legs extended if there was room. The men sat in chairs inside the church. This is typical Sudanese culture. I squatted with the women and enjoyed my meal immensely, the fellowship even more. The women were so surprised that I could speak a small bit of Dinka. The people really love when you can speak their language, or that you at least try. This is so important if one wants to reach a people group. Learn the language first, if possible and if there is time.

Each evening we walked to town for some marketplace evangelism. There are very few foreigners in this area so we were an unusual site to see. We carried a portable speaker/microphone set which helped to draw a crowd. We told stories and gave personal testimonies and always ended with prayer for healing, salvation and deliverance. There are many Muslim believers this far north and even they stopped to hear what we had to share. We noticed a man who was mentally challenged and naked and we were told that he refused to wear clothes. He was very kind and gentle, although he was a very large man and he couldn't speak intelligently, instead making guttural grunts and noises. On our first evening in town he came over while we were preaching and ambled forward with his hands raised. We stopped our preaching to pray for him and he fell to the ground. He started saying, "Jesus, Jesus, Jesus". That evening we bought some clothes and to help him out. Unfortunately, the next day he was walking around naked again. Oh well, you win some and you lose some.

When I lived in Aweil in 2013, I ministered to the street boys so they came running when they saw me, shouting, "Mama Carolyn!" and throwing themselves into my waiting arms. It was a wonderful reunion. On our last day we had a youth program just for them, just like old times. We bought big sacks of flat bread from our old bakery just across from the church where we held our conference. The bakers remembered me and were happy to see me again. We also bought some other treats for the boys, meeting with them in our old meeting place in the center of town, as if no time at all had passed. And just like old times, I shared a message before we ate. As I was trying to organize the boys to keep them in a line to receive their food, they began to fight and push each other and chaos ensued. In the midst of all this chaos an old man was led in by his grandson who was pulling his grandfather along with a stick. The old man was blind. We saw him move around our chaotic group and he sat down next to Wildra and one of our pastors. I continued to restrain the fighting boys.

Two of the boys had scratches on their faces and were bleeding, and some of the boys were still pushing each other. I was so focused on bringing order to the boys that I didn't hear the old man shout at first. The boys started pointing to the old man. I had heard him the second time. He shouted, "I can see!", in Arabic. In the midst of total chaos this man was healed of blindness! Even the boys were excited as they knew this man and knew that he had been blind as long as they could remember. Hallelujah! Oh, what a day it was! As we were leaving the boys asked me if I came back to start the program again. It broke my heart to tell them that I couldn't. I was so sad to leave them again.

When we retired to our rooms this evening I couldn't stop thinking about the day's events. So many times, in my worldly travels I find that church's want everything to be perfect before any healing ministry can begin in order for God to move and do a miracle. The perfect music must be playing, an organized line of people all standing thus and thus with assigned catchers behind each one, some churches (especially in Africa) requiring the sick to sit in a chair at the alter while others require them to kneel, the healer with anointing oil in hand, so much order to make sure God moves. Yes, all of this order is right and the humility is wonderful to God but, it doesn't have to happen in order for God to do what He wants to do.

I love ministering in Africa because we minister so many times in chaos on outreach, people crowding around and pushing to get close (Hmmm, sounds like Jesus' outreaches), some wanting to steal from your backpack, others trying to touch places on your body, but if one can focus on the Lord and the person in front of them, well, God will move. God just showed us that He is also very present in the chaos of things. He goes where there is faith, not necessarily the perfect scenario. He sits on a wooden bench while boys are fighting ten feet away. He strolls through the marketplace where men walk around naked. Amidst all of the suffering in Aweil, the people are still so hungry for God, so encouraged that He would come to visit them. I love the simple faith of the people of Africa. This simple faith is why they see miracles as an ordinary occurrence. They believe it and expect it. There is so much freedom in this!

This morning we called the airlines desk in Aweil and were told that our luggage was not coming until the day of our flight back to Juba. We told them to just hold it at the Juba airport and we would collect our luggage when we land back there. We were still wearing the same clothes as when we first arrived, therefore, it was necessary to retire to our rooms early enough each night to allow us to wash our clothes. Jumping and dancing and kneeling and sweating in the church can get quite dirty when the floor itself is dirt. We washed our clothes in the little sink in our bathroom and hung them to dry in our rooms, draping them over a plastic chair or hanging them from our mosquito nets.

Meanwhile, we wrapped ourselves in our bedsheets as if it were a toga. We were quite the hilarious sight. But, all joking aside, we also learned just how powerfully we could minister when we had nothing to distract us, nothing to do but read our Bible, alone in our rooms each night, no western comforts, just the word of God and the presence of God. Our focus was fully on Him because we had nothing else, absolutely nothing else. It was an intense week, one we will never forget. The fire of God was surely with us and in us.

After seven days, today we departed for our home in Yei. Our luggage was waiting for us in Juba. We were happy to see our luggage but vowed to definitely travel lighter on future outreaches. And now, we go back to life as usual as we plan another walk about outreach.

During our time in Aweil the civil war felt as if it were far away from us, the clashes being a distant memory. As we prayed together in the church, we really had such hope that this would be the end of it so that we could return to some sense of normalcy. But, this was not to be. Our lives would soon change forever. The five-year anniversary of our independence was just two days away and people were seriously hoping to finally celebrate peace this year, although no plans were made to have official celebrations in the town square. We didn't celebrate last year because the conflict was too severe and this year the tension still ran high. Little did we know this day that a catastrophic day was about to come upon us.

Chapter Twenty-Two

On July 7, 2016, today, just two days before Independence Day, in the nation's capital city of Juba, the beginning of the end has come upon us. Our nation is once again in a state of great turmoil. The two armies are fighting each other with a vengeance, killing each other in the streets, using AK47's, Techno's, and heavy artillery and gunships were flying overhead. It seemed as if someone had thrown a match to a fuel truck, the explosion rocking the entire nation. It was so sudden and unexpected that we were all in shock, not knowing which way to run nor who the enemy was and where safety could be found. The incident sparking this tinder box began at the city checkpoint when the soldiers from each side of the conflict began firing at each other causing all-out vengeance to ensue.

The streets have emptied and everyone has rushed home or into the nearest building terror stricken, locking their doors, shutting the windows, throwing themselves on the floor and under their beds and furniture, crying out to God Almighty while listening to the chaos beyond their thin mud walls. At one point, about a week into the clash, we heard gunfire on every side of us as we lay on the floor quietly during the barrage of gunfire. For three days we were held captive in our houses. During this time our brave cooks still continued to cook simple meals as I ran back and forth with plates of food for 130 children each meal. We all remained inside trying not to let fear grip us.

By the fourth day of that barrage it grew quiet at last and I was able to travel into town in order to acquire information from the Commissioner on the current situation in our city. Soldiers were everywhere, on the streets, in the markets, sitting in front of commercial buildings, ever alert. I could see their restlessness because they were itching to help their comrades in Juba and felt as if they were far from the frontlines. Three other cities besides ours are also experiencing great turmoil due to this latest clash. One third of the armies of South Sudan are in our region of the country. The army barracks at the edge of our city is of considerable size. We have been praying for them to remain stable and calm and to help keep the peace here.

We have learned that on July 8th the border to Uganda has closed once again. We remain vigilant because of the news we are hearing, that trucks loaded with goods coming from Uganda have been shot at and hijacked. The news has come across the media wires and this war has become more real to us now than ever before. The trucks which were shot at or hijacked are very large eighteen-wheeled trucks with large twenty to forty-foot shipping containers loaded onto the bed filled with goods and produce. Every truck has turned back upon hearing the latest news. There are hundreds of trucks now sitting at the border, hoping that this latest clash will wane, just like it did in 2013. The produce traders now risk losing all their investment as the produce wilts and rots in the heat of a metal shipping container sitting in the hot sun on the border. The traders too are frustrated with the fighting.

I have continued to encourage our church that Jesus will always come in the mess of things, reminding them of the testimony of the blind man who was healed in Aweil. Jesus will come when we cry out in the mess of things to show Himself strong. Our family at Iris South Sudan is comprised of at least six different tribes yet we have no tribalism here. When I arrived at the Iris Base in 2013 as Director, I told the children that we would not involve ourselves with tribal politics, telling them that it does not belong in our family because we are all from one tribe, the Kingdom of God. The children embrace their heritage and culture but their pride is only in their citizenship in the Kingdom of God.

Our hearts grieve together for all tribes across the world. Even in the midst of the chaos here in South Sudan, we still grieve for America. Many Africans have commented that if America falls then we all fall. Americans just don't realize how much Africa prays for them and depend on them to do what is right and good, walking and leading in righteousness. We are all beacons in the darkness, called to keep our lamps full until the coming of our King no matter what.

It is now Friday night, July 9th, the second night of fighting on the streets of Juba. We have gathered as a family in the center of our compound, under the heavens, stars blinking as a blanket of lights, and we prayed for our nation and worshiped God as if we were standing before His throne. We danced before Him and poured out our love for Him so completely, knowing that we are held in His hands and are kept hidden in His secret place, even in the openness of our compound. We did not fear the night nor the rain of gunfire in Juba, or even when it came close to us. We trust God. Throughout the ensuing days many of us continued to pray and intercede for the nation and for our families. Our children are faithful to pray because they know that God answers. I am so blessed, so very blessed to have a prayerful and worshipful family.

We are now six days into this present conflict and my heart is heavy as I write this. The people of our city sit in their houses in fear because of the bloodshed by those whom we have trusted to protect us, those whom have taken an oath to protect the people of South Sudan, the military might of this nation. It was absurd to believe back in 2013 after the coup attempt that two armies under two different leaders with two opposing views could walk together in unity. A clash was destined to happen, and so it has.

Most of the major towns and cities from Yei to Juba have now emptied out, entire towns, as people run into the bush or to the borders because of the violence! There is no one left in Layna, the town between here and Juba, except for soldiers. All of the foreigners in Yei have left for Uganda except for us here at Iris and three Americans at the other children's home. Ninety percent of the shops are closed a full week after the clash started. Most traders have left for good, fearing to come back, not trusting peace to last.

We continue to sit here on our compound, with our children at play, trying to maintain some sense of normalcy as we watch along our fence line, witnessing the village emptying out, people walking by on our bush trails with their belongings on their heads and backs, fear upon their countenance, escaping from those who are called to protect us. One small family has even taken up residence in an abandoned goat shed near our front gate having nowhere else to go. I am grieved that we cannot take in refugees we aren't familiar with for fear that they might belong to one of the fighting tribes. It could even bring violence to our home.

In Yei we have not experienced the violence that was so destructive in Juba last week, although there have been sporadic raids on homes this last week. One incident occurred at the hospital in town. A soldier decided to fire his AK47 into the air inside of the hospital numerous times, angry because the doctor was unable to save a dying comrade. This incident has instilled even more fear into our townspeople, never knowing when a soldier would snap and start firing his weapon. The anger in these men is tremendous and so destructive.

Army troops have been moving on all sides of our compound, silently staring through our fence as they walk the perimeter, the children warily watching them. Today we counted eighty soldiers passing through in full battle gear.

No one was smiling or joking around, the soldiers remaining very serious and ever alert. The trader's trucks from Uganda are nonexistent these days, everything grinding to a halt, the traders deciding it's just not worth their lives to make a few bills. The few shops that remain open present empty shelves. Can you imagine walking into your grocery store to find that there is nothing left on the shelves but a few spices? What do you do now?

There are no longer any planes coming in or going out of the country for fear of landing here and being hijacked or shot down. The bush alongside the major roads is now filled with bandits and soldiers, which army they belong to we don't know, but they wait to take advantage of fearful mothers and fathers who wish to escape the bloodshed. As for us, we couldn't escape if we wanted to, not with over a hundred children in tow. We are stuck here on our compound, basically hostages in our own town.

We press ever closer to God because He is our only hope. There is no other help. No one is coming to save the day, not World Food Program and not UNICEF. Only the hand of God can save us. We just harvested some acres of peanuts this week and will harvest some acres of corn next week. The children didn't take me seriously when I told them a few weeks ago that we will now have to work for our food and I have reduced all of our meals to half portions. I went into town to investigate the situation and only 20% of the shops are still open, and of those, maybe fifteen have food. Once it's gone, it's gone. The Commissioner who was here in 2013 is no longer in office leaving the office vacant. We literally have no help.

We even have one child who is trapped in Juba, right at the epicenter of the fighting. Eliezer, who is thirteen, left last week with Jendina, one of our caregivers, to be fitted for his prosthetic leg after his leg was amputated six months ago due to an out of control infection. We found him this way in the village and brought him here to care for him. Eliezer and Jendina have been trapped for four days, lying on the floor, eating only a lump of porridge once a day, while bullets and RPG's have been raining down around them. We only know this much because Michael, one of my older sons working in Juba, informed us of the news when they did not return to their compound, as they were staying there.

We were able to make phone contact with them and for now, they are okay, although they cannot walk around or go outside, only able to crawl along the floor for fear of being shot. They have no more food in this place, or water, so we are seriously praying for their release and for a way back to us. A few days later we are told that Eliezer and Jendina have finally been rescued and are safe, but still in the tension of Juba. We are told that Eliezer is not doing well emotionally because of the trauma of the last few days. My heart is beginning to feel the pull and weight of what is coming. It is no longer this country's war, but it has become my own, happening to my people, my friends, my family. I can no longer separate my heart and mind from any of this. Oh Jesus, stay ever closer to us.

Chapter Twenty-Three

I have received extremely sad news today and my heart is crushed with the weight of it. My pastor in Juba, at Dar Jebel, the one that helped us with our outreach to Terekeka, has been dropped to his very knees. I just learned that he had to run with his family because their area was heavily bombed last night. In the process of running, his little boy of seven years just stopped breathing. No bullet hit him, he just stopped breathing. Fear had gripped his heart and it stopped. He is now with Jesus and being laid to rest today. I am grieved and crushed and crying because I knew and held Isaac so many times. He was going to be like his daddy, a preacher man. Now he is gone. This is the part of war that people don't see. The innocents are very angry and are crying tears of grief because they just want to be free and those in charge are not bringing freedom. Instead, these soldiers are stealing the freedom that so many gave their lives for. Has it all been for nothing?

I gathered our staff together this morning, along with our children, and we worshiped together and thanked God for keeping us so close to Him, and for protecting our Juba family at the children's center there, where many of our children came from in 2014. We are tired and we are crying for peace, a peace that has refused to come. Some of us fell to our knees and we began to weep and sob for God to consider us, to come and meet us here in our circumstance and to respond concerning these terrible men who have robbed us of our peace. So many people in this nation have been so faithful to pray and to keep crying for peace, waiting for the solution from heaven to come, trusting and believing and praying and crying, even as we bury the dead. My heart is breaking and I feel such anguish. I don't know how to express this without upsetting the children. Jesus, Jesus, Jesus.

I do know that revival comes with the smoke and fire of sacrifice. I have to believe that revival will come out of this, that dry bones will stand and that the Spirit of the Lord will fill us again and again. We do not walk around with hanging heads, we cannot or we lose hope. We do not sit and cry and complain, instead we get up out of our beds each day, we go to our fields and we work to bring in the harvest. I tell the children that this is the picture of what God desires of His church, to keep bringing in the harvest. After we prayed today, many of us went to the houses in our village closest to our compound to pray with our neighbors for the peace and protection of the Lord. Our neighbors were encouraged, filled with a new hope and joy. We arise each day because His joy comes new every morning. Today we are full of joy because Jendina and Eliezer are finally home with us once again. Hallelujah! We refuse to run away or even hang our heads, continuing to clap and dance and praise our God from whom all blessings flow.

Although I have made no plans to evacuate I remain wise, exploring our options. Right now, we are diligently working on our immigration papers for every single one of the children and staff and their children. We hope to be ready to leave if that day ever comes. There is an open door right now for this to be accomplished if all of the offices cooperate with us. It has never happened before, where the government says that they will do this for the orphans who are in our care. We are praying for favor with the officials that have the ability to make this happen. I believe that God can do this. We trust God, one step at a time.

It is very traumatic to live in a constant state of alertness, wondering where the next bullet will hit, wondering if the soldiers walking by would try to take our boys to fight, wondering if they will come back in the night to rape our girls. These things are happening right now all across the nation. Sleep is not deep, rest always punctuated by an ever-alert body. My mind is ever consumed with the next step to stay one step ahead. I start my days the way I always do, sitting in His Presence and I wait. He always comes.

These days the range of emotions and thoughts that one goes through on the quest for truth and faith in a really hard place are wide and varied. God always shows us His faithfulness and He is always good because that is His nature. This night I found myself battling a spirit of fear so great that I could not sleep. I sit here on my bed, tucked inside my mosquito netting on a four-inch piece of foam, holding my Bible, and I pray. The Lord then revealed His love for me in this scripture and it gave me hope:

(Philippians 1:27-28 (The Passion Bible)):

"Whatever happens, keep living your lives based on the reality of the gospel of Christ, which reveals Him to others. Then when I come to see you, or hear good reports of you, I'll know that you stand united in one Spirit and one passion – celebrating together as conquerors in the faith of the gospel. And then you will never be shaken or intimidated by the opposition that rises up against us, for your courage will only prove as a sure sign from God of their coming destruction and that you have found a new life."

This scripture has delivered me from fear. If I see my reality as that of the Kingdom of God and what He says, not being moved by the reality of what is happening around me, then I can have peace in knowing that greater is the One in me, Jesus Christ and His Spirit, than all who would be against me. If I keep my peace, if I bless my enemies, if I feed them and give them water, if I hold on to hope, then I will not be overtaken by chaos and anguish of heart. I will remain in His love, which keeps me in perfect peace, casting out all fear. Only the Word of God can keep me focused and peaceful in these trying times.

We have been waiting, waiting, waiting, for what, we don't know. As for myself, the most difficult place of rest is in the waiting, the not knowing. There are so many questions in the waiting. I find it easier for my heart and mind to operate from a place of chaos and activity than not knowing what is next. This is the place where trusting God becomes even more crucial, in the waiting. It is a battle to arise each morning when I
awaken with a heaviness of heart, already feeling so weary. I am angry at this war and how it consumes us. Situations are occurring that I can't even talk about without feeling the desire to point my finger, shouting, demanding that people be held accountable for the atrocities that have happened and are still happening in this nation.

One of the housing complexes in the capital city, which houses many UN personnel, has come under attack by evil men. During the uprising on July 7th, a handful of UN ladies were trapped in this housing complex as the fighting broke out in the morning hours. Soldiers suddenly came rushing in under the guise of rescuing them and began to gang rape the women, one being an American. I have also learned that soldiers were regularly raping young women, not even eighteen yet, near Dar Jebel. Every day I mentally prepare myself for the day ahead, every single morning, before my feet hit the floor, because there are always problems and rumors and bad situations such as this that threaten to jar me from a place of rest.

Each night when we lie down to sleep, we are restless, wondering where the shooting will be tonight, what news will we hear in the morning? Our bodies may sleep deeply all night yet we awake tired. Unconsciously, our bodies and minds are on high alert to what might happen in the night so that none of us sleeps deeply or restfully. Whenever I hear a noise even related to a gunshot,

I sit up and my ears perk up, listening, waiting, wondering. After discussing this with the older children, they agree with me wholeheartedly on this issue. Each day there are bad reports that we must filter through. We share how we are feeling and we pray with each other, standing against fear.

Today I read a message from Ambassador McPhee, the US Ambassador to South Sudan, which was sent out to all U.S. citizens still residing in country. She was forced by circumstance to make an announcement that the US was not sending in CIA agents in order to sneak in thousands of military troops to take over the country. There have been forged, fake documents circulating around the country, which the government or the people believe to be real. The documents are overflowing with grammatical and spelling errors that any educated person could see. The documents were published on the internet and no American with an education could possibly have written them. Yet, the people who are posting this propaganda are luring people into believing such nonsense, thereby putting our very lives (Americans) in even more danger.

We also read on the internet that the South Sudan government supported a protest this week in Juba which was against any additional UN involvement in this conflict and against any type of help concerning this conflict. They don't want their dirty laundry aired in public for all to see. The Japanese call it "saving face". The United Nations humanitarian workers are being harassed, causing medical and food distribution flights to transport much needed food to critically malnourished refugees in the north to be grounded indefinitely. I just cannot understand the insanity of it all. What would cause people to purposely keep food from the starving masses? All I can assume at this point is that I don't know the whole story. I just know that it looks bad.

Chapter Twenty-Four

My compound manager left for town this morning to attempt to restock our food pantry. Later, upon arriving home he informed me that he was almost arrested for buying food for our children, the soldiers accusing him of buying supplies for the rebels. Immediately I wrote a letter to carry in all of our vehicles stating that we were an official NGO responsible for feeding and caring for orphans. Anyone on my staff who makes purchases now carries this same letter, so that we can be free to continue our work of caring for these children unimpeded. We have now been forbidden by soldiers to use our big truck for any type of purchases in town, instead making several trips into town with our Land Cruiser to buy food in small batches so as not to make the authorities suspicious. It is so absurd to think that missionaries would participate in this conflict by buying food for rebel soldiers. What is wrong with this picture? There is so much about this conflict that is absurd.

These matters are made even worse by the fact that the soldiers who are harassing us on the roads have not been paid in months, probably not even this year, and they too are desperate for food. The rebels also receive no pay and are pretty desperate for food themselves, making everyone an easy target. The World Food Organization (WFO) compound in Juba was robbed by gunmen of 45,000 tons of food in one night, which was earmarked for the internally displaced refugees. The robbers are now selling it on the black market, in open view of everyone, no one doing anything about it. Whether the thieves were soldiers or rebels, no one is saying.

This is the fallout of war. It lives at our doorstep. What cost $50 yesterday is $100 today and will probably be $200 tomorrow. If things don't change soon we will be forced to evacuate regardless. We seriously need the government to approve the children's immigration papers in order to steer clear of the refugee camps in Uganda. Running is not an option with over one hundred children. Where would we run to? Will we be gunned down, moving targets? I can't go there in my mind. If our papers are denied and the need to evacuate becomes a reality, the children would very likely be deposited into an Internally Displaced People's (IDP) camp in Juba without us. Foreigners are not allowed in the camps except as part of the UN force working there. We cannot just leave them at a camp because terrible things happen even there. The stories of rapes and alcohol abuse, cholera and typhoid, and a myriad of other issues is terrifying and heart wrenching to witness. In the year 2010 I was part of a UN delegation which was requested to investigate incidents at the Congolese refugee camp in Lasu, South Sudan. These atrocities were rampant there. There is never enough security in the camps to control these things. My mind has been so busy all my waking hours trying to think ahead and plan ahead, every waking hour, to find a way for all of us to escape from here, alive and together. This is the war at our door.

In the midst of these worries we struggle to keep the children occupied since most of the school teachers have fled across the border to safety. School is no longer in session anywhere except across town at the other children's home. If we don't keep the children busy, they start to worry or become depressed from too much time on their hands thinking about the lack of a future that they are possibly facing. Each day we go to the fields to dig, even though we know that we might not ever see the harvest, but someone will. Even me, I go with them and dig every day, maintaining an appearance of peace and joy, the children being aware of the danger but seeing that I am not too concerned because I put my trust in God alone. This is the war at our door.

Yesterday a staff lady, Amina, and one of our older girls, Eliana, had a sudden and acute asthma attack, both residing in the same house. We have ten children's houses. We weren't really sure if it was asthma because there are no doctors left in our town to diagnose them. All we knew was that it was a strange lung situation where they could not get their breath, gasping and struggling to breath. Neither of them had ever had asthma, so why now? Miraculously, inhalers were available at one of the town pharmacies, which was nothing more than a small wooden shed, a ten by ten-foot structure. Typically, the inhalers didn't work leaving the ladies still in distress. Desperate, I watched them labor to breathe and was at a loss as to what to do except pray. We had been through this before with Isaiah and the Lord healed his lung. He would do it again.

I took a flask of anointing oil and proceeded to anoint the house and every child and adult within. Then I prayed a prayer of deliverance on all who were being afflicted, casting out tormenting spirits and asking for the infilling of the Holy Spirit in every space that had been swept clean. We then worshipped the Lord and thanked Him for His kindness and mercy toward us who believe in Him. This morning, the two who were gasping for breath yesterday were breathing normally, as if it had never happened! Praise the Lord Almighty Jesus! We now believe that the spirit of fear had gripped them, stealing away their very breath. Fear can actually rob us of our breath if we allow it to take hold. We have learned a valuable spiritual principle today. The children have also been experiencing bad dreams and fighting fear, therefore we prayed together and anointed all.

Earlier this week I had gone on a run along the perimeter of our compound to relieve my stress, the stress of carrying this heavy responsibility and the constant decision making, and as I was running I almost fell to my knees in the middle of the path to cry. I really wanted to cry. Instead I looked up to the heavens and talked to God, telling Him that I can't do this on my own, that I am tired and I can't take much more and neither can the children. I'm so tired of hearing only bad news day after day, night after night. I kept running down that dirt trail flanked by teak trees, feeling as if I were in a forest of worry, and I told Him all of these things as I ran on.

This is the hardest thing I have ever had to do, staying in a place that looks so hopeless. The children have been congregating in our prayer hut every single morning to worship and to pray to God for His help and protection. I have been staying up late into the night and arising early to pray to God, drawing ever closer to Him and leaning on His strength which is given to me through His grace and mercy. The gunfire in the night is constant, every single night now. Sleep evades me these nights as I lay awake to be alert in case the soldiers come close to us.

Our governor, who appears to have concern for his people, came to our town more than once to reassure us that he is doing everything possible to ensure our safety. He has declared this city a city of refuge, a city of peace, stating that he will allow no guns to be toted around our town. He gives the impression that he is serious, the people seemingly encouraged, which is needed right now. I don't know how he will stop the soldiers from carrying their guns in town. They have a job, he has a job. Who has the bigger gun?

I went to see the commissioner again to obtain permission to take these children to Uganda. Again, he asked me to be patient, that this will all blow over. He asked me to continue to care for these children while also asking me to take in two more children who have been separated from their parents, if he doesn't find any relatives. They have been residing at his home since their abandonment. This is just another product of war, abandoned children or orphaned children. The numbers increase daily. I assured him that if we could be of assistance then we would help in any way we were able, considering our low food supplies.

In Juba, our friends at the children's home are even planning to "dig a trench for the kids to hide in because there are rumors that more assaults are coming and that the lion will roar again". Rumors are a large cause of people fleeing to the border, believing everything they hear, fearing the worst, or the soldiers stir up the people and they flee believing these rumors are true. The nation has been without phone service since July 9th, almost two weeks ago. Praise God for internet or else I would know nothing beyond our fence line.

In town, the people that are seen on the streets are at about 50% as compared to normal traffic. Our town is emptying out before our very eyes. The shops that are opened are at about 30% stock compared to what is normal. All prices have increased by 100% which is disastrous for the people of this nation. They are literally starving to death, many families arriving at the hospitals severely malnourished. Some of the shopkeepers who are still here are so happy to see that a few of the foreigners are still around. They shake our hands vigorously and exclaim how happy they are to see that we have stayed. It gives them some hope. I am really surprised to see some of them still here, still doing business. They are more concerned with making money than their own safety.

The only good thing that has come out of all of this is the quality and quantity of time we spend in the presence of the Lord each day. I have fully encouraged the children to spend as much time in prayer as they need, the more the better. All day long He is ever before me in all that I do. I love this closeness and this dependence upon Him. I am still learning to let Him carry all of my burdens, and I find myself weighed down sometimes trying to carry them alone. It is a very difficult thing to be responsible for so many lives and so much decision-making to just let it all go and not worry. Daily I hand these things over to God, even hourly.

I have been meditating on James 1:2-8:

"My brethren, count it all joy when you fall into various trials, knowing that the testing of your faith produces patience. But let patience have its perfect work, that you may be perfect, lacking nothing. If any of you lacks wisdom, let him ask of God, who gives to all liberally and without reproach, and it will be given to him. But let him ask in faith, with no doubting, for he who doubts is like a wave of the sea driven and tossed by the wind. For let not that man suppose that he will receive anything from the Lord; he is a double-minded man, unstable in all his ways."

It is paramount for me to hear from the Lord, to gain his wisdom. When I hear from Him I have to believe with full faith what He tells me. He gives wisdom to everyone liberally, as much as is needed. I cannot afford to be tossed upon the waves by doubting Him and myself. I choose faith and I choose to believe that it is Him I am hearing. This requires me to stay so close to God that I can hear even His whisper. There have been a few people that have contacted me through the internet, asking me if I knew what I was doing. Some have gone so far as to accuse me of purposely putting the children's lives in danger and not making wise decisions.

I cannot comprehend why people would think that they had even an inkling of what we are going through. Unless one is in this situation, how can they know how to deal with anything? People don't have a clue what I am faced with each day, the decisions I must make, the lives I am responsible for. I would rather listen to God's voice any day, over the voice of my accusers. These people have now been blocked from my internet accounts as I don't need those who know it all right now.

I have also been meditating on Romans 5:3-5:

"And not only that, but we also glory in tribulations, knowing that tribulation produces perseverance; and perseverance, character; and character, hope. Now hope does not disappoint, because the love of God has been poured out in our hearts by the Holy Spirit who was given to us."

Where there is no testing of our faith, there is no growth. We would never mature into the hope that God has given us. Many of God's people quit and give up because they have lost hope. Hope is the only thing that keeps a person moving forward. Without hope, there is only defeat. I pray that I never lose hope. When one loses hope, they lose their life.

Every day we fight the good fight of faith and sometimes we crawl but we continue to move forward, inch by inch. There is nothing that can separate us from the love of God, nothing. Not height, nor depth, nor width, nor length, nor the devil, nor angels (Romans 8:38-39). God always wants the best outcome for us. My friend has come to be with us during this time and she told me that when we were praying the other day she saw wings behind me and she saw my skeletal frame as being made of titanium. I had a picture of the bones in Ezekiel being called to rise up as a great army, standing strong. This encouraged me to imagine my frame as titanium, lightweight yet stronger than anything, because of Christ in me. I could picture these children with titanium frames. They have withstood more than most adults I know and are still standing strong.

(As I look back now I laugh because last year in 2018 I underwent two surgeries, one for two discs in my spine and one for my ankle, which I broke and dislocated, where titanium discs and titanium screws and plates were implanted. Little did I know.)

We continue to press on in all circumstances. Our faith in God is not the real test. Faith in ourselves to hear Him clearly and to do what He asks of us, no matter what others may say, no matter what circumstance we find ourselves in, this is the real test. This is where our faith is tested, radical obedience, with the assurance that He loves us. Abraham took the ultimate step of faith and His whole life was blessed because He fully trusted God. We continue to pray for peace in this nation and for God to change the hearts of man because no one else can. Unless He changes the hearts of man, man is doomed to destruction, mostly by his own hand. I've asked many to keep us in prayer as we face each new day and each new trial with great faith and perseverance.

Chapter Twenty-Five

It is now Saturday night and the children are inside their houses with doors locked and lights out and I myself am preparing for bed. I suddenly remembered that I had forgotten to take my nightly medication. I went to the desk in my house to retrieve it and as I reached for my medication, I found a swarm, thousands of ants, in my house leading an organized assault through the window pane. I had no bug spray and quickly decided to try and sweep them onto a dustpan to jettison them outside. There were too many for me to keep us with!

They just kept coming, so many ants that I lit a fire inside my house with paper from my trashcan to stop them from going everywhere, sweeping the flaming paper back and forth under the window, roasting ants the entire time and lighting more paper to throw on the window sill where they were still coming in! I know, it's ludicrous to think that anyone would purposely start a fire in their house. This was the only thing that worked. Faintly I heard a noise in my kitchen and ran to investigate and discovered another swarm, hundreds of ants attacking a large lizard, killing it in a matter of minutes, the fat lizard curling and squirming, fighting for its very life, trapped between the screen and the window pane.

At this point I ran to check all of my windows and found another swarm at my bedroom window attacking another lizard! The lizards didn't stand a chance, the ants were that lethal. I ran outside to call for help and stopped dead in my tracks, almost falling down, and found that my house was completely surrounded by killer ants, lines running and weaving up to every single window, every single one! This was a demonic attack because they swarmed every single window. There were trails coming from every direction, converging on my house. I can't even imagine what would have happened if I had gone to bed. I can't even go there right now. I called for the watchmen to come and help me, "Help me! Come quick! Bring ashes from the kitchen!!" I had two fires going in my house and my eyes were burning and I was yelling "JESUS!"

The boys came flying out of their house, running across the compound to help me, lighting even more fires all over the house! The watchmen ran over with a wheelbarrow filled with ashes from the kitchen cook fires in order to smother the ants. After almost an hour every line of militant ants had retreated back into the bush, as if someone had blown the bugle with the command of retreat. The situation was just so crazy because all advancing lines instantaneously turned back. There were three varieties of ants in this attack, which is unheard of as they stick to their own kind. To see them working in unison, under one commander was way beyond my comprehension. They don't join together to attack anything. This confirmed to me that it was a demonic attack.

Rebecca and Sandy also came running from the missionary housing to help me and were in shock because they had never seen anything like it. They too were lighting fires. At every window someone was waving a fiery torch across the swarm of ants, roasting them alive as they fell like rain. After we had gotten the victory, I marveled because not a single ant had bitten any of us, not even finding them on our clothing. This alone was a miracle. Last year I unknowingly walked into a trail of ants and one attached itself to my pinky toe. When I tried to pull it off of my toe, it actually drew blood. This type of ant literally digs in and grabs on. One cannot simply just brush them off.

At the end of this present battle, there was one dead ant on my person which was lying dead on the top of my shoe. It must have fallen as we were roasting them. My house smelled like a campfire so after everyone had gone back to bed I left all of the windows open. Before retiring to bed, zipping up tight in my mosquito net, I walked once more around the perimeter of my house to ensure that this army did not reattack. I slept peacefully, knowing that the Lord had protected me and always would.

I awoke to a clear, bright morning, the smell of smoke long forgotten, as I went to greet my staff and the children. I thought about the way we greet each other in the morning. In South Sudan the customary greeting is to say "Salam Taki", which means, "Peace to you." These days I don't say this lightly anymore, I listen to what this really means. Peace is yours. We say this every day, peace is yours. Yet peace constantly eludes us, each and every day, unless we stay close to the One who brings real peace, Jesus Christ. After the ant attack last night I was able to sleep in great peace because I knew the Lord would not sleep concerning me. The SPLA and the SPLA-Opposition Forces are still fighting from Juba to Yei in all directions, both sides suffering heavy losses, no one really knowing what the real casualty count is as reporters are not allowed anywhere near the battle zones. When reporters do manage to enter into these areas, the news tends to be inflated. Unfortunately, bad news sells stories and brings higher ratings.

Most people are now without food, unless they grow it themselves or they can pay triple the price for whatever is left in the market, which isn't much these days. All of our Face Book followers were very excited for us when I posted that it was a good day because we had food and water and were safe. By no means does it mean that we are now seeing trucks roll into town carrying an abundance of food supplies. It just means that for this day we have food. If the fighting does not stop soon the entire country will be running for the borders if only to eat and stay alive, including us.

I am worried about Eliezer who was trapped in Juba when the war broke out. He refuses to talk about it and his auntie Jendina doesn't laugh like she used to. During one of the recent shooting incidents in our city Jendina held her trembling hand to her heart, her breathing became rapid and full of fear she said, "My heart, my heart." All of us now flinch or jump or run when we hear shooting. I told Eliezer that God is our very present shield and He will protect us. I also encouraged him not to be discouraged about not being able to obtain his prosthetic leg. We would fly to Uganda if we had to in order to obtain that much needed leg. I think Eliezer's fear stems from the idea that he would not be able to run in the event that we needed to run. He feared being left behind.

Our gates remain open during the day in order for our neighbors to come and use our borehole thereby, keeping them safe also from bandits and soldiers. This also gives us the opportunity to hear the news from outside. This week the comment was made that when our neighbors hear the sound of our worship every night, and many mornings throughout the week, they are encouraged because they know that God is with us and that they are safe if they stay close to where God dwells in our small community. This really encourages me that people feel safe because they feel God's Presence in our village. When discouragement tries to steal its way in, God reminds me of this. We really are making an impact for His glory right here. I have been hearing of entire churches closing their doors because all the congregants have left, although many of the pastors remain, putting their faith in God alone.

During the daylight hours, the soldiers seem to go quiet, allowing me to continue with ministry so that I am still able to preach and teach three times a week. Today I went to visit and have lunch with the mother of one of our staff, the mother being blind. She went blind when the coup occurred in 2013. She told me that she was fine for a bit and then lost her sight completely. We prayed for her healing and shared a meal with her.

One thing I noticed was that her granddaughter led her into the house and showed her exactly where her chair was, as if she didn't know where it was. I was surprised because the house is extremely small, one room, and she had been blind for over two years so I assumed she would know by now where things were. The granddaughter, Chaltere who led her into the house lives with us on our compound along with her mother. Her mother is one of our caregivers. Only one other girl lives with her and I think that one goes to school so I really did wonder why she needed to be led. I never asked. God would use this scenario to teach me later.

This week I also went to visit a widow who lives next to our church. She is very frail, reed thin and tired and has been for some time. She has two sons that have not been good to her, one a soldier in the last war but who is now not mentally well and I'm fairly sure that he has a few demons. He lived with her for a few months then left suddenly. Her other son was in prison and we helped to pay his release fee for the purpose of him coming to help his mother. He came to stay for a bit then he too suddenly left. I feel so sad for her because these two men were lazy and I noticed her waiting on them most times. We take dinner to her every Sunday after church and invite her to share every meal with us and we always care for her when she is sick, the children always informing me if she is sick. She has become a part of our family.

I really pray for the Lord to take her home if that is His will. This is the first time that I seriously prayed for someone to go home to the Lord. I have watched her labor over the years and have even sent some of our children to help her at times. She works so hard to get what little she has and it breaks my heart. She carries large loads of firewood on her head, which she chops herself, she plants and harvests her own garden by herself. I don't know the Lord's plan for her but He must have a plan if He is keeping her here on this earth. She does come to our lady's fellowship each week and I see that it is the highlight of her week.

Chapter Twenty-Six

Lately, since hearing about the rapes in Juba, I have been battling a spirit of fear, most especially concerning my girls. I don't think that I could mentally cope if this happened to them, I just couldn't. I have been praying for three nights now and last night I heard the Lord tell me to "face my fears", to go to the place where these things are occurring, to Juba. One of my daughters, Awek, is from the Dinka tribe, the tribe who lives in the area of Juba that I feel to go to, to the large Army Battalion Headquarters Barracks. This is the headquarters for the entire South Sudan Army.

Awek has an uncle who is an Army Chaplain in the Episcopal church so I asked her to call him for me. We were told that foreigners are not allowed in this place so I knew I was asking for the impossible. If this was really from the Lord then He would open the door for me with no striving on my part. I talked to the Chaplain tonight on the phone and he has welcomed me to come and seems even eager to have us come, also being very impressed at our boldness to come. I pray with all of my heart that we bless them and love them so wonderfully.

Two years ago, when we took a team to Terekeka, just north of Juba, I remember pointing at the mammoth structure which loomed over the Battalion Headquarters and I made the comment at that time that one day I would preach there. This is now the timing of the Lord, almost two years later. I pray that His message comes from my lips with such anointing that it will break any yoke and even bring peace to their hearts and minds, encouraging them to be peacemakers in a nation desperate for this. The people are seriously tired, many crying in frustration, including me.

My word for this week is that I can do everything that I need to do because Christ strengthens me to do this, having no strength in and of myself. I can do nothing good in and of myself. It is only through Christ and His blood that any good can come from my life and my highest call is to give Him my all, every day trying to do this, giving Him even my worries and fears. I have no choice but to trust Him. Just as Peter said in the scriptures, "Lord to whom shall we go? You have the words of eternal life." (John 6:68)

Today, August 8, 2016, Awek and I arrived in Juba and we spent the afternoon with our friends at the Children's Home there. We ministered to the small children and a bit later, after the little ones had gone to bed, we organized a trauma healing prayer session with the older girls. They have been in this city of chaos and tension for a month now and we could see it in their eyes, ever alert, a heavy weight upon them. After we prayed and ministered to the girls they were so encouraged and remarked that they felt tremendous peace for the first time since all this began. Prayer and ministry to people in stressful situations is so important as it releases them from anxiety, fear, stress and trauma, even delivering them from bad dreams and sleepless nights.

On my flight to Juba today I was still fighting fear. My stomach was recoiling at the thought of entering this city, but as I disembarked from the airplane and walked into the airport, I felt all of my fear dissipate. It felt as if a heavy burden had been lifted off of my back and for the first time in a month I am walking in total freedom from the bondage of fear. Many years ago my spiritual mother told me how she would something afraid until the fear left and now I told myself the same thing, that I would come to Juba and do this afraid if necessary. I slept peacefully this night and I trust God and His plan and purpose in this.

Sunday morning has come and we are waiting for a taxi to take us to the Army Barracks at the edge of town. As we approached the fortress of their headquarters, I felt very small, its imposing stature dark against the morning sky, the face of it looking as if it would open its mandibles and swallow me up. The entire time we were walking, I surreptitiously glanced back a few times, as if it were following me, watching my every move. We met with the Army Chaplain in the marketplace as arranged, he and some of his leaders agreeing to meet us. We greeted each other, as we smiled and shook hands. I then spoke in the Dinka language, "I greet you in the name of Jesus." If there was any ice it was broken wide open with this. The Dinka absolutely love to hear white people speaking their language and consider it an honor that we would take the time to learn it.

As I looked around, I noticed many people watching us with hooded eyes as we walked by, unsure as to why whites were here. Again, foreigners are not really allowed or even wanted here, this being Army territory. I found out after church that they also do not trust the Americans these days. We were only allowed to come because my Sudanese daughter accompanied me and she has family here. It also helped that I was retired military. The Chaplain was very interested to hear my military story as we shared a meal after church.

An elderly man who was part of the escort group informed me that he knew we were from God because we walked for two miles through the mud and tall grass to get to the church, which was deep inside SPLA territory. There are no roads, only small footpaths and our feet were covered in mud up above our ankles as we sometimes sank ankle deep in the muck. The old man chuckled as he commented that no whites will do this unless they are coming with God. I had to chuckle myself because all day they made a big deal about the "whites" coming to see them. I was exhilarated because I was in my element once again!

After church some of the congregants escorted us to Awek's auntie's house for a feast. We were graciously seated on short, sturdy, bamboo chairs and took hot, sugary milk together. The weather was quite comfortable because of the recent rains. Juba is normally a miserably humid and hot place. We then took some "boon" together, which is a local coffee spiced with ginger, very black and strong, clearing my sinus passages into the next continent. All of this milk and coffee business consumed two hours with no one sitting with us.

Awek told me that this was normal protocol for the Dinka although I found it somewhat odd and even a bit uncomfortable. There are always children around, anywhere in Africa, so there really was no lack of companionship for Awek and I as her cousins entertained us with smiles and giggles, running up to touch my arm and darting off again. African children who aren't around many white people usually do this to see if we are real and perhaps maybe our skin feels different.

The women prepared the feast while the men seemed to be absorbed with an elder's meeting inside the hut. Finally, in the late afternoon, everyone retired inside the chaplain's humble abode to eat, enjoying all of the delicacies of the Dinka cultural food, my favorite being kisra, a paper-thin bread like dough, tasting a bit sour as it is left to ferment, using this to dip into the meat sauces. I was in heaven. After the meal, we again took boon together, the men gathering around and each in turn spoke their piece to me, one by one, taking whatever time was necessary for everyone to fully speak what was on their minds, no one in a hurry. This is typical fellowship in South Sudan, especially with the Dinka.

Many of the men shared with me about their distrust toward Americans and that after getting to know me, they now see that we are not all against them. My heart was so grieved that they felt hurt, whether it was a valid hurting or not, and when my turn came to speak I lowered myself to my knees, quiet tears choking my throat as I asked for their forgiveness for my people causing them any hurt. They were moved by this, seeing my sincerity and accepted my apology.

We then prayed together as we stood as one, singing hymns together and praising God for His faithfulness to keep us safe in this place of turmoil. On this day I enjoyed the most meaningful fellowship that I have ever experienced in South Sudan. I told the men that this is the fellowship that the Lord is attracted to, every nation and every tribe being together in unity as one, forgiveness offered and accepted without reservation. I really believe that we have bridged a very large gap between our cultures, at least the church culture. The chaplain told me that Awek was also a bridge between our two cultures.

As our day came to an end, the chaplain escorted us back to the market where he first greeted us, walking along the still soggy path, moving from house to house and greeting our neighbors as we shared the gospel of Jesus Christ and His love for all people, also praying for the sick along the way. As we walked, the chaplain suddenly stopped me and handed me his gumboots to wear. He took them straight off of his feet and handed them to me, going barefoot himself. I was so astounded because grown Sudanese men do not walk barefoot in public, ever, especially men of stature such as this man. I have never ever seen this in my time in South Sudan. This was true humility and honor and friendship. When God is in everything we do, His light shines through in the most amazing ways. I will never forget this man or this moment.

As we flew back to Yei my mind was filled with wonder. How on earth was it possible to have such sweet fellowship with the people of this tribe, in the midst of a civil war, knowing that this tribe was part of the cause of it? I had to see for myself that we were all the same, innocent victims in a war that most of us didn't want. In America we have a saying, "The squeaky wheel gets the grease". There are three other wheels, yet only the one gets the grease, the attention, because it is loud. It's the same with this war. Only a few wanted it whereas the majority did not. Unfortunately, the loudest and most forceful men took it upon themselves to be the voice of the people, exerting power that wasn't theirs to take. I needed to remember this in the months to come. Little did I know just how caught up in it I would become.

Chapter Twenty-Seven

These days most of the children in South Sudan are not attending school due to school closures as most of the teachers have quit and disappeared across the border to Uganda in the refugee camps. Our primary school is the only school in Yei that is still operating a full schedule. We have even accepted children from other schools, at no cost to them, so that they can continue school. Our secondary school children are also not in school so we have instituted our own school here on our compound. The missionaries have volunteered to teach the children as best as we can, at least preventing their minds from stagnating with all this sitting around and doing nothing constructive, keeping them sharp and focused. We cannot let this war consume us. Daily, we think of new ways to keep our children focused on God and school, continuing as much as we can with the normal things of life.

It is now Saturday night and as I lie in bed I hear gunfire erupting as we always do not far from our compound. This night it carried on for two hours, until midnight. The action drew extremely close to us and I prayed that the children were on the floor and staying low and at one point I heard a woman wailing as if someone had died. I just knew that someone had been killed, it was that kind of wailing. Our compound was dark, no lights on as we are still in blackout for our safety. As I stood there looking out of my widow at midnight, the moon illuminating the fields, I wondered what loss this wailing woman had suffered in the night. My heart grieved for her. The next day we heard three different accounts as to what had happened last night in town. We can only guess which one is true.

Our Commissioner explained over the public address system that one of the soldiers went rogue and decided to discharge his weapon at the army barracks resulting in the other soldiers chasing after him while also discharging their weapons. The local news reported that the two armies were in a firefight with each other throughout the night. Lastly, one of our staff told us that her neighbor had become angry because the storm had blown his roof off thereby causing his family to become drenched and out of frustration he proceeded to fire his weapon into the air. For all I know, each one of these situations could have taken place simultaneously as many shots were fired over a long period. The longer this conflict continues, the more frustrated people become.

The truth is that we have tribes that hate each other and want to kill each other off completely. Belonging to either one of these tribes puts one's life in danger, regardless of age, gender or status. Meanwhile, Americans have been accused of taking sides just because we speak out against injustice. This puts the Americans in danger, which by the way includes most white people, whether one is really an American or not. Today I learned that one of the tribes in this fight told an independent tribe in our area, not having any involvement in this conflict and remaining neutral, that if they don't pick a side then after they are finished destroying the other tribe and capturing the capitol they will come after this independent tribe. The independent tribe, being innocent in this conflict, is now being threatened for not getting involved by not choosing a side. If this wasn't so real life I would just laugh right now. It is all so ludicrous, beyond making sense, to even try to debate it or make sense out of it.

I have desperately been working to find a way to send two of my children, Awek and her brother, out of our city immediately because their very lives are now in danger. This cannot happen fast enough for me or for them. They have been fighting the fear of even walking home after school so I have pulled both of them out of school, not allowing them to leave the compound for any reason even though the girl is nineteen years old. We try to hide them as much as possible, without confining them to their houses, because the armies are always very close to us and they can tell which tribes the children belong to just by looking at them. Each tribe has very distinct facial features which are unmistakable.

One morning we watched as eighty soldiers walked by our fence line, staring seriously into our compound, which instilled fear in our smaller children, the older ones counting the soldiers as they marched by while we were still in our houses peering out through the cracks in our shutters, looking on silently. This crisis was now in our backyard, literally. I began to make connections in Uganda in case we received permission to leave. We really needed to get out somehow.

I have talked with our friends at the children's center in Juba about Awek and her brother and they believe it would be best, for now at least, to get them to Juba, where it would be much harder to indiscriminately attack people because of tribal affiliation. We obtained plane tickets and had the children wear caps and jackets, trying as best as we could to disguise them. I took them myself to the airstrip. It was crowded with people, at least two hundred. There were people of every tribe and tongue of South Sudan and other nations trying to get out of the country. There was one flight to Juba. Only our two children were on it. I learned why as I walked them to the plane. It was full of cases of cigarettes! From stem to stern, port to starboard, floor to ceiling, full of cigarettes!

I stood there on the dirt runway, people crowding around me trying to gain access to the plane, staring in through the copilot's door, wondering where these two would sit? I could not believe what I was seeing, there were no seats, just cartons upon cartons of cigarettes. I saw one seat nestled behind the pilot. My children would need to squeeze themselves onto this one seat. At this point, I didn't care. The reality of the situation was that the children's lives took precedence over safety. I had to trust God on this one. I prayed for them and watched as the plane lifted off into the great expanse, wondering if I would see them again, and where. My heart felt the first of many pains for my children.

Our children continue to work on our farm planting crops. Most people have quit planting because they know that they won't be here to see the harvest, so what's the point? We refuse to engage in this defeatist mindset. We carry on as best we can. Every day more and more things in the market are no longer available. We can no longer purchase eggs, an important part of our weekly sustenance. We can no longer purchase lentils, another weekly meal. We can no longer buy potatoes, one of our staples. Every day I am told that this and that are no longer available. I have been buying and stockpiling as much as I can while it is still available. If the situation doesn't change soon we will be eating maize flour porridge and nothing else. We are only able to buy greens if village women feel safe enough to harvest them, and if they feel safe enough to walk to the market to sell. Our sweet potatoes are in the ground but they won't be ready to harvest for another two months. We might not have the most well-balanced diet but we will eat something. We share what we can with our closest neighbors, the women in my ministry group.

We continue to trust God even though I have been experiencing a bit frustration, feeling like a hostage in this country as no one can go anywhere. Every road is closed, there is no way out or in by road, which is how most people travel. The entire country is frustrated and fearful, praying for the intervention of heaven. This weekend, three government officials from Yei were ambushed on the road and two of them are now dead.

Food and supplies no longer to come into the country. Obtaining hygiene items such as girl's pads, soap for bathing or to wash dishes and clothes and toilet paper are becoming a real concern. The lack of these items alone can create a breeding ground for bacteria and sickness, bringing dysentery or cholera. We are very close to becoming prisoners of war, although not held at gunpoint or imprisoned, just imprisoned in our homes because we are restricted from any movement.

I awoke this morning to hear the news that the inconceivable has happened. Last night, in our town a nun was shot and killed by soldiers, rebel or otherwise, we don't know. She was from France and has lived here a very long time and everyone knew her. Last night she was driving an ambulance early in the evening just a bit after dark. She had ventured out on a humanitarian mission, her second run of the evening, carrying sick people to the hospital, when she was stopped by unknown soldiers and shot at point blank range, then left for dead, the ambulance gone. I cannot believe this. I am just in shock. The boundary lines have been erased. There are no longer lines of demarcation.

I pray for all people who are still here. We are being told by our friends who live closer to the river in our town that dead bodies have been floating in the river, decapitated men, women, even small children. We were also told by others that huts are being set on fire with families still inside, soldiers waiting outside, ready to shoot them if they manage to escape the flames. When I say soldiers, I don't have any idea which side they are from. We just hear, soldiers. Jesus come, please come! I am crying and crying out to God to please come! My heart aches with the pain of this.

Chapter Twenty-Eight

We have left the month of August behind and have learned that our town market is out of beans. This is when my heart kind of misses a beat, just one, but it's a miss. This is our main staple. We eat beans every day, for lunch and most nights for dinner. There is never a day without beans. Some of our children refuse all food and will only eat beans for every meal. Without beans we become part of the malnourished statistic. I pray that greens will continue to be available. As long as we have something to eat, we will be okay a bit longer. I have a reserve of beans stockpiled, but they will be finished in less than two weeks. No beans in the market puts our town in crisis mode. Mama Heidi called me last night and told me that if there is anything I need I should just ask her. I replied, "Just send beans!" Of course, that cannot happen because anything coming in will be hijacked and stolen.

It is difficult to navigate the days and hours of our lives, never knowing what the days and weeks to come will bring, wondering if my children will even have anything to eat. The village women still come every week to our fellowship, the only ministry I can do these days. This week I spoke about Jesus and how He is our hope, the One we depend upon, and we have a future only in Him. We cannot put our hope in the soldiers or in our president or in the market or in beans. All of this hope; governments, man's wisdom, has begun to unravel and will one day fade away. There is only one hope, the One who told us that if we hope in Him we will not be disappointed (Isaiah 49:23).

I would be lying if I said that I arise from sleep every single morning full of joy and peace. I wake up many mornings, dread fighting to overtake me, fear threatening to knock down the door, even before my feet hit the floor. I have to press on and pursue this hope, pursuing Jesus. It is a good fight of faith and if we don't quit, we always win. Do not be deceived. Our enemy, Satan, is very real. He only seeks to kill, steal and destroy. Our fight is very real.

This week our Primary School students completed their second term exams and all of the students were called together for one last assembly with our incredible teachers who remained for these little ones. The headmaster (principal) told the students that if it were not for the people of Iris Ministries remaining here and keeping the school open in faith, that even the teachers would have run away. The Headmaster also told the students that our faith is what causes many people to remain on their land, to have faith and to keep moving forward. Iris Ministries remains because we cannot leave but also so that we may encouraged our neighbors who have chosen to remain, to keep their hope in God.

Last week our team went to the prison in town twice to encourage the men incarcerated there. The guards told us that if the prisoner's families run away, the prisoners don't receive much food because even the prison can't buy food that isn't there. Neither can they release the prisoners or crime will run rampant. Because of this, there are men and women in the prison who have scarcely eaten. Our team brought some of our precious bags of rice and maize flour to the prison, even though we are struggling ourselves.

Jesus said, "for I was hungry and you gave Me food; I was thirsty and you gave Me drink; I was a stranger and you took Me in; I was naked and you clothed Me; I was in prison and you came to Me." (Matthew 25:35-36)

Jesus did not add a disclaimer to this that said, "unless it is during the time of war, then care for yourselves only" or "unless you find yourself a bit low on provisions, then you must hoard them for yourselves".

If we see these things and do not help we are not walking in His grace and mercy. Jesus will reward grace and mercy and He will help us in our time of need. If we do these things that He commanded us to do, then we are telling Him, "God, I trust You and I trust Your provision for all of us who call upon Your name." David declared in Psalm 37:25, "I have been young and am now old; Yet I have not seen the righteous forsaken, nor his descendants begging bread."

The Hebrew word for righteous has a two-fold meaning. One of the Hebrew words is, *mitzvah*, which means a good deed or a commandment (loving and serving God). The other word, *tzedakah*, means to bring charity, justice, and fairness to our neighbor. When David says that the righteous are never forsaken, he is saying that those who love God and also love their neighbor, by actions and deeds, they will not be forsaken. There is never a better time to help our neighbor, through acts of righteousness, than this time that we are in. We need each other.

We are escalating our plans to evacuate. The roads have been completely shut down for almost two months and we are now eating our reserve food. We have been discussing our options in order to decide our next move. If we must run, who will go with who, as in which children will go with which adults? If we can only take so many out, which children go first? Can you imagine having to plan how to group kids in case we can't all leave together? This is something that parents should never need to plan. It is unimaginable. It feels as if an iron anvil has taken up residence in my stomach. I am heavy with anguish to have to even think of this type of planning.

We contacted a Ugandan Charter airplane company who can get everyone out in one day but the cost is hefty. We have been electronically scanning all of our paper files in case we lose these important documents in transit. This includes 130 report cards for all of our children, for up to ten years for some who have been with us this long. The children have some idea of our plans but we have decided not to concern them with too many details in order to keep them from worrying. I have managed to keep our older children somewhat abreast of the evacuation plans. The boys are becoming fearful of being taken as child soldiers and some of our boys are actually old enough to be in the regular Army.

The situation here continues to grow more dangerous to our wellbeing. One of my spiritual sons is in the rebel army. He came to see us today. He put his life in danger to come and plead with me that we needed to go. He said that everyone in his team in the rebel army knows who we are and that they are all trying to be careful for as long as they can, not causing any gunfights to ensue around our compound. The only reason they don't start shooting is because they know we are here and that we care for children and many in our village. He asked his higher ups if he could come and tell us to leave so that we wouldn't be caught in the crossfire. This young man used to work at the dam in our village, where people had their cars and motorcycles washed. Every time I drove past I would stop and say hello. I prayed for him and his friends quite often. Sometimes we hired them to level the road after the heavy rains came. I have given some of the guys Bibles, and have given them food and drink many times. They love us and we love them, and they sincerely wanted us to get out unharmed. I took him seriously.

We have been talking to government officials about evacuation to no avail. Everyone is asking the impossible of us. Because we cannot obtain permission from these officials to take our children to school in Uganda, we are stranded here, in these dangerous times and this dangerous place, where there is no immediate educational future for them, if we manage to stay alive. My pastor and his family of nine tried to leave the country yesterday by a back road. He was almost distraught because he sees the bodies floating in the river near his house where the community comes to wash clothes. He fears for the lives of his family. He left today with my blessing and help. I gave him enough money to pay off the road criminals.

Later today he was back, his head hanging in discouragement. They didn't even make it out of our town before they were turned back, all their money taken from them. He was heartbroken. I have decided to pay their airfare of $1,500 to get them to Uganda. They will leave in two days. The only way out of South Sudan anymore is by plane.

We had also come up with a plan to get most of our children out of the country. We discussed the option of chartering planes for all to go to Uganda. We didn't have the funds to do this but we believed that if this was of God then He would make the way. We took all of the paperwork that we had concerning the children's history with us and proceeded to the immigration office to apply for visas to Uganda. Within hours the immigration office had given us travel papers for all of the children! I was in shock and jubilant at the same time. It was decided that I must remain on the compound while the other missionaries took the children to the airstrip. I would remain behind in case something went wrong and they needed rescuing. One of the missionaries stayed with me. The children were so excited. I then called the charter air company and asked them if they could come to take our children to Uganda.

As I stated earlier, I did not have the funds to do this. The Chief Operations Officer from Iris Global in Redding, California had asked me a week ago if there was anything they could do to help us. I replied by email and almost jokingly told him, "Yes, I need about $30,000 for charter airplanes." Well, he took me serious and today I received an email from him stating that we did in fact receive the entire amount, $30,000! Oh my gosh! Are you serious? On top of this we also received an additional $24,000 to pay the school fees in Uganda from another organization in the U.S. This was the most amazing miracle since I did not know either of these donors. I had no idea who they were. I can't even explain how I feel, I am so overwhelmed with emotion, and I am crying tears of relief. Someone in the world cared enough about our plight to send all this money. Only God can move on hearts like this. This was a gift from the heart.

Here we are two days later and the children are running around to gather what small items they will be allowed to carry on the plane. I hugged them all goodbye and prayed for them, tears rolling down my face. They would be going to the other side with Brian and Dorinda and two of our mamas. After I prayed, the children climbed into our tipper truck and waved as they drove off, the dust cloud behind them obscuring them from my sight as tears rolled down my cheeks. It was a scary moment because we had no idea if this would work, taking over one hundred children out of the country, but we were desperate.

Two hours have gone by and I am starting to worry. No one is answering their phones. "Where are they?" After three hours I have become agitated and feel as if my stomach is dropping out of my body along with my heart. I sent one of my staff on a motorcycle to go and check on them because they had taken both of our vehicles. I wanted to go myself but my small staff who remained with me wouldn't let me go. "You need to stay here because if something happens to you who will rescue them?" At this point I began rocking back and forth, praying in the spirit, travailing in prayer for these children and my staff. Suddenly my phone rang. It was the charter air company telling me that they had to cancel the flights and turn the planes around. They were told by the airstrip personnel that if they took these children out of the country they would be shot out of the sky. Our plan had fallen apart like a crushed egg. She also advised me that it had cost $9,000 to stage the planes at the border and this money could not be refunded. "Jesus! What do we do now? Where are they???"

It had now grown dark and had begun to rain. I was beside myself with worry, pacing back and forth, imaging all sorts of terrible scenarios, when suddenly the tipper truck rolled into the compound with all of the children in the back, drenched and crying. I ran to them crying tears of relief and couldn't get them out of the truck fast enough in order to hold them close. We were all crying as our tears mingled with the pouring rain, standing there in our now dark compound, feeling as if we were never going to see the light of day again. After I had pulled myself together, I asked Brian, "What happened?" Brian then told me their bizarre and frightful story.

They had passed the checkpoint with no problem, only cursory glances at their immigration papers. Upon arriving at the dirt airstrip, the children alit from the vehicles and stood off to the side of the registration building. Brian went inside to organize their paperwork and told them that charter planes were coming for them. Within minutes three army techno's sped into the airstrip, sliding to a halt at the front door. The soldiers jumped down and approached Brian, pointing fingers in his face, accusing him of stealing children out of the country. They would not listen to him as he tried to show them his paperwork signed by government officials.

They then walked over to the children and yelled at them to get back in the tipper truck. All the while they were waving their weapons around instilling fear in everyone. The soldiers told them that they had three minutes to get the children loaded and get back to our compound now! Everyone was afraid and thought that they would be arrested or even shot. In fact, they did threaten at this time to arrest the director of this group, me. Our staff member who tried to check on them using his motorcycle was stopped by soldiers and accused of working for the rebels. They told him that he must be a rebel because he was driving a motorcycle. They told him to go home and to never be seen on the road again.

This was the hardest day so far and our hearts were deflated as we pondered what to do next. We were wrung out, no strength in our minds to think and we knew that we needed to be fully accountable from now on, not missing a T crossed or an I dotted. We prayed together and then fed the children, although no one was very hungry. We praise God for the rain because this would at least keep the soldiers quiet tonight. My team and I met in my house to pray and to ask God what our next step should be. We all heard the same thing, that we needed to do everything with honor and due diligence. The Lord spoke to me that Iris Ministries is not finished in South Sudan. Even if the children are released to Uganda, the ministry will continue. Lying in my bed tonight I tried not to think about the day's events. I just thanked God for protecting us and the children. Tomorrow would be another day.

Chapter Twenty-Nine

After eating breakfast this morning, I tried to keep the children encouraged and as we were walking out of our front gate to go to our garden, I was taken aback and astounded as we watched at least five heavily armed military vehicles come down our bush dirt road, straight at us. We stood there motionless, stunned as they stopped practically at our feet. You can only imagine what was going through my mind at this point. I thought that surely they were here to arrest us for yesterday's fiasco. My heart was pounding on the inside although I remained steady and calm on the outside. The leader of the group stepped down from one of the heavily armed vehicles and walked up to me, striding as if this was an everyday occurrence for him, to pull his battalion of vehicles up to the front gate of a children's home.

He looked me in the eye, somewhat surprised that I wasn't running in fear, and quietly asked me where the road to a certain village was. I held up my right arm and pointed the other way, never taking my eyes off of him. I told him that he would need to turn his vehicles around in order to get on the correct road to the village in question. He then turned around without saying another word, climbed back up into his vehicle and proceeded to make a road with their vehicles right along our fence line, mowing down our crops and whatever else was in their way! After moving around to the backside of our compound, the soldiers set up camp right there at our primary school. I was in a state of shock I think, even a bit pissed off, to put it bluntly. What the heck were they doing here, within throwing distance of over a hundred children?

I wondered what they were doing here as I watched them set up their equipment. Were they really going to have a battle right here? The younger children on the other hand were excited to see the soldiers and their equipment. This was exciting to them, to see big army trucks and guns. I sternly directed them to stay inside the compound until I knew what was going on. I then walked up to the top end of our compound where the missionaries lived for a better view to see what they were doing. After some time, the morning sun now high in the sky, a young soldier strode across the field of knee-high elephant grass, coming directly to me as I stood at the fence watching, my hands on my hips, a look of continued disbelief on my face. He politely greeted me and told me to tell the children that they would hear a loud boom but to not be disturbed as they were only test firing one mortar. I confirmed with him that it would only be one. He replied in the affirmative. I really hoped that it was true and that they would then leave, but from the looks of things, setting up camp, I knew that they were staying.

As he strode back to the school compound I ran down to our living compound to calmly tell the children what was going to happen. "They are only test firing one mortar which will make a very loud noise so don't be afraid", I told them. Now all of the children were excited because they had never seen a mortar launched and I found it very difficult to contain the older boys so I allowed them to watch because we were inside our fence and not in their range of fire. After some minutes they launched a mortar. Then they launched another. Then to my horror another and another and another until they had launched twenty-six mortars in ten minutes from their location! At this point I was more angry than afraid. Did they not realize that there would be retaliation from whomever they were bombing? Did they not realize that we were now in danger?

I waited for about fifteen minutes before walking up to the school with two of my older boys to inquire as to their motive for firing mortars from a children's home compound. I walked with purpose up to their encampment and politely asked to see their commander. They were fairly startled I think to see this white woman walking right up to them, bold and unafraid, after just witnessing the launching of all those mortars. The commander came over and looked at me with interest, and invited me to have a seat. I told him that I was in the American military for many years and I knew what launching these mortars would mean for us. "I am not a clueless missionary", I told him. He then began to ask me questions about my military career. I decided to practice patience and answered his questions. He offered a slight apology and told me that he was only following orders and that as a military person I should understand this. Actually, I did. I was quiet for a moment and I responded to him.

I told this commander that even though I understood his position, we both knew the inevitable was going to happen. There would be retaliation from the rebels, and soon. It was at this point of our conversation that I felt the Holy Spirit move me to pray for these men. I asked the commander, "May I pray for you and your men before I go back to the compound?" Surprisingly, he replied, "We would appreciate your prayer." I prayed that not one of his men would be hurt or killed. I also prayed over them the scripture in Matthew chapter five, when Jesus told the people that the peacemakers are blessed and they will be known as sons of God. I prayed that these men would be transformed and bring peace to this hurting nation.

After I had prayed for the men, I told them what I felt was God's heart to do for them. "Your men must have food and water if you are to remain. Is someone bringing these things?" His response was a negative so I told him that I will have my boys quickly bring you these things. After living in this country for so long I pretty much figured out that they did not travel with food and wood for fires or even dishes for cooking. He was surprised I think because moments ago I was pretty upset and now I wanted to help them. I had just heard from the Lord. I was not too happy about this request from the Lord, but I am ever obedient and I put away my anger, choosing to love these men instead. The commander told me that his men had not had anything to eat since yesterday.

My boys and I went back to the compound and I told the other children to go inside and close the doors and windows because things were going to get crazy in a short while. After making sure all the children were inside and settled, the boys and I brought some small bags of rice and maize flour and beans and a few other items, including dishes and cookware and two jericans of water and cups. I told him that I understood that he was just following orders and it wasn't exactly his fault. But I did tell him that I was still upset that they were there. I asked him if they were going to leave any time soon and he replied that they would stay until they were told to move on.

As the boys and I walked back to the compound we found that all was quiet within. Within the hour all hell broke loose. For the next hour there was a barrage of gunfire coming from both sides of us and all around us. We were terrified and locked inside, lying on the floor, hands over our heads, wondering if this was to be the end of us. Many of the girls were screaming and crying. We prayed and we prayed and we prayed. We could hear men yelling and boots running through the bush. Some of the gunfire was so close I imagined our buildings being hit by the bullets and prayed that the children remained on the floor, not looking out windows. Finally, everything grew quiet, even our screams and crying. I then heard men talking and knew that at least this fight was over. After it had been quiet for about fifteen minutes, I tentatively walked outside. I proceeded to go to every house to see if everyone was okay. The girls were all okay. Praise Jesus, praise Jesus!.

I then ran up the path to the boy's houses, which were extremely close to the soldiers who were camped nearby, and as I rounded the corner, I saw the older boys sitting on benches outside, against the wall. I looked at them as if they had lost their minds, even speechless for a moment. I practically yelled at them, "Have you been out here the entire time?" They sheepishly nodded their heads yes, their eyes not able to meet mine, instead staring at the dirt beneath their feet. "Have you lost your minds? Do you think that these bullets will dodge you? You could have been killed", I almost yelled at them. In a gentler and concerned voice I told them, "Never, never do this again. Do you understand?" They looked at me, nodding their heads in the affirmative and I continued to explain to them that I would not be able to handle it if any one of them died. My heart cannot handle the loss of one single child. I loved them too much to just let this go. They told me later that they wanted to know what was happening so they came out to stand guard so that if they needed to protect us they would. Boys becoming men before their time. Their hearts are so beautiful.

I also went up to check on the soldiers when I knew it was safe to do so. The commander told me that his men were okay and there was no loss of life as far as he knew. I told him that the Lord had protected them this time. The next time is never guaranteed. Only the Almighty God can guarantee anything. The Commander asked if his men could come and take more water from our borehole. I gave them permission because I'm sure they would have taken it no matter what I said. For the next week our boys filled their water cans and carried them to the gate so that the soldiers would not come onto our compound, putting us in more danger than we already were. Meanwhile we began to ask around town where we could stay. We had to get out now.

Tonight, right before dark, as we were with all of the children in our library for evening prayers like we always do the soldiers had come onto our compound to get water. I think that they didn't want to wait for us to bring it to the gate for them, deciding to come get it themselves. As they were filling their water cans, a rebel soldier was spotted up on a ridge just opposite our compound. The soldiers at the borehole quickly squatted down to take aim. I had to yell at the children to, "Get down now!" We were in the direct line of fire! I started to pray seriously.

After a few minutes of silence, the soldiers then stood up. I assume that the soldier on the ridge ran off. We must leave this place, we must! After some phone calls, later in the day we found a place in town to evacuate to. We are packing it up tomorrow morning at first light. We received permission from another orphanage on the other side of town to come and stay with them temporarily where it was a bit safer. We were told that we could come but that we couldn't stay for long and needed to make other long-term plans. We were so very grateful to them. I don't know what we would have done without them. We were running out of food and the war had come to our door. We had nowhere to run except to the arms of the Father. We were literally in His hands now.

The night passed quietly praise God. I was so worried that there would be more fighting and couldn't sleep at all. My adrenaline was in overdrive. We arose at sunrise and I called the children together in our library before breakfast. I explained where we were going and how we were going to organize ourselves. I paired each older child with a younger one and told the pairs that they were to go nowhere without each other. They must remain joined at the hip until we arrived safely on the other side of town. "I really need you to help me with the smaller children okay?", I told the older children. I explained, "I need you to be men and women now, putting away childhood and stepping into a greater responsibility than ever before, even for the lives of those I am giving you to watch over. Will you do this for me, for them?" This was the day that our family changed forever. We had a bond that nothing could break. We had a great love for each other and we were committed to do whatever it took to watch over each other. Even as I write this book almost three years later, this bond is still strong in all of us. We truly see ourselves as a family, no longer a children's center, a family that loves each other and watches over each other.

We hurriedly fed the children tea and bread and we told them to hurry and bathe. We also told them to take their school backpacks and to put just a change of clothes inside and anything else that they wanted that could fit in their backpacks or that they could carry. I felt that we would possibly come back for the rest of our things when the soldiers left. I told the older boys that we would be the last ones to leave the compound because we needed to take all of the solar equipment down and get it ready for transport to the other orphanage. I knew that anything we left behind would be looted and the solar equipment would be the first to go.

As the boys were climbing onto rooves to rescue our solar panels, I was directing the children onto the big tipper truck, little ones first with Dorinda and Brian. I told the other children to stay close by just in case chaos broke out again. As the first truckload departed, I left one of the missionaries in charge and I went to help the boys with the solar equipment. Four hours later, after three trips in the tipper truck to transport all of the children, six missionaries and two mamas, I was finally able to take a breath. The fourth and last trip out carried my older boys and all of the solar equipment and as many mattresses and blankets as we could take. We learned that we would be sleeping on the concrete floor indefinitely.

In the stillness of the afternoon, no gunfire, no children's voices, no pots rattling in the kitchen, no dinner bell ringing, I went around our compound to ensure that every door was locked up tight and windows were closed. I took one last look around, sadness in my soul, and walked to my motorcycle where Wildra, my friend from Poland, was waiting. We were the last ones out. I had never heard our compound this quiet. It felt so final. The entire compound was deserted. My heart ached with the hurt of it and I had to fight back my tears, needing to remain strong for these children and my team. I kept telling myself that we would be back soon. As we drove out on the dirt road, the village was like a ghost town. We could see the soldiers in the bush watching us silently as we drove out, their weapons held at the ready, their stance relaxed, sentries in the tall elephant grass, the grass yielding to a gentle breeze flowing across the silent fields. It looked as if they were respectfully saluting us as we left, knowing who we were and how we had helped them as much as we could, their eyes following us until we were out of sight.

Kindness always opens doors. I had not been physically off of the compound for weeks because of the threat by the officials to have me arrested for constantly disturbing them with my requests for our children to be allowed to leave this war-stricken town. My team felt it best that I stay out of sight for my safety. Now, as we rode out, seeing the empty huts and empty yards, some with laundry still on the line, doors closed up tight, some left ajar, I just felt numb. Even the animals had deserted the village, leaving behind empty pens and empty fields. Our village, which had been full of life, goats and sheep and chickens and dogs running about, children yelling and laughing at play, mothers calling their children, fathers laughing and talking as they bent their backs to the work of the day, it was all silenced now in the wake of the mass exodus. It was as if everyone had gone for a funeral, leaving everything behind but themselves. For three miles we didn't see another living being. The war had come to our door and had chased everyone from theirs. It was a day that would forever be etched in our memories.

Upon arriving at the children's center across town, we settled the children in as best we could. There were very few beds available for our children which meant most of them slept on the hard cement floor with only a thin sheet beneath them. We were just so grateful to be safe for a little while and to have other people to go through this with. The children of this center that we have somewhat displaced were not happy with ours being "in their space". They had plenty of room but it was as if we had invaded their home, taking up residence, uninvited. We had welcomed thirty-six girls two days before Christmas, two years earlier, and I guess I thought we would be welcomed in the same way.

Our children felt horrible because the other children were accusing us of eating their food. I asked the leadership of this center to please tell their children that we contributed more than our fair share. We were not beggars. I had hoped that we would be guests. Our children were so brave and so humble, never complaining and serving anywhere they were needed. We were refugees in our own country among our own people. I am still so very grateful that we had someone to take us in and I know that our children were too and that is why they never complained. We were just happy to be alive.

Chapter Thirty

The missionaries and I went back to our compound every day for three consecutive days to check on things, still praying with the soldiers, although no longer feeding them. Every day more and more of our belongings were looted, foxholes were being dug, and the army was settling in. By the fourth day all of our dishes were gone, everything in all ten children's houses and everything in our offices and missionary houses. The only house left untouched was mine. Meanwhile, we have been to every government office in the city only to be told, "So sorry, there's nothing we can do, go to the next office."

By Friday I was so upset after being told yet again by the governor's office, "No", that I cried in their office out of frustration as I shared my heart for these children, telling them that I haven't eaten for seven days (I was fasting) and that I refused to eat until I got some justice for these children, that this is how important it is to me. I had to make them understand that we were never going to leave these children and we were never going to stop fighting for their freedom, for their lives.

After my meltdown I made a final visit to our ever-emptying compound, solemnly sitting in my still intact house, staring out at a compound with no children, a compound that used to be our home, and had to turn it all over to God. I handed Him the children. I handed Him the compound. I handed Him the ministry. I fully submitted everything, leaning into Him. I was at the point of no return and I was willing to fight to the death if need be. We are in an amazing place spiritually, fully dependent on God, fully at His mercy because there is no just judge in the land who will fight for us.

After weeks of doors closing on our requests we have now been referred to Juba, the seat of the nation's government, to continue our petition to evacuate the children to Uganda. Our goal is to secure their freedom of life, liberty and happiness in Uganda and away from the craziness of this war. I have been plowing through the South Sudan law, hopefully having found a few things that might work in our favor. The team has agreed that I am the one to proceed to Juba, armed with as much knowledge as I could muster and the full backing of God.

But, today as I sat in my house I knew that this truly would be the last time that I would sit here in this chair in my living room. I leaned my head back, closed my eyes, let out my breath and my heart looked to God. I heard Him whisper the words, faintly, "Step by step." I repeated them quietly, my lips moving, my mouth breathing out the words with ever exhaled breath and I was reminded of the day that I had lunch with the blind lady just some weeks ago. While I visited with her, we were called inside for lunch. Her granddaughter then led her into the house and I wondered why she would need help to go inside her own house because she had lived there for some years.

And now, sitting here in my house thinking of this blind lady, I heard the Lord in my spirit, "Don't assume that you know anything from now on. You will need to hold onto Me and let Me lead you like the blind woman and trust me completely. You can make no decisions on your own nor assume that you know what to do. Follow me completely." The Lord also clearly revealed to me that this entire season ahead of us would be like Moses' journey out of Egypt, where he had to follow God step by step, not knowing from day to day where they would go and how it would look. They had to keep their eyes on the cloud and the fire and move with it. We are moving with the Holy Spirit and this next week might have my team moving in three different directions at once, Juba, Yei, and Uganda.

The next day, my team made one more trip to the compound without me. Everything was gone! Every house had been looted and papers were drifting all over the compound, school notebooks, books, letters, pictures, clothing. In the children's houses, the beds had been torn apart, mosquito nets dangling from empty bed frames, caught on the splintered wood rails, metal boxes thrown open, hinges bent, and what few clothes remained hanging over the edges like withered leaves on a rainy day. Every day when I think that things could not get any worse, it gets worse. This battle is real, especially the battle in our spirits. We are gaining victories in all of this but the battle is incredibly intense.

I am still fasting because I need to stay focused. Any tiny distraction can derail so much. Seriously, it is that intense. I have given up all food, taking in just six ounces of juice once a day to maintain my strength for the battle ahead. Wildra will be going with me to Juba and has also been fasting with me. I have seen the benefits of fasting before in my life, in that my spiritual senses are ever alert and precise, enabling me to be aware of the minuscule details that will make a difference in the long run. If one is fasting in order acquire things from God it is the wrong reason for fasting. Fasting to hear God better is what true fasting accomplishes. When we eat and we are satisfied we tend to become too comfortable in our waiting, not putting forth much effort in prayer. The most intense battles are won through prayer. Prayer paves the way in the spirit for the natural to be accomplished. It is essential that I hear God clearly and precisely concerning these matters that I am fighting for. Our very lives depend on it.

Today we spent the entire morning at the Secretary General's office just to obtain a small stamp of receipt on a letter from Iris Ministries South Sudan to this office which states that they acknowledge our decision to release all of our children who are no longer children according to South Sudan law. Those who are eighteen years old will be released from our care officially on paper. In real life they continue to be under our care of course. This is the only way to legally move these particular children out of the country and across the border into Uganda. The letter that the Secretary General gave to us in return, which acknowledges our letter, was so confusing and vague that even I was not sure if they were in fact considered legally released. We were worried that the soldiers at the checkpoints and the immigration officers at the airstrip would also think the same. We needed God's hand to be in this every step of the way.

Before we left for the Secretary General's office we had gathered the children and staff to worship and pray over what we were about to embark on. They understood that they had a part in this and that they were an important key to their own release. They needed to pray just as sincerely as we do for them. We had just begun to worship when I was told that the Secretary General would see us now. I instructed them to keep praying if they wanted to and when they were finished to leave te church the way they found it. Hours later, at least four hours later, we had finished our business at the Secretary General's office and drove back to the compound of the children's center we were temporarily staying in.

As I drove through the gate I noticed that none of our children came to greet us as they usually do and were not even visible around the compound. I wondered where they were and upon further investigation I was amazed by what I encountered! I heard the children's voices singing and headed in that direction, back to the church where we had left them hours earlier. Tears came to my eyes as I gazed in wonder at the children because every one of them were still praying and worshipping! These beautiful children are so close to the

Lord and love and trust Him so much causing me to be so grateful for them and for the gift that God has given me to be their mama. They are so full of faith and trust, just as Jesus said we would need. My heart is full even though we are walking in this desert place. Having each other is what carries us through each and every day.

We then shared with the children the great news that the older ones would be allowed to leave and attend school in Uganda! They were so thrilled, some even crying tears of joy, others whooping and hollering, and still others were quiet and a bit sad knowing that they might not see their brothers and sisters again for a long time. It was bitter sweet rejoicing and we knew that God had opened a big door for us. We just needed to keep walking with Him. I told the older ones who were to leave that they would leave tomorrow and to pack what little they had and be ready first thing in the morning.

After a restless night, everyone woke up early in order to say our goodbyes and receive prayer. With the official letter in hand and fifteen "no longer children" but young adults loaded in the Land Cruiser, they left for the airport amidst tears and joy mingling together as we waved them out of sight. Originally, we were planning to charter a plane which would have been close to $7,000. The first attempt to get the children out was a disaster because we were stopped, the children forced to turn back, the planes cancelled and all the money was non-refundable. It was a huge blow to us. We lost $9,000 that day. My team pleaded with me not to go to the airstrip because they still feared that I would be arrested as the governor was still not happy with me. Brian would be the one to take them to the airstrip, along with Haley, who would travel to Uganda with them.

This time the charter air company told us that they would not charge us for the positioning fee, instead they would take our children out first and then fly back in to pick up the remaining regularly scheduled passengers! This is huge, especially that they would take us out first, delaying the schedules of everyone else. They were just as much a part of our journey as we were. The lady that I kept in contact with told me that she was always praying for us.

About twenty minutes after the Land Cruiser left the compound for the airstrip I received a phone call from Haley. They were stopped at a checkpoint on the way to the airstrip. The soldiers had denied the children permission to travel and were told to turn back. The things that went through the minds of those children, young people really, one could only imagine. Here they are on a now deserted dirt road, a band of soldiers standing in front of the vehicle, armed and ready, as a belligerent armed soldier forces our children to move over so that he can climb in with his weapon, ordering them to go back to National Security. Our children and missionaries were under arrest.

Earlier this week I had befriended a man from this office because we have our military background in common. He was also the military commander in charge of the military action which took place at our school so I felt like I could talk to him. When we arrived at National Security, this man came to our rescue. The plane had just landed and they were still a twenty-minute drive away and they still needed to come back to the compound to pick up the second group of children. We didn't know if the plane would wait that long. They usually land, offload, onload and go, being about a thirty-minute process. We were asking them to wait forty minutes.

During this fiasco I was at the compound pacing when I decided to seriously pray because my heart was in a bad place toward these men and this war. I laid on the concrete floor, my face pressed to the ground and I refused to arise until my heart was right. I felt a seed of bitterness and anger taking root. I began to lose my love for these people who were stopping us in the face of all this adversity these past two weeks. My heart became like David's, angry with my enemies, tired, overwhelmed and so close to being done with humility! I lay there until my heart loved again. I was also praying to keep my focus on those who were at the airstrip, praying for their paperwork and their safety.

Meanwhile our vehicle raced back to the compound after dropping the first group of children at the airstrip. Brian had to beg the pilot to please wait so that he could drive back to bring the remaining children. He raced into the compound and told the remaining children to throw their stuff inside and get in the car now! They raced back to the airstrip on the same deserted dirt road which was littered with so potholes and speed bumps I'm surprised we didn't crack an axle, throwing dust into the air, this time unimpeded by the soldiers at the checkpoints. Brian skidded to a stop and parked the vehicle on the edge of the airstrip where every other vehicle was parked.

A large cargo plane had also landed at the airstrip, larger than any we had ever seen in Yei. As it was preparing for takeoff the pilot spun up the engine and the high pitch of the engines blew out some of our rear windows, shattering glass all over some of our boys. No one was harmed and crazy enough, our vehicle was the only one that was affected, yet we were parked by many.

The airstrip had become intense over the last few weeks because everyone was in a hurry to leave this country. There were at least one hundred people standing around all day, even spending the night with no shelter, waiting for a plane to take them out yet they had no reservations. An older boy who was under the care of our partners in Juba walked fifteen kilometers every day for a week to try to get a plane out. After a week he finally had a seat on a plane. Whenever a plane landed, everyone, and I mean everyone, crowded the plane, pushing and shoving, handing babies over the crowd, begging you to please take their baby at least. It is heartbreaking to see and have no power to help them. These were South Sudanese people begging to get out of their own country.

Haley took the children to the check-in desk and the soldier assigned to the airstrip denied the children permission to leave. They accused the children of plotting to come back to do harm to the soldiers. They accused the white people of thinking that they could do anything they wanted. It was a horrible scene and the children were frightened, their hope fluttering precariously in the wind. Again, I called the National Security office and that Major who had helped us was still there. He talked to the soldier and told him to release us immediately. The soldier hung up the phone, handed it back to Brian and turned to the children. He told them that if they come back to South Sudan, do not come back to do harm. How insane is all this? This is what we were up against at every turn.

After I talked to Haley I was back on the floor praying in earnest and after some time I got up from the floor to go outside to see what was taking them so long. Three hours had already passed. Why wasn't our vehicle back yet? Did the children make it out? Where are they? As these thoughts raced through my mind, the Land Cruiser pulled into the compound and the first thing I saw was the shattered windows. Not knowing why, my heart almost stopped in fear. What had happened? Where are the children? Did they get shot? Brian jumped out of the driver's side door upon seeing my face, my hand to my heart, immediately waving his hands in a gesture of "It's okay" and he gave the thumbs up and mouthed, "They are out, they are safe".

My legs felt like jelly. My heart exploded with relief and gratitude. I fell to my knees in sheer relief. I sobbed huge, wracking sobs, my heart bursting inside of my chest. All I could do was sob, "Thank You God, thank You God" over and over, hearing in my spirit, "Today you have truly given birth to these children." I didn't fully realize until that very moment just how much I loved these children. I loved them with all that was in me. I would love them forever. Having a mother's heart does not necessarily mean that one has physically birthed a child. Having a mother's heart is when you would do anything to make them safe, anything, even giving up your very life if need be. Sixteen of mine were finally safe. Now I had to remain focused to get all of the others to safety.

This was a win for us. I felt a new sense of purpose. We were so encouraged. The other children were somewhat somber, missing their older brothers and sisters and wishing they too were in Uganda so we gathered together to keep the remaining children encouraged to not give up their faith. We promised them that we would not give up until every last one of them were out. We were committed to this and to them. We prayed together, trusting God and completely gave ourselves into His hands this night. Everyone felt a bit better and went to their floor space to sleep. As I looked in on them, my heart was full. I knew somehow that God would do this for us and I knew that I couldn't quit. I silently made a promise to them, "I will not quit on you" as I looked upon them lying on the floor, some of them with nothing but a blanket to cushion them against the hard concrete, and I thought about how brave they were, how very brave. God, help us all to get out of here.

Chapter Thirty-One

I have been in Juba for two days. Wildra traveled with me, leaving Brian, Dorinda and Sandy with the children in Yei. In Yei, we had revisited the Secretary General's office and the Governor, asking for permission to take the rest of the children to Uganda since we had no place to live anymore and no way of acquiring enough food to feed all of our children. We asked the director of the orphanage where we were staying to write a letter that would explain our situation, that we were only welcome to stay with them for a limited time and that we must find an alternative soon. They stated in the letter that there was not enough food to feed all of our children and theirs. Of course, he denied us permission and recommended we go to Juba to plead our case. This morning I am exhausted as I write letters to the Country Internal Affairs Office, the Country Foreign Affairs Office, UNICEF, the Commission For Refugees and Relief, and so many other ministers who are headquartered in Juba.

I received an official letter from the Governor in Yei granting us permission to seek help in Juba from these offices. The fight for our children will continue to be fought here in the capital city. Our team has been dispatched to three different places in two countries two countries. Haley and my pastor were in Uganda to settle those children who flew to Uganda into their boarding schools. Myself and Wildra are here in Juba, and Brian, Dorinda and Sandy are in Yei with the children. We are still full of hope but some days, most days, are really tough and it takes fighting the good fight of faith in the face of extreme opposition to keep going. The government officials want to help us but they are also trying to protect their jobs, understandably so.

Every day we communicate to officials at every level of government that we need their help and advice. In the midst this I also needed to travel to Uganda once again to withdraw money from our account at the bank. It is such an inconvenience and a wasted expense. Little did I know that this trip would be different, life changing for us and nothing wasted or pointless. God knows every step of the journey before we do. On the flight to Uganda I was sitting next to a man who knew someone who worked in a government office that we needed to see. This was a divine connection and when everything was said and done, this man became a crucial connection. Without him, I don't know if any of this would have happened. A few day later, when I returned to South Sudan, I immediately contacted the man that he told me to connect with. He was expecting me, the man on the plane having called him.

The man in this office had such empathy for us, seeing all that we had gone through so far. He actually had a true desire to help us so that these children could have a normal life once again, in their own home, not having to sleep on the floor, feeling like refugees in their own country among their own people. He started our paperwork right away and guided me through the process, telling me which letters to write to which offices. He didn't have all the power but he did have the connections. At the orphanage that I was now staying at in Juba, my friend, who is the director, also had many connections. She made an appointment for me to talk to the United Nations (UN) the next day.

As we walked onto the UN compound, through mountains of security, I was so hopeful that finally we would have the UN on our side after they heard our story. We were led into a large conference room and we waited. Three people came in to meet with us, one American and two foreigners from other nations. I told them our story and asked if they could help us. The lady told me that they couldn't help our children to leave the country. They were only authorized to work within the confines of the country. They had no authority and were under the direction of the President of South Sudan in most matters. The only thing that they offered us was to put the children in an Internally Displaced People's (IDP) camp.

I was stunned and asked her if she knew what happened in IDP camps. I could not believe the disconnected response of these people! I could not believe that they were this dispassionate about innocent children having been run off their own compound by soldiers and mortars. Maybe they had become immune to the cries of the innocent? I passionately replied to her, "This is not some mission to us. This is not some project that I am working on. This is our family and I will not leave them, ever. These children would go to an IDP camp over my dead body."

I don't think she had ever met anyone like me, one who would do anything for foreign children that weren't even hers. She looked at me as if I was crazy. There was also a UNICEF representative in the room. I asked her if they could help us with mattresses or blankets because our children were sleeping on concrete floors. We had literally lost everything and nothing was available in the markets because the roads had been closed for two months. She told me that they were out of funds and didn't have anything in the warehouse for us. I stood up, keeping my anger in check, and thanked them, telling them that I would continue in my search to find someone who would help us. Needless to say, when I left there I was deflated. I even wondered what they were there for then? Are they only helping children in Juba and forget the rest of the country? It was a known fact that Yei was the most dangerous place to be right now. I resolved to put this behind me, harboring no bitterness, and continue moving forward.

This morning, after yesterday's let down at the UN I visited the Office of the Mayor of Juba. He was very empathetic to our cause and truly wanted to help us, even offering us a compound in his city at no charge for rent. He explained that a lady from Egypt had had an orphanage there but abandoned the work earlier this year and left country, abandoning the compound and the children living there. We immediately went to see it, thinking that this might at least bring our children out of a dangerous area, but upon inspecting it we found that it was in a terrible state. It would take a large sum of money, which we didn't have, and a lot of time and work, which we also didn't have, to make it livable again. The compound was also located in a dangerous part of town, across from hotels and bars, or discos as they call them here. I didn't want our children exposed to this sort of nightlife. I gracefully declined it for the reasons stated and thanked him for being so helpful.

We were once again back to square one. I then spent the next two months sitting at the offices of the Minister of Gender, the Minister of Education, the Minister of this and the Minister of that every single day except the weekends when no one was available. There were many days where we sat all day in one place waiting for an official to see us and just as many times leaving at the end of the day without having talked to a single official. I never had an appointment at any of these offices. My modus operandi was to show up every day and wait until someone received me. If we knew that someone would be around on Saturday, we went on Saturday. At lunch time and at the end of every day, we hopped on a motorcycle taxi which took us back to our temporary home. In Africa, motorcycle taxis are the fastest and cheapest way to move around the crowded cities.

Almost every person in the offices that we visited was sympathetic to our situation and were willing to help us solve our problem. Some were astounded that we were still in the country and fighting so hard for the children.

Sometimes I was so emotional when I spoke about our plight that I couldn't help but cry out of frustration that things weren't moving fast enough or that there were more requirements to fulfill every time that we thought we had fulfilled them originally. There was a desperation in my soul because I knew firsthand what was happening in Yei. It hadn't improved, instead, only grew worse.

The staff in the offices we visited only knew the news as they heard it through filtered venues. When I told them the truth of what I had seen and knew, many of them were surprised. Many people who truly emphasized with us had the best intentions, but told me that we would be okay, the war will end soon, just be patient, your children are safe where they are, and on and on. The news reports were so false. The people weren't being told the truth because the government couldn't risk a revolt from the people. Most of the news reports painted the government as doing everything they could, painted the rebels as evil men, painted the war as almost over and soon everything would be okay because this was the only news that was being allowed on the public media airwaves. I was desperate for people to see the truth of our situation at least.

Each day starts early, about 5:30 am. After twelve days of fasting food completely, we finally relented and tailored our fast to eat one small meal at the end of the day for the next two months. I really need to stay in this place of clarity and precision, of hearing God, of going with Him step by step. In the early mornings I read my Bible and sit before the Lord to see if He has anything specific to tell me for this day. Wildra and I then compare notes and pray together and wait to hear from the Lord again.

Every morning, we arrived at a government office at least fifteen minutes prior to their doors opening, paperwork in hand, so that when the doors opened we do not delay in making ourselves known. Almost every Minister's office presented the same decor, two full-sized couches in front of an immense desk, the couches running lengthwise on either side of the front of the desk with an assortment of coffee tables in between. Many a time I entered an office and was asked to be seated on the couch. Often the Minister addressed me from behind the large desk, towering over me which intimidated me just a bit. I don't know if this was purposeful in order to intimidate people or to give the impression that the owner of the office had the upper hand. Some of the Ministers were very humble and came out from around their oceanic desks to sit with me and meet with me at eye to eye.

When we arrive at any of these offices, we actually spend more time waiting than anything else we do. Many times, while we waited, we pray for people in these offices and minister the gospel to them. We are finding that people actually look forward to the times when we will return to their offices, even the top leadership. We have found that they especially like to be prayed for. Although what we are doing is so time consuming and frustrating, we never leave an office without offering to pray for people. Our first mission is Jesus.

I carry sheaves of paper and every kind of list of information concerning the children, background information concerning how the children came to be with us, biological information, and school report cards. The file is thick and we carry numerous copies to provide whenever they are requested. The office that finally launched us in the right direction and finally has us moving forward, and which gave me hope was the Minister of Gender and Social Welfare. We have spent most of our time talking with her assistant, the man we were connected to on the airplane trip to Uganda to withdraw funds. There were so many divine connections and appointments that I could not remember anymore how I came to know some of the people in this process. My mind is usually overwhelmed with trying to gather and consolidate all of the information that was required of us. Every time I deliver what was requested, I am told to go back and bring something else. I have never been to an office yet that told me what I needed in full detail, what I actually needed upfront. Many times all that was needed was a stamp or letter from another office.

The office that has caused me the highest degree of stress is the National Security Minister's office. People call this monstrous building with no windows "the blue house" because it is multistoried and blue. This is also where the foreigners are detained whenever they are arrested for a national security incident, no passport and any number of things that foreigners may be involved in, and rightly so I think. It is very high security and once inside there is no leaving unless someone allows you to go. Cars are not allowed to stop anywhere near the entrance gate so, if one needs to see someone inside this building and arrives in a taxi, like we us every time, we must be let out a bit down the road. This office was ultimately instrumental in allowing us to take the children out of the country legally. If this office says no, then you might as well forget trying anyone else. They have emphatically told us that there is no way we will take over one hundred children across the border. I keep trying. I refuse to quit.

There is a story in Luke 18:1-5, about a persistent widow. She continued to knock on the godless judge's door late into the night, crying out, "Get justice for me from my adversary." The judge finally relented and said, "because this widow troubles me I will avenge her, lest by her continual coming she weary me." If this judge, who was unjust, answered and helped the woman, then how could God, our just judge, deny our cry for help? I have become this persistent widow, refusing to be denied until I find justice for these children.

The soldiers have now migrated to the side of town in Yei where our children are currently living. We have run from the fire into another fire. The soldiers shoot their weapons in the night so close to the children's home that the children actually believe that the soldiers are on the compound walking around in their heavy boots, clicking the magazines on their weapons as they walk by the houses. Dorinda told me that one night they hid in the bathroom and prayed because they heard boots on the porch and a weapon being readied for fire. Dorinda cried for hours that night, silently, because she was so afraid of our children being taken.

It is so difficult for my team and the children in Yei because they can't see what we are up against with the different offices here in Juba and why it is taking so long and the hurdles we are trying to jump through. They are just as desperate for our children to get out of this mess as we are. I feel so overwhelmed sometimes with all of the decisions needing to be made daily while at the same time assuring my teammates that I am moving as fast as I possible can, doing everything I can without delay. There have already been numerous times that I thought we were about to get our approval, just to be told that we needed more signatures, someone else's permission or another stamp or more paperwork. There have also been many times that I have said to myself, "I can't go on, it is too much for one person, I can't do this God." It seems that whenever I feel like I am at the end of my rope, God opens another door and we move ever closer to the goal. The streets of Juba are quiet these days but the tension in the city is thick and palpable. At night, the streets empty out considerably as we fall asleep ever alert for the next volley of gunfire to ring out.

Chapter Thirty-Two

Today, as we were sitting in a certain Minister's office waiting for another letter to be typed and printed, the power went out. This is quite common in every city where there is power. Yei rarely has power these days because of the shortage of diesel. Five minutes after the power outage, the minister came out of his office looking a bit worried, his suit coat draped over his arm and brief case in hand, he told us to come with him quickly because there is trouble on the street. I asked him, "What kind of trouble?" He just said, "I need to get you to your compound because it isn't safe for you on the street. You should not take a boda. I will take you but we must hurry." There is a rumor that the President of South Sudan is dead. This news has released considerable tension in the people throughout the morning. As we were in the car the President was addressing the nation over the radio, declaring that he is very much alive and would be driving through the city streets to wave at the people this afternoon so they could see for themselves. The minister who took us home told us to stay off the streets for our own safety.

Although I wasn't really afraid, I praise God that this man felt obligated to take us home safely instead of just leaving us there to fend for ourselves. It turned out that nothing radical happened on the streets today. Days like this are days wasted for us, a day further from our goal, another day of fighting the good fight of faith when every day is crucial.

We are once again sitting in the Minister's office to continue where we left off yesterday to obtain a letter, signed and stamped. Each day we drove past the President's palace on our motorcycle taxis (bodas) and we prayed for the President and this nation each time we passed by, from two to four times a day. Lately I have even begun telling myself that if I have to go all the way to the President to get these children to safety then I would. And one day, a day like today, because of a day delayed, I found myself at the President's palace!

The President isn't the man that I came to meet with today., at least not on this trip, but it was someone else who worked at the palace. I found myself at the palace because we were led to the wrong office it seems, and as I stand here inside of the visitor's entrance to the palace I think about all the offices that I have had to go through to make it even this far. Only God could open these doors for me. I am not acquainted with people of high stature in this country except for the governor of Aweil, who is now the President's Chief of Staff. If I do find myself going that high up the chain, he is the one I would see. While I was involved with the street children in Aweil, his was the first office that we visited. He then invited us to have dinner at his house on two separate occasions because we were the only ones doing something with the street children at that time. After standing at the entrance for some minutes our driver came and escorted us back to the car and took us to the correct office. I felt as if my accidental arrival at this place just might be prophetic and I declared even more that I would be back if we couldn't get the help we needed.

I also have an appointment with the U. S. Embassy Ambassador. As I arrived at the U. S. Embassy, the first face I saw was a United States Marine. I was so encouraged by this, as it reminded me of home. Something about it just made me feel better. After I was escorted inside, I was led to another conference room and offered a cup of coffee. A few minutes later a lady came in and introduced herself as the Ambassador's assistant. Apparently, the Ambassador was not feeling well so once again I relayed my story to yet another person in the hierarchy of democracy after which she proceeded to tell me why she could not help us. I felt like hitting the record and replay button, same story, different person, same country, different city. I'd heard it all before, how no one from my own country could help us except to evacuate me out of this country, leaving all my children behind to fend for themselves. I know very little about foreign policy but what I did know was that they weren't much help to me. Again, I thanked yet another person for humoring us (not really said that way) and went back to my little room at the children's center feeling defeated.

I then had a "John the Baptist" moment, the moment when John, in Matthew 11:2, sent the disciples who had come to see him in prison to Jesus with this question, "Are you the one or should we look for another?" He was in prison. This was not how it was supposed to end. He spent his life preparing the way for Jesus and was probably expecting to see the kingdom of heaven come with all its glory. But prison? This wasn't what he expected. Where was Jesus? I too felt like this. I have given my life for everything that I believe in. I said yes when no one else would to these children and to God. Where are You God?

This cannot be how it ends for us. What was the point of it all then?

I sincerely felt discouraged all day. When I returned to the compound at the end of the day I just stood there in the yard as tears of discouragement rolled down my face and I looked up to the sky, my arms outstretched in questioning, crying out to God, "Are You ever going to do this? I have kids still in a war zone. When is this going to end?" Later in the evening while I was in my room face down on my bed, I once again I handed everything over to God, trusting Him, believing that He would come and that He was not hurt by my moment of doubt and discouragement. I told Him that I knew He was for us and I know He will save us and I know He will come in His perfect time.

October has now faded into the wind as we step into the month of November and I am running out of options and offices. I don't know what else to do or where else to go. "God, I need Your wisdom, I need Your providence, I need Your connections." Today, Saturday, is another really hard day for all of us. We truly thought that we had every permission and authorization needed to leave this country and continue on with our lives in a safe place. We made all the plans and coordinated everything only to be halted in our tracks at the very last minute. "Go back" was the command. There is nothing we can do. No explanation, no sorry, no thank you very much, just go back. We are just devastated, especially the children.

I wailed and sobbed and cried, crying out to God that, "I just don't understand this. I can't understand this at all." I felt like David did when he would cry out to God. When will you deliver us God? When will You come and save the day? My couch is soaked with my tears! Are You coming? I am trying very hard not to be discouraged. I stood outside today, Sunday, and looked up at the sky once again and cried out to God, "When will you come?" I spent the rest of the evening encouraging myself in the Lord, truly knowing that He would come. I was just frustrated and He understands me. God is so kind. He knows how we feel and He knows the end of a thing right from the beginning. He knows how this will end. I must continue to trust Him.

This morning I pulled myself together and was ready to face the giant once again. This has been the hardest journey of our lives for all of us. It is so taxing on our minds and even our bodies. There is still gunfire, almost nightly, and the children are still not in school. They are allowed to sit in classrooms with the "regular" students at the children's center where they are staying temporarily but are not allowed to touch the books or even participate in classroom activities. They are only allowed to sit and watch, asking no questions, and never allowed to put pencil to paper. I don't understand this mindset that would so persecute a child who has no fault in any of this but to be born in this country. To be told not to touch a book because they might spoil it is insanity at its best. I wanted to scream. How can people, teachers, be this cruel? What is the world coming to? Oh my gosh, we must get out of here. We keep telling our children that one day they will get their double portion for all their trouble and to be faithful and to be kind and to remain humble. One day they will see their reward.

The people who have taken the time to know our children have seen how beautifully gentle and humble and obedient they are. I receive so many compliments from visitors who say these things. Some of the children are here with me in Juba and I was told by the director here that our children are starting to influence theirs in a positive way. Our children have been so amazing through all of this. They don't complain even though I see the sheer boredom on their faces from sitting here all day long and not being allowed to participate in school. I see the sadness in their eyes that they don't even have a place to call home. Wednesday night I played worship music and I watched our children and instead of joy, I saw homesickness in their eyes. It was too much, all of the memories of a better time in our prayer hut with our family. How do I continue to encourage them to hang in there? How do I tell them that one day it'll really be okay. This is what frustrates me the most, not being able to do anything quick enough.

Many times, the Lord speaks to me in dreams. When I don't see the answer to my questions, I sometimes receive the answer in dreams, although I have never particularly asked God to give me an answer in a dream. I usually have a dream and write down what I thought it meant and then I forget about it. I learned how to interpret my dreams by reading many books on this subject so I felt fairly confident in my ability to interpret. I had become so frustrated because I wasn't seeing much movement towards our goal of rescuing our children. I was desperate and I asked God to give me a dream. I needed a dream, an answer. That night I dreamt! I awoke and immediately knew that God had answered my prayer. My dream was a confirmation of all that we have been working toward and where we were headed.

I dreamt that I was in a car with Wildra following a moving truck, the type that moves household goods and furniture cross country. In my dream, we were in Juba, South Sudan and as the truck approached a roundabout we followed it as he drove around the turn and took the road that we had just come from. The back door of the moving truck was open and there was furniture in the back of it. Three of my small boys were jumping and playing on the furniture, full of joy. I just knew that we were going to make it out. This dream spoke to me and I just knew that things were going to "turn around" and that I would go back for the children and we would move to a safe place. This was what I needed to hear and see and I was so encouraged.

Chapter Thirty-Three

We have been sitting in government offices for two months every single day, all day long, sometimes groveling, sometimes crying, sometimes just zipping my lip after being told yet again to go back to an office that I've already been to five times. God has been teaching me so much about grace and humility and how, when I look at the big picture, we really don't have it so bad, as do many other countries right now. Listening to the world news unfold, I have seen where entire cities have been bombed and devastated by wars and earthquakes and hurricanes. Praise God that we are all still together, although a few miles apart. Praise God that we have food and we have shelter. Praise God that He protects us and watches over us through the night. Praise God that we have a God that we can trust.

We are continuously vigilant and ever diligent as we press on, never giving up the fight for justice for these amazing children of God. We will keep running this race until we can't run anymore and even then, the Lord will continue to strengthen us as He always has. He doesn't quit on us so how can we quit on Him or the children. Next week I will sit again in government offices, smiling and saying the right things and doing the next thing they ask of me, keeping my eyes and heart fixed on Jesus and this mission that I am called to. This morning I found an especially significant scripture which is so fitting for us right now.

"From one man He made every nation of men, that they should inhabit the whole earth; and He determined the times set for them and the exact places where they should live. God did this so that men would seek Him and perhaps reach out for Him and find Him though He is not far from each one of us. For in Him we live and move and have our being." (Acts 17:26-28)

God determines the exact place where we will live. If He determines that the place is Uganda, then He will set us there and there is nothing that man can do to stop it. I have to believe that I hear Him, that I am doing my part, and most of all, that He is doing His part, working everything out for us because we love Him. Wildra left today to go back to Poland. I will miss her so much because she is a dear friend and she kept me steady and focused through the roughest parts of this journey. She always knows just what to say to me and at the time that I need to hear it. Sandy has come to join me here for this last leg of the race. We too shall run it together.

I have just returned from yet another meeting and was told that we can take the children to Uganda if we can obtain the permission from at least one relative for each child. Are they kidding? Do they know that this is impossible? Most of the people of Yei emptied out of town and poured over the border two months ago, including the relatives of the children and are now in the refugee camps. There are close to two million refugees in the camps, many still in the intake centers who have not even been documented. How on earth are we going to do this? How do we find anybody in this mess? I called Brian in Yei and I also called our pastor in Uganda. This was our very last chance. If we can't do this, it is not happening. I prayed to God as I have done every step of the way. I told Him that there is no way on earth that we can make this happen. It is humanly impossible. We seriously need His help to find all of these relatives. My pastor in Uganda started calling. I kept praying.

One week later Brian called to tell me that we have the phone numbers and permission from every relative except for ten children! This is beyond an incredible miracle, it's God's amazingly, incredible providence. How my pastor did this, I cannot fathom. I know without a doubt that God's hand was on this. This was not humanly possible, especially not in just one week! But Jesus looked at them and said, "With men it is impossible, but not with God; for with God all things are possible." (Mark 10:27)

Brian faxed the information for the children to me and I took all of our forms back to the Minister's office. She told us to leave them with her and that she would call us tomorrow. I gave her the packet and told her that I would be back tomorrow. I never waited for a call back when told that someone would call me. I always went to the office and waited for my answer. I went back to our home and prayed and prayed and fasted. I spent the evening in my Bible and praying. And now the next morning our approval letter is waiting for us! But, we were told that we still needed National Security's permission. They would have the final say.

We immediately drove to the National Security building, the Blue House, and asked to see the Security Minister yet again. We had been to this building many times before but had never been invited up to any office and had only been able to communicate our concerns through his assistant. We waited for the assistant in the lobby area. After fifteen minutes he came down to meet with me and quietly looked at our papers. He looked up at me and said, "I cannot give you permission to take one hundred children out of the country." I asked him, "Why didn't you tell me this two weeks ago? Why have you let me have hope only to do this, to deny us?" I said these things as tears rolled down my face. "Do you even care that children are homeless because of this war."

There was nothing more to say because he had closed his ears to us, having no emotion at all concerning the fate of these children. I felt the seed of bitterness rising up again in me like bile. I left that place not just as a deflated balloon but a squashed, stepped on and drug through the mud balloon. I still believe that we were denied because of job security issues. People are afraid of making a decision that could bring repercussions. I couldn't blame them but that didn't stop me from being completely frustrated and angry. We have hit the end of the road. There is no place to go from here. I can't bear the thought of going back to Yei and telling the children that we are stuck and they can't go to school or have beds to sleep in. I just can't bear the thought of staying in such a dangerous place and not knowing if we would be able to even obtain food anymore. I didn't know what else to do. The last stop was the president of South Sudan. I would go there. I asked my Sudanese friend who had been helping us how I could make an appointment with the President.

She then told me that her uncle is one of the highest men in the land next to the President. If we could get an appointment with him then we would have a chance, again, our last chance. I asked her if she would call him for me. She called him and asked if we could come and see him. He invited us to come the next day. At this point I didn't bother to get excited anymore. I am becoming so used to the word NO, that I don't even expect a yes to really be a yes anymore. My heart can't take another let down, so my mindset at this news was as if it were just another appointment in a long line of appointments. I went to bed that night numb. My mind had had enough and my body needed rest. I didn't pray, I didn't eat, I just slept. If God was going to do this, He was going to do it His way and I would accept His way.

This morning I woke up tired but I prayed again for God's favor as I had every other time. I was not going to give up on the children nor God, ever. My Sudanese friend, Akat, came with us to her uncle's office. It was in the Blue House! Oh no, here we go. We entered the same building as we did every other time. We were actually going to see the Minister whom the assistant kept us from! When we arrived in his office, he kindly invited us to come in and have a seat. His office was small and crowded. It contained his desk and a few chairs pulled close enough to his desk to shake his hand, which is what I did before I sat down. Akat greeted her uncle with a hug and pleasantries before we were all seated. His manner was gentle and his voice encouraging. He smiled and asked me, "What can I do for you?" I told him our story.

"Sir, thank you so much for inviting us here today. We have been here in Juba for just over two months and have been to many offices to seek permission to take our children to a safe place. When the conflict entered our town of Yei we decided to remain. We thought that it would be a repeat of the 2013 conflict when everything calmed down and the roads opened up and the traders bringing food to our town again."

I continued, "That didn't happen this time. The army came very close to our compound and a battle ensued, causing us to involuntarily abandon our home and everything in it in order to get to a safe place. It was extremely dangerous where we were living and, the armies on all sides of us so we had no choice but to flee. The leader of the soldiers even asked us why we were still there."

"The children are now staying at another orphanage on the other side of our town. The director of this orphanage told us that we needed to find an alternative place to stay rather than living with them. They can not house us or feed us indefinitely. Currently our children are sleeping on the floor, not able to attend school, and the conflict continues in our town, gunfire every night, causing our children to be afraid. They are traumatized.", I explained to him.

As I tried to keep my emotions calm, I told him, "We are just requesting permission to take the children to Uganda, where it is safe, where they can be free to go school again and where they can sleep peacefully at night without fear. We have donors who have already sent the funds to sponsor all of their school fees and we have a man, the governor of Luwero, who has invited us to come and to stay as long as we need to."

I continued, "The governor of Yei sent us to Juba with a letter and we have been to all of the Ministers and all of them have approved our papers. We were then told to return to National Security as our final step, and upon reaching here your assistant regretfully denied us without a reason, telling us that he cannot allow these children to leave South Sudan. We are here to seek permission from you to take the children to Uganda and to safety."

The room was silent, the clock ticking, ticking, ticking. He quietly looked at me, as if considering what to say next. My hands were trembling and my stomach was in knots. I knew that whatever his answer was, it would be final.

There really would be no other option. Oh God, I silently prayed. Then he said to me, "Who am I to stand in the way of the future of these children, the future of our nation, to stand in the way of their education and safety?"

"You have my permission to take the children to Uganda. I see that you care for these children and I cannot deny them their future. I ask of you to raise them well so they may return here to become the leaders one day who will bring change," he said.

I cried tears of gratitude. Through my shaky tears I asked, "Really? Is this really true? Will there be another obstacle to stop us?"

He replied with a smile, "No one can stop you. My name is known everywhere. This is my phone number. If anyone tries to stop you, call me immediately. I have the authority to allow you to leave and there is no one who can cancel this. Trust me."

My tears were still coming as I shook his hand. I felt a relief that cannot be described but the closest I can come is to say that it felt as if the anvil in my stomach had been replaced with cotton. My heart felt the lightness of peace indescribable. I then asked him when he wanted us to return to pick up the authorization letter. He told me, "No, no. You remain seated. My secretary will type it right now as you wait. There is no reason to delay. When do you want to leave?" I told him we would like to leave tomorrow if we could and that we would leave by charter plane which was already paid for. He was happy about this as he informed me that the roads were too dangerous. "Leaving by plane," he said, "will also save me from having to send a military escort with you." He really would have done this for us. This man truly had concern for the innocent victims of this war.

I just couldn't believe it. One letter, one friend in the right place at the right time, one man in the right place and everything turned around in an instant when yesterday everything looked impossible. I left his office letter in hand and so much thanksgiving. I cannot say who this man is or even what office he is from so as to protect him and us. I am just so grateful to him and I am so grateful to God for making all of this happen for us. I am practically running home to tell the good news and to call our charter plane service to set things up. I am praying for a green light from them for tomorrow.

When I got home I immediately called the charter service and I asked Rhonda if the planes could come tomorrow, Friday. She said that she didn't have any planes available but that they could fly in on Saturday. She was very skeptical about us having the authorization to leave because we had cancelled twice already at the last minute. I told her that this man was the highest authority in the land, that no one was above him. I faxed her the letter and she believed me. Rhonda called me back and told me that the three planes would also not be available now until Sunday. I was very nervous because we were so desperate to get out before anyone changed their mind, as had happened in the past.

Rhonda asked me to wait until Monday when more people would be around. She said that we would be alone and exposed at the airstrip, fully exposed to anyone wanting to stop us or hurt us, even attacking the plane which would put her flight crew in danger. Monday would be better as it was a regular flight day for them and no one would take notice of the plane landing and leaving, nor would they think too much about all of us being, over one hundred of us, as there were hundreds waiting every day. Knowing all of this I still insisted that we must leave on Sunday, we simply must. I felt such a desperation because of all the delays and I knew from experience that just one day could make a difference. We had to leave!

We agreed on Sunday as flight day but, instead of three planes they would only send one. One plane, flying in and out three times over the course of five hours minimum. My heart dropped a bit but I knew we had to do this no matter how it happened. My biggest fear was that someone would stop us and revoke our letter or we would be surrounded once again at the airstrip. I could not wait around for that to happen, I just couldn't. Everything was set, Sunday, November 13, 2016, we would go. After confirming all details Rhonda called me back and made me promise that I would stay in Juba until the last plane landed in Uganda safely. She insisted I not go to Yei, telling me three times. I promised her that I would stay in Juba in case we were stopped yet again and that I would fix it if this happened again. I told her that I had the phone number of this man who had given us the letter. Rhonda still made me swear that I would not go to Yei. I promised that I would not.

Chapter Thirty-Four

Today is the most important day of our lives. It is early Sunday morning, November 13, 2016, and the children arose and bathed quickly. No one had slept much last night, everyone still a bit uneasy about the plan working. We were excited, nervous, and afraid of being stopped again remembering the outcome the last time we attempted this. We were surrounded by soldiers and were turned back. It was very disheartening. We didn't want to go through that again. No one could eat. All were quiet and subdued, knowing the importance of this day. We packed what little we had, some having nothing, and loaded the children into three tipper trucks to take them to the airstrip in one trip.

Our friends at the children's home helped us with the transportation and we are so very thankful for them. They were our refuge for almost three months and I can't imagine where we would have gone or how we would have eaten without their help. Although we had money there was no food left in the market so the director had to literally transport beans and maize flour in by airplane which was quite expensive. As we drove off, giant teak trees lining the dirt road, an early morning dew still clinging to the day, no one looked back. It was time to look ahead.

At the first roadblock the vehicles were stopped. Our hearts stopped. The soldier looked at the name and signature on our papers, he looked at the children, and he allowed us to pass, never saying a word. Every road block after this waved us through and no one stopped us. This man's name carried that much weight. There were no questions asked, no threats, just quiet obedience, the soldiers allowing us to pass. Our final journey, our exodus really did look like the parting of the Red Sea, but Pharaoh's army was no longer chasing us, although our hearts were still anxious.

The trucks finally arrived at the airstrip at 0830. The plane was to land in Yei at 0900. At 0930 the plane still had not arrived. I called my friend at the charter company and she told me that the plane was on the way, first having to stop in Arua, which was just on the other side of the border from us. Then 1000 came and went. I was becoming frantic, pacing back and forth, sitting down, standing up, bowing my head and dragging my hands through my hair, holding my head. My insides are a terrible mess. I am still stuck in Juba and not able to be with the children as all of this is happening, feeling powerless, unable to help. Finally, at 1030 the plane landed in Yei. Our children have been standing in the morning sun, afraid and anxiously looking at the bush perimeter of the dirt airstrip, the only people out there. I told Brian to text me with constant updates. I had to know what was happening, minute by minute. His texts began,

"First plane loaded."

And then, "First plane is in the air."

My heart leapt at the news yet my mind is still with the remaining children. From the other side, in Uganda, the YWAM Arua team is waiting for our children. Also, Haley is on the plane with the first group of children. The flight time to Arua from Yei is twenty minutes and those twenty minutes felt like an hour. I couldn't eat, I couldn't drink, I couldn't sit still, instead pacing back and forth in my tiny room with my phone glued to my hand.

Finally, Brian texted, "First plane landed in Arua! Second plane heading back to us."

I cried with relief. "Oh Jesus, Jesus, thank You, thank You!" My insides were still a mess. I was pacing back and forth. I was praying so hard. I sat down, I stood up, I paced, I sat down... I was so sick inside because of nerves. I hadn't eaten in two days. "Please hurry! Please, please hurry!" I tried to sit and calm myself, impossible.

Yei airstrip, "Second plane is here." I was up and down, still praying and pacing.

"Second plane loaded and off the ground." I am crying again, trying to stifle my sobs from erupting like hot lava. We still had one more plane to go. By this time, I was running on pure adrenaline. On the other side, YWAM Arua was there to meet our children, help them with their visas and then transported them to their base. The director remained at the airstrip the entire time to ensure that we all made it safely out.

YWAM Arua then texted from Arua, "Second plane landed." Ten minutes later, "Second plane returning to Yei."

I am praying so hard for that plane to safely return for its last trip, no complications. It feels like an eternity since that second plane took off from Uganda.

"Where is it? What is taking so long. Please God, let there be no hiccups or bumps. Please, God. I could not handle it if any of our children were left behind, I simply couldn't."

From Brian in Yei, "Third plane landed!"

Oh my God this is really happening. Tears are rolling down my cheeks. Pacing, crying, praying, "Jesus thank you, thank you". Almost there.

"Third plane loaded. Last plane, we are in the air!"

I sobbed tears of relief, my tears gushing like a waterfall as they pour over my cheeks. I can't believe it. We are free! I pumped my fist into the air! I am still crying as the adrenaline wanes and peace comes to my body. Within thirty minutes I received a video from YWAM Arua of the plane landing with a final text,

"Third plane has landed in Uganda!"

My knees felt weak as I slipped to the floor, almost passing out in utter relief. My insides were a mess and I was crying so much, sobbing in relief. My babies are safe! We are free at last! No more fear in the night! It is a day I will never forget as long as I live. It has been the longest day of my life. Still on my knees, I thanked God for never leaving us, for strengthening us daily, for saving us this day. I arose and I quickly grabbed my carryon bag and raced to the airport, ready to get myself out of the country. When I came to Juba a little over two months ago I thought that I would only be here for one week. I had only brought two changes of clothes. Little did I know just how long this would take. Every office that I went to, I wore the same two dresses every day. I could have gone to the market and bought more but it just didn't feel right knowing that my children also had nothing. I didn't even have the strength to go shopping, my mind always so fixed on our quest.

Now that I am free to leave and know that I will be allowed to leave with no glitches, I was still a bit nervous. My name is now known in this country, the woman who took over 100 children out of the country. I have no doubt that I am on their radar, especially since that incident where they had recorded my phone conversation. I still don't think that the governor of Yei is too happy with me either. I even asked the man from the highest office to write a letter specifically to the Governor, telling him that the children are leaving with this man's approval and to thank the Governor for all his help. I had dropped it at his Juba office on Friday afternoon.

Although the Governor had given me permission to go to Juba, I hadn't gone straight to the office he told me to go to. I felt that I had received wisdom from the Lord to go to another office first. Upon learning of my movements, he was not happy about this change of plans and that I didn't do what he told me to do. So, I kept praying until my plane was in the air, thinking that I could still be arrested at any time. I have finally boarded the plane for Uganda and I am so relieved.

I feel like I am the main character in a 1,000-page epic novel and I am on the second to the last chapter where the hero wins the battle leaving only the last chapter which will take me into the future. I would still need to wait two more days before I can reunite with the children because they also need a day's rest after all the stress they've been through. I also know that YWAM is praying over them and ministering to them. Again, I am so thankful for YWAM. From the beginning they have been praying for us. From the beginning they were there for us. I am so glad that we fell into their arms on this side of the border.

After arriving in Uganda, I went to see Rhonda at the charter air service office so that I could personally thank her and meet her in person. She worked with us through all the difficulty and numerous glitches, always let me know if things were not safe and joining with us in prayer. She really did want to see us make it out. The day that we had chartered the plane that first time and had to cancel, Rhonda is the one who told us that the soldiers would be at the airstrip, even before the children arrived there. She knew many things before they happened. I asked her how she knew these things and she could not reveal her source but told me to trust her which I did. Today I walked into Rhonda's office for the first time and we looked at each other, recognition dawning on us at the same time, and we immediately hugged each other so hard and I cried again. It was an emotional meeting for the both of us.

I sat down by her desk, across from her, and we relived some of our story together, recounting the times in which she had warned us of danger. Rhonda then grew very serious and she asked me, "Carolyn, do you know why I told you to stay in Juba yesterday?"

"Yes, I do," I responded. "You wanted to make sure that I would be there in Juba in case something went wrong again."

"No," she replied, "that isn't the reason I told you to stay. I told you to stay in Juba because," and she hesitated here as if trying to determine whether she should tell me or not. I asked her, "What? What is it?" She replied, "I insisted that you not go to Yei because there was a price on your head. You were supposed to be shot in Yei on Sunday. If you had gone to the airport, you would be dead."

I was incredulous, somewhat shocked, and asked her, "How do you know this?"

In all seriousness she looked at me straight in my eyes and replied, "You know I have my source. I can't say anymore, only do not return to Yei. It is very dangerous for you to go back there."

As I took all of this in, I honestly did not feel any fear because I knew that I was right where God wanted me. I also know that his purposes for me are not finished yet. As long as I have a purpose in His kingdom here on the earth, He will protect me and I will continue to go where He say go. I put Rhonda at ease and reassured her that I would not return to Yei anytime soon.

I praise God for Rhonda, for listening and for not telling me the reason on the phone. I think if I had known this yesterday I would have been in a state of real fear, for the children and for myself. I don't know who would want me dead, but I have some ideas. I am just thankful that I wasn't there yesterday. God knows the plans that He has for me.

I praise God for YWAM Arua. Youth With A Mission is an incredible ministry that was founded by Loren Cunningham and his wife, Darlene in 1960. YWAM's mission is to "know God and to make Him known" and has bases in over 181 countries with over half of the organization's staff from non-Western countries. The directors of YWAM Arua, a couple from America, with their amazing children, met our children at the airstrip in Arua and carried our children to safety. They helped us to navigate through customs and immigration and brought our large family to their base for two days rest and ministry before our final journey to Luwero. Their hospitality was a beautiful landing place for our exhausted children and staff. We are so grateful to them and their staff for making us feel so welcome to be a part of their family.

From the very beginning our journey we really connected with the story of Moses and the Israelite's journey in the Bible. I have spent the last three months only reading and meditating on the Book of Exodus. I was so encouraged by Moses' and Aaron's steadfastness in the face of so much rejection, sometimes by their own people. Every time the Pharaoh said, "No!", Moses immediately sought the wisdom of God. Even on the journey out of Egypt, Moses did not make a move without first seeking the very face of God. He followed the cloud by day and the fire by night. I made a decision then, to be like Moses throughout our journey, trusting God and never giving up.

I remembered what the Lord told me as I sat in my chair on our compound for the last time in September, "Step by step. Don't assume that you know anything apart from Me. You will need to hold onto My hand and follow Me like the blind woman and trust me." I cannot emphasize enough the importance of God's timing, especially in complex situations. If we try to force things because of impatience, we will miss the open door or the breakthrough that is needed to turn it all around. Nothing good can come from our own efforts. God's plan is always perfect, even if the wait is long and chaotic. In Him we find rest and peace. Peace is not the absence of noise and chaos, but the essence of God's presence in every situation, especially in the midst of chaos. If you follow God's counsel you can never go wrong.

Chapter Thirty-Five

Today is the big day and I'm so excited to finally see the children! Haley and I rented rooms at an Anglican Guesthouse in Luwero so we are standing outside on the front lawn, having received a phone call from Brian that the bus has just reached town. There are so many emotions inside of me and so much has happened that I find it difficult to settle down. What will it be like to reunite after so long apart. Are they happy? Of course, they are, but it's been such a long journey. Are they still traumatized? Where do we go from here? There's the bus! They are here! Tears of thankfulness and joy are again running down my face. I have cried so many tears through this, this tough soldier who is now a mother. Everything changes when you have children.

When the bus pulled in and stopped, I stood at the door of the bus and hugged every single child so tight, telling each one that I love them as I finally felt the fulfillment of our long journey together yet apart from each other. There were many smiles and tears of happiness, of relief, of love as we held each other close. Although we wouldn't want to do this again, the journey here from Yei was so exciting for them with so much to see and learn on the way. I asked the little ones about the plane ride and the bus ride and they excitedly told me all about what they had seen. "We saw monkeys! They came up to the bus and we threw them some cookies!" And another said, "I was fearing when the tiara (plane) was leaving the ground. How can this get in the air? I held on to the seat so hard!" And still another, "We had to sleep on birris (mats) made from hard bamboos at Arua. We stayed with YWAM. They are very nice." I could listen to them all day, their voices music to my ears.

Our entire family then walked to the back lawn of the Guesthouse to sit under the trees and worship and pray together, thanking God for all that He has done on our behalf. It was a beautiful sight and all I could do was let slide tears of relief and joy unspeakable, even now tears fill my eyes in remembrance as I write this page of memory. My children know by now that I am a big crybaby when it comes to my love for them and that's fine with me. Crying isn't a big part of the culture of the Sudanese people, most disguising their emotions under the guise of happiness or anger, although there is crying at funerals. If I cry for anything, let it be for these beautiful children and for Jesus and I will cry tears of joy into eternity. After we worshipped together we immediately settled the children and mamas in their temporary home. Evening was coming soon and we still needed to cook dinner for over one hundred now! How I have missed this.

The Chairman (Governor) of Luwero has been so kind to us. He owns two boarding schools, which are located next to the guesthouse where we have been staying. We had decided to board all of the children in school, even the little ones, at least until they went on Christmas break in two weeks. We had no other option until we found a place large enough to house all of us. The children were so happy just to be in school, any school. They have missed so much and now need to catch up. The next two years will be a tough road to navigate. Our children are already two years behind Ugandan schools in their curriculum and the added struggle of missing half a year because of the war didn't help matters. All of our primary school (elementary school) children have automatically been set back one school grade. Our secondary school (high school) children were able to catch on and catch up by the end of the year, enough to pass, some barely.

In the two days that Haley and I were waiting for the children to come from Arua, we worked every waking hour to buy school supplies, metal storage boxes, hygiene products, shoes, underclothes, bedding, which included mattresses for over one hundred children, and so much more. When the children walked into their new school dorms and saw their individual footlockers filled with all new supplies, their new beds and linens and towels and bath buckets, it was like Christmas day for them! They were beyond happy! Our efforts to organize all their footlockers, including locks and keys, and stenciling their names on each box was a labor of love, so much love poured inside these trunks. My heart was so happy, beyond happy I think. I felt lighter than air.

Most of our children have been sleeping on the floor since early September 2016 with no beds to call their own. You can imagine how it must have felt to spend their first night in a bed with fresh sheets and blankets that were their own. This morning they looked happy and rested. In two weeks, they will begin their summer holidays (December – February), the first month of which we will still be living at the school and guesthouse until our new compound is finished.

The Chairman has been such a blessing to us in every way. He is building a large house for his family, although his sons and daughters are fully grown, as he wanted a place for them to always be able to come back to. It has a very large living room and seven large bedrooms with a private bathroom in most. We told him that we might not be able to stay in Luwero because there was no place large enough to accommodate our big family and we had no funds with which to rebuild. He immediately told us that he would turn his house, the one he is building for his family and that was almost finished, into our new home. I was stunned by his generosity. Yes, he would charge us rent, but this was his house. It is beautiful. We said yes!

Over the next month, the work was accelerated to include two large dorms, outside latrines and bathing shelters and a kitchen. The day we moved in the dorms were still in progress so we were all packed like sardines in the house! The living room was filled with the boy's bunkbeds, three tiered. The girls were stuffed into three office spaces along with four mamas. My staff took up residence in four of the bedrooms. We didn't care how packed in we were because we were finally together in one place and we were so thankful to have the freedom to move around our small village. I really have never seen the children happier in all the years I have been with them.

The most noticeable change I have seen in the children is the true bonding of family. My heart's desire from the beginning, back in 2013 when I first accepted my role as mama and director of the children's center, was for us to be a family and not just another institution. Everything that we tried to bring this in just never seemed to fully click. In Yei, the children were divided between ten houses and many times it seemed as if they were in competition with each other, between houses, making it difficult to see ourselves as family when there was so much separation. Since we have been living together here in Uganda, for the first time I see the connect, this true bond of love that can only come from having gone through the trials that we have been through together. I am reminded of the saying, the family who prays together stays together. I am finally seeing my heart's desire come to be, family. The children do not view themselves anymore as living in a children's home or institution. This is our family home. Each day when the children arrive home from school I always say, "Welcome to your home!"

Since I didn't have a huge compound to run and we were waiting for our house to be finished, I found myself with a lot of time on my hands. I used this to my advantage to reconnect with some of our older children, our teenagers. The repeating theme among them was, "For the first time we feel like family, like someone will truly fight for us and will not leave us." Unfortunately, children in orphanages see people come and go constantly which inhibits them from truly connecting with people at the heart level. Many times, especially after missionaries have "done their time" and have left that particular mission field, the children ask me, "Why don't people stay? What did we do wrong? Why don't people like us?" This breaks my heart because it is never their fault.

I try to convey to new missionaries that when they commit to a mission to please look at the bigger picture than just their own small part in it, to look at the peripheral, the other people in God's plan, before deciding to leave or quit. This one thing keeps me from quitting when I become overwhelmed to the point of wanting to quit. I made a commitment to these children and to God. Commitment is covenant and cannot be broken without hurting someone. When missionaries come and go at their whim the children are the ones affected and their self-esteem. They always think it's their fault that people don't stay. It does not matter what you tell them, trust me. They will always think that if they were better then maybe people would stay. When you hear from God to go and give yourself to a children's home, please, please, commit for a good amount of time and really be prayerful about leaving. Make sure it is from the Lord. Then make sure that you tell the children what the Lord is saying to you. Don't just leave, thinking that they'll be alright. They won't be in their hearts.

Chapter Thirty-Six

We are just two weeks away from our first Christmas together in our new home. I have decided that it will be the biggest and best Christmas ever! I have reserved the Anglican Guesthouse banquet room and grounds for our celebration. Outside on the beautiful lawn where we first worshipped and prayed together, there will be large white canopy tents for shade and presents! Inside, the banquet room will be set up like a church, able to hold at least 200 people! We have invited many guests already. A team from the Harvest School in Mozambique has just arrived and they have raised almost $5,000 to give our children the most beautiful Christmas ever! We can feel the excitement building as we draw ever closer to the big day. The missionaries and the team from Mozambique, about ten of them, have been busy shopping for presents for two days, and so much candy that we might need to make a visit to the dentist by the time we are finished!

The Harvest School team has also come to help us minister to our family (friends from Yei) who now live in the refugee camps. They have lost everything and now live underneath a small, one room, tarp and wooden pole structure, the inside floor being hard packed dirt. There are no mattresses or blankets, just plastic mats. There will be no Christmas feast or presents brought to the refugees, the innocent victims of this ongoing war in South Sudan. This war is never far from our minds because we feel the pain of those in the camps. We want to go before Christmas to share what we can with those we love, our people of South Sudan. There are sixteen of us and we left before dawn today, Monday morning, heading north to the Rhino Refugee Camp which is on the northern border of Uganda where over 12,000 of our Yei family and friends live. The camp is very large, almost 40,000 people, but the area that we visited was newly inhabited, just in the last two months, by the new arrivals from Yei, Morobo and Maridi. When possible, the Operation's Managers (OPM) of the camps like to place new arrivals together with people of their tribes and according to their location in South Sudan, thereby avoiding tribal hostilities within the camps. The drive will take us at least eight hours from Luwero.

We arrived at Rhino Refugee Camp late this afternoon and were embraced by our friends and neighbors. There were tears of joy and thankfulness as we practically threw ourselves into each other's arms, meeting up with long lost friends and even staff who worked with us. Our hearts were undone with compassion and love for our friends who have also journeyed so far amidst such hardship, only to arrive to no water, no medical care, no shade trees, and lots of rocky ground and scorpions and intense heat. Even though they were in a refugee camp our friends have made this place as much a home as is possible, building their temporary homes out of the bright white plastic UN tarps. Since the floors were made of packed down dirt, when it rained the water ran in small rivers, forcing its way into the houses from under the hems of the tarp walls.

Water is extremely hard to find under the ground in this arid place and I was told that for now one borehole pump served all 12,000 people because the camp was so new. The influx of refugees has severely stressed the UN's capabilities to move fast enough to provide the services desperately needed here. Water is currently being trucked in to supplement what comes from the one borehole, sometimes leaving the people two and three days without water. Water is needed for cooking, bathing, and washing clothes and dishes. Imagine trying to accomplish these things for a large family that only receives two jericans a day. Impossible.

The refugees have been on half food rations because the UN has run out of funding, their food storage warehouses standing empty. This camp is ten miles from any medical facility and there is no transportation available to get anyone to a clinic. We were told by the camp chief that every day one or two children die, every day, for lack of medicine that is readily available all over the country except here in this deserted piece of Uganda. The camp is so new that clinics and pharmacies are yet to be set up. This is how rapidly the refugees are streaming in like a river from across the border in South Sudan. This is the part of war nobody reports to the public. It is a hidden killer, adding to the wartime fatalities and most are children.

After visiting with the chief, we returned to our friend's small plot of land and quickly set up our tents and prayed. Our hearts were already broken hearing about the children dying and seeing the pitiful state of the people around us. We then set out to visit people in their small tarp shelters to hear their stories and struggles, to pray with them, cry with them, hold them and encourage them in the Lord. Everywhere we went we saw hopelessness, people who were so tired of carrying their burdens who had just resigned themselves to this desolate place. Most of the people we met were heartbroken because many didn't know where their loved ones were, becoming separated during the chaos, children from parents, husbands from wives. Many people were working in their fields thus leaving small children at home with an older brother or sister. When the chaos struck, everyone ran in different directions as far away as they could run which caused so many families to become separated from each other. There are now thousands of orphaned children in the camps, no one knowing where the parents are, if they are even alive.

Many told stories of carrying as much of their belongings as they could only to have everything taken from them along the way by bandits who ambushed them along the way and dared to take advantage of their plight. Others told stories of being chased from their homes at the end of a machete, escaping death at the hands of terrorists who didn't even know or care what side of the war they were on, if any. Some of the bandits causing such terror were doing just that, simple banditry, taking advantage of a bad situation. The people who now live in the camps are non-participants in the feud between the tribes. They just want to live in peace. Many different tribes are here and they are dwelling together, united in purpose, to pray for the peace of their country and to live in peace.

One man told us that this is the third time in his life that he has had to run to Uganda from war in South Sudan and he is just tired, just plain tired, and has decided that he will live out his life here in the camps. He doesn't ever want to go back home as it was too disheartening to keep losing everything. We prayed with so many and we were moved beyond words by the faith of the people. They had such faith in God, never complaining or angry at God, instead placing anger where it belonged, on evil men who cared only about their agenda. The people told us time and time again that it was only God who brought them out and only Him who kept them safe still. The faith of these refugees surpasses that of anyone I know. They have nothing, yet they have everything.

The next day we arrived at the tarpaulined church structure where we would spend the next two days. The people worshiped God with all their hearts and they lifted their hands in thanksgiving yet they have nothing. They praised a God who is so much bigger than all of this and they have completely offered the throne of their hearts to God, for Him to be seated there. I am undone even as I write this and continuously moved to know God more and to draw ever closer to His heart, knowing that He is our best and only hope. Over the next two days we talked about persevering faith, hope and love, about forgiveness, and about new hearts and about peace.

It was not a one-way conversation with the team preaching to the church, but there was a kinship between all of us. We too had lost everything although we weren't living in a refugee camp, but we were still without a home. The people know that they need to love and forgive those who hurt them and caused their livelihood to be taken from them. All of us together needed to forgive so that we could move on with our lives. We bent to our knees as one in the dirt, tears sliding down many cheeks, some from the pain and hurt and some from repenting of our anger, me included, at those who had done this to us, asking for forgiveness and choosing to love our tormentors in the face of this evil, having left us with nothing but our very lives.

As we ministered, we found a spirit of forgiveness sweeping through the camp as well, being confirmed as we visited more houses over the next two days. The local pastors attending our conference shared with the community just how important it is to forgive. Forgiveness releases the poison from our hearts and lets the captive of our hearts go free. We no longer need to feed and house this anger toward our enemies. We felt that God was doing something new in this place and in us and that forgiveness and peace were going to be the new normal so that God can take us back into our country with this spirit of forgiveness and peace and love for all. After the long days of the conference and going out to minister to the people in their homes afterward, we spent our evenings sitting under the canopy of heaven, the stars shedding their light on our hearts as we interceded and worshiped together, praying for the people, our people, most especially for water to come and for children to live and not die.

Today is our last day at Rhino Camp before we go back to our town and we have just learned from the camp chief that yesterday was the first day that no child had died in the camp! Our great and loving God has heard the cry of His people. We lifted our hands in thanksgiving because we know it is only God who can help the people in this desolate place without no amenities just as he did in the desert with the Israelites after leaving Egypt. We all belong to Him, yesterday, today and forever.

Tonight, we are preparing for our crusade at the local football pitch where hundreds will come to watch the Jesus Film. Upon arriving at the field we encountered many people who had already come and we began to preach right away about the power of light and darkness and making wise choices about which one to agree with. I had organized with my children to help me with a skit so they dressed up like demons. Our main reason for bring some of our children on this outreach was for them to see and experience the aftershock of war and what happens to those who have no help. We don't shelter our children from real life but, instead we encourage them to see it for what it is. As we began the skit, about three minutes into the action, the very moment that we began to enact darkness with demons snarling and hovering, the sound system started to sputter out.

This was a new system that we had just bought some days before coming on this trip and this was the first time that it had been used. Along with the sound system sputtering, a powerful dust storm that actually looked like a tornado surged through the sky toward us, sucking and swirling everything in its path! The windstorm hit us with such power and force that it blew down our firmly anchored movie screen, blowing dirt and debris all over our equipment and the people. Right across the road three grass thatched houses immediately caught fire as the embers from cook fires blew onto their flimsy homes! I could have cried for them because they had already lost everything once coming here and now this within weeks of arriving.

I was preaching that God is mightier than all powers of darkness when this happened and I didn't let this craziness stop me, but I continued preaching and declaring the word of God and rebuking the wind while the team persisted in resetting and anchoring our movie screen. My lungs and throat choking with dust, I continued to preach, my voice raw, giving it everything I had. In the midst of my message I also stood against the tempest! The people all around were covering their faces and eyes with clothing and whatever they could find on their persons. When the wind finally moved on and the dust settled we all gave a big cheer. It was a perfect end to my message about light overtaking darkness when all was said and done!

The audience knew that the surprise storm was caused by an evil spirit trying to shut us down because the skies were clear with no clouds or rain in sight and we were in the middle of the dry season. Demonic activity is very evident in Africa, many of the people visiting witchdoctors for cures and curses, so they are familiar with spirits. Once witchdoctors accept Jesus as Savior and Lord, they actually see the spirit of darkness for what it is and can easily identify it. In the West, there are also many demonic spirits but the people just don't see them. These spirits are very good at disguising themselves as depression, suicide, horoscope writers and many others.
We were finally ready to watch the Jesus film and afterward, another message was preached by Brian. Hundreds gave their lives to the Lord or rededicated themselves to follow Him. Jesus continues to have the victory when we place

our hope in Him in all things.

The name of Jesus was lifted high in Rhino camp, day after day. Right before our very eyes we saw people regaining their hope. People began to smile again from the inside. The camp chief told us that we were the only whites who have been allowed to stay in the camp thus far. Others have asked but were told that they could not come in right now because the refugees were still adjusting after having gone through so much and they didn't want all these white people running around taking pictures. When we asked him why we were allowed he told us that Iris Ministries is well known and recognized in South Sudan as a reputable ministry who cares for the orphan, and our reputation for doing good and doing what is right is known. He also told us that he knew we were not there for any other reason except to love and encourage them.

There were seven of us from the Iris South Sudan team and by the last day we all commented that we really wanted to live there in the camp with the Sudanese people because it felt like home. We cried when we said goodbye to everyone because it felt like we were leaving home again. Our hearts are so pierced with love for our people, a love that only Jesus can bring. As we drove down the road towards Luwero, we were silent for a long time, reliving in our minds the weekend that we had had, one that would be etched on our hearts for some time to come. One of the Harvest School team members commented that although he was leading this team, at first he had struggled to fully engage in the outreach and that by the time we left, he too had tears rolling down his cheeks. He said that he has never cried on any outreach, that this one had touched him deeply, the pain and the love of our people. The love of God leaves a mark on a person if one allows Him to touch deeply.

Chapter Thirty-Seven

We are back in Luwero and Christmas day has arrived, the atmosphere festive and joyful. We only have one car, a seven-passenger van, so we hired a bus to bring all of the children from our new compound to the guesthouse where we had stayed for two months to celebrate the Lord's Day together. Last week all of the children received new clothes to replace everything we had to leave behind in South Sudan at our compound in Yei. For the first time, all of the children had fancy tennis shoes and nice dress shoes which was never possible for us in South Sudan. I thanked God because we could still be in South Sudan, eating beans for Christmas dinner, having no presents, amidst gunfire and fear. But thanks to the grace of God, we were here in this beautiful place. We are so thankful. I pray that we never forget what He has done for us.

My message in church was about Jesus being our present. The gift was here and He never quit giving of Himself to all who would receive this gift of His love. This year especially, we know how amazing this gift is. The altar was full of children who wanted to keep giving themselves to the Lord and to what His plans were for their lives. None of the children were in a hurry to leave the alter as all of the missionaries and pastors and mamas gathered around the children to minister love to them. Unwrapping presents was the furthest thing from our minds in that moment. The true gift was right here in our midst, the presence and the love of God. I don't think that there was a dry eye in church this day. We were just so thankful.

After church we had the most splendid feast! Most of the children have never eaten chicken so this was the first time for them. Everyone had bottles of coke and French fries and plates piled so high with food, feasting to our heart's content. Afterwards we gathered outside on the lawn under the big white tents where tables and tables were filled with presents. The children have never had wrapped presents because this too was not possible in our small town in South Sudan. This was a new experience for them, unwrapping presents! The team bought the children a television along with their first play station. There were new bicycles and small iPods, which were donated for our teenagers, everyone receiving a new Bible and so much more!. It was our second most wonderful day, the first being our escape to freedom.

I have never seen our children smile and laugh so much as I did this day. By the time we drove home at the end of the day, we were filled to the brim with love and joy and our stomachs were also full! I cannot stop thinking about where we could have been right now if not for the Lord and that man in the National Security office. I can't even imagine what our Christmas would have been like. I really pray that the children will never forget what God has done for them, what He truly has given them where so many are still without hope in their country. I know that I will remind them many times over the coming years.

I used to wonder why in the Bible, the writer seemed to constantly repeat himself, retelling the same story, even using the same words. Now I know that it was so the people would never forget what God has done for them. When we don't remind our children of these things, it becomes lost to this generation and they will forget what God has done in their lives. Never grow tired of reminding children how God has moved in their lives. Every Sunday our church service begins with the sharing of testimonies, of how God has moved on our behalf during the week. This starts our church service each and every week.

On New Year's Eve we gathered together in our new country for our annual New Year's Eve Prayer Day to fast and pray for the coming year. Our children really look forward to this day, never failing to ask me each year, "Are we having prayers tomorrow?" Even our small children will sit for the entire day, fasting right along with the rest of us. A child will embrace the things that we embrace. If we embrace worship, our children will embrace worship when taught from a young age. I came into the lives of these children when many were still young, not even teenagers yet and they were introduced to fasting and soaking and to the Presence of the Lord. We fasted four times a year along with teaching how to hear the voice of God and to feel His Presence, so much so that they began to look forward to these days each year. Today as we begin our day of Presence the children spread themselves out on a beautiful acre of grassy lawn, the sun shooting light through the tall and resplendent African trees swaying in the soft breeze as we open our Bibles and wait for His presence and we prayed to the Lord for His will in our lives and to reveal mysteries to us. I did also ask Him not to give me a word like He did last year, about having to have great faith and great trust. I don't know if I can handle another year like that!

When the day was done, I invited those who felt to join me to continue the fast and to press even closer into the mysteries of heaven and what the Lord had for us this year. I continued my fast for ten days, one glass of juice a day my only sustenance. The children have never fasted for more than a day so I was extremely surprised when twenty-three of our teenagers said they were continuing the fast also. Over the next nine days they never once complained and each one was able to fast all the way through with no food, just juice! Just when you think you know your kids... It's incredible where this journey of faith has taken us this year, through the fire of testing and trials into a richer faith in the Father's ability to do all things for us and be all things to us. Jesus is the reason for our being here in this new country.

During these first three months in Luwero we have lost five of our team missionaries for various reasons. Not only we starting over with everything else but now we are starting over with an entirely new team except for Hailey and I. The children were a bit sad because no one seems to stay longer than two to three years. Some go back to school, some to other types of ministry, and some go back home. Children's ministry is one of the more difficult ministries only because children are very needy. They need love, reassurance, validation, expectations, order, discipline, and a myriad of other things. It is a 24-hour ministry and when I go to bed, I am always ready for a knock at the door.

The wonderful thing right now is that we are all living together in one big house so my door isn't far away, it's just around the corner. My door is literally always open and some of the older girls actually hang out in my room without my permission. This tells me one thing. They know their identities as daughters. I love tis and the desire of my heart has been fulfilled. The Lord has something new to show me every day, if I open my eyes to see it.

Chapter Thirty-Eight

On January 16, 2017, I had to return to South Sudan to take care of some important paperwork with some government officials. Very few people know about this trip because I want to keep a very low profile and stay under the radar, as I'm not sure about how things have been in country since I left in November, or if there was still a price on my head. I had to revisit some of the government offices in Juba to bring updates concerning our children's well-being and to obtain school records for our high school graduating class. There was no avoiding this trip. Believe me, I really didn't want to go because I now had a new fear of being discovered there and possibly putting my very life in peril. Needless to say, when we fasted those ten days, for myself, it was to bring clarity concerning this trip.

My flight to Juba was uneventful and it was 122 degrees when I hit the tarmac. Five days later when I left it was even hotter. As soon as I made it through passport control, my phone rang. It was a friend from National Security. He said, "Hey are you back in Juba?" I was shocked. How did he know I was here? My name is definitely on someone's list. This caused me no small concern the entire time I was in Juba. I grabbed my suitcase and caught a motorcycle taxi at about 10:00 a.m. on Friday morning. It felt as if someone had turned on a blow dryer and put it in my face at 40 miles per hour. Unfortunately, I was sick the entire time I was in Juba, so I felt even worse as I had work to do. I learned the locations of so many latrines needless to say! I knew that the sickness was a result of the severe stress and anxiety that I was feeling again, being back in this country, knowing what I knew.

Although the city seemed calm there was still a tension in the air and high security all around. I didn't hear a single gunshot while I was there and this put me a bit more at ease, although I was still in a hurry to get things done and get out. The South Sudanese pound is now 10,000 South Sudanese pounds to one hundred dollars! This time last year it was about 2,500. The economy has spiraled out of control and is set to collapse unless something happens quickly to turn things around. People everywhere are hungry, approaching me for money, any coins I could spare. Most cannot afford to buy food at the current market prices and the dry season is upon us. The time when they should have been planting, the nation was thrown into war so there were no crops to harvest in November to tide people over until the next season. I was able to help microfinance one widow so that she and her small girl could survive. She is going to open a small tea shop or make Kisra bread to sell to restaurants. Kisra is a very thin sour tasting bread. It is thinner than a crepe, very delicate, and is layered in sheets, to be used for dipping into meat sauces and one of my favorite foods.

My heart breaks now as I walk the streets and see the suffering and I find tears flooding my eyes as I look at all the human suffering that I have seen in the last six months. Sometimes I wonder how my heart can take it all in and not hold on to it. I weep for the children who have no voice in this, for the widows and abandoned wives who struggle to survive and care for their children alone, for the man who has lost his dignity because he has to resort to begging so that his family doesn't die of starvation. My heart breaks and I cry out to God. This is the fallout of war where war never leaves your door. This is what most people never hear about, only the missiles flying and people being shot. There are many more being shot with starvation and homelessness than were ever shot with a gun. Starvation is a much slower and painful death, especially when you watch your own children die in your arms, wishing you could cut off your arm to feed them. But I must let go of the pain and move on for the sake of my children. They too must move on, looking toward the future.

On this visit I was also able to visit with my Sudanese pastor for the first time since I left Yei last September. We were so delighted to see each other and the Holy Spirit was so tangible in our conversation as we testified about all that God was doing in Yei and in Uganda in our children and in the refugee camp. "Revival is breaking out in Yei," my pastor told me with great enthusiasm. The people have nowhere to turn except to God. There is no other help, nor food, nor are there white NGO heroes coming in to save the day. Pastor and his team go to the streets every Friday and blow the shofar and shout, "Repent, for your salvation is at hand!" Every Saturday morning the people gather at the town square and he has a revival service where hundreds come each week and each week people receive their salvation in droves. Pastor's church can't hold the masses anymore. Jesus is moving on hearts all over Yei!

I also talked with my pastor in the north in Aweil, and also my pastor friend in Akuem. These two pastors are testifying to the same things, that people are running to the churches because there is nowhere else to go. The people's eyes are opening to see their need for a savior and they know that only Jesus Christ can save the day. In the midst of chaos and war, peace is here, the Prince of Peace. I always say that peace is not the absence of war and chaos but the Presence of the Prince of Peace in the midst of it all! This has been our hearts desire in South Sudan, to see revival, however God wants to do it.

My trip to Juba has come to an end and no danger has come upon me, praise God. I wasn't able to accomplish much as people are not easy to find these days. I was glad to finally step onto the plane and breathed a sigh of relief as it lifted into the air, South Sudan fading into the distance along with the last sunset I will see over this country, at least for some years to come. The Lord has spoken to me that Iris Ministries South Sudan is not finished here. I know that one day I will be back. I still pray for lasting peace and for my pastors who live here as they continue to do the work of the ministry.

Chapter Thirty-Nine

Three years have gone by and it is now 2019 as I sit here in our new temporary house to write our story. The journey continues with new joys and along with it, new struggles. Throughout this entire journey faith in God has been the cornerstone of my spiritual life. There have been so many times, even in these last few years of living in a peaceful place, where I have had huge mountains in front of me and I can either stare at those mountains or I can look to God. Each week, each month, each year I face struggles and trials as I raise these children in a foreign country in a culture that is not their own. Many of my children are in boarding school. Here in Uganda, once a student reaches a certain grade level in school, if they are not boarding they miss so much extra instruction which does not benefit us at all because the children are still a bit behind in their education.

As a parent of teenagers living away from my immediate supervision, the need to trust God has increased, and trusting God is what I have sown into these children over the years. If I spend my time worrying about them and the many new influences around them in boarding school I would chew my fingers off. Although we teach them still I also continually hand them over to God and trust that the seed that has been sown in them, and continues to be sown, is good seed and our prayers for them are enough. God hears me and He knows my heart for the children and His heart is even more for them than the enemy is against them. During the holidays I pour love and God into them as often as I can and I make it a point to be physically here for them and try not to travel while they are on break. I do what I can and I trust God for the rest. He is faithful.

When I told the Lord all those years ago, "Yes, I will care for these children," I was afraid. I thought, "I don't have all the money I will need to even feed them! I don't know enough people to raise this kind of money! What do I do?" I told the Lord that I will do this as long as He is with me every step of the way.

If He leaves us then we die because we have no one else. I remind Him many times that I did not ask to be the leader of this crew and I did not want to be the proud owner and operator of a children's home. Do you know that when you don't seek position or promotion that is when God promotes you? He is looking for people who don't love money and who don't seek fame or position, someone that He can trust to take care of His business with a heart after Him. Even though I sometimes stress about these things, in the end I remind God again that I never sought this out. I just answered the call from a place of obedience and love for Jesus, and I have always loved these children.

Since then, with my yes, we have had an amazing partnership. He has never failed us and I have been in some really tight spots. Just last week I had a board meeting to discuss which of the children would not be able to go to school for this next semester because we literally have no money for the school fees. The meeting didn't accomplish anything except that we would wait to see what our beginning of the month budget would be and then we would decide.

That Friday night I did not feel like worshipping at all. I had no strength left but I was still the iPod worship leader. I laid out African mats on the floor, I turned down the lights and I invited all the children to come and sit with me and Jesus. We sat before the Lord, the children having no idea what was happening with our finances. As I sat before the Lord and listened to the music, my heart began to melt and tears silently rolled down my cheeks. I told the Lord that I have nowhere to go, I have no one to turn to. I have only Him and that I can't do any of this by myself. I poured out my heart and committed yet again to trust Him and Him only.

The next day I received an email from one of our sponsors who told me that she was sending a large check. She asked me how much I needed and I almost told her that it was more than she could provide. Instead, I was honest and told her we needed X amount of dollars for immigration visas and food and school supplies and fees and that this amount would meet all of our needs. The next day a check for the full amount was already in the mail! I was in awe that somebody would just give away this kind of money to someone they had never met. I always pray to God that I want Him to keep me honest and to expect a high degree of integrity from me. This is a lot of money and I never want to misspend even a dime of it. I praise God for people like this who release so much to us. And I praise God for the ones who send what they have, be it ever so small, because this is probably a lot of money for them. I am reminded of the story of the widow's mite,

"Then one poor widow came and threw in two mites, which makes a quadrans. So He called His disciples to Himself and said to them, "Assuredly, I say to you that this poor widow has put in more than all those who have given to the treasury; for they all put in out of their abundance, but she out of her poverty put in all that she had, her whole livelihood." (Mark 12:42-44)

I am so grateful for the faithful, the cheerful givers, no matter how large or how small, I am grateful.

As to my testimony, the next day I received another email from a foreign ministry who informed me that they were sending a check which would be enough to cover all of our school fees! I had just received a double portion! God is the one who moves hearts and He is the one who knows the times and seasons of our lives. I chose faith instead of defeat. I chose to take my eyes off of the mountain and put them on Jesus. Every single time I do this Jesus responds. Of course, it isn't always as I imagined it would be, but every problem is solved and we are never left begging for bread.

As children of God we really need to trust Him as our Father, in all things. When most of the disciples left Jesus because they were offended by His teaching concerning eating His flesh and drinking His blood, Simon Peter responded to Jesus when asked if he too wanted to leave, "Lord, to whom shall we go? You have the words of eternal life?" (John 6:68)

From whom do you seek your wisdom? Is there really someone on the earth that you trust more than God? So many times during our fight to be free of war people questioned my judgement and my decisions. I knew I had heard from God and I had to stand against opposition in order to walk out what He had spoken to me. Too many people have a fear of man, what others might think about them, just as Saul did when he was in a critical place in battle.

Samuel told Saul to wait for seven days because he would come to give the sacrifice right before going into battle. The seventh day came and Samuel hadn't shown up. His men started to scatter. Saul then decided to make the offering himself. When Samuel came, at the appointed time, he asked Saul, "Why have you done this?" That day the kingdom was taken from Saul because he feared man and not God. (1 Samuel 13:8-14)

Do you see how Samuel came at the last minute? Do you see how Saul grew impatient in the wait, how fearful he became because he looked around at men and not up to God? I often ask God, "Why do You have to come at the last minute for me?" I know that He knows I have faith but if He never tests my faith then when I really need it I will fall, I will fear the mountain. I can't even count how many times He has come at the last minute, the very last minute, when all looked like it was lost. I have learned that God is never, ever late. He once told me, "There are no emergencies in My kingdom." Did you get that? Nothing is an emergency to Him. Nothing takes Him by surprise. You have heard this message so many times but do you believe it? It is not until you face the mountain that your faith will truly be put to the test. My life scripture, the one that is the core of who I am, is this, "When the Son of Man comes, will He really find faith on the earth?" (Luke 18:8). I want to be among those who say yes.

I praise God when He tests my faith because these are the times that I praise Him in the middle of the storm even when I don't feel like it, when I have no more strength. I praise Him and I tell Him that I have no one else, that I cannot do this by myself and I don't want to. To whom shall I go? You have the words of life. Even in my darkest night I have to believe that He is holding onto me because there is no one else who will. I have over one hundred children who depend on me for their every need. I have eighteen staff employees who also depend on me for their salary and their medical care and their children's school fees. I carry a huge weight and sometimes I forget who really carries it. I have to tell the Lord that this is His ministry and not mine. I have to tell Him that these children are His before they are mine.

I remember sitting on the floor in a hotel room in South Sudan after I had lost everything I owned the first time. I sat there looking up at the ceiling, my knees pulled up, my arms resting across them. When I looked up at the ceiling with the bare lightbulb dangling there, I felt such peace because in that minute, that very minute, I experienced His truth when I decided to give Him everything, to fully give Him everything. I gave Him my material possessions, my fears, my hopes, my trust, my disappointments, my calling, my ministry. At that moment, I knew that it was always His and never mine and this was such a relief to me. I felt so much weight lift off of me. Suddenly these things didn't matter to me anymore. Suddenly I smiled and I experienced what it must have been like for Him when He walked the earth with nothing but His clothes on His back, all of the weight of things lifted off. I had nothing to be concerned about anymore. Little did I know that the Lord was teaching me and preparing me for what was yet to come. That day he told me to not hold tightly to the things of the world. I always thought that He didn't want me to be materialistic. No, He wanted me to hold tightly to Him, to trust Him.

Our Father is so pleased to give us everything that we need, everything that our hearts desire according to His will. If we don't trust Him, if we don't have faith in Him and what He can do, then are we not holding onto the things of the world?

"Without faith it is impossible to please God." (Hebrews 11:6)

How can we please God when we reject what He has offered because we choose instead to trust in our own abilities or in the things and people of the world? Faith is the substance of everything that we could ever hope for. What do you hope for? You must have the substance of faith for that which you hope for to even begin to come to you from your Father. Faith is a real thing, it is a substance that we can touch. Even our salvation came from that first step of faith. If we believed then, what happened? Oh, I wish you could see how true God is to His word. He is looking for faith.

Do you know that Jesus is going to return for His perfect bride? Yes, of course you do. Many people think that Jesus will come back when we get our act together, when we get the whole world to turn to Jesus, when we get clean enough because He is returning for that spotless bride, is He not? Let me show you what the Lord showed me. Lately I have been reading the Artscroll Tanach, the Jewish Bible. Look what Solomon wrote in the Song of Songs.

"My faith is firm as a wall, and my nourishing synagogues and study halls are strong as towers! Then, having said so, *I become in His eyes like a bride found perfect.*" (Song of Songs 10:8)

The bride that Jesus is coming for is the bride of faith. When He comes will He really find faith on the earth? I want to be found full of faith, even in my discouragement, even in my complaining, even when I cry in frustration, "Are You going to save me?" At the end of the day you will always find me full of faith because the alternative offers me nothing? People always ask me, "What is the biggest revelation that you have had in this incredible life of yours?" Faith. I have had, and am still having, a deeper revelation of faith and what that looks like to Jesus. Every time I think that my faith cannot get any bigger, I face another mountain bigger than the last and I have to reach down deeper for bigger faith. The kingdom of God is in us. Faith is in us. We just need to reach in and grab it and refuse to be moved by the world and its constant motion, waves and winds.

Chapter Forty

Looking back on our journey I know that another huge game changer in my walk with the Lord has been the prophetic words that the Lord has given me in any season. I'm not talking about prophetic words spoken by others to me although these words are good confirmation of what God has already spoken to me, but they don't decide my direction. I've had people prophesy over me and many times it was right on, as if they were reading my journals. I have also found that too many who rely on the prophetic word from other people to move them in any direction end up lost in the wilderness because they didn't wait to hear from the Lord for themselves. I've had prospective missionaries tell me that they were called by God to South Sudan, swearing that it was from God, only to turn around some months later and tell me that they aren't coming as God has called them elsewhere. This is not God's character. He is not a wishy-washy God, a double minded God who changes His mind with the winds everchanging direction. At least let's be honest and reveal the truth of why we might have changed our mind and not blame it on God, right?

It is so important to journal because when you receive a word from the Lord and write it down you can always look back and say, "Wow, see, God told me this six months ago!" The word of God tells us,

"Call to Me, and I will answer you, and show you great and mighty things, which you do not know." (Jeremiah 33:3)

When I need to hold onto a promise, especially when I am going through a great trial, I need the word that the Lord spoke to me. His word cannot be contradicted by any person or any circumstance. If He said it, it will come to pass. Six months before the civil war escalated the Lord gave me a very sure word. He told me that I would need great faith and great trust and that I have been this way before and He is with me. When everything started spinning out of control in July of 2016 and I needed solid footing, I remembered the word the Lord spoke to me six months previously on New Year's Eve . The time had come for my faith and trust to be great. This is what I held onto during that first month of terror and the weary months that followed. When discouragement set in, I remembered His word spoken to me, from His Spirit to my spirit, that He would be with me and that He would bring victory, and I reminded Him, and others, of this word. I stood firm in it.

Hearing from the Lord for yourself is so important and I cannot stress this enough. We cannot be moved by our feelings. Too many people use the excuse, "I just didn't have peace about it." And they use this as an excuse to not do something that is uncomfortable. When Dorinda heard from the Lord about coming to South Sudan, she didn't change her mind just because there was a war on. Her own mother asked her if it was a good idea to come and Dorinda told her mother and her friends that she had heard from the Lord so she needed to go when and where He said to go. Was she afraid? Yes, she was a bit afraid. She didn't walk around and say, "I feel perfect peace about going into a war zone."

Sometimes we don't feel perfect peace even when we are in the center of His will. I sure didn't feel perfect peace when we lived in a war zone but I knew that I was where He wanted me to be at that time. I didn't let my feelings direct my feet. And I have to believe that God did something unexplainable and incredible in our children because we stayed, especially after the first war crisis happened in 2013. David could have killed Saul and solved all his problems. The people loved him, Jonathon loved him, no problem! But, David heard from the Lord that he was not to touch the Lord's anointed. David walked in obedience even though it was terribly uncomfortable for what, fifteen years? He even lived in the midst of his enemies towards the end of Saul's reign, right there with the Philistines. Do you think he felt perfect peace? I think not.

When we become so familiar with the word of God that it reverberates in us, whatever the situation that we find ourselves in, then that word is all that we need to direct us on through to victory. It is the only thing we can hold onto when everything goes south. When the Lord gives you a specific word which is meant just for you and your situation then this word becomes a life saver, it becomes a shield against the enemy. If I did not have faith in God or trust Him when the army encamped on our compound I would have fled, possibly into the bush with all of our children, or even across the border by myself. Who knows? I never became impatient after I knew what His plan was. I was sometimes discouraged and I sometimes wondered if we were ever going to get out of our mess, but I still waited on the Lord and His timing. Why? Because I had a word from Him. His word to me and His promise to these children are what saw us through the craziest time of our lives.

The children understand this and they pray the Word of God. During the crises I began to look up scripture that we could declare and believe for ourselves, to hold onto to keep us safe and focused.

"No weapon formed against you shall prosper, and every tongue which rises against you in judgment you shall condemn. This is the heritage of the servants of the Lord..." (Isaiah 54:17)

"I have been young, and now am old; yet I have not seen the righteous forsaken, nor his descendants begging for bread." (Psalm 37:25)

"My times are in Your hand; deliver me from the hand of my enemies, and from those who persecute me." (Psalm 31:15)

These are just a few but there was so much scripture that we hung all over the walls of our prayer room and each night when we prayed we would remind ourselves that these words from the Lord are meant for us, His children, today, yesterday and forever and we prayed them, boy did we believe them and pray them!

I believe that all of these promises from the Lord are what kept us in more peace than if we had nothing to stand on or cling to. We really thought about those who claimed no God and we prayed for them, that they would encounter God through this. They had nothing to hold onto but each other and unfaithful leaders. If we as parents teach our children the wisdom they need to carry them through life then we should teach it so they will remember it therefore doing what is right and good. Brushing our teeth and bathing are good and needed and so we teach our children to do these basic things. Eating a balanced diet and getting exercise are good for us so we teach our children how to do these things. Shouldn't we also then teach them to speak the word of God over their lives? This is just as important as these other things, even more so. It is not enough to take them to church and hope they "get it" or drop them at Youth Group and hope they are learning something. Would we depend on someone else to bathe our children and feed them each day without investigating what they are being shown?

I was a teacher for thirteen years and many of my students had parents who never once asked what they were learning in school or how they were doing in their school work. Parents just sent their children out the door and expected that they would learn everything they needed to learn to get on in this life. Is every one of your children's teachers a spirit-filled, Bible believing

Christian? What do they believe in? These are the people who are teaching your child how to live. Not me, I question my children and ask them what they are learning and I preach at their schools. I'm fairly involved. I remember when I was a young girl, about twelve years old, I knew nothing about how my body would change at the age of twelve or so. When I got my first menstrual cycle I cried and thought I was dying. I shakily told my mother and she laughed and then she handed me a tampon and told me to use it, that what I was going through was normal. That's it, nothing more, not how often or how long or how strong. There was no explanation from her or even how to use this tampon. I sat in the bathroom and cried because I couldn't figure out how to use it. I will never forget how awful I felt that day. Can you imaging your child going through a great struggle and having no idea how to deal with it, having nothing to believe in or hang on to? We must equip our children.

If we don't teach our children the word of God, when sickness comes and doctors cannot fix it, they will just sit and cry, not knowing what to do or who to believe or even how they should pray. When disagreements come in their marriages, instead of praying the word of God over their lives and spouses, they will just throw in the towel and become bitter or severely depressed as I was, or even worse. The promises of God bring peace in every storm. Worship from a place of destitution or depression or even hopelessness can restore the soul to a place of rest and peace. Bringing the sacrifice of praise when we don't feel like it is what makes it a sacrifice. We just might need to let go of our anger or depression or worry or bitterness so that His love can penetrate even the hardest of hearts. Praise does this. It breaks through when nothing else can. How many testimonies have we heard about people who were in the darkest moments of their lives and they began to listen to the word of God or a certain song and everything turned around for them, causing them to give their lives to the Lord? Many people in prison have come to the end of themselves in that place and when they attend the church services, many of them give their lives to the Lord, saying that this was what helped them make it through doing their time.

There is something so powerful about praying and worshipping and reading the word of God. All of my spiritual life, every morning I wake up and read the word of God before I go anywhere or do anything. I cannot start my day without it. Even when I don't feel like it, I still read the word. It feeds my spirit just as I would feed my body. When we are sick we are told to eat something so that we can regain our strength. Is it any different concerning our spirit? If we don't feed our spirit, it will become a dry and empty place, a hole that we don't know how to fill.

Eating the word of God fills this hunger and nourishes our spirit. In John 6:53, Jesus told the Jews who were following Him, "Most assuredly, I say to you, unless you eat the flesh of the Son of Man and drink His blood, you have no life in you."

He further states, "For My flesh is food indeed, and My blood is drink indeed." (John 6:55)

His flesh is the word. If we don't eat the word we have no life in Him or in us. John wrote his book to the church and in it he tells us, "In the beginning was the Word, and the Word was with God, and the Word was God."

Do you see how the word "Word" is capitalized, making it more than just letters on a page? The Word was a person, the person of Jesus Christ. Further in this same chapter of John's book, in verse 14, John explains to us, "And the Word became flesh and dwelt among us, and we beheld His glory, the glory as of the only begotten of the Father, full of grace and truth."

Jesus Himself told us that if we don't eat His Word then we have no life in us. People are going to church and they are still dead. They have not fed themselves and don't even know that they are dying. Oh, I pray that the saints get this. Life comes through Him, through His Word, His word.

My children are prayer warriors. They know how to pray for the sick, how to rebuke demons, how to pray for wisdom and they believe that what they pray will come to pass. They know how to pray the Word. We have had too many testimonies of how God came through for us to not believe it was always Him. They are now becoming serious readers of the word of God so that they can stand on their own with a God that they know personally and having done all, to stand.

Since I came onto the mission field in 2009, I have written updates, letters home each week for the last ten years. As I was reviewing our history through these updates I found one that shows how faith worked in me even recently and not in a war zone.

"I had a talk with our children and told them how proud I am of them for being so patient and so resilient through all of this. They too want a permanent home and not a rent-a-compound where we currently live, where there is no room to play and no land for digging and planting, always wondering where we will keep getting water. The local community wants to charge us a high price to use their borehole and they become a bit frustrated because there are now an extra 150 people standing in their water line. I certainly don't blame them at all. We also have to truck water in because 150 people just need a lot of water. Tomorrow I start our land hunt. I don't have the funding but I have the faith. When I find the land that God says will be ours, I know the funding will be there. That's just who He is."

Even though we usually had no money in the bank, I knew that the Lord would come through for us to have land of our own. Our funding either comes through Iris Global in Redding, California or through my Carolyn Figlioli Ministries account in Texas, America. The testimony that came out of this land hunt is incredible. After looking for land for a few months I found the perfect plot. I was so excited because it looked so much like our land in South Sudan. When I showed our staff employees who are from South Sudan, they agreed with me wholeheartedly. Everyone was so excited and we just knew that this was the place that God had for us. Before I ever made an offer on the land we started praying over this land, walking every inch of it, declaring the word of God over it and then we thanked God for making it ours. After all this, then I approached the owner and asked for a price. After he told me the price I asked if we could drop it just a tiny bit. In Africa, one is expected to bargain, no matter what you are buying, a t-shirt or a plot of land. So, I felt to bargain him down just a bit as a matter of protocol. He agreed to my bargain. I then told him that I needed to check my bank account to make sure I had the funds available as I hadn't checked my account in Texas in over a month and I knew we didn't have it in the Iris account. Upon checking my account, I discovered that I had almost the exact amount that was needed, just two hundred dollars more than was needed! Trust God! Trust God! Hear from God. Declare the Word of God. Believe God.

God has given me so many testimonies about faith and prayer and His Word. There is no way anyone could ever tell me that God does not answer prayer. We must ask ourselves, "Is the position of my heart right? What are my motives for asking this? Do I really need this?" If our answers align with the will of God for our lives, we then mix it with faith and the word and we wait. Yes, we wait. If it is still simmering, then spice it a little more with faith and some more word. I believed for one year for our land. I waited for His timing. He came. Remember, there are no emergencies in the kingdom of God. The wait is where faith breaks through or the lack thereof will shut it down. When I find myself struggling to have faith for a thing, I ask myself, "What is the alternative? Worry and stress? Have I done all I can from my own strength? Is this anything I can have control over?" Then I put my mind at ease and I refuse to worry. What is the point of worry? There is no point. Has worry ever solved anything? Keep telling yourself these things. Step into a life of faith.

In the New Testament faith is mentioned over four hundred times. It is the benchmark of our religion, oh wait, of our faith? In the book of Habakkuk, God Himself acknowledges that the just in any generation shall live by faith, not by sight.

"Then the Lord answered me and said: "Write the vision and make it plain on tablets, that he may run who reads it. For the vision is yet for an appointed time; But at the end it will speak, and it will not lie. Though it tarries, wait for it; Because it will surely come, it will not tarry. Behold the proud, his soul is not upright in him; But the just shall live by his faith." (Habakkuk 2:2-4)

You and I are the just of God, the ones who won't look around and let ourselves be moved by our circumstance or our feelings. Trust God, walk in full faith, believe what He tells you, and you will see great and mighty things here on the earth.

Acknowledgments

First, I want to acknowledge and honor my biggest hero on the planet, my mentor, my friend, my boss, Heidi Baker, Co-founder of Iris Global. She constantly shows me what true humility and complete dependency on Jesus Christ looks like. Although I've known her for over ten years, every single time I am with her I learn even greater grace and mercy toward those who are hurting and suffering in the world. She inspires me to never, ever quit. In our type of ministry there are many days over the course of years where we do feel like quitting, like we just can't go another mile. That's when I hear Heidi's voice in my head and heart, "Carolyn, if you don't quit, you win, Jesus wins." And I can go another day. Heidi, I love you so very much and besides the call from Jesus on my life, you are the reason I remain and don't quit. I pray that we both run into heaven, into the arms of the King, straight off the mission field, when our race has been run.

I want to acknowledge and honor Ted and Nancy Boersma, without whom we could never have made our great escape. We would still be sitting behind enemy lines, fearing for our livelihoods, wondering if we would even eat another day. When Iris Global made a cry out on our behalf for a rescue attempt by charter planes, no one had that kind of financing. Ted will tell you that neither did he. But like he says, "God didn't ask me for a dollar amount, He just asked me if I would help. So, I wrote the check. I didn't have it but God did, and the check didn't bounce." Ted is the most tender-hearted man who cannot talk about Jesus without wearing his heart on his sleeve. He and his wife Nancy have become family to so many of us at Iris Global. I love you two so much and pray that someday you can come meet all these beautiful children that you helped to rescue.

I want to also acknowledge Operation Boat Angel who made it possible for all of our children to be enrolled in school in Uganda immediately upon our arrival in our new country. We needed school fees, uniforms and supplies and we had nothing. We lost everything and came out with only the clothes on our backs. You made it possible for them to not miss a beat or to feel the loss of everything they have ever known. I pray that one day I can meet you face to face to bow to my knee and say thank you.

I would also like to acknowledge Ronald Ndawula, the Chairman of Luwero District Uganda. We had never met before this war, you did not know me, yet you heard of our plight and insisted I come to your district to make our new home here. You welcomed us with open arms, converted your new family home, which was still under construction, into our new Children's Home. You then built your home right on the other side of the wall from us! What kind of man purposely chooses to give up his home to a people not his own, and then chooses to live next to 135 noisy, excited, happy children? Ronald, you are my hero. You have never, ever not helped me and I have needed a lot of help from you over the last three years. You are what servanthood looks like, you are what unconditional acceptance looks like. This tribe that came to live in your town didn't have the greatest reception, but you told people that we were different. You believed in us and saw us for who we are, children of God. I am forever your friend and advocate. I see your heart for your people and it blesses me so. I love you friend.

And lastly, but most importantly, I acknowledge, honor and sincerely love my amazing team of seven missionaries, and my two amazing friends who came to help us out of the worst of it (you know who you are K and W), without whom any of this could have been accomplished. Every single one of you were vital in our journey out, but you were even more vital in the years leading up to it. Your love for these children will never be forgotten by these little ones. They say that because of this amazing team that they finally see that they are worth fighting for. When I wrote this book, I decided I could not take the liberty of telling your stories because only you could do that. I could only tell my part in it. I always look back and say, "I had the BEST team for what we needed to get done at that time." I could not have asked for better or found better even if I looked for a year. I am so thankful for each one of you and I will ever love each one of you and wish I could list you by name but I know your privacy is important to you for a number of reasons. Some of you are still running your race on distant shores and I can only pray that you keep running and finish strong. We are all on the same team, even if continents apart.

There are so many others who, although not an intricate part of this particular story, have been with us through the thick and thin of things for years, even up to ten years, standing with us financially and prayerfully. I could never hope to list all of you as the list exceeds 300 people. But I do want to say thank you Cornerstone Church in San Antonio, Texas under the leadership of John and Matthew Hagee, for always being there for me. From that first bullet into the trenches, Papa Hagee, you personally called me to tell me you would come and rescue me if I just say the word. I have never had a papa in this world who loved me enough to come for me. You truly carry the Father's heart. You and now your son Matthew have given so much to us and continue to help us until now. Words could never express my gratefulness for you. Cornerstone Church will always be my home church, my home family. Thank you for always standing with my family here in Africa.

I also want to thank Ark Revival Ministry under the leadership of Phil and Connie Thompson, who love me and my children with unreserved love and support. You also have been with us since that first bullet flew and stand by us still. When I travel to the USA, you are the first to make sure I have what I need while there. When I come to preach at your church, you first make sure that I am ministered to, refreshing my weary soul, filling me with new strength. Your support and love for me over the years could never be measured in words. Thank you for loving me and us so wonderfully!

And thank you Gwynne and Larry Wright, my family, my best friend, friend to my children. Gwynne, you have been with me through the thick and thin of it for over twenty years, yet you still stand in the gap for me and with me. You are the first face I see when my plane touches down and the last one I see when I take off again, every time. My heart swells with love for you my sister, my friend, my very best friend. I could never find a friend closer than you except for Jesus, who is the One who caused our paths to cross. Our friendship has truly withstood the test of time.

And finally, because I cannot keep this up or I would use two hundred pages, thank you for my secret prayer team who prays for me when things have hit the fan and I have hit a wall! I love you Karen Park, Lestra Gross, Diana Hagee and Sandy Farhart. I've had some pretty dark nights of the soul and could not imagine finding my way out without your prayers. When things get really dark, I always know that I can call on you to come find me and lead me on. My heart explodes with love for each one of you.

How You Can Get Involved

Carolyn Figlioli is still leading the work in Uganda of caring for these children. She now cares for 135 children fulltime who live with her and she also reaches out to the village community with various projects.

Many children in Uganda cannot attend school because of the lack of school fees. One of the works of Iris Ministries Uganda is to help eligible children attain their education through the sponsorship program at Iris Ministries Uganda (IMU). IMU also partners with a local Ugandan Children's Center under the sponsorship program, providing baby formula and porridge for malnourished babies or those who have no mothers.

Lastly IMU provides subsistence and hygiene products for the Luwero Battered and Abused Women and Children's Center operated by the Luwero Police Department. These ladies are usually waiting for new placement or trial and the children are kept until another relative is found.

If you would like to sponsor any of the children or projects at IMU, or are interested in visiting the Iris Ministries Children's Home in Uganda, please contact Iris Ministries Uganda through their email, carolynf@irisglobal.org.

Donations may also be sent to:

Carolyn Figlioli Ministries
410 Spyglass
McQueeney, TX 78129 USA

All donations are tax deductible and the full donation goes straight to the children and projects at IMU. All royalties from this book also help fund our projects.

LIST OF ILLUSTRATIONS

ACKNOWLEDGEMENTS

Mrs Katherine Halverson, historical research and publication division, Wyoming State Archives.
Jack D. Haley, assistant curator, Western History Collections, University of Oklahoma.
Janneyne Longley Gnacinski, West Allis, Wisconsin.
Mrs E.L. Metcalf, Greve Coeur, Missouri.
Mrs J.A. Knight, Amarillo, Texas.
Christopher L. York, Belton, Texas
Roy W. Fletcher, Giddings, Texas.
Elmer O. Parker, assistant chief, Old Military Branch, National Archives, Washington D.C.
Mrs Sarah Randles, archives division, Rosenberg Library, Galveston, Texas.
Joseph W. Snell, assistant state archivist, Kansas State Historical Society.
Richard E. Folkes, clerk of the district court, Lee County, Texas.
Staff at the Masonic Lodge, Waco, Texas.
Barker Texas Historical Centre, Austin, Texas.
Texas State Archives.
Austin Public Library.
Wyoming State Archives.
Mrs Lucie Price, Austin, Texas.
Ray Seaton, Wolverhampton, England.
Allan Radbourne of the English Westerners' Society who gave much help and encouragement, especially with the need, when writing about the Old West, to distinguish fact from fiction.

My thanks to Ian Arnold
'a good man to ride the river with'.

1

'Don't you think it is hard to kill me for my sins and give Wes Hardin only twenty five years?' - Bill Longley

In 1878 the town of Giddings in Lee County, South East Texas, had a population of about four hundred, mostly farmers, cotton pickers, storekeepers, blacksmiths, ranchers and odd-jobbers. Some of them had bought land cheaply under the Homestead Act sixteen years previously and, by fair means or chicanery, had added to their acres and grown prosperous.

It was a typical, normally peaceful county, which rang the school bell weekdays and the church bell on Sundays. Since the turmoil and confusion of the reconstruction period after the Civil War, the county had begun to settle down.

On Friday, 11th October everything stopped in Giddings. Normal day-to-day activities were suspended. There was no school and the general stores were closed. It was not a public holiday, but the appearance of four to five thousand people, converging on the town from miles around, suggested a harvest celebration or a hoe-down, some popular festive event. There was excitement in the air as families travelled on horseback, in wagons, on buggies or on foot along the dusty highways and rough bridle paths. They exchanged banal remarks about the weather, greeted one another and some, who had come long distances were already tucking into food hampers. Children, too, were in the crowd which flocked to a destination a few hundred yards from the Houston and Texas railway line. In a rough field everyone jostled for position and waited for an event without precedent in law-abiding Giddings. This was the appointed day for the public execution of William Preston Longley, Wild Bill, accused of thirty two killings, but sentenced to hang for the murder of a man he claimed had murdered his cousin; an outlaw who finally agreed that he deserved to die.

Not for long did any casual sightseer, a stranger to this part of Texas, remain unscrutinised. Law officers were watching for anyone carrying a weapon, to confiscate it until after the hanging. A special watch was kept on all those close to the gallows. Scores of special deputies mingled with the crowds, ready to seize anyone who made a move to interrupt the official proceedings. It was rumoured that an attempt would be made to snatch the condemned man from the gallows, or on his way from the local jail. His younger brother, Jim, who had been arrested with him on the murder charge and later released, was known to be on his way to Giddings and Sheriff Jim Brown suspected he might be involved in a rescue operation.

The morning had begun overcast and heavy clouds threatened rain. By day-break hundreds of people had left their farms and stores unattended to get the best views near the foot of the gallows. Throughout the morning they sat and chatted. As the sun broke through the clouds at midday, they opened their hampers and ate chicken-legs and sweet potato pie. 'Nice day,' they said, 'for a hanging.' By early afternoon deputies, standing four deep around the gallows, with rifles and pistols ready, had to heave back the crowds. This was what Sheriff Brown feared. If too many people pushed close to the gallows, it would be easy for someone to fire a pistol causing a panic and in the chaos try to snatch the prisoner and get away on a waiting horse.

This was the first judicial hanging the town of Giddings had known. The sheriff was determined it should proceed according to schedule, but he was aware of Longley's extraordinary reputation for cheating death at the last moment. Many people believed that Longley's guardian angel would not desert him at this fateful hour.

For weeks Sheriff Brown had studied reports, based on rumours and speculation that plans were being made to free Longley from prison. An official investigation into these rumours had pronounced them groundless, but Brown was not convinced. Each moment increased his anxiety. Longley had been served his favourite meal of turkey and apple pie. He seemed remarkably cheerful in his cell. Was it, wondered the Sheriff, philosophical resignation at his impending fate or the optimism of a man who knew he would be rescued before the law could take its course? In many ways he admired his prisoner. He liked his chivalrous nature. In jail Longley had been a model prisoner, in spite of the long, complaining letters he had written to newspapers. The Sheriff respected Longley's family, law-abiding and devoutly religious. It was a tragedy and a strange twist of fate that such a respected pioneering family should have produced one of the most notorious desperadoes Texas had known; a killer who, by his own confession, had sent at least thirty-two men to their graves, though he had been tried for only one.

During the months between the trial and the day of execution Sheriff Brown sat in his ranch house wondering what had set Bill Longley on his gunslinging life of crime and lawlessness. He tried to imagine him growing up in these very surroundings, sitting at the long hardwood table while his father read passages from the family Bible. For it was the Longley home the Sheriff had bought eight years before when the family, ashamed of the reputation their outlaw son had brought on their heads, moved to a neighbouring county.

Brown was a good friend of Campbell Longley, who was respected throughout Texas as a pioneering settler and one of its first Freemasons. It was a hard, unenviable task that Brown now faced, presiding over the execution of Campbell's son. But the law had to be upheld and he was an instrument of the law, regardless of his personal feelings. The Sheriff looked at his pocket watch, as he had done every few minutes in the last three hours. 'One twenty-five,' he said. 'Time to move the prisoner out.'

The twenty-seven year old prisoner, looking neat in a new grey suit sent to him by a cousin as a birthday present five days previously, was brought from his cell. A faint smile hovered around his mouth and broadened into a grin when he saw what precautions were being taken to guarantee a safe passage to the gallows. If he had been given time to stop and count he would have counted one hundred special deputies, fifty of them on foot and the rest mounted, under command of Captain Z. P. Egleston. The foot guard, commanded by Captain W. G. McLennon, stood ready to march in columns of four. They were drawn up around a dougherty wagon, a kind of ambulance used by the army to carry sick and wounded. The Sheriff had spent three months selecting his deputies. Each man's record had been carefully vetted. The final, hand-picked list was reckoned to represent the best deputies in Texas. A visiting head of state could not have expected a more impressive escort.

'All this just for me, Jimmy?' Longley asked the Sheriff, as he set foot on the iron step plate of the wagon.

'Just for you, Bill,' the Sheriff replied, helping the handcuffed prisoner to one of the transverse seats. The canvas side curtains were tightly strapped down and on the chain-supported platform, normally used for carrying luggage, a guard supplemented those who sat either side of the prisoner inside the wagon. At a signal, the dougherty moved forward, flanked by the special deputies. It was not far, only a few hundred yards, to the place of execution. Every yard of the way Sheriff Brown looked apprehensively toward the roofs of general stores, saloons and shacks, half expecting to see a rifle appear over the eaves. If anyone were determined enough to attempt a rescue operation, he would have to do so in the next few minutes and it would take a strong party to break through the massed ranks of his well-armed deputies.

Brown was not put off by the fact that Longley had never belonged to a gang, apart from his early and brief association with Cullen Baker's raiders. He had been a loner, but not without his admirers, especially those who despised Negroes, toward whom Longley had displayed a paranoiac and often murderous loathing. There were plenty of sympathisers, Brown realised, who might try to save Longley at the last moment.

As the wagon drew near to the crowds Brown noticed a large number of Negroes among them. 'They'll be glad to see him gone,' he said to one of his deputies. 'So will the state of Texas,' came the reply. How much had been spent and how much manpower employed by state agencies over the years to bring William Preston Longley to justice, no-one had accurately estimated. At various times the army, vigilantes and the Texas Rangers had pursued him. Reward notices had been posted throughout the state. Time and again Longley had eluded his pursuers, through sheer daring or luck.

As the wagon moved slowly through the silent crowds, held back by more special deputies, children were lifted onto the shoulders of their brawny fathers to get better views. Some of the womenfolk had turned out in their best clothes, balmoral skirts with basque or muslin waists; paletots (a long-sleeved jacket buttoned like a military tunic) or sacques (the female version of the sack coat worn by fashion-conscious men). Others were in their simple working clothes, ready to return to their fields, barns or household chores when the execution was over.

A murmur of excitement and expectancy rose when Longley was escorted from the ambulance wagon and marched to the foot of the gallows, where two priests and the judicial hanging party were waiting. He was slightly stooped, but walked without any sign of fear. His thick black hair was neatly combed over the nape of his neck. It was difficult for those in the crowd, aware only of his reputation and never having set eyes on him before now, to reconcile his calm and composed forebearance with the description of him by Sheriff Milton Mast, who had arrested him, as 'the worst man in Texas'.

There was something almost dandified about his curling black moustache and strip of beard cut squarely at the point of his chin. Only the piercing black eyes suggested the cool tenacity for which he was famed. He could have been mistaken for a Mississippi river-boat gambler, handy with a derringer. Except that Longley had not time for a vest-pocket pistol. His weapon was a Colt, man-sized, or a self-cocking Winchester rifle.

Sheriff Brown had insisted on Longley being handcuffed in spite of the extensive armed guard. He was taking no chances of the prisoner getting his hands on any kind of pistol and only when the rope was round his neck would he release the handcuffs. That moment was drawing near - and still the Sheriff feared a last-minute rescue attempt.

There was a rickety step-ladder to the platform and the third step shifted under Longley's 150 lbs weight. 'Look out!' he called, in jest. 'The steps are falling. I don't want to get crippled or fall and break my neck.' His laugh was heard by those nearest in the crowd. It was not the forced laughter of a man trying to conceal panic; rather, the easy laughter of an outlaw whose charm (the other side of his enigmatic personality) had often captivated young women. Twelve years as a desperado, being hunted through the South West and all over the Great Plains, through forests, deserts and swamps, had not dimmed the lustre in his eyes or dulled his sense of humour. Reaching the platform, he turned to look directly at those who had come to see him hanged. He recognised several relatives, but his parents were not among them. The one person he was looking for was his brother, Jim. Whenever he had returned to the family farm during his years of wandering and hiding from the law, it was Jim with whom he had spent most of his time, teaching him how to shoot and hit the trunk of a tree six times while riding past at full gallop on a piebald. And it was Jim Longley whom Sheriff Brown imagined would now make a play, if he was rash enough to take on more than one hundred deputies, to snatch 'the worst man in Texas' from the gallows.

2

'I was a man before I was done being a boy' - Bill Longley

The formal admission of Texas to the Confederacy on 1st March, 1861 meant little to Bill Longley. At the age of nine he was more involved with Webster's Blueback spelling book and McGuffy's series of readers than the tumultuous affairs which occupied his father and fifteen-year-old brother, Alexander. He had heard something about an attack on Fort Sumter and knew that a leader named Jefferson Davis was in charge of military operations in the South. More was heard at school about Davis than George Washington during these restless times.

Many of the Longley family's neighbours were turning over their ploughs to their womenfolk and young boys while they responded to the Confederate call for three thousand troops from Texas. A vast war game was underway, it seemed to young Bill Longley, who in the school ground enacted with his friends the skirmishes their elders talked about at supper and around the saloons of Evergreen. Instead of playing their usual games of Bull Pen and One-Eyed Cat when they came out of the small, timber-framed schoolhouse, five hundred yards from the general store and the blacksmith's forge, the boys and girls hovered near groups of men under the shade of oak trees, discussing news of the Civil War. There was a new word they memorised but had difficulty in spelling - secession. Bill overheard someone say that Texas was no longer part of the United States, but belonged to the great Confederacy.

'What does secession mean, pa?' he asked his father. 'Why ain't we in the United States no more?'

Campbell Longley did not know how to answer the question. At heart, he was a Unionist, but first and foremost he was a Texan. Whatever his adopted state decided he would go along with it, not out of weakness but because he owed his livelihood and security to Texas. At the same time, he was disquieted by the admission to the Confederacy. His political vision was based on Washington, not Richmond. But he was not rash enough to declare these principles openly. Only his sympathies were for public consumption and these were known to be close to the grass roots of Texas.

'There's some trouble going on, but I expect it'll be over afore you're much older,' he told his son. 'I hope so. Think of Texas as your country. This is where we belong.'

Throughout the summer and autumn young men were leaving Lee County to join a mounted regiment of Rangers or to enlist in the Confederate army. In the winter it was decreed that all able-bodied men between the ages of fifteen and eighteen were to be enrolled in companies, ready for immediate call-up in the Southern cause. Bill was tall for his age, with firm muscles, and he showed a rare capacity for leadership in one so young. On the rough ground outside the schoolhouse, he was put in charge of the younger children for organised games. In some ways he was a surrogate teacher. The children of Lee County looked up to him as a natural leader and felt protected if he were in charge of them.

'Will I be able to join the army soon?' he asked his father.

'Lad, you're only nine years' old. Just forget about this war and tend to your learning.'

'Will you have to go to the war?'

Campbell Longley was forty-five, with a wife four years' younger. They had six children, three of them boys. 'No, I won't have to go,' he said.

Age and family commitments ruled out immediate enrolment. As the war raged on, decimation of the Southern armies would make the initial age categories meaningless. The manpower contribution of the sparsely populated state would reach at least 50,000. In the winter of 1861-62, before the confederacy's conscript law brought in compulsory active service for all able-bodied men aged eighteen to thirty-five, there was confusion in the state's thirty-five brigade districts. None of those on military stand-by knew if he would be required and there were optimistic forecasts of a quick end to the war with a Confederate victory.

Campbell Longley was not one of the optimists. He was aware of the North's military and industrial capacity. Although he did not anticipate an early call-up himself, he realised that if the war dragged on much longer, his son, Alexander, would be conscripted. At night, after working his land, when the family gathered for supper and bible readings, he prayed for an early end to the war.

For Texas to be embroiled in a Civil War, which threatened to destroy the pioneering work with which he had been closely associated, was painful and distressing to him. In his youth he had fought in battles. Bloody campaigns were familiar to him. He had seen men die, some quickly and others in agony. But he regarded himself as a peaceful man, devoted to the religious ordinances of New Testament Christianity. The name of Campbell Longley was respected throughout Texas and in his own county he was a church elder to whom people brought their personal problems and from whom they sought advice. Ten years before the Civil War began he took his first degree, later becoming a charter member of the J. D. Giddings Lodge, No. 280, at Evergreen. As one of the state's first Freemasons, he was part of the civil Establishment and took pride in the prestige he had earned coming from Tennessee to help Sam Houston form the Texas Republic.

Campbell Longley - he dropped the prefix Mc from his name before his marriage - was born on 30 September, 1816, near the Little Pigeon River in Sevier County, Tennessee, the son of Joseph and Priscilla Patterson Longley. His grandfather, William Longley (1760-1841), of New Jersey, fought in the War of Independence for the Colonists, was discharged from the army in Maryland and lived in Virginia before moving to Tennessee with his wife, Mary, and settling there with their eight children. Joseph was born in 1795, fought in the war of 1812, and died in 1830, leaving a widow and nine children, the youngest a few months' old and the eldest, Campbell, fourteen. It was on Campbell, with eight brothers and sisters, that much of the domestic burden fell. He had to help their mother run the farm. There was no time for more schooling. He had to apply himself to the hard, practical tasks of making the farm self-supporting. From the start, taking his father's place, he displayed a tenacity of purpose which not only toughened his sinews but produced in him a spirit of self-reliance that would reach its peak in Texas during the war against Mexico. No matter how hard he had to work, his religious education was not neglected. His mother took care of that.

Through his membership of the Church of Christ, he began to take an interest in the social and political affairs of the territory, where most people were Baptists or Methodists. This interest led him to think of the outside world. Work on the farm in Jackson's Purchase, McMina County, where the family had moved when he was twelve, in time proved irksome. He was getting restless. His brothers, Alexander Preston and William Tennessee, would soon be in their teens and would be able to help with the chores. Two other brothers, Caleb and George, were old enough to do some of the light work around the farm. These were the considerations he put to his mother when he announced his intention of volunteering to help Sam Houston fight the war against the Mexicans in Texas. At first she was horrified and refused to let him go. His persistence, and the fact that he was now nearing manhood, forced her to give way.

David Crockett's fame as a frontier hero had not been diminished in the state by his loss of office as a Democratic Congressman in Washington. He was rallying support and seeking volunteers to go to Texas. Young men were flocking to join his band of fighters. Campbell Longley was eager for action and enlisted with a company of one hundred men under Captain Augustus Parker, of Georgia. The states of Georgia and Tennessee provided the weapons and ammunition, but the recruits had to provide their own wagons and horses.

Parker complained that there was no time for proper military training. Guts and courage would be the substitutes for military skill. If anyone did not feel capable of withstanding the rigours and dangers that would inevitably occur, the instruction was to fall out now. No-one dropped out. The company made its way to Nashville, to be met by a civilian named Joseph Clay, who was in charge of sleeping arrangements. Volunteers in small and large companies were arriving daily. Excitement rippled through the town. Most of the volunteers were young men, like Campbell Longley, yearning for new adventures; anything to relieve them of the monotonous grind of farm work. Others were mercenaries, ready to take up any cause that gave them the promise of reward, probably in the form of land grants.

A hard core believed passionately in the cause of wresting Texas from the Mexicans, either as a self-governing Republic or as an integral part of the United States. There was a festive spirit in Nashville. Cheers greeted the arrival of each new group of volunteers, who soon numbered well over one thousand. A huge barbecue was held to celebrate, with effigies of General Antonio Lopez de Santa Anna, the Mexican dictator, hurled into the flames. The way the volunteers celebrated their arrival at the point of embarkation for Natchitoches, Louisiana, one might have assumed the fight for independence had already been fought and won. Girls who normally would have withheld their favours, saw nothing wrong in 'accommodating' the fighting-fit young men who had rallied to Crockett's call. Many of these raw backwoods fighters spent their last night in Nashville drinking and making love, but by morning they were ready for the next stage of their journey.

All fares on the paddle-starner taking them to Natchitoches were paid by Mr. Clay. As the steamer churned the muddy water of the Cumberland River, Longley turned to Captain Parker and said: 'Joe Clay's the best friend we've met since we started. He's got a heart as big as a pumpkin.' A look of wry amusement came over Parker's face. 'Hmmm. . . maybe. But what do you know about him?'

'Nothing, really,' said Longley. 'I guess he's rich, though, to pay all these fares.'

'He's a partner in the firm of Sterling C. Robertson and he owns forty leagues of land in Robertson colony - and that means if Texas goes down, he goes down with her. If Texas goes up, so does his fortune. He's got a very definite interest in the outcome of this war. So the 250 dollars-ahead fares are a pretty good investment.'

Longley and his fellow volunteers were disappointed by missing the battles which were pending when the volunteers set out from Nashville and fought while they were still en route. Prisoners taken by the Mexicans met a terrible fate. Though assured of clemency, they were taken under Santa Anna's orders to the plains and butchered. It is estimated that more than three hundred prisoners, taken at various points along the coastal plain, were massacred and fewer than thirty managed to escape. The Mexicans disposed of the bodies by throwing them in a heap and burning them; this happened with the bodies of Jim Bowie, William Travis and the rest of the defenders of the Alamo, which fell on Sunday, 6 March 1836.

'Remember the Alamo!' It was with this slogan that Houston rallied his men and took Santa Anna's army by surprise while the Mexicans, jubilant after their Alamo victory, were enjoying an afternoon siesta at San Jacinto, on 21 April. The battle lasted under twenty minutes and the Mexicans were routed. Those who did not die or were taken prisoner fled across the Rio Grande. The way to full independence was now open.

Campbell Longley voted for General Sam Houston as President of the Texas Republic. In September, he and all the other men who had volunteered to serve under Captain Parker were honourably discharged. Longley took stock of his possessions: one suit of clothes (torn) and a pair of shoes (tattered), plus a few dollars. He had come through unscathed but had little or nothing to show for his labours on behalf of the emerging republic.

Intending to return home to Tennessee, he boarded a ship and fate took a hand. The ship was caught in a storm and wrecked. Another ship came to the rescue of those on board and Longley was taken with other survivors to Matagorda. After recovering from the ordeal, which had left him in a state of nervous exhaustion, he decided to stay in Texas. His movements over the next two years are unknown. Possibly he worked on farms. In 1838 he applied for a land grant and because of his services to the republic as a volunteer, he was given 320 acres. This confirmed for him that his future livelihood was in the state and he abandoned whatever plans he still had of returning to his home state.

In a letter to his mother, brothers and sisters, he explained that he wanted to make his home somewhere between the Rio Grande and the Red River, where the opportunities were incalculable and a spirit of adventure was all anyone needed to make a start. He made his way to Austin County and there met an attractive girl of seventeen named Sarah Ann Henry. When they married, on 26 July, 1838, he was established as a farmer and small landowner. Texas had gone its own way, having gained recognition as a republic from Washington. He did not doubt that in time it would gain statehood. He was proud to think of himself as a Texan. The

Longley's first child was born the following year and christened Mary Catherine. Two years later another daughter, Martha, was born and a third girl, Frances Caroline, after another three years. (By 1867 they had had ten children, nine of them surviving.)

Six years after settling in Texas, Campbell Longley helped to establish the first Church of Christ west of the Brazos River in Austin County. As a lay preacher he was invited to preach sermons and lead prayer meetings in adjoining counties. An obituary notice, after his death at the age of ninety-one in September 1907, summed him up as 'a brave soldier, a good citizen, a true friend, a good husband, an affectionate father, a bright mason and a faithful Christian'.

The first son, Alexander, was born in October 1846, and was followed three years later by George Washington. The sixth child, William Preston Longley, was born on 6 October, 1851 two years before the family moved to Washington County. At this time Campbell Longley, aged thirty-three, was a Justice of the Peace and was farming 316 acres of land. In 1854 the Washington County Texas tax assessment books valued his land at Elm Creek at 1,580 dollars. He also owned a Negro slave (valued at 900 dollars), two horses worth 200 dollars, 60 head of cattle (300 dollars), oxen and wagon (225 dollars), making him a 3,205 dollar property owner in that county alone. He also had 2,380 acres in Bexar County valued at 2,380 dollars and 1,066 acres in Nueces County. A year later he added a further 30 head of cattle and another horse to his stock.

By the end of the 1850s - fifteen years after the admission of Texas into the United States - he was a Washington County Commissioner, a school trustee and the owner of one hundred head of cattle and nine horses, a man of considerable substance and influence in his county. Within five years, from 1854 three more children were added to the family - Elizabeth, Joseph and James Stockton.

Campbell's brother Caleb, five years' younger, had come to Texas in the 1840s to settle in Washington County with his wife, Ardelia, and owned one hundred acres, two horses and 30 cattle. Both families were prospering in 1861, when the Civil War broke out. Campbell had taken care not to align himself with either side and he continued to devote himself to his civil responsibilities, including service with a special detail to care for war widows and their children.

Apart from young men leaving to join the colours, life went on much as before in Washington County. The Longleys had another Negro slave to help till their land and gather the crops, but they parted with fifty head of cattle to the army. This was the family's only contribution to the Confederacy. The war had been raging for two years when their son, Alexander, was conscripted. Three months short of his 18th birthday a message came that he had been killed. The circumstances of his death were never known in detail. He was reported to have been shot by a sentry guarding Union lines while he and other Confederates were about to make a surprise attack.

Billy had doted on his brother and his death caused him to fly into a tearful rage, shouting that he would 'kill every damned Yankee' who crossed his path. His parents waited for his distress to subside and then, in their grief, tried to explain that this was a sacrifice thousands of families had to endure. That evening, after supper, Campbell Longley opened the family bible and by the light of a kerosene lamp, read from the Revelation of St. John the Divine, Chapter 21: 'And I saw a new heaven and a new earth; for the first heaven and first earth were passed away; and there was no more sea. . . And God shall wipe away all tears from their eyes; and there shall be no more death, neither sorrow, nor crying, neither shall there be any more pain; for the former things are passed away. And he that sat upon the throne said, Behold, I make all things new. . .' The words did not mean much to Billy, not yet turned fourteen. He could not understand his father's calmness, but he was compelled to respect his authority and scriptural guidance.

When General Robert E. Lee surrendered his army to General Ulysses S. Grant at Appomattox Court House, Virginia, nine months after Alexander's death, Billy was still at school. His teacher was Dr. G. D. Wilkinson, a medical graduate. Social history was not part of the curriculum. This was taught elsewhere, in the woods. Wandering by the creeks and through the oak woods, a mile or so from the schoolhouse, Billy noticed what appeared to be a scarecrow dangling from a branch. As he drew closer he saw that it was the limp body of a white man, around whose neck was a sign with two words painted on a strip of wood: 'Yankee lover'. For a few minutes he gazed at the swaying body in horrified fascination. Then he ran home to tell his parents.

'Keep out of those woods,' his mother commanded.

'Why'd they lynch him, ma? Was he like one of them Dozier boys?'

'No, not like them. Just keep away from there, do you hear?' Some years before, two Dozier brothers, convicted of a crime, had been strung-up from the strong, spreading branches of an old oak that served as the Evergreen court house. Children were always scrambling up the four foot wide trunk to look for the rope mark around the branch.

Little public interest was taken in Billy's discovery of the lynched 'Yankee lover'. The consensus in Evergreen was that the hapless victim must have got what he deserved. Lynchings were frequent in the so-called reconstruction period, when the Carpetbaggers arrived from the North and attempts were made to enfranchise Negroes. The shock waves of the immediate post-Civil War period were felt more strongly in Texas than those of the war itself. Geographically, the state was in a favourable position to avoid the worst traumas of the war. Military activities were confined to the border areas. While General Sherman's troops were pillaging and setting fire to the crops in Georgia, the crops in Texas grew and were harvested, mainly by Negro labour from Louisiana and Arkansas, sent to Texas for safe keeping.

Jefferson Davis, a cotton planter before he was elected President of the Confederate states at the outbreak of war, looked on Texas as a warehouse for the Confederacy. Supplies could be sent through Mexico from Texas and cotton shipments made to Europe to finance the Southern war effort. Texas emerged from four years of war with adequate food and money, only to get embroiled in another kind of war, between old Democrats and the radical reconstructionists. During the war a large number of Unionists had joined the Confederate forces out of fear of what would happen to them if they didn't do so. Mobs had caught and murdered hundreds who had tried to escape to the North. Others had swallowed their principles and taken the oath of allegiance to the Confederacy, staying at home to serve in special details. If Unionists now thought it was safe to declare their true allegiance in Texas, they were seriously mistaken. The South had lost the war, but hatred and prejudice remained, reinforced by the exploitation of the Carpetbaggers, opportunists and radical reformers who arrived carrying their belongings in bags made from carpets.

Campbell Longley believed in a reconstituted Texas, faithful to the Union. Voting the Union ticket, he declared, was the only way to establish permanent peace. He made no secret of this view among those in Evergreen who thought that Texas could and should go its own way in defiance of Federal military rule. Anyone but Campbell Longley, voicing such unpopular opinions, would have been lynched. His reputation as a church elder and commissioner, his work during the war for widows and their children, for whom he had tanned leather and made shoes, saved him from violent reaction. As the social and political divisions became more hostile, he began to despair of a peaceful community being established and his preaching, he felt, fell on deaf ears.

The state's frontier spirit militated against easy reconstruction. Communities scattered over wide areas had relied in the past on their own forms of protection, mainly through vigilante groups or law enforcement officers. Given this sturdily independent outlook, together with the sectarian violence which characterized the post-war period, and it is not surprising that an atmosphere for lawless, self-determined behaviour was established. It was in this atmosphere that Bill Longley spent his most impressionable years.

Carpetbaggers from the Northern states were proclaiming to uneducated Negroes their rights under emancipation. Southern loyalists were regarded as traitors; disbanded soldiers, ill-fed and many of them destitute, were looting and pillaging on their homeward journeys. Civil authorities were impotent as insecurity, unrest and violence spread through the state like a plague. When it was obvious that the existing civil officials were not going to be recognised by the Federal government in Washington, there was nothing to stop banditry and anarchy triumphing over law and order. Guerillas, highwaymen, bands of robbers, looters and desperados behaved as if the state were 'open house'. In Austin, the state treasury was ran- sacked. Stage coaches were held up every few miles between the Rio Grande and San Antonio. In 1865, the year the war ended, 47 white people and 51 freed Negroes were murdered. The following year the murder total was 170 and in 1867 it rose to 347.

Fears that rampant lawlessness would lead inevitably to military government and repression were voiced in the newspapers. Editorials appealed to honest citizens to restore order. Local police forces and 'home guards' were set up, but they were powerless to diminish or even contain the rampaging virus which seemed to be lodged in the bloodstream of Texas. On 20 August, 1866 President Andrew Johnson, a Southern Democrat from Tennessee, who as Vice-President had succeeded Abraham Lincoln, declared the end of insurrection in Texas. His proclamation took an optimistic view, in contradiction of the facts of life in the state, that peace, order, tranquility and civil authority existed throughout the United States. On such wishful thoughts, official dreams were based.

A more realistic assessment came from Texas governor, James Webb Throckmorton, an anti-secessionist, swept into office by 40,277 votes against his opponent's 12,168, on an anti-radical platform. In his inaugural address he spoke of a conquered province exercising only such privileges as the conqueror in his wisdom and mercy would allow. The loyalty of Texans was doubted, their integrity questioned, their aspirations for peace and restoration maligned. The frontier was unprotected by the Government and was a marauding ground for Indians. Devoted frontiersmen were filling bloody graves, their children murdered, their wives and daughters carried off and tortured.

The new governor, who endorsed President Johnson's restoration policy, was woe-begone, but no-one in Texas who sincerely wanted the restoration of civilian government and the establishment of law and order, could quarrel with his observation. The future did indeed seem, as he put it in his address, inauspicious and life in Texas was, to say the least, uninviting.

Under the Evergreen oak across the dirt track from his school and outside the inn where Dr. J. H. Stockton had entertained General Houston a few months before the Alamo, Bill Longley heard grown-ups talk about Throckmorton and denounce the radicals and Negro suffrage. What he could not understand was why Negroes had been freed. He had grown up thinking of them as slaves, not as a result of white oppression, but as the natural order of things. There had been no conflict between his father's religious precepts and the two slaves working on the family's farm until released under the terms of emancipation.

The state's economy was suffering from lack of cheap labour. Flushed by their new-found freedom, many Negroes were refusing to do menial jobs on the land except for high rates of pay.

'It's gone to their heads like rot-gut whisky,' was a common remark. 'Cuttin' 'um loose is like panhandlin' whisky to Indians on the frontier.'

Out of school, Billy, now grown to six feet in height and weighing 150lbs, had to work harder on the farm to make up for the loss of Negro labour. Farmers everywhere were complaining of crops having to remain unharvested because the cheap labour they had relied on for so many years was no longer available. Sweating and weary after a day's work in the fields, Billy found both solace and stimulation in whisky. The impression it made on him was to last his entire life. Given a choice between a bottle of whisky and a six-shooter, it is said that he would have taken the six-shooter to rob a liquor store!

The farm work developed his physique, toning and shaping his muscles, as similar work had done for his father in Tennessee. His black hair and black eyes set off a lean and hard appearance. He moved with the grace of a Comanche Indian, especially on horseback. But not to everyone in Evergreen was he a handsome, athletic youth. To some his eyes had a snake-like intensity which unnerved them and his introspective manner could be deceptive. He was inclined to explode into extroverted arrogance after drinking whisky.

Towering over other youths of his age in the county, he enjoyed being their idol. It confirmed for him that he belonged to a chosen race, the Texans. For further confirmation of this superiority he looked around for 'lesser breeds' and 'enemies' against whom to demonstrate his courage. He did not have to look far. 'There's only one thing better than a Carpetbagger and that's a rattlesnake,' ran a popular sentiment of the time. Calfskin boots were protective against the bite of a rattlesnake. The Carpetbaggers were more deadly and inscrutable. Generally, they ignored the old Negroes as being too set in their Uncle Tom ways to change politically and take advantage of emancipation. They concentrated on young, impressionable Negroes, headstrong enough to do whatever they were urged. Carpetbaggers and 'uppity Nigras' became Bill Longley's chosen enemies. There was no point, he felt, in listening to arguments between radicals and conservatives about whether civic officials should take the amnesty oath.*

Nor was the sixteen year old Bill Longley much interested when on 30 July, 1867 General Sheridan, commander of the Fifth Military District of Louisiana and Texas, issued an order removing Throckmorton from office 'as an impediment to the reconstruction of the state under the law'. The impact on him of two or three Unionists, Carpetbaggers or Negroes strung up by the roadside, with a sign 'Thus to Traitors', was more dramatic and enduring. The youth had learned to hate. He hated the sight of Negro soldiers, some of them undisciplined, sent to maintain order and he was further inflamed by their Union uniforms. It was the Union that had killed his brother.

In Jackson County, 300 Negro troops were sent to prepare a railway line, but groups of them broke away and plundered nearby plantations, inciting local Negroes to join them. In Galveston, Negro troops went on a rampage. The local Bulletin reported 'a reign of terror' and called for the military authorities to take control, warning that otherwise citizens themselves would retaliate. Texas, said General William E. Strong, an Inspector General, quoted in the New York Herald, was in the worst condition of any state he had visited, 'the population hostile in feeling and action toward Washington'. Whites and Negroes everywhere, he claimed, were 'ignorant, lawless and starving'. A few months later he roused the indignation of Texans by recommending a military campaign through Eastern Texas 'such as Sherman's through South Carolina, to improve the temper and generosity of the people'.

Another top-ranking officer, addressing the Reconstruction Committee, suggested that the condition of Texas was due to the fact that, unlike other Confederate territories, 'she had never been whipped' and her women were rebellious. If a war broke out with

*I. . . do solemnly swear (or affirm) in the presence of Almighty God, that I will henceforth faithfully support, protect and defend the Constitution of the United States and the union of the states thereunder, and that I will in like manner abide by and faithfully support all laws and proclamations which have been made during the existing rebellion with reference to the emancipation of slaves. So help me God.

another country, he said, Texas, except its German population, would go over to the enemy. With the interaction of so many stresses and strains, as Texas lurched, fumbled and groped toward a semblance of balanced government, it was inevitable that scapegoats would be sought and found. Unionists accused diehard secessionists of trying to regain control; Southerners found themselves disfranchised and their property confiscated.

Men like Campbell Longley, ready to accept a reconstructed state government supervised by Federal authorities, were alarmed by the breakdown of civil order and a resort to violence to settle grievances. Instead of being condemned, outlaws were being hero-worshipped. The law of the six-shooter seemed stronger than the remnants of laws still on the statute books. Branches of the Union League and the Grand Army of the Republic were seeking, through Negro registration, to gain political control. The conservative Houston Telegraph warned that Texas could pass into the hands of Negroes, who would then tax land out of white ownership.

Hysterical overtones played on Bill Longley's mind and shaped his judgements. In this highly-charged atmosphere he felt a need to assert himself. He had the essential physical requirements, but something he lacked - a six-shooter.

The best range of guns were on display in Houston, a few hours' train journey away. He had enough money saved to buy a pistol, but not enough for the train journey. But that was no problem. All he had to do was work his passage by feeding lengths of pine wood into the locomotive fire hole. Many youngsters got around the country this way. It was known as 'taking the Pine road'. Some travellers he met claimed to have covered all 35,000 miles of railroads in the east without spending a dime on fares, just by feeding the burners, and living on the one-dollar station meals.

In a woollen shirt and slouch cap, to look the part of a fireman, he boarded a Mogul freight engine, which had three driving wheels each side and a front truck with two wheels. Brassware and paint gave the engine a bright, jaunty appearance as it rolled along the track, spitting sparks and cinders around and out of the funnel stack.

Houston was a startling contrast to the rural way of life in Evergreen. As a near-frontier town, it was wide open, a rough but

Campbell Longley, the outlaw's father, was a respected Texas citizen, a Freemason, preacher and a pioneer of the state after the war with Mexico.

exhilarating Baghdad of the Bayou. Longley's expression stiffened as he noticed the large number of Negro troops, who had replaced the disbanded Texas Rangers. He didn't like the look of the large lead balls on leather thongs they carried on their wrists. He decided to give them a wide berth and not go looking for trouble. Nor was he looking for pleasure in the town. All he wanted was to buy a six-shooter and return home. To carry an appreciable sum of money in a money-belt or purse after nightfall was an invitation to have one's skull crushed from behind. Robberies-with-violence were commonplace. Most of them remained 'unsolved', though leading citizens drew attention to the nature of the attacks and the lead balls carried by troops.

Houston was all things to all men and all sorts of men gathered there, to slake their thirst after months on the cattle trails, to sport with Amarylis in the shade of a bordello, to gamble, play poker, monte or faro, or just drift about and see which way the winds of reconstruction would blow. From all around, Negroes were converging on the Freemen's Bureau, set up by act of Congress. The Bureau looked after the welfare and interests of Negroes by arranging educational programmes, supervising labour, contracts and wages. To many ill-informed Negroes, it was a place to pick up free clothes, shoes and even teams of mules to work the land they expected to be distributed to them once it had been taken from their previous bosses.

Near the Bureau, Longley found a store that had just the kind of weapon he wanted - a Dance revolver, made by J. R. Dance and Bros., of Columbia, Texas, a model manufactured during the war for the Confederacy. A Dragoon-pattern forty four, with a flat frame, was to give him at least this much in common with the renegade Apache, Geronimo, who also used a Dance revolver. Happy with his choice, he tucked the revolver inside his coat and wandered for a while through the streets, watching veterans of the war, in faded blue or grey uniforms, wander in and out of saloons. Early in the evening he stumbled on a group of drifters roasting potatoes and meat over a campfire and asked if he could join them. They didn't object and he joined in their talk about 'uppity' Negroes and the way they were being stirred up by the Carpetbaggers. There was talk of joining the Ku Klux Klan, which had just appeared in Texas to counter the activities of the Union League and the Grand Army of the Republic. Klan membership was expanding rapidly. Longley listened to the ways in which it was being established in various parts of the state, but while, in general terms, he agreed with its aims and objects, taking oaths and dressing in a hood and sheet had no appeal to him.

'Why's it called the Ku Klux Klan?' he asked.

'They use Springfield rifles and that's the sound the musket hammer makes,' he was told. 'Like this - "klick-kluck".'

After talking for a while, Longley and one of the youths broke away from the campfire circle to stroll around the town. There was no train until morning and the only thing to do was while away a few hours and doze the rest of the night by the campfire. When they came to Preston Avenue their way was suddenly barred by a burly Negro soldier. In his right hand he was swinging his ominous lead ball.

Where, he demanded, were they going? Didn't they know it was against the law to wear grey? Longley had not noticed until then that his companion's clothes were grey, the colour of the Confederacy. The clothes were ragged, but could have been mistaken for the remnants of a rebel's uniform.

'These ain't rebel clothes. I wus too young to join the army,' the youth protested.

'No arguin', boy. Tek off dem clothes. Give me yuh jacket, yuh cap and shoes.'

Longley's companion backed away and then stood his ground, facing the soldier and his expression had only one interpretation. If the soldier wanted his clothes he would have to take them from him. The silent challenge was accepted. Swinging the heavy ball, he made to bring it crashing down on the youth's skull. But in the time it took to raise his arm and swing the ball, his chosen adversary had whipped out a six-inch bladed knife and plunged it into his stomach. With a cry of pain and astonishment the soldier sank to his knees, the lead ball falling to the ground. As he writhed in agony, the two companions ran and did not stop running until they were almost breathless. Though deaths in Houston were frequent, practically a nightly occurrence, they expected a hue and cry. Soon scores of Negro troops would be searching for them, if the knifed trooper were still alive and able to describe them. On the outskirts of town they hid in the undergrowth and managed to sleep for an hour or so before dawn. By daylight it was too dangerous to be seen together, so they separated and Longley made his way back to the railway station, to work his way back home on the next freight train.

At home he said nothing about the incident to anyone and busied himself in target practice. The Biblical injunctions that the Longley family honoured, as best they could, did not extend to pacifism. Like other families in Texas, they were true to the frontier way of life, which put an emphasis on self-protection and that, of necessity, meant skill in the use of arms. Campbell Longley encouraged his son to perfect his marksmanship by blasting away at cans and rocks placed on fences or thrown into the air. The boy had a steady hand and it was not long before he was a more accurate shot than the seasoned Civil War campaigners who had returned to their farms in the county.

Some of these embittered ex-Confederates regarded it a moral duty to try to disarm Negroes. Their justification was the claim that Negroes were easy prey for the Carpetbaggers. Consternation turned to anger and violence when some of the more hot-headed Negroes deliberately rode horses through the crops of their former owners to demonstrate their contempt and shouted insults, such as 'White trash!' to those who had for so long held them in bondage.

If, in his youth, Bill Longley had been blessed with the kind of reflective detachment that marked the final days of his life, he might have distinguished between the hard-core trouble-makers and the more circumspect Negroes, who were treading carefully the free ways now open to them. In his single-minded view of the situation all Negroes were alike - dangerous when given too much freedom and far too dangerous to be allowed to carry arms.

Longley and another Evergreen youth, named Johnson McKowen, decided to do something about it. Together, armed with six-shooters, they rode about the county looking for Negroes to disarm. If there were two or three Negroes together and all of them armed, they rode clear. Usually, it was the lone Negro, unprotected by friends, who became their quarry and victim. Doubtless the impulse in these highway misadventures was bravado rather than perverted civic conscience. Barely did anything exciting happen around Evergreen and lynchings in various parts of the county had lost their sensationalism. At the age of 16, standing six feet tall and with a six-shooter never intended to be confined in its targets to cans and rocks, Longley felt a compulsive desire to assert himself. He did so on the Camino Real road just outside Evergreen.

One afternoon a Negro appeared on horseback, riding up and down, shouting insults against white men. Among those whose names he spat out was Campbell Longley. Possibly he had been drinking and did not know exactly what he was shouting.

When he saw Campbell Longley's son riding toward him, the Negro raised his rifle and fired, but as he was pitching in the saddle it was impossible to aim accurately and the shot went wide. Longley's answering shot was on target. The fellow dropped from his horse with a bullet through his brain. Longley dragged the man's body several hundred yards into a wood and left it in a ditch, covered with sand. Then he stripped the saddle and bridle and hid them in the wood. Longley congratulated himself on doing what he had just done, unaided. He hadn't needed McKowen's help. Any time he wished, he could take on an adversary alone. Already, he had the lone killer's instinct.

For a while, the two continued their partnership, breaking in mustangs and Arab-Barb short horses to ride in local races. Lexington, north of Giddings, was a lively place for race meetings. On one occasion when Longley and McKowen arrived there to enter one of their horses for a race they found that whites were outnumbered by Negroes and a confrontation seemed likely. The Negroes looked suspiciously at the two youths. Fearing they might be recognised as having disarmed their friends, Longley and McKowen decided that discretion was the better part of valour and withdrew from the race. They reckoned that even if they won there was no chance of being able to collect the prize money. Soon after arriving back in Evergreen they heard that Negroes from Lexington were celebrating the flight of 'them white boys' past Yegua Creek. Their flight had earned them a reputation for cowardice.

This was more than they could stomach. If anyone laughed at them he would have to answer for it. Goaded by what they heard from someone who had been in Lexington and ridden back to Evergreen not long after they had left, Longley and McKowen retraced their earlier journey. It was getting dark when they arrived and a carnival atmosphere was building up in the village. People were singing and dancing jigs in the streets. There was much drinking and a great deal of merriment.

Longley and McKowen spotted the Negroes they had seen earlier in the day. They were grouped together, dancing, and had not noticed their arrival. McKowen must have lost his nerve at the last moment, for he remained some distance away, content to watch as Longley in a state of excitement and bravado, spurred his horse and charged into the group, firing his six-shooter. Two Negroes fell dead instantly and one or two others were injured in the fusillade. Their maddened companions tried to drag him from the saddle but in the panic and confusion he managed to control his terrified horse and ride away, without a scratch. The carnage was all over in under a minute. Longley had no concern for the consequences. Apparently, he did not expect the forces of law to be marshalled to capture him. There was little law in this part of Texas and he was sure that most people in the county - most white people, that is - would condone what he had done.

There was no question of his going into hiding and becoming an outlaw. On the farm he continued to chop cotton and in his spare time he trained horses for races. The races were important because the prize money enabled him to buy another six-shooter and the ammunition he needed for target practice.

By the time he was seventeen he had a number of accomplishments. He was an excellent marksman; he could ride a horse well, be it a Morgan, Quarter Horse or Pinto; he knew how to work on a farm, cut cotton and plough a straight furrow. He also had a taste for liquor, bourbon or rye, though he was partial to Cobblers (whisky or wine mixed with fruit juice). On the farm, to slake his thirst, he usually carried a corked bottle of rye. On trips to Houston or some other place where most saloons were restricted to warm beer, gin, brandy and rum, he would do his best to find a bottle of Irish or Scotch whisky.

When he had been drinking, the dividing line between bravery and bravado, or between self-assertion and reckless exhibitionism, did not exist. He was a law unto himself and would brook no argument. It did not take long for his reputation to range far beyond the boundaries of Washington County.* His temper could flare up like a flash storm. A popular story, no doubt apochryphal, described in later years what happened when a Negro porter on the Houston and Texas Central railroad asked a passen-

* Absorbed by Lee County in 1874

ger not to stick his feet across the gangway. Every time he came along the gangway, the same boots obstructed him. Finally, the porter lost patience and kicked the passenger's feet out of the way. When he was informed by the conductor that the passenger was Bill Longley he ran to the rear platform and jumped off the train!

In the summer of 1867 a one-ring circus came to Evergreen. There were several of these travelling circuses in the West. Usually they had a few lions and elephants and one or two clowns. Travelling was far from easy and the two-horse wagons were often bogged down in mud. Farmers were hired to haul the equipment. When Longley and his companions tried to gain admittance to the circus in Evergreen, an attendant noticed they had been drinking and tried to turn them away. They shoved him out of the way, strolled inside and instead of going to the seats, strode into the ring and at gun-point forced the clowns to dance an Irish jig, then a 'back step'. When the dancers slackened, shots were fired at their feet and there was a stampede for the exit. In the panic the tent was torn down. One of the audience, Will Grant, reporting the incident in *Frontier Native*, said that the show was broken up and everyone scattered. He was so terrified that not until he reached home did he realise he had left behind his small sister.

Justice James Brady, of Bastrop County, was incensed.

He wrote to the civil board of 5th Military District of Texas, describing what had happened at the circus, 23 miles east of Bastrop:

> 'Four men, supported by a body of armed men, entered the circus, drove the deputy sheriff away and robbed the freedmen of their pistols and money. Two men named John Wilson* and Long (sic) appeared to be the leaders of the gang. One boasted that they shot Paul Brice a freedman. Wilson is a citizen of Burleson County and two years since murdered a freedman at Bastrop, named Record, for which crime he has never been arrested.'

Two days before the circus rumpus Justice Brady reported that two white men (one of them Longley) and a freedman named Cook went to Brice's house, ten miles from Bastrop, shot him and drove off his horses. The Justice of the Peace was getting more

* Longley's brother-in-law

alarmed about the activities of Longley's band and on 11th February was again in contact with the civil board, declaring that a band of armed men, headed by Wilson and Longley, were murdering, robbing and ravishing coloured people in that section of the state, the gang being principally citizens of Burleson County. He asked for military assistance to enforce the laws.

On 30th March, Joseph Jung, sheriff of Bastrop County, heard from the sheriff of Liano County, Charles Wagner, that Wilson and Longley were about 70 miles from Liano, about to start a cattle drive. The Liano sheriff requested information about what reward money was offered for the arrest of the desperados and where they were to be delivered. Nothing came of this information. Perhaps Sheriff Wagner delayed too long while waiting for precise details of the reward.

At home Campbell Longley's authority was weakening. His wife had relied on his religious strength of mind to keep their eldest son in check. She was worried about the stories she heard of his riotous adventures, though it is not known whether the killings of three Negroes were ascribed to him in the Longley household. It was clear to the head of the family that the boy was bent on going his own way and was not bound by the conventions and religious ethics laid down in his boyhood. Campbell Longley prayed for guidance, but had to admit that the course of his son's life was getting beyond his control. The degree of guidance or authority exercised by Billy's mother cannot be determined. It must have been slight, for in later years in his letters to newspapers and in his interviews with reporters, he made no special references to her. Nor is it known if she shared wholeheartedly her husband's disciplined religious life, which today would suggest some bigotry or at best, excessive high-mindedness.

Sarah Ann Longley died on 14 April, 1890. Campbell Longley married again, a young wife, who found she had little in common with him but long after their separation could claim to be the 'oldest' widow of a man who had fought in the Texas war of independence.

Various strains, religious, political and social, must have worked sub-consciously on Bill Longley's mind. His education had been fragmentary, work on the farm sometimes superseding classes. He had grown up close to the arbitary violence of lynchings, commonplace during the war. His father's Unionist principles were not shared by the families of most of his friends and the religious observations of his home life were difficult to relate to what he saw and experienced outside. He was born into a community without any cultural traditions, except what some of the settlers, many of them German migrants, had brought with them but had not successfully transplanted in the heated atmosphere of a state still unsure of its identity and destiny. To all this has to be added the 'frontier spirit' divorced from most of the civilising influences of the east, which to him was an unknown world. The race was not only for the swift, but for the toughest and the hardest.

In many ways Longley had outgrown his family life. He was physically stronger than his father, restless and eager to assert himself. His father was respected for his support of Houston in wresting Texas from the Mexicans, but as a Unionist, not admired. Bill Longley did not care about being respected. He wanted to be admired. There were men and women in Washington County so demoralised by what was happening in Texas that, without qualm of conscience, they could admire a headstrong youth who openly boasted that he intended to kill Carpetbaggers and 'uppity' Negroes.

3

'Some killed for a grudge then some for a woman and some because they liked it' - Bill Longley

Whatever efforts were made by the military authorities to enforce the rights of freedmen according to the laws of Congress, after the civil war principle and practice were often in violent conflict. Time was needed, several generations, in fact, to obliterate the vestiges of slavery. Unionist radicals, however, were in a hurry and were determined to enforce on Texas what was being forced on other conquered states. This is where Texas differed from other Confederate states. The war had been waged in excess, elsewhere. Only in border skirmishes had it made any physical impact on the territory. Farmland, towns and villages had not been devastated. The state had not been left, as had Georgia, ravaged by sword and fire. Its wounds, to many Texans, were being inflicted in the aftermath and in a sense a new war was being fought, between the old civil authorities and the military command. Texans could not consider themselves 'conquered'.

The Longley family, in spite of its Unionist leanings, had not questioned the right of landowners to own slaves. Now they were witnessing the consequences of imposing a new order on conservative traditions. In the general store at Evergreen and the shack that served as a saloon, stories were told about what was happening throughout the state as Negro troops became responsible in many districts for the enforcement of law.

At Victoria (first cattle capital of the west and one of the first three towns incorporated by the Republic of Texas) Negro troops took over the jail, freed two Negroes convicted of horse stealing and hanged a white man awaiting trial accused of killing a Negro.

A Negro in Bosque County, charged with raping a white woman, was released by order of a Bureau agent who threatened the Sheriff with trial by a military commission if he refused to comply.

Against this background freedmen were being murdered by enraged secessionists, to such an extent that in a report of inspection of the Freedmen's Bureau affairs in Texas, General E. M. Gregory, who had organised the Bureau, declared that Negroes and Union men were trembling for their lives and preparing to leave the state. Criminals responsible, he claimed, were always acquitted in the civil courts.

General Sheridan agreed that conditions in the state were so bad that the trial of a white man for murdering a Negro would be a farce. Casualties inflicted on white settlers in the border areas by Indians were far exceeded in the interior by outrages committed by whites on Negroes.

A farmer and landowner named Alfred Evans wrote to the state governor giving details of what happened to three negroes on their way to Austin County.* The letter recently came to light in the archives of the Texas State Library in Austin. Writing from Salado, Bell County, Evans set out what he called 'a truthful narrative of a most brutal murder and robbery, which was perpetrated about 8 miles below the town of Evergreen on Sunday evening, the 20th December'. Two of the freedmen, Green Evans and his brother, Pryor, who was about eighteen, were travelling from Bell County with an older black man named Ned, to visit relatives and friends. They had been Evans' slaves and it is likely they had assumed his surname as indication of ownership.

At Evergreen they were accosted by three white youths, who wanted to trade horses with Pryor. The Negro boy, having a good mount, refused and they carried on. A few miles beyond the village the youths caught up with them, disarmed them and at pistol-point, led them away, saying they were going to teach them some manners; a fair intimation that they were going to be rough-handled or worse. Realising what he was in for and seeing no reason why he should be treated in such a manner, Green broke away and ran. He did not get far. A bullet struck him in the back of his head and he fell dead. The other two scattered and eventu-

* See Appendix One

ally Pryor found shelter with two other freedmen in a house, where a young white man volunteered to go out and bury Green's body. The Negro had been left where he had been shot, his pockets turned out and his money, about four dollars and thirty cents, taken.

Two days later, when Pryor reached home and reported what had happened, Alfred Evans joined him, another brother, Burrill, and his step-father, to find the culprits. After some difficulty, they established that Longley had been one of the three and they persuaded a magistrate to issue a warrant for his arrest. A deputy sheriff went to Longley's home but returned to say he had gone into hiding. Evans was advised to get military support at Brenham. It was clear to him, however, that this would be futile as Longley's friends were probably keeping a look-out and a military search would be a waste of time. Furthermore, though people in the neighbourhood appeared to have no liking for Longley and his companions, believing that the sooner they were brought to justice the better it would be for the peace of the community, they were afraid to lift a finger against them.

Alfred Evans was clearly a decent-minded man who had not used his position as a slave-owner in the pre-war period to subvert his humanitarian principles. He was a gentle patriarch, but not in a condescending way, to the Negroes who had worked his land for him and after emancipation still felt responsibility toward them. He was infuriated by what Longley and the two other youths had done and appealed to the governor to offer a reward for their capture. He shuddered for the safety of society if they were left at large.

This, to Longley, was nothing more than an escapade. It is doubtful if he gave the murdered Negro much thought even after getting word that a warrant had been sworn out for his arrest. While it is in keeping with what is known of Longley's temperament and his accuracy with a six-shooter, to assume that he was the one who killed Green, it should not be assumed that he was the one who turned out the unfortunate Negro's pockets. The killing would have been enough for Longley without compounding the crime with robbery.

His attitude toward Negroes would today be termed pathological, bordering on insanity. In his mentally-disturbed condition he equated them with the social misery being endured by Texas in the reconstruction period. It was, in effect, the classic casebook prejudice, the singling out of a scapegoat to account for the ills and adversities that oppressed an independent way of life he had been brought up to believe was synonymous with Texas.

Certainly, there were numerous instances of Negroes abusing new-found freedom and of arrant disregard by some Negro troops of the civil rights of white people, but in Longley's dementia, frequently enflamed by whisky, the Negro race itself represented the evils brandished by his father's biblical fulminations.

While he could denegrate Negroes with the moral support of a sizeable section of the county's population, he could also use them to boost his ego. A youth such as Bill Longley, hero-worshipped by callow juveniles in Evergreen and grudgingly admired by their elders for his physique, handsome features and derring-do, needed to reassure himself that he was capable of defeating sworn or imagined enemies. Any challenge to his self-esteem was an attack to be resisted and crushed. There were times when he would go out of his way to prompt a challenge as if to demonstrate, if only to himself, his ability to overcome it and go his own way. He could work well on the land, industriously and conscientiously. Given a more settled disposition, he would have made a successful farmer.

Reacting querulously to the conditions of his time and against a strict parental upbringing, he lapsed at an early age into waywardness which, combined with a psychotic attitude toward Negroes, led to a murderous trail of lawlessness and, in another context, extraordinary adventure.

He fed on his notoriety like a boe-weevil in the cotton crop.

Aware of his reputation, he was not at all times secure within it emotionally and felt the need to boast of his exploits, especially to newspapermen who, for a time, had free and easy access to him when he was in jail awaiting trial. It was in these interviews and in his long, rambling letters to editors that he revealed the nature of an outlaw overwhelmed by vanity, mistakenly interpreted by unwary observers as precocious innocence.

There was too much guile in Longley, too much assertiveness and braggadocio to make sense of any view of him as a headstrong youth who mistook recklessness for manliness and recognised too late the error of his ways. Even confessions of his crimes smack of self-conscious postures, as if seeking the admiration of those who had condemned him.

A few months after the shooting of a Negro on the Camino Real, three Negroes, two of them mulattoes, tethered their horses in Evergreen and went into Stockton's Inn. Like other such inns or saloons in remote, rural areas, it was hardly anything more than a not-so-glorified shed with an earth floor, a place, not of ease and comfort, but for slaking the thirst or getting drunk when there was nothing better to do. When the three men, strangers to the district, returned to the hitching rail one of them was heard to call out that Evergreen was a dangerous place for coloured people. If that were so, he shouted in the general direction of bystanders, let anyone try to molest them and they would regret it! Longley was not within earshot but someone hurried to him and told him that some 'goddam Niggers' were looking for trouble and were not scared of it. It was enough to set Longley's blood boiling. Joined by two companions, he ran to the inn and arrived just as the Negroes were riding away.

'Come on,' Longley urged, 'let's get our horses and follow them.'

They caught up with the party eight miles away, in Burleson County. Longley's intention, he afterwards claimed, was to force them to abandon their weapons and send them on their way. When he ordered them to drop their guns, one of the Negroes fired his pistol at him, but the shot went wide. Longley's shot, from his .44, pitched the Negro from his saddle. It looked as if a gunfight were about to start, at point-blank range. But sensing the danger they were in, the other two Negroes galloped off. Longley and his companions decided not to give chase. They were satisfied with killing one man.

'I guess they won't come around these parts again,' Longley said, with the cool detachment he was to demonstrate time and again in such situations, unmoved by the sight of a dead man lying in the grass at his feet.

He was wrong about the man's friends not returning. They came back the next day, with a large number of other Negroes, to collect the body of their companion and bury him. They did not, however, try to seek Longley out, fearing retribution from all the whites in Evergreen if they began a rumpus.

Even so, law officers in the county were worried. They had become increasingly aware of Longley's violence. At first it had been unpredictable. Now it was only too predictable. They were under pressure from the military authorities to halt the spate of killings in South East Texas and to deal forcefully with anyone who might be stimulating local genocide. Two weeks after this particular killing, the deputy sheriff of Washington County rode with a posse to Evergreen to arrest Longley. Accompanying them were the two Negroes who had ridden away after the sudden attack on them. Tightly-knit communities such as Evergreen had their bush telegraphs. It was virtually impossible for a strongly-armed posse to ride from one part of the county to another without word preceding it. Longley was warned before the posse were even in sight of Evergreen. He had time to saddle his horse, pack a few provisions and disappear into the scrub oak to the west before the deputy sheriff and his men reached the Longley farm.

The posse knew it was useless to follow him there. It would be difficult, if not impossible, to pick up his trail. There were hundreds of places in the scrub where a man could hide for days. All the deputy could do was warn Longley's parents that a watch would be kept on the farm and their son would be arrested and charged with murder as soon as he returned. Grief and shame had come to one of the most respected families in the county. To all intents and purposes, Bill Longley was now an outlaw. It would take more than his father's standing in the community to save him from the due process of law if he were caught. Nor would it do much good for the Longley's to plead that, at seventeen, he was still a boy. He had grown to six feet and looked two or three years older, strong enough to subdue most men his height. Furthermore, he showed every sign of being able to take care of himself. Bill Longley was too shrewd to hide out in the scrub for a couple of days and then return to the farm. He knew a guard would be posted, looking out for his return. He pushed on through the scrubland, roaming through several counties far beyond Evergreen. There is no record of his exact movements, but his trail can be picked up later at Karnes County, where he found work helping to look after the stock of a farmer, John Reagan. Until this point he had often gone out of his way to find trouble, either for the sake of excitement or in drunken rages. This time he rode straight into it.

Range wars had broken out and there were feuds between cattle families. Some of these feuds had the intensity and retributive force of medieval family feuds in Europe. A process of elimination usually determined who won. Strangers were immediately under suspicion in case they had been hired as gunmen and were seeking advantage under the guise of ordinary farmworkers and cattlemen.

After a few days at work on the land and tending the stock, Longley became friendly with a man named Charlie Taylor, who was on the Federal 'wanted' list for various crimes. Physically, the two had much in common.

Both were tall, dark and lean. This no doubt explains why Longley, riding through Yorktown, was ordered to halt by troopers mistaking him for Taylor.

Longley's impulse was to turn and make a dash on his horse. A dozen mounted troopers went after him. Some of them fired at him from the saddle, but to hit any kind of target from a galloping horse depended more on luck than judgement. The troopers must have known this and hoped the sound of rifle fire would cause the pursued rider to stop. Longley's response was to turn in his saddle and fire five shots from his six-shooter, all of them wild. Two or three miles beyond the town he was well ahead and out of range of the troopers' Spencer rifles and .56-50 tapered shells. One of the pursuers, however, a sergeant in charge of the sixth Ohio Regiment detachment, had a fast horse and after six miles, managed to overtake him. One bullet was left in the chamber of Longley's pistol. As the sergeant drew alongside, ready to force him off his horse with the barrel of his rifle, Longley rammed his pistol into the sergeant's midriff. The pistol hammer caught in the soldier's jacket. As Longley pulled it back, the hammer was released and the pistol discharged. The sergeant fell dead from his horse. It cannot be judged for certain whether Longley intended to kill the soldier or merely to frighten him away by ramming the pistol against his body, the shot occurring accidentally. All that is known is that he left him there for the oncoming troopers and made good his escape.

It was now impossible for him to return to Karnes County, even to collect his belongings. For a while he was undecided whether

William Preston Longley. 'Wild Bill'.

to press on in the hope of finding another job, or return to Evergreen. It was likely, he decided, that a watch on the farm had been withdrawn and if he were careful he could get to the farm house without being observed. His expectation was correct. After dark, he was reunited with his family. His parents were happy to see him, but worried in case law officers should make another periodic visit. The military government, he was told, had offered a thousand dollars reward for his capture. One can be sure that instead of alarming Longley, the reward excited him. It confirmed his self-importance and, in a bizarre way, acknowledged that he was a force to be reckoned with beyond the confines of his small home community. It was the first time he had been 'evaluated' and it must have given him a perverted satisfaction.

In the circumstances, Campbell Longley realised that a lecture on civil obedience and a reminder of living according to the Christian virtues could have no bearing on the situation. At the same time he did not have the mind to urge his son to give himself up and rely on the mercy of the court. Several years' hard labour was the least he could expect now that the military authorities were cracking down on all killers, irrespective of whether they had killed whites or Negroes. The reward notice troubled Campbell Longley. While the family could count on the goodwill of most people in Evergreen, there were some for whom the temptation of one thousand dollars would override any respect they felt for the Longley's. The longer Bill stayed, the greater the danger. There was only one course open to him - to leave the county, to get far away and try to settle down to what Campbell Longley described as 'a God-fearing, upright life' where he was not known.

The visit lasted one night. In the morning, provided with money and food, the young outlaw was on his way again. His parents agreed that when possible, he could return on short visits, provided he did not approach the farm until after dark and did not try to renew his friendships in the community. This time he headed north-east into the counties of Marion, Cass and Bowie, where Cullen Baker's outlaw gang operated and had so far managed to elude the Federal authorities, mainly through Baker's knowledge of the swamplands and forests.

Longley decided to get out of Texas entirely, judging that no part of the state was safe for him. He crossed the border into

Arkansas, where Baker's gang also roamed in the counties of Miller and Lafitte. Here he could get work as a cow hand. Fate intervened. Before he was able to find employment he met a renegade named Tom Johnson and they struck up a friendship. Johnson, glad to have company, invited him to spend a night in his log cabin in the woods. Longley was tired after his long journey and needed a few days' rest. He agreed and learning that Johnson was also on the wanted list, knew he had nothing to fear from him. In the cabin they brewed coffee, ate a meal of pinto beans and sourdough biscuits and turned in for the night. Soon after midnight they were roused suddenly by half a dozen men who came bursting in and pulled them from their beds. Too dazed from sleep and the unexpected intrusion, Longley and Johnson were not able to put up any resistance. Their pistols were out of reach and hardly before they knew what was happening, they were brusquely dragged outside.

'That's him!' Longley heard one of them shout, referring to Johnson. 'That's the horse thief.'

So it was Johnson they wanted. He had told him he was on the wanted list, but not for horse-stealing, which was regarded as a grave offence; as bad as murder where frontier justice was concerned. Longley pleaded that he had nothing to do with it, that he did not know Johnson and was only spending the night there. His plea was ignored. If he was with a horse thief, it meant he must be a horse thief too.

These men were not law officers. They were vigilantes and that meant one thing; not an arrest and trial before a jury, but a lynching. Struggling and kicking, the two youths were dragged to an oak tree and with their hands tied behind their backs, they were set on their horses. Two ropes were slung over a branch and nooses placed around their necks. There was no chance of escape. Everything had happened so quickly that Longley found it difficult to convince himself he was not having a nightmare. Johnson seemed resigned to his fate. Longley cursed his ill-luck. Normally, he would have slept rough, in the woods. A chance meeting had put him in this position. The rope around his neck had not been put there by those who had been searching for him around Evergreen. He was simply a victim of circumstance.

The vigilantes did not waste time inviting last words or prayers. As soon as the ropes were in position they swatted the two horses and the men's legs struggled for the ground they could not reach. They were left dangling. But for a thousand-to-one chance this narrative would have come to an abrupt end - the end of Bill Longley's life. The rope around his neck did not slip. The knot caught under his ear. This, but for another thousand-to-one chance, or more, would not have saved him. He would have died of slow strangulation. As they rode away, one of the lynchers turned and emptied his six-shooter at the swaying bodies. One of the shots, as if guided by a guardian angel, split the rope just above Longley's head and another hit his money belt. His weight was sufficient to make the split rope snap. When this happened the hanging party were out of sight in the woods and did not see or hear their victim crash to the ground, unconscious.

Somewhere in the woods, Johnson's thirteen year-old brother had heard the commotion. He had been in another cabin when he was wakened by the pistol shots. Reaching the site of the hanging, he clutched at his brother's legs, trying to raise him and relax the pressure of the rope. It was too late. Johnson's neck was broken and he was dead.

After a while, Longley regained consciousness. He was gasping and coughing. The boy cut the strand of rope from his neck and untied his hands. Together, they cut down Johnson's body and carried it some distance to a cabin where his parents lived. For a few days Longley remained in the woods and was given provisions by Johnson's distraught parents. He marvelled at his good fortune in surviving the lynching, but alone he was vulnerable. If he happened to run into the vigilantes again he would not be so fortunate. In a gang, he decided, there would be greater protection.

Baker's gang were notorious killers and robbers, but he had heard they never harmed Southerners and robbed only government trains and wagons. To some people Baker was a Western Robin Hood, to others with a greater sense of realism, a murderous braggart. It was inevitable in the prevailing social conditions and with so much resentment in former Confederate territories against military law, that outlaw bands attracted mindless popular support when they posed as defenders of Southern interests.

Baker was quick to appreciate the fact that common robbery and thuggery could be given a seal of unofficial approval while he voiced sympathy for the South and maintained a diehard attitude toward the Federal government. He was able to exploit the best, or worst, of two worlds. In his band were those who had no feelings whatever about the Union and the old Confederacy and cared only for the fruits of plunder.

There were those who mistakenly saw in Baker the mainspring of a guerilla war against the Union which might, in time, lead to a resurgence of Southern power and influence. Whatever means Baker used, justified their own ends. It was, therefore, a conglomerate force, disparate and yet united, that Longley joined once he had made contact through the outlaw world's communications system. He was surprised to find that Baker knew of him. Baker had heard too of the miraculous way he had survived the lynching. He was glad to have him join his band and explained that he was engaged in guerilla warfare against Negroes, Carpetbaggers and northern sympathisers. The south, he said, may have been defeated but it was only a setback and the cause had not been lost.

Longley was probably not too impressed by this specious argument. He had not come to join the band to fight for a political cause. His only interest for the present was finding protection to save his own skin before deciding where to go and what to do. There was double protection in belonging to Baker's band, for the gang was also helped to some extent by farmers and homesteaders who professed ignorance when troopers questioned them about the gang's movements. Baker's popular reputation, based on altruistic motives, found favour with the Giddings Journal: 'It must be known that Cullen M. Baker would not rob the Southern people, but his principal glory and pleasure was in robbing the Government trains and in protecting the Southern people from the scalawags and swell-head Negroes.'

Little is known of Baker's early life. During the Civil War he fought on the Confederate side and afterwards formed his gang of Confederates to continue the war in his own way. If this was his true initial intention, it was soon overtaken by looting for its own sake and he showed no reluctance to enlist desperadoes without Southern persuasions.

It was not long before eastern Texans, demoralised by the effects of reconstruction and the repressive measures taken by the military authorities to overcome survivals of Southern allegiance, turned Baker into a folk-hero. They needed a homespun superhero to defy the Federal garrison at Boston in Bowie County. In their minds, the vainglorious Cullen Montgomery Baker was transformed into heroic proportions.

One story, widely believed, shows how much his credibility was exaggerated by those who were morally and spiritually depressed by Carpetbagger rule and military government. Armed with cap and ball pistols, he is said to have spurred on his mule and gone shouting and laughing to stampede twenty troopers who had followed his trail to the edge of a forest. The story goes that he chased them twenty miles to their Boston headquarters, the farmers along the road shouting encouragement: 'Give 'em hell, Cullen!' At Boston the troopers fled to the safety of houses and public buildings while 'the old swamp fox' shouted for them to come out and face him, fired bullets in the air, hurled rocks through the court house windows and proclaimed his doctrine for the suppression of 'Carpet-baggers, jayhawkers and yeller-bellies'. Then, quietly, he rode away.

This was the kind of fabricated tale that many people wanted to believe about Cullen Baker as a Texas freedom fighter, while they ignored the truth about him as a desperate outlaw. The story is more indicative of the public mind in east Texas at the time than of the man himself.

Federal troops were under orders to spare no effort, night and day, in tracking him down. In the north, a Unionist report described how a military unit, after several days, picked up his trail through a cornfield and surrounded a thicket where he was sleeping. Baker heard them creeping toward him and snatching his pistols, shot three of them dead before getting away.

Pulp fiction writers and journalists latched on to such reports and popular legends, weaving them into colourful and highly inflated accounts of his exploits. Little or no care was taken to distinguish between fact and fancy. So persuasive was the legend that a Northern newspaper, castigating the authorities in the South for failing to capture him, declared 'that this lone rebel would dare to ride into Federal headquarters at Natchitoches, Louisiana, alone and horse-whip the General in command there, is preposterous'. It was certainly preposterous, though not in the way the paper meant. The general in command at Natchitoches said it was news to him. Baker had never come there looking for trouble with a horse-whip.

This and other press reports, however, worried the authorities in Washington. Baker was a menace, not only as an outlaw but as a popular hero, whose description of a typical Carpetbagger struck a responsive chord in the hearts of Texans:

> 'A man who has no stock in the country beyond his satchel and yet by the grace of reconstruction, he rules a black crook convention. He lacks guts, red blood, starch in his back and a grain of brains.'

Troop reinforcements were sent to eastern Texas to assist in efforts to capture him. For a week operations were intensified. But Baker was elusive and disappeared with his gang into the swamps. Not all his men were unswerving in their loyalty to him. Several could not stand the pressure of being hunted constantly by troopers and they returned to their homes in Arkansas. Baker was glad to have Longley to help fill the gaps. In the forests they planned raids on wagon supplies but in spite of their dexterity with Dance and Colt revolvers the story of their two-man attack on a well-armed Federal wagon supply train defies belief.

Emerging from the woods, they were said to have attacked the quartermaster's wagon, guarded by four troopers. Baker 'shot the wagon driver and forced the others to flee', and he and Longley then drove the wagon into the woods to loot it. The outraged commandant at Jefferson promptly offered a reward of one thousand dollars for Baker, dead or alive. It is more likely that only a single wagon was involved and that Baker had much greater assistance than one man.

Late in the spring of 1868, the Baker gang captured a number of vigilantes who were helping the military search. While they were trying to decide what to do with them, one man began talking about two horse-thieves he had helped to hang. Longley did not recognise him. In the darkness of the woods he had not seen clearly the faces of the hanging party. But he had no doubt that the prisoner was referring to that incident. What was intended as a boast by the nervous captive was, in effect, a fatal confession. Longley, who had been serving Baker well, asked if he could deal himself with this particular prisoner. Baker agreed.

The luckless vigilante, now aware that Johnson's companion had survived the hanging, was bound and taken to the same oak tree close to Johnson's cabin and hanged the way Longley had been strung up. As a *coup de grace*, Longley fired six shots into his body, 'just to make sure,' he said later, taking care that none of the shots creased the rope.

At this time the price on Baker's head was far greater than that on Longley's. In Austin, General J. J. Reynolds was determined to capture him and was confident that a reward of one thousand dollars would have the desired result. Longley realised that with Federal troops and vigilantes forcing them to hide in the swamps for days at a time, his safety within the gang was by no means guaranteed. In fact, his position was far more precarious. So far, they had made skillful use of Baker's knowledge of the woods and swamps. As more troops and vigilantes poured into the area, their chances of evading capture or death in a gun-fight receded rapidly. There had been several narrow escapes, too close for comfort.

There is no record of what the Baker gang did with the vigilantes they captured. Possibly, they met a fate similar to that of their companion, to whom Longley had administered his own form of poetic justice. To have released them, even miles from their base and without their horses and guns, would have been a compassionate, but foolish risk.

Reward notices were being nailed to trees in several counties. Instead of being alarmed, Baker was exhilarated by the price on his head and the trouble he was causing the military authorities. New recruits were coming from Arkansas to join his band, which he now regarded as a small army, over which he gave himself the rank of captain. In future, he announced, he was to be called Captain Baker.

In this respect he was taking a lead from such Southern diehards as Jack English, Fred Bickerstaff and Robert Bob Lee. The latter had served as a cavalry captain with Nate Forrest's rebel riders. All of them were carrying on a wild and vain campaign against the military authorities. The Civil War had left them with a strong fighting spirit they had no desire to sublimate. Furthermore, they grossly over-valued their own ideals.

Bickerstaff, from Sulphur Springs, had lofty social ideals and a highly strung temperament. He, too, was reputed to have captured and burned a military supply train, almost single-handed. Seeing that Federal forces were being organised to cover the areas where outlaw groups were operating, Bickerstaff suggested that his, Lee's and Baker's bands should combine. By themselves they were heavily outnumbered by Federal units. Together, they would be a formidable force and be in a better position to harass and disrupt the search parties. Baker's vanity was the stumbling block. Under the proposed command, he and Bickerstaff would be field leaders under the overall authority of Lee. What Bickerstaff had in mind was leading a popular uprising against the military government. Baker did not want to lose his own authority and independence. Nor could his imagination embrace a civil uprising. He had no ambition except to continue his raids and survive. Nothing came of Bickerstaff's wild and ambitious scheme which might possibly have succeeded. Baker survived for another year in the six counties he regarded as his territory - territory where, if he could 'take care of five per cent of the meanness, I'll have a lifetime job cut out for me'.

It must be conceded that Baker was a superb guerilla leader, wily, mobile and never trapped into doing what was expected of him. He knew how to make use of the terrain, where and for how long to remain hidden. After the seizure of his ablest lieutenants, Matt Kirby and Seth Rames, he was not enfeebled. His answer was to divide his raiders into small groups, one of them led by Longley, and to embark on a series of quick hit-and-run raids. The swamplands afforded excellent cover after an attack. The uncharted swamps and dense forests were as familiar to him as the canyons of New Mexico to Geronimo. Baker would allow his campfires to smoulder to lure his enemies and then, when they thought they were creeping up on them, ambush them from the rear.

For a time Longley enjoyed the excitement and Baker had no cause to regret putting him in command of a small group of raiders. Eventually, however, the excitement wore off. The pattern of making raids, snatching loot and disappearing into the swamplands or forests for several days while search parties passed by began to get tedious. It was time, he decided, to break away and strike out on his own. Baker did not try to prevent his going. He thanked him for his services and wished him well. His departure was accepted in good grace and proved timely. A few months later, on 6th January, Baker was shot and killed by a man named Joe Davis.

News of his death was at first disbelieved by his strongest admirers, who claimed that no one would ever get the better of 'the old swamp fox'. Because of his notoriety, which had grown to legendary proportions, the rifle with which he was shot took on a mystical quality. It became the prized possession of Davis's son, John T. Davis, and was kept in the family for sixty years until sold by deed to T. U. Taylor, Dean of the School of Engineering at the University of Texas and subsequently presented to the State Library at Austin, suitably inscribed. This, visitors are told, is the rifle with which Cullen Baker was shot in the brain.

Baker's death foreshadowed deadly retribution for other outlaws who had suggested an alliance to him. They had been living on borrowed time since he rejected the plan, their own bands being too small to withstand for long the forces assigned to tracking them down. Two months after Baker's death, Robert Bob Lee was killed in a Fannin County ambush and, in April, Bickerstaff was shot dead in Alvarado. All had one thousand dollar rewards on their heads, by Special Order No. 17, dated 27 August 1868.

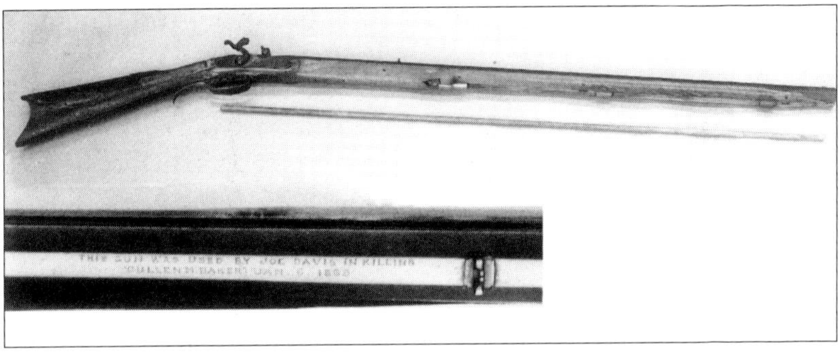

Above: The gun that was used by Joe Davis to kill Cullen Baker on January 6th, 1869. It is a Pennsylvania rifle made by H.E. Leman and was presented to the Texas State Library by T.U. Taylor in the 1890s.

4

'I may carry a gun a long time and never need it but when I do I'll need it mighty bad.' - Bill Longley.

Six months with Cullen Baker did much for Longley's self-sufficiency, resourcefulness and grit. His rawness had gone and his experience had toughened his sinews, but he suffered from homesickness. Thoughts of home beat on his mind like the intensity of the sun. In spite of the risks, he was determined to return to Evergreen - at least, he would be able to satisfy his curiosity by finding how the land lay.

Cautiously he reached home after dark and was dismayed to hear that in his absence the situation had worsened. Negroes were helping troops to track down law-breakers. Troops had been to the farm a number of times, often becoming belligerent when his parents told them they had no news of his whereabouts.

The family had been threatened, prized objects in the house had been wantonly destroyed. The troops, said his father, might reappear at any time to make further searches of the barns, lofts, cowpens and fields. If he were caught in Evergreen, the entire family would suffer. Longley's parents wanted him to go.

They had not been happy at his decision to wander about with his brother-in-law John Wilson, a hardened, pugnacious and wanton character. The two together unleased such a reign of terror in the district before they split company that extensive efforts were made by a company of the 11th Infantry to capture them and a military reward was offered for them, dead or alive.*

A Bastrop magistrate in fear of his own life at their hands, wrote to the military authorities at Austin describing the incident when Wilson and Longley caused havoc at the circus after forcing a sheriff to leave at 'double quick step'.

* See Appendix 2.

Evergreen then was in a parlous state, with little semblance of law and order. Rape, rapine and robbery. were commonplace. So was murder. And many of these crimes were attributed to Longley and Wilson, the latter being regarded by Brevet Captain J. Whitney, who applied for and received permission to offer the reward, as the worst of the pair. Whitney said in a message to his commanding officer that they should be shot on sight. They had openly boasted of killing some eighteen freedmen and they intended to kill more, threatening to take the county into their own hands and defy arrest. This 'territorial claim' was a gross exaggeration, for Longley and his brother-in-law knew they had to keep on the move to avoid capture, in spite of professed law-abiding people ready and willing to help them. Whitney did all he could to track them down, with patrols searching the woods and guarding roads. One search lasted six days and nights. He was confident of success, but did not achieve it. The desperadoes proved too elusive and too well informed, by farmers, of where the army searchers were operating. The reward was not enough to tempt anyone whose life thereafter, if one of them escaped, could not be guaranteed.

Whitney confessed that trying to find the two outlaws was like looking for the proverbial needle in the haystack. He needed secrecy in which to plan his searches, but the entire county, he complained, was aroused and there was no chance of his movements being undetected.

He paid tribute to Campbell Longley, 'a very good man' for trying to prevent his son from associating with Wilson. Wilson's father, known throughout the county as Dog Wilson, was another matter. Whitney could not prove it, but he suspected that Stephen Wilson encouraged his son's lawlessness, especially when he was drunk. Dog Wilson had caused a commotion at the circus by shouting that no Yankee or anyone else would take John Wilson except by shooting old Steve. In a drunken state, he announced at the circus that his son and Longley would soon be in town and then there would be hell. He was right. Shortly afterwards the pair arrived, robbed a Negro of his pistol and caused a rumpus at the circus.

For disorderly conduct and drunkenness, Dog Wilson was fined 100 dollars by Whitney and bound over in the sum of 1, 500 dollars to keep the peace.

Whitney regarded Longley and Wilson as being 'beyond the pale of civilisation'. He was prepared to visit Evergreen every month to bring them and other offenders to justice. His hopes, after laying a trap for them, were dashed when the uneasy partnership ended. Apart from their activities, which apparently included rape as well as murder, they had little in common. After a few months they agreed to go separate ways. Longley preferred to be alone and his involvement with a gang led by Ben Brown had, it seems, been through his brother-in-law's associations. It is not possible to trace accurately his movements after the split. In all probability he found work away from the county as a cotton-cutter, fence repairer and general farm handyman before his occasional return visits home became too unsettling for the family.

Campbell Longley had to think seriously about his son's future. Occasional visits were becoming too frequent. The authorities might get word of them and put the farmhouse under constant surveillance. The only hope of evading capture was to go far away, to Utah, where a relative was going with his family to live in a Mormon community. This was Charles M. Tyler, who in 1854 had married the Longley's eldest daughter, Mary Catherine. The family were taking with them a herd of cattle and were now in winter quarters on the Little Arkansas River, before continuing their long journey. Billy was told he could catch up with them. They would be delighted to take him with them and would help him to settle in Utah* whether or not he became a Mormon.

It sounded a good idea, At least in Utah there was scarcely a chance of the military authorities or bounty-hunters catching up with him. The best way to make ground and earn money for the journey was to team up with a cattle drive on either the Chisholm trail or Goodnight-Loving trail, The first branched out of Texas into New Mexico Territory and turned north along the Pecos River and then over it and the Canadian River into Colorado. He could leave the trail at Pueblo and move across country into Utah, or he could pick up the Chisholm trail, opened in 1867, north from Brownsville to Abilene, Kansas.

He decided to go southwest and from Gainesville try his luck with the first herd of cattle that came along. Ten miles from

*The mountain territory had been settled by Mormons for 21 years but was not then a state of the union.

Gainesville on the Elm Fork he encountered a large herd and sought out the trail boss, John Rector, from Beeville, Texas. Rector hired him at the customary rate of one dollar a day with food provided. He also gave him a fresh horse and told him he could turn his own horse in with the extra horses taken along for emergencies. Rector was probably making a hundred dollars a month. Longley did not care for the sullen look of him, but he needed the job, which promised to take him toward the route followed by his brother-in-law.

Rector, like other trail drivers, collected most of his steers from South Texas in the brush country where thousands of cattle had been left unbranded during the Civil War. In the north he could get about twenty dollars a head. Even those he bought in Texas did not cost more than six or seven dollars a head. He expected a sizeable profit. But life for the cowboys and the horse wranglers was hard and tiring. There was danger from Indians and rustlers, treacherous river crossings, dust storms, hail storms that could cause a herd to drift off trail, and rarely was it possible to cover more than ten or twelve miles a day. Calves born on the way had to be shot or sold to local farmers and days could be lost on cow-hunts, rounding up strays.

One of Longley's tasks was to ride up and down the herd, making sure none of the steers became separated, and to keep a look-out for Indians. In small groups, Indians were not interested in attacking an entire herd, they preferred quick, surprise raids from the rear, snatching one or two steers at a time. The greatest danger came from outlaw bands, demanding two or three dollars a head to let a herd pass unmolested. Failure to pay up meant a stampede.

Late one evening, following one of the sudden stampedes, Longley found himself alone with the cook when one of the cowboys rode up with the news that the herd was ten miles away. It was nearing nightfall and wolves were howling on the prairie. The chuck wagon was at a lonely spot and easy prey for Indians or outlaws. Prowling wolves ventured near but the three men did not want to use their guns to scare them away for fear of drawing the attention of Indians or outlaws. They took turns keeping watch through the night, Longley hardly slept at all. By night he preferred to be in the woods or a sodbuster's dug-out, not

Outlaws like Longley often 'hid' themselves on cattle drives such as this, as hired hands. This herd of Texas cattle was pictured at Dodge City, Kansas in 1878

exposed on the prairie. There were cheers and sighs of relief when the herd returned next day.

Tired of the cow-hunts and watching for marauders, Longley asked to stay with the chuck wagon and assist the cook. Rector agreed. The chuck wagon, an essential part of any cattle drive, was presumed to have been devised by Colonel Charles Goodnight, born in the year of the Alamo (1836) on a farm in Illinois and taken with his family ten years later to the plains of Texas, where he grew up among Longhorns and 'learned cow'. A four-shelved cabinet was built into the back of a chuck wagon with a tailgate that was lowered to serve as a working table. The four-wheeled wagon was loaded with pots and pans, tin plates and cups, iron forks, knives and spoons and dutch ovens for making sourdough biscuits. A large water barrel was slung on the side and under the wagon was a coonie, a cradle made from cowhide to hold firewood.

There was no shortage of meat. Apart from the herd itself, there was plenty of buffalo, wild turkey, possum and prairie chicken to hunt and add to the stew pot.

It was customary on the drives to offer passing strangers chuck from the wagon. But when two Negro soldiers rode up and asked for grub Longley told them they had nothing prepared. Grumbling, the soldiers rode on. One of the cowboys watched them and pointed out that they looked uneasy on their mounts. It seemed to him they had stolen the horses. He and another cowboy went after them.

An argument broke out and one of the cowboys was shot and killed. The other hastily rode back to camp and related what had happened. Longley and several others took off in pursuit but the two horsemen were far ahead and there was no time to follow their trail.

Using axes and knives, they dug a shallow grave for the dead cowboy but no one, Longley later recalled, bothered to say a prayer over it.

As the drive continued, the weather signs indicated an impending storm. Stake pins were hammered into the ground and the chuck wagon was chained to keep it secure. By midnight the camp was thrown into turmoil by a violent wind, which hurled anything movable over a wide area. The storm terrified the herd and caused another stampede. Only the chuck wagon was still in the same place when the storm died down. It took a whole day to retrieve the cattle and spare horses.

This disorder did nothing to help Rector's temper. He was known to have a violent disposition, likely to flare up at the slightest provocation. He was anxious to get his herd to one of the cattle towns in Kansas and the delays were infuriating him.

Longley found that Rector was unpopular with his men. All they could say in his favour was that unlike some of the trail bosses, he did not object to carrying a ten-gallon keg of whisky on the chuck wagon and chipped in to replenish the keg when it ran dry. This was because he was partial to whisky himself. At night he refused to stand guard at any time and usually drank himself to sleep on whisky.

When he was drunk in the daytime, he would ride into the herd, stampede the steers and curse his men if they did not round them up quickly.

Tempers were badly frayed on the drive to Kansas. Rector and one of the herders came to blows. Longley did not see the fight but when he heard about it, he said 'He'd better not run on to me that way'. One of the hands told Rector what Longley had said.

'Is it true what I hear you said?' Rector demanded, confronting Longley at the chuck wagon.

Longley stood his ground and said it was.

That was enough for Rector, his temper inflamed by whisky. He reached for his Colt. He was too slow. Longley beat him to the draw. Rector did not have time to get his pistol out of its holster. Longley's first shot struck him in the chest and five more shots followed. The first shot was enough. Firing five more suggests a maniacal hatred of Rector with Longley setting himself up as a figure of vengeance on behalf of the cow herders who loathed their boss.

According to Longley in one of his letters written from Giddings Jail; 'the boys were glad of it' but they advised him to give himself up at Fort Sill in Indian Territory and said they would testify on his behalf because it was self-defence.

They did not know that Longley was a wanted man. If he faced a trial, his record in Texas might come to light and he would be turned over to the military authorities. The only sensible thing to do was leave the herd. Another cowboy, Tom Davis, said he had had enough of cattle driving and wanted to go with him. The cook gave them, supplies of pinto beans, dried fruit, flour, sugar, salt and chewing tobacco from the chuck wagon and they set out for Wichita in Kansas, one of the towns on the Chisholm trail. It meant a long and dangerous ride through Indian country. Bands of Cheyenne and Sioux roamed the territory, but after crossing the Red and Washita Rivers without a sign of Indians, they felt safe. Caution gave way to carelessness. Late one evening, after crossing a stream, they killed two wild turkeys and roasted them over a camp fire. Until then, they had taken precautions, camping after dark to rest and then moving on before bedding down for the night in case they had been seen making camp. This time they did not bother to repeat the procedure. Their horses were tired and there appeared to be no marauding Indians in the area. After the turkey meal, they settled down beside the camp fire and allowed it to smoulder as they relaxed. Davis, who was about Longley's age, nineteen, looked up at the clear, starry sky and said it was good to live out in the open.

'Not in open Indian territory,' Longley said.

'Oh, we're fine here,' said Davis, who began telling amusing stories.

Longley half-listened, but his mind was concentrating on a wolf's howl in the distance.

'I'm not so sure that's a wolf,' he said.

'There are plenty of wolves around here,' Davis said.

'Could be an Indian call,' Longley suggested. 'Maybe we should move out.'

'It's too dark,' Davis said. 'We're O.K. here. There's nothing to be scared of.'

Soon Davis was asleep but Longley stayed awake. He was uneasy. Around two o'clock he was still wide awake and noticed his horse turn suddenly, as if startled by something. Raising his head from his saddle, which served as a pillow, he saw a figure creeping toward his horse. The horse tugged at its tether. Quickly, an Indian ran forward and slashed at the rope with a knife. Longley saw the flash of the blade in the moonlight. The next moment Longley was on his knees, his six-shooter in his hand, but he did not want to fire and risk hitting his horse. The Indian saw him, dropped his knife and fired a gun. The shot whistled past and then other Indians appeared from a cluster of rocks, firing arrows. Davis was roused and grabbed his gun to fire at them. The Indian who was trying to steal the horse appeared to be the only one with a gun. The others, four of them, had only bows and arrows and presumably knives.

'Rush 'em!' Longley shouted, as arrows struck the ground a few feet from them.

Before the raiders had time to put more arrows to their bows, Longley and Davis were on them, firing their pistols. One of the Indians fell dead. The others turned and ran, disappearing among the rocks and bushes.

Returning to saddle their horses and get as far away as possible before daylight, Longley and Davis found their blankets had been torn by arrows.

If Longley had not stayed awake, they would have been killed as they slept.

In the excitement, Davis had not noticed an arrow strike his arm; it was bleeding, but he was not badly hurt. Longley bandaged the wound and they rode on for ten miles, stopping to bed down again when the sun rose.

During the next two days they saw a party of Osage Indians, leading two horses which they had obviously stolen, who might have been their attackers. The Indians did not see them and there were no further incidents until the two travellers were riding down a pleasant valley toward Wichita. Buffalo (more accurately, bison) were grazing in the valley, but seemed restless. A cloud of dust appearing over the horizon indicated what was happening. Indians were evidently stampeding another part of the herd, driving the creatures over the edge of a ravine, which was a practical way of killing them. Taking cover below the bank of a deep creek, Longley and Davis waited and listened. The thunder of hooves became louder and louder until it seemed to be almost on top of them. Longley asked Davis to hold his horse while he climbed up the bank to peer over the plain. Buffalo were running in all directions, but there was no ravine to which any were being driven and none was being shot down. He noticed several riderless horses among them. Then he saw two bands of Indians. They were not hunting the buffalo, They were hunting one another. At a rough estimate there were 300 Cheyennes and 150 Osages.

Some had tied themselves to their horses and were hanging dead, bouncing against the sides of their mounts.

This, it seemed, was to ensure the dead did not fall into the enemy's hands to be mutilated.

Heavily outnumbered, the Osages were in full flight. Those who fell behind were surrounded by the Cheyennes and butchered with tomahawks.

Longley watched the gruesome battle as it continued for two miles down the creek.

'Then I thought the victorious Cheyennes would be certain to retrace their steps to see how many of the enemy might be found on the ground, so I thought we had better be on the move,' he wrote afterwards.

Riding hard, Longley and Davis followed the course of the Arkansas River and next day reached the place where Charlie Tyler and his family had wintered their cattle en route to Utah. The family had left a week before in two wagons. At the rate they were moving with a herd of cattle, Longley thought it would be easy to catch up with them in a couple of days. As they began following the trail they met two men who said they were searching for two Texans who had stolen a pair of buggy horses. There was a reward of two hundred dollars for the capture of the thieves. Longley and Davis said they would look out for them. Forty-five miles from Abilene they stopped at a grocery store run by a man named Cook, who had become friendly with Longley's brother-in-law during the winter lay-up. While they were talking inside the store, two men rode up. Davis, remaining outside with the horses, recognised them from the descriptions they had been given and called to Longley.

Longley came out and looked at the men's horses. He said nothing, but returned inside, had a stiff drink of whisky and crept round the back of the store, coming behind the men who were trying to trade the horses and were asking Davis what he would offer for them.

As soon as Longley levelled his six-shooter at the two would-be traders, Davis jumped on the step of the store, drew his pistol and called for them to drop theirs.

'I'll die first.' answered one, later identified as Joe McClellan, wanted for killing a deputy marshal in Abilene.

Longley responded to this provocation by shooting him from his horse. As he fell, McClellan fired an aimless shot, which struck and mortally wounded the storekeeper. The other horse-thief, named Shelley, raised his hands and surrendered. Longley had in mind killing him on the spot, but paused to consider whether the reward was 'dead or alive'. He decided not to risk losing the reward money if two dead men could not be identified. Rash and impetuous, Longley could also be coolly calculating. Efforts were made to tend the storekeeper, but he died after fifteen minutes. Longley and Davis then set out with their prisoner and the two horses, to deliver them to Abilene. It was the first time either Longley or Davis had been near the cattle town, then in its infancy but flowing with whisky and money. It was a prostitutes' and outlaws' paradise, with little semblance of law and order, and when the cowboys were on the loose after long and dry cattle drives, it was said that hell was now in session.

This was a few months before the townspeople petitioned for the right to elect city officials and the short, ill-fated law enforcement of Tom Smith, who was succeeded as marshal by James Butler Hickok.

Longley had no time to enjoy the rip-roaring pleasures of Abilene. All he wanted was the reward money and then to catch up with his brother-in-law. Not only was the hundred dollars reward paid; added to it was a sum contributed by some of the town's more stalwart citizens. The extra money gave Longley an idea. Instead of riding on to find his brother-in-law, he could travel more comfortably by train to Salt Lake City by way of Kansas City, Missouri, and Fort Leavenworth, where he could stop for a few days to look around. Davis decided that Abilene was as good a place as any to stay for a while and when his money ran out he could team up with another cattle outfit.

After selling his horse, Longley journeyed by rail to Leavenworth, but found there was little to do but go from one saloon to another. In one of them he fell into conversation with a farmer and mentioned that he came from Texas.

'You oughta be ashamed of it' came a voice from a nearby table. Longley turned and was met by a hostile grimace from a soldier.

'Ashamed of what?' Longley asked.

'All Texans are thieves,' said the soldier, backed up by his drinking companions.

'My father lives in Texas and he's an honest man,' retorted Longley.

'If I was from Texas I'd be damned ashamed of it and keep it to myself,' rasped the soldier. There was a roar of drunken approval from around him.

Longley advised him to 'go slow' but the soldier persisted with his taunts and shouted: 'In Texas every man's a thief and every woman's a whore!' They were his last words. Longley would take no more insults. A single shot from his Dance revolver ended the soldier's life.

Covering the other soldiers with his pistol, he backed to the saloon door and then ran in the darkness to his hotel to collect his saddlebags. Within a minute he had bundled together his few belongings and was dashing to the Missouri river to board a steam ferry. Luck was with him all the way. The ferry was leaving as he jumped on board and by the time the soldiers from the saloon reached the levee he was half way across the wide Missouri. Once on the other side of the river, he lost no time boarding a train bound for Omaha, Nebraska. In the early hours, the train pulled into St. Joseph, Missouri, and a conductor came down the aisle announcing that passengers going on to Omaha had to change trains. Wearily, Longley stepped from the coach

Merchants Hotel, Abilene, the scene of many shoot-outs and one of Longley's haunts

The Long Branch Saloon, Dodge City, Kansas. Longley spent many a wild night here.

straight into the arms of two law officers. As they seized him by the arms, a third arrived and removed his pistols.

'What's going on?' Longley protested.

'Just a little joke,' said one of the officers. 'We're taking you to a safe boarding house until we hear from Fort Leavenworth.'

Too late Longley realised how quickly telegraphed messages could overtake trains. A report of the saloon killing and a description of the killer had been telegraphed to the police and military authorities in St. Joseph and the officers had been sent to meet the next train from that side of the river.

If he had anticipated this he would have taken a horse and ridden into the hills.

Now he found himself locked in a brig, waiting for a troop of soldiers to return him to Leavenworth. For the next three weeks he was kept in close confinement in a Leavenworth guard house and passed the time whitling wood. Talking to his guards he learned from them that he was to be court-martialed and probably shot. This was highly unlikely as he was not a military prisoner, but he knew that one way or another he would be tried and hanged.

As the days went by he became friendly with a sergeant of the guard who admired the 'violin' he was shaping out of pine wood with his whittling knife.

'That's some piece of craftsmanship,' remarked the sergeant. 'Where'd you learn to do that?'

'Just picked it up,' Longley said. 'You can have it when I've finished it.'

Next day he finished the carving and gave the 'violin' to the sergeant as a gift. Now came his one and only chance. He still had some money, about fifty dollars, all he possessed.

'Fifty dollars, all I've got, if you'll let me get away from here,' he offered.

The sergeant could have pretended to agree, taken the money and kept him shut in the guard house, Instead, he proved amenable to the offer and facilitated the prisoner's escape. Exactly how, and how he covered up for himself afterwards, is not recorded. Within a short while Longley was free again and on his way by foot into open country. Though he was a stranger in the territory, he did not find it difficult to get help. Most people, he discovered, were hostile toward the soldiers and resented their presence. News of the saloon shooting had spread and the consensus was that the soldier had got what he deserved. None of the people to whom Longley turned for assistance in his escape considered turning him in. They gave him food, money and clothes.

By day he slept and by night he walked, until he reached Atchison, where he felt it was safe enough to board a train. By this time he had cut his shoulder-length hair and was wearing false whiskers. Even his own parents would not have recognised him. The description which had gone out over the telegraph wires bore little resemblance to the figure on his way to Cheyenne City in Wyoming Territory.

Rollins House: the Court House in Wyoming Territory.

5

'I may be a killer, I may be a murderer, but I never stole a horse.'

- Bill Longley.

Longley described Cheyenne in a letter to his parents as follows: 'If enough people here get down on a man they just take him out and string him up and later they have a big spree on the strength of it'.

It was a hard-bitten cattle town where cowboys from the Goodnight-Loving trail and the Western trail poured down their throats more potent concoctions than Arbuckle's coffee, and chewed tobacco with Calamity Jane (Martha Jane Canary), who had worked as a labourer on the Union Pacific railroad and drifted into Cheyenne the year it met the Central Pacific at Promontory Point, Utah.

Short of money, Longley toured the saloons to get into card games in the hope of making a few dollars. In one of these games he heard about a party of 130 men going to the Big Horn mountains on a mining expedition. Gold had been discovered and in spite of a Government decree, enforced by the military authorities, that civilians were to keep out of Sioux territory, there were plenty of prospectors willing to defy it and risk their lives in the search for gold.

Not all the soldiers stationed at forts in Wyoming were conscientious about their orders. Some were pleased to help the miners at a price, if only by turning a blind eye.

Longley made contact with the leader of the expedition, William Littlebury Kuykendall, who later became a judge. In 1917, Kuykendall wrote in his memoirs:

> 'Today thousands of people in the Black Hills are living and prospering in comfortable, happy homes.

> Beautiful towns are located in and around them.
>
> Churches and fine schools abound. Across the line in Wyoming in the very center of the last stand of the Sioux, the same conditions exist. There, ranchmen live in peace and comfort, without fear of an Indian foray. Livestock of all kinds graze unmolested where buffalow ranged and the Indian in war paint was monarch of all he surveyed.
>
> Amidst these quiet scenes stand the monuments placed to mark the spots on which the Fetterman and Custer massacres occurred. It is very doubtful if many of those enjoying all this splendid good fortune know or realise the exposure and danger passed through by those of us who sought to bring about such conditions or, knowing, ever stop to think of the many civilians as well as soldiers who gave their lives that they and their little ones might live without fear of the merciless savage.'

If the 'savage' indian was merciless it was in defence of an ancestral home, doomed five years later after the Indians' pyrrhic victory at the Little Big Horn.

At Fort Laramie, in January 1868, a Federal commission had been told by the chiefs of the Sioux and Cheyenne that Red Cloud would launch a major war, if necessary, to defend the sacred Black Hills and a subsequent treaty re-defined Sioux territory, stipulating that the lands of the North Platte, Black Hills and Big Horn mountains were barred to white settlements or occupation without consent of the tribes.

Like so many other treaties, it was fragile. There were not enough troops to keep out traders, speculators and prospectors. To the Indians, the Black Hills, covered by thick pine forests which made them appear black from the plains, were the sacred domain of the Great Spirit and the springs and pools (the Great Spirit's tears) were pure and full of healing powers.

An offer of sixteen million dollars by the government for the Black Hills was no inducement to the Indians. Their natural shrine was priceless, a symbol of their spiritual culture.

Crazy Horse, who later led the Sioux and Cheyenne against Custer's force at the Little Big Horn, expressed the tribal sense of values when he said 'One does not sell the earth upon which the people walk.'

Kuykendall, aged thirty-five when he led the miners' expedition into the Black Hills in May 1870, showed scant sensitivity toward this spiritual heritage.

In the winter of 1869-70 four men, including Kuykendall, met in Cheyenne to discuss ways of getting rid of the Sioux from the territory north of the North Platte River, where white men were not allowed to settle or even travel.

Many of the Indians were far from scrupulous in the way they observed the line of demarcation. The more headstrong looked on the land as a sanctuary from which to raid white territory and snatch cattle and horses. In a number of these forays several white men had been killed.

There was one sure method, the four conspirators agreed, to open up the land - a public announcement that gold had been discovered. A gold rush would soon override any claims the Indians had to the territory. A public meeting was called in McDaniel's Theatre the next night and it was crowded. Taking the chair, Kuykendall announced that the purpose of the meeting was to organize a Black Hills and Big Horn expedition.

Excitement swept through the theatre when he said that gold had been discovered there.

But an expedition, he maintained, had to be properly organized to guard against attacks by Indians. Small groups of prospectors going into the hills would soon be massacred. A large, well organized expedition, would stand an excellent chance of mining for gold.

There was unanimous agreement about this and he was made president of the organizing committee, with a Colonel Farrar as secretary.

Over the next few weeks letters poured in from potential prospectors from other territories and states, asking for details and permission to join. When a list was drawn up it contained the names of two thousand men. All were to be armed with repeating rifles and each man would have one thousand round of ammunition. Everyone was asked to bring enough supplies for six months.

The expedition was set and ready to move when President Grant issued an order prohibiting the expedition from entering the Black Hills, scheduled as its first objective.

A presidential order unnerved most of the expedition's members. They did not want to get into trouble with the government and military authorities, who would have the task of enforcing the order. All but 130 dropped out.

Judge Plesants was the Judge of District Court, De Witt County for forty years. To him credit is given for bringing many hardened criminals to trial.

Kuykendall decided to go ahead with those who were left. He made sure they were properly outfitted and divided them into two companies, with himself as commander.

This small-scale expedition came to the notice of Colonel King at Fort Russell. But instead of putting an outright ban on it, he issued a modified order, restricting the expedition's range. Kuykendall was instructed to sign an agreement that he would go no further than South Pass country.

Finally, on May 20, 1870, towing a six-pounder cannon presented by Major John Talbot, of Cheyenne, the expedition set out from Fort Russell. They did not need scouts to inform them that they were being closely watched, every mile, by the Sioux. The Indians followed at a distance, on both flanks. No doubt the sight of the cannon dissuaded them from attacking. Outside Camp Brown they broke away without having made any attempt to harass the expedition.

Most of the men in Kuykendall's party were middle-aged and looked to the expedition to provide them with enough gold to live comfortably in old age. Longley was the youngest by ten years. He knew nothing about gold prospecting, but was willing to learn and he enjoyed the thrill of the adventure. At night he did his share of guard duty when the wagons were placed in a circle, not so much as a protection against Indian attack as a means of keeping the cattle safe.

Small groups of Indians crept near, on foot or horseback, fired haphazardly at the wagons and fled when the fire was returned. In the daytime they kept well clear of the cannon's grapeshot.

'We travelled through a country that beggars description in beauty,' Longley recorded. 'We were now on the old California trail and were never at any time out of sight of a grave.' Nearly every grave had been desecrated by Indians. As the wind got up the miners noticed feathers flying in the air. Somewhere a wagon train had been attacked, its occupants killed and their feather beds ripped open and emptied. Scattering feathers from beds never failed to amuse the Indians.

When they reached St. Mary's ranch the miners were confronted by a grisly sight. The ranch, an old Overland Stage stand which for some years had been occupied by herdsmen, was now nothing more than a smoking ruin. Close by were the bodies of five men and two women, horribly mutilated. Their throats had been cut, their hands and lips cut off and they had been scalped.

When they saw that the two pregnant women's entrails had been ripped out, several of the miners were sick.

'I never slept a wink that night,' Longley recalled. 'It was a nightmare I could not shake from my mind.'

Signs indicated a party of about one hundred Indians. The massacre had occurred no more than a few hours earlier.

After burying the bodies, the miners camped near the smouldering ruins and next day travelled on into country teeming with antelope, buffalo and elk. The wildlife and scenic splendours did not diminish the shock of the mutilations they had witnessed. Longley wondered if it was wise to move further into Indian country.

'We've got the cannon,' a miner reminded him.

On the third day one of the party said he was going to look for some game.

'Better not go alone,' Kuykendall told him.

'It'll be all right,' the miner replied. 'I won't be long.'

By nightfall he had not returned and in the morning a search party was sent out. They found his body in a ravine, almost shot

Front Street, Dodge City, Kansas. Longley took no notice of the sign and had to be asked to surrender his gun!

to pieces. Evidently he had put up a fight. Around his body were thirty empty cartridge shells. The Indians had taken every shred of his clothing.

Five days later the expedition reached South Pass, a mining town, The miners there were glad to have their numerical strength increased.

Indian attacks had grown alarmingly and many miners and soldiers had been killed in sudden raids. Kuykendall did not want to delay. He was for pressing on, in spite of the danger.

While in camp on the Little Agie creek a guard, posted on a hill, shouted that there were plenty of elk moving about. Close inspection through binoculars brought the elk into focus and revealed them as Indians, about thirty of them.

Kuykendall ordered a cannon shell to be dropped among them. As the gun was wheeled round and the sunlight flashed on the casing, the Indians took fright and fled behind a hill. It was necessary to use the cannon.

'Even if we didn't have any shells, the cannon would scare 'em off,' said Kuykendall.

When the expedition reached Fort Brown, an officer warned against moving further north. He estimated there were at least one thousand Indians in the locality and it would be suicide to continue, even with the cannon. Still Kuykendall was undaunted and decided to ignore the dangers. Rough roads receded and gave way to sagebrush seven feet high, which had to be cut away for two hundred yards to get to the Big Wind River (later called Merritt's Crossing, after General Merritt, who led an expedition against Chief Joseph).

Provisions were taken across the river on a raft.

Near the Wood River, with the Big Horn mountains away to the right, the expedition was overtaken by two companies of the Second Cavalry, commanded by Lieutenant Whelan, who had orders to return the miners to Camp Stambaugh, near Miners' Delight.

Kuykendall inspected the orders and observed that they instructed the officer to turn the miners back if he found them in or moving in the direction of the Big Horn mountains. 'We're moving away from them,' he argued. 'We're on public domain, not on an Indian Reservation. If you try to stop us, the responsibility will rest on you.'

A conference was held and continued well into the night. It ended with another agreement for Kuykendall to sign, this time giving an assurance that his men would not go into the mountains.

Satisfied that he had performed his duty according to the letter, the officer and his company left in the morning and the expedition set up camp beside the river.

Eighty men were left in camp while the rest were divided into three groups to prospect the headwaters of the river.

Longley, in one of the groups, seems to have spent as much time appreciating the beauties of nature as prospecting for gold. Hot Sulphur Springs moved him to eloquence. Later, he described it as 'a place on earth which could have been called the sportsman's paradise.' Wildlife and fish were plentiful. He sat and watched the water boiling up in the centre of a bowl-shaped basin, close to a mountain range which was covered all year in snow.

The miners forgot their fear of Indian attack as they panned for gold and hunted blacktail deer and mountain sheep for their meat. On a sheep hunt Longley and a miner named Miller returned later in the day to the spot where they had hung up a sheep's carcass and found two young grizzly bears eating it. They shot and killed both grizzlies, but the death cries of one brought its mother crashing out of the woods, teeth barred.

'I thought my time had come, sure enough, 'Longley said. I started pumping lead from my Winchester at her. I thought if she got too close I would try my six shooters. I broke one of her fore legs with a shot, but Miller got a shell hung in his rifle and yelled to me to take care of her while he went up a tree.

'I kept pumping lead at the old bear and on she came until she was only a few yards away and still going strong, to all appearances. So I threw my rifle down and in another minute was sitting by the side of Miller several feet from the ground in the cedar tree.'

The wounded bear shook the tree and gnawed it, but after several pistol shots in her back, dragged herself away.

After what remained of the sheep had been taken to camp, other miners set out after the mother bear, which was found dead in a pool of water in a canyon. They skinned the 900 lb creature and divided the meat in camp.

'All hands had plenty of bear meat and it was very fine,' said Longley.

Again, the expedition moved on, deeper into forbidden territory. Near the Grey Bull River, which joined the Big Horn River in the foothills of the Big Horn mountains, they ran into a determined Indian resistance. Two miners were killed and another was badly wounded. A further attack occurred when the miners entered a canyon. Huge rocks were rolled down the slopes. One rock, weighing at least 500 lbs, dislodged a score of rocks and caused an avalanche. Several men were crushed by boulders and two wagons were damaged beyond repair. The canyon was eight miles long and every yard was a hazard. It was a running battle all the way.

Once they were out of the canyon and in a position to use the cannon, they were unmolested. Several miles from the canyon, they stopped to make camp and tend to the wounded.

That night a man put on guard fell asleep. In the morning a 'court martial' was ordered. In effect, it was a 'kangaroo' court of six of the ablest men in the party.

Kuykendall presided. At the start of the expedition he had made it clear that discipline was to be strict and punishment for any lapse severe. The expedition was organized on paramilitary lines.

Sentence of the 'court' was death by firing squad.

The wretched miner was taken blindfolded to the edge of a hastily-dug grave. Longley was one of the firing squad, which had six rifles, three of them loaded, the rest unloaded so no one would know whether he was an actual executioner. Three bullets struck the condemned man, who toppled into his grave.

Longley's terse account was : 'We buried him and travelled on and soon reached the Grey Bull River.'

At the river they were stopped by five companies of the Second Cavalry, commanded by Captain Gordad, with orders to get them to Camp Brown. Kuykendall admitted he had been given previous orders not to proceed further into Indian territory, but insisted it was only verbal advice without official authority, which had to be in writing.

This excuse did not impress Captain Gordad, who told him he could be court-martialed and shot for disobeying orders in such 'a dangerous and explosive part of the country', especially when

President Grant was trying to placate the Indians, not stir them into violence.

Kuykendall realised this was the end of the expedition. They were forced to return under military escort.

The expedition had been a failure. No gold had been found and several men had been killed.

'Thus ended the first expedition and effort to get the Sioux out of the country,' Kuykendall wrote in his memoirs.

> 'We had driven the entering wedge, however, which eventually accomplished it. The fever was on, resulting in about 150 men from Montana in 1872 invading the country where the Custer massacre occurred in 1876. Among them were many of my men. For 13 days they fought and whipped Sitting Bull's band but had to get out of the county as they could not prospect.'

Kuykendall seemed to want it both ways. In his memoirs he pleaded the case for getting the Sioux out of the territory and then blamed the Indians for breaking the treaty.

> 'We of that day in Wyoming knew the Indians had not observed it for a day and were breaking it at the time when we planned to get them out of the way.'

In 1879 he might have contemplated the words of Chief Joseph, of the Nez Perce, in an appeal to President Hayes to allow the survivors of his tribe to return to their former land

> 'I have asked some of the Great White chiefs where they get their authority to say to the Indian that he will stay in one place, while he sees white man going where they please. They cannot tell me.'

Or the words of Sitting Bull

> 'What treaty that the whites have kept has the red man broken? Not one. What treaty that the white man ever made with us have they kept? Not one. When I was a boy the Sioux owned the world Where are the warriors today? Who slew them? Where are our lands? Who owns them?'

Longley, like most of the men in the ill-fated summer expedition, had no social-political motive for joining it or any special awareness of the tragedy being enacted between the indigenous population and the newcomers.

He was after gold and adventure. Being without gold at the end of it, made it imperative for him to look for work. Kuykendall could offer him nothing, being more concerned with rebuking easterners for their condemnations of lawless whites for Indian massacres:

> 'These easterners, without knowing details, even said that the white men had no right to be in the country, that they had no business to attempt to redeem it from a wilderness and the savage conditions then existing. And this they said in fact of the fact that pioneers in many of the eastern and southern states had to and did do the same thing in settling their own states from the Atlantic Ocean west and it is more than probable that the ancestors of some of our latter-day sentimentalists were engaged in making what they considered good Indians just as our miners did.'

For all the dangers, Longley had enjoyed his excursion into Indian territory and would like to have gone into the Big Horn mountains.

Though he felt relatively safe from lawmen at Camp Brown, he prudently changed his name to Tom Jones. His aliases were always chosen at random, common-sounding names that made him seem fairly ordinary. Under escort to the camp he had struck up a friendship with some of the soldiers, who suggested that if he had trouble finding a job he could join the army as a teamster driving a six-mule Federal supply team between Camp Brown and Fort Bridger.

Many of the prospectors, adventurers and tramps were almost destitute, lacking even the possession of a horse or mule to return to the settlements of the Union Pacific railroad. Longley was in that category.

On June 22, at Camp Stambaugh, he performed one of the most extraordinary acts in his life. He had gone to northern parts of the mid-west to escape from the military authorities in Texas and the South-East. He knew that his name was on the military's wanted list. He had shot and killed at least two soldiers. It is likely, though, there were no records to prove that he shot down troopers while he was with Cullen Baker's raiders. There was, however, a military price on his head, yet in spite of this he enlisted under his own name as a private in the United States Cavalry and signed on for five years. He was assigned to B company.

It could be that he did not associate the army in that part of the country with the military authorities in Texas. To a Texan another state was another country. Possibly, he did not think that his enrolment would be recorded in Washington and checked against the army's wanted list (evidently it was *not* checked).

Even so, it is surprising that he should have enlisted under his own name when he had taken pains previously to disguise his identity, with aliases, no matter how far he was from Evergreen. He would not have had to prove his identity to enlist. The army had a large number of drifters, ruffians and wayward adventurers who regarded military service as nothing more than a job to keep body and soul together and would as soon spit at an officer as salute him or call him 'sir'. It is doubtful, however, if B company had more than one recruit wanted by the army for murdering soldiers.

Is it reasonable to suppose that Longley enjoyed the peril of being at close quarters to the army when, in other parts of the country, it was offering a reward for his capture? The irony must have occurred to him for he had a sharp mind and by this time had developed a taste for danger, which is often the indulgence of those who have failed to find reward or satisfaction in the ordinary routines of life.

By using his own name on enlistment - it can be seen today in the preserved muster rolls - he was 'pushing his luck' but his record went undetected.

He soon found that the army was not to his liking. One of his tasks was to take supply wagons to Fort Bridger and this meant constant exposure to Indian attacks. At Dry Sandy Creek a supply team was hit by 130 Indians, who wanted the army mules. One soldier was killed and several men were injured. The mules had to be written off the supply list. In less than two weeks Longley had had enough. On July 3 he deserted. Most of that day he rode, pausing only to rest his mule and in the evening, in what he described as 'a country that God forgot,' he stalked an antelope to provide him with meat. for the next few days. Over his camp fire he broiled antelope steak, without thinking of the smoke curling high over a ridge, visible for miles around. Later, his sleep by the smouldering fire was interrupted by the kick of a boot - army issue. Instinctively, he reached for his Colt, but it was in the hand of one of the soldiers who surrounded him.

His freedom had lasted for one day. Immediately his desertion had been notified, a reward for his capture had been set at thirty dollars. This was shared by the soldiers who apprehended him at Big Sandy, after they had returned him to Camp Stambaugh.

For more than a month he was kept in confinement and sometimes, during exercise periods, was forced to walk carrying a sandbag weighing one hundred pounds, and prodded by a bayonet when he stumbled.

On August 26 he was court-martialed and sentenced:

> 'To be confined at hard labour under charge of the guard for a period of two years, wearing a ball and chain weighing twenty-four pounds; to forfeit all pay and allowances during that period; and at the expiration of sentence to be returned to duty with his company.'

The proceedings, findings and sentence were approved and confirmed, the sentence to be 'duly executed at the post where the prisoner's company may be serving'.

Through the intervention of Lieutenant James N. Whelan, his enlisting officer, he served only three months of the sentence. Whelan, known to his men as a human and kindly officer, took pity on him and procured remittal by testifying to Longley's ignorance of the service.

For the next twelve months Longley adapted himself to army life and was put in small parties to hunt beef and game for the command. According to some reports, he worked a crooked deal with a quartermaster named Gregory to supplement his army pay of 75 dollars a month. The scheme was for the quartermaster to issue full rations of corn for the mules and for Longley to feed them half rations. Corn was two dollars a bushel. What was not fed to the mules could be sold to the miners who did their trading near the camp.

When an officer inspected a mule that had died from natural causes and not through being half-starved, Longley had it removed. The next night he dragged it back to the compound and reported that another mule had died. The same procedure was repeated and the official record showed that three mules had died. Longley took two of the best mules to a mining camp and sold them for 250 dollars each. When he returned he told the quartermaster he had sold them for a total of 350 dollars to some miners leaving for Helena City, Montana, and gave him half.

These lucrative diversions helped to make his official duties more bearable, but regimental discipline, slack by modern standards, did not suit him. He resented taking orders, and on June 8, 1872, he again deserted from Camp Stambaugh.

Somewhere on his desertion route he met a man named Tom Johnson, who had a plan for opening a saloon at Miners' Delight, not far from Camp Stambaugh. The miners there had nothing to do in their spare time except drink and gamble. A shack with a bar, Johnson explained, would be the next best thing to a small goldmine. He was looking for someone to invest in the stock and share the running of the saloon. Longley was not keen to stay in the area and risk being caught to face another court martial, which would mean three or four years' hard labour. On the other hand, the army would not expect him to stay in the vicinity and would probably concentrate their search for him to the Sweetwater Mountains and Green River City, further south.

The army pay he had saved he pooled with Johnson's savings to buy barrels of alcohol, two brands of whisky, one brand of wine, rum, tobacco and cigars which they hauled from Bryant, on the Union Pacific railroad, nearly one hundred miles to the mining camp.

'There was no law at all,' Longley wrote later, a surprising lamentation by one who had gone there to elude it. 'It was simply the rule of claw and tooth and the weakest went to the wall.'

He might have been describing any of the mining camps that sprang up in the mid-west wherever gold or silver was discovered. Such camps, rough and squalid, were usually shorn of the normal benefits of civilized living and characterized by their violence. Crime was rampant because there was no one, in these isolated camps, to enforce the law. Greed could easily get the better of men who had staked all they possessed in a gamble to get rich quickly. Violence was precipitated, too, by the absence of women, frustration finding expression in quick-tempered outbursts and vicious over-reaction to petty disputes. Gambling, around which most of the squabbles revolved, was the only way of passing the time when not mining - gambling and drinking.

In the winter at Miners' Delight tempers were as short as the days. Brawls and shootings were so frequent they were taken for granted as part of the life of the camp. Life was cheap. When someone was killed, by gun or knife, he was dragged outside and buried and that was the end of it. No one considered reporting the death. Anyone who had not managed to stay alive got what he deserved. Such was the code of life and sudden death at Miners' Delight. It did not bother Longley, whose own code of conduct ran parallel to it. In any case, he was on the other side of the bar counter and while dispensing drinks, was not involved in the brawls.

The winter was unusually hard, with more snow than usual and bitterly cold temperature. No mail could be sent out and none could get through to the miners, whose tempers were consequently soured.

On Christmas Day, Longley and Johnson, not entirely for altruistic reasons, did their best to instill a festive spirit by providing free drinks. Once loaded on free drinks, the miners could be expected to spend lavishly for the rest of the day. This hospitality went to the miners' heads and a day which began as a jamboree ended in drunken gunfights and knifing incidents. The evening of Christmas Day produced a bout of mayhem. When the violence had subsided, seven men were dead. There is no record of any subsequent investigation, initiated either by the civil authorities or the families of the men killed.

Though inured to the violence, Longley tired of the camps' monotony. There was nothing to do but serve drinks, play cards and wait for the winter to pass. By the middle of January, when the weather turned mild, his nerves were on edge. Miners' Delight was getting him down and he was restless. Someone, sharing his feelings, came up with the idea of a deer and bear hunting expedition, and a party was formed.

In spite of weather-lore warnings that a mild spell in January usually meant a blizzard was on the way, they set off on horseback, with five pack mules, and headed toward the Rattlesnake Hills. The snow was hard under the horses' hooves and the sun was bright in a cloudless sky. The freedom of the open country after being confined to a smoky, whisky-fumed saloon, was exhilarating. For eighteen miles the hunting party of eight men rode along singing mining ballads and were unaware of the blizzard until it struck them. It seemed to come out of the blue sky. Dense clouds of thick snow threatened to engulf them as the blizzard snapped down from the mountains. If they had been experienced plainsmen they would have banked the snow around them, scooping away that which fell in the enclosure. In this way they would have protected themselves and their mules from the freezing wind. Instead, they panicked and tried to struggle on, heads lowered against the wind. With every aimless step they moved further into a disaster area. As night came on they were numb with cold, miserable and desperate. They knew if they stopped, their horses would freeze to death, so they kept on moving, losing all sense of direction. The snow, whipped into great flurries by the raw wind, pounded them through the night. Just before daylight they stumbled on a cluster of rocks, which gave some protection from the wind. On the verge of exhaustion, one miner lay down behind the rocks, wrapped his blanket round him and fell asleep. Two hours later, when his companions tried to rouse him, he was dead.

Gradually, the wind died down and the snow ceased. But the fallen snow was too deep to dig a grave for the dead man. They left him where he had frozen to death and as they moved away, wolves moved in to tear his body to pieces and fight over each piece.

Longley felt sick as he watched the starving creatures tear at the body of George Pierce, who at Miners' Delight, before winter set in, had read aloud letters from his mother and sisters urging him to return home. Pierce had replied that there was good money to be earned in the mines and though the work was hard, he was enjoying it and would return in the spring.

For a day the party dragged on, hoping to come across a prospector's dug-out or a trapper's shack. Most of their provisions had been lost in the snowstorm. They were hungry and so were their horses and mules which had not eaten since they set out. At nightfall the mules were turned loose and left to cope with the wolves. 'We were so tired we could have slept in the snow,' Longley said. 'That would have meant freezing to death like poor George Pierce, but it was only the thought of being eaten by the wolves that prevented us lying in the snow and dying there.'

The following night an elderly Frenchman in the party froze to death after sitting, close to exhaustion, behind a snowbank. In the morning Longley saw a Mexican lion tearing at his body.

The six survivors abandoned their horses, which could only stumble in the snow, and trudged on. 'Our feet were frozen but as we pressed on we could walk better,' Longley recounted.

'About noon our feet began to thaw out and they hurt so bad we could not walk at all. We got on top of the highest hill we could find and began to watch, for we knew help would be sent out. About the middle of the afternoon we saw them coming. Talk about a shipwrecked sailor being glad when he saw a sail come in sight and turn in his direction.' They carried us on their horses and our feet were swollen so badly they had to cut our boots off our feet.

One man's frostbite was so severe that he died soon after they reached Miners' Delight. It was two months before Longley and the other four survivors fully recovered.

When he was well enough and fit to be on the move again, he had to plan his movements carefully. Captain A.E. Bates' muster roll showed that he had deserted. Not that he was 'B' company's only deserter. Six other privates had deserted around the same time. Colonel Innis Palmer was not the kind of commanding officer to shrug them off. After more than two months, Longley doubted if efforts to find them had been relaxed. In Texas he was an outlaw. In Wyoming he was a deserter. His immediate dilemma was a choice between travelling where the army might pick him up or where Indians might do so. He decided to take his chance in Indian territory and he made his way toward Snake River, his idea being to make a wide detour west through Idaho Territory into Utah.

For several days he saw no one and felt as if he belonged to a world inhabited exclusively by wild life. One morning he was awakened by dogs barking. Had the soldiers, with dogs, picked up his trail? He listened intently and judged the barking to be that of small dogs, not the breeds used by the army.

Setting out to investigate, he climbed a bluff and from the top looked down on an Indian village. Tepees were set up on both sides of the stream that flowed through the valley. From his vantage point he estimated there were about two hundred Indians in the village and they had a large number of dogs and Chickasaw horses.

He could see a scaffold where buffalo meat was dipped into boiling brine and left to cure. The meat reminded him that he had not eaten for two days. He hadn't killed any game because he was afraid a shot would give him away to any cavalry scouting party or hostile Indians.

Was he to continue on to the northern plains, half-starved or should he go down to the Indian village and ask for meat, putting himself at the Indians' mercy?

If they saw he was alone, walking boldly into their camp, it was likely they would not harm him. Leading his horse, he walked slowly into the village. Men, women and children gazed at him, but their stares were curious, not hostile. As he moved among them he was relieved to find they were Snake Indians, regarded by many whites as semi-civilized. At Camp Stambaugh he had learned that some of the Shoshone even spoke broken English and the tribe were currently at peace with the white man, after a period when no trapper had been safe on their reservation.

When he made known that he was hungry, an earthenware bowl of broth was handed to him and he was invited to sit and eat it. It was a kind of broth he had never tasted before. The squaw who had made it watched him eat. Making signs that he wished to know what it was, she pointed to the dogs that were running about. Dogs were not pets for the children, but an extra source of meat and broth.

Finding himself a centre of attention and welcome in their midst, he was in no hurry to depart. And when he was shown to a tepee to rest he knew he could stay as long as he liked and would be safe there.

The Shoshone (Snake) Indians' lodge and encampment where Longley found refuge for about a year.

6

'You kill one man and then another and after that it's easy.' - Bill Longley.

Weary after his wanderings, Longley had taken a calculated risk by stepping into an Indian encampment. Again, he appeared to have a guiding star. The way he was received by the Snakes can be imagined. He would have been left to sleep beside a fire in the centre of the tepee and when he woke, would have been given slices of buffalo meat pounded with dried berries, a staple Indian diet. His threadbare clothes would have been replaced by a soft buckskin shirt decorated with strips of white weasel skin, breechclout and moccasins.

From his reminiscences, it is known that he was given two pistols. These, he concluded, had been stolen and the Snakes wanted him to teach them how to use them properly. This is where he came into his own in the village. Setting up a target, he showed the warriors how to fire accurately at it while riding past, just as he had instructed his young brother, Jim, at an oak tree in Evergreen. The Indians enjoyed it as a war game and in return taught him how to hurl a lance, wield a stone-headed club and fire arrows almost as quickly as he unloaded a six-shooter.

He was surprised by the readiness with which they accepted him. No one troubled him as he wandered about the village, watching the children at play and the women scraping, curing and tanning deer and buffalo hides. One of the children's games was to creep up and steal strips of buffalo meat. The braves, he discovered, encouraged this as a means of training them to sneak up to an enemy's camp when they were older and steal horses.

After a few days of contenting himself by decorating a lance with beaver fur and resting by the stream, he found the squaws beginning to dismantle the tepee and pack them with their bedding robes on the travois. The village was moving on, following the buffalo.

Some of the women were attractive in their elkskin or buckskin dresses and knee-high leggings. Elk teeth necklaces set off their braided black hair. He hoped that if he went with them, to the next camp site, a squaw would be offered to him. He hadn't been with a woman for some months, but he would have to wait on the generosity of his hosts when they reached the head of the Big Wind River.

Again, the women did most of the work, setting up the tepees with the openings facing east toward the rising sun in honour of the prime diety. The ground inside the tepees was covered with water and dried grass, which was set alight to make a hard floor.

Until now Longley had thought of the plains tribes as one, with various branches. Watching the braves prepare themselves for raids, he realised the extent of tribal hostilities. Such tribes as the Snakes, Bannocks and Utes had been at peace, but one tribe often made raids on another, to steal horses or kill a traditional enemy for the sake of tribal glory. Stealing a horse or touching the body of a dead enemy led to special honour and veneration within a tribe.

He was fortunate to have stumbled on the Snakes. Had they been Crows they would probably have killed him on the spot.

The Snakes were impressed by his horsemanship. He was not as agile on a pony as an Indian, but good enough for them to invite him to join a 24-strong raiding party into northern Wyoming and the southern tip of Dakota.

Before long, they encountered a party of eight Sioux braves, herding some army horses stolen from Fort Laramie. The Sioux put up a vain fight against overwhelming odds and succumbed after being surrounded. Five of them were killed. The other three got away while the Snakes were rounding up the eighty horses, a rich prize that would bring honour to the raiding party on its return to camp. The three escaping Sioux would inevitably be back with a much larger war party to take revenge, so there was no time to rest.

The Snakes travelled day and night to get out of range, but three days later were surprised near the Panther Mountains by one hundred Sioux. The Snakes were caught in the open and in a running battle three of them were killed and the horses lost.

Longley brought his six-shooters into effective use, but the Sioux, armed with bows and arrows, lances and tomahawks, did not hesitate to charge against the gun-power of the Snakes.

There was only one possible escape: into the mountains. Riding furiously, Longley and as many Snakes as could break through the frenzied attack, reached the mountain range and followed the narrow trails as darkness came. All night they stuck to the trails and in the morning ran into another party of Sioux, about seventy, heading for the Red Cloud agency. Longley and the surviving Snakes found themselves trapped in a canyon. The slopes were too steep to mount. All they could do was dismount and seek protection in the chaparral. The decision saved their lives.

When they saw their enemies had abandoned their horses, the Sioux went after the horses. A live horse was worth far more than a dead Indian.

It was one hundred miles back to the Wind River village and the chances of reaching there on foot, with Sioux raiding parties roaming the area, were remote. On the open plains they would be vulnerable. Even so, there was no alternative. They had to try. Mile after mile they walked, looking anxiously for Sioux, and then in a valley they sighted a miners' camp. Not knowing how many miners were there and whether they would agree to barter mounts, the Snakes closed in and fired on the encampment not to kill but to scare away whoever was there. The miners scurried for cover and the Snakes took what they wanted, sixteen horses. To arrive back in the village with more men than horses would be a disgrace. There were still two or three braves without horses. Longley was for going back, but had to fall in with a plan to go to Crow Creek and try to snatch horses from the Crows. It was a simple and successful raid. The Crows, doubtless thinking that a larger band of Snakes were bearing down on them, offered no resistance and watched from a distance as their horses were taken.

By the time the Snakes arrived back at their village they had been away for six weeks and were greeted as noble warriors. They did not describe how the Sioux had taken them by surprise and chased them for ten miles near the Panther Mountains.

A victory dance was held and Longley joined in the rejoicing. But the Sioux were not to allow the killing of their warriors to go unavenged. A few nights later they made a raid on the camp and made off with two squaws and 75 ponies.

A war party was sent after them and Longley went too. The trail was followed for twenty miles before they overtook them on the plains. Several Sioux were killed and the squaws and ponies retrieved. Two Sioux were captured and taken back to camp.

Hardened as he was to frontier life, Longley was sickened by what happened to the prisoners. First, they were tormented by the squaws and children and then tied to stakes and burned alive. He did not join in the celebration. His idea of killing an enemy was to do it as quickly as possible, not to gloat over a slow and painful death. Yet there was nothing he could do as the Snakes danced and whooped around the roasting captives. He was astonished that the victims accepted their fate without screams of pain.

> 'They were cooked or burned until nothing remained but bones. It was past midnight when the wild and hellish orgy ceased. Until my dying hour the fearful din and the pictures of the appalling scene will remain in my brain and memory.'

He tried to conceal his revulsion, knowing that if he showed his disgust of what to an Indian was natural justice, he would lose the prestige he had gained in the tribe. It suited him, for a while, to be one of the Kool-sapti-ka-ra (Buffalo eaters) under their chief, Washakie * or Pina-qua-na (Smell of Sugar), a tall, handsome half-breed with firm control of the Eastern Snakes.

Washakie did not object when Longley said he would like to lead a raiding party to get more horses. A party setting out to convince the Sioux that the Snakes were not all squaws would always have his blessing. This was not exactly what Longley had in mind. Either through devilment or perverted bravado, he was thinking of a hit-and-run raid on the military corral at Camp Stambaugh. His popularity among the young bucks put the scheme in his mind. It would show that he was fearless even against the dog-soldiers and at the same time give him satisfaction in striking back at those who had been hunting him. Secrecy

* Credited with one of the wittiest speeches in relations between the Indian and white man. When the Indian Bureau tried to persuade him to turn to farming, he summoned what little English he knew and declared 'God damn a potato.'

Washakie or 'Shoots the Buffalo Running', of the Shoshone (Snake) tribe, with whom Longley lived for a year while the army searched for him, after his desertion.

was essential because Washakie was anxious to avoid any kind of friction between the tribe and the white man.

The party set off in the direction of the Sioux reservation but once away from the Snake lodges, turned and headed toward Rollins Springs.

A Second Cavalry company was patrolling in the region of Whisky Gap and it was here that a fight broke out between Longley's Snakes and the soldiers, ending in several Cavalrymen lying dead, Taken by surprise, the company did not have time to organise a proper resistance and were deprived of thirty head of horses and mules.

In triumph, the raiders pressed on toward Camp Stambaugh. A mile or so from the post they fell upon three men herding mules and added another twenty head to their stock. This should have been enough for a small raiding party, but success made them crave more adventure. An army wagon train provided it. The soldiers could not have made it easier for them. They had stopped to set up camp for the night and had not troubled to post guards, assuming that in the vicinity of the Camp Stambaugh there was no need.

Resistance was out of the question as the Snakes, led by Longley, appeared suddenly, disarmed them and collected together another forty mules. Longley was in his element but knew he was living precariously. Soon, the whole of Camp Stambaugh would be roused. It was time to return to the village. En route, they halted a stagecoach heading in the direction of Fort Hall and forced the driver to exchange his team of horses for six skinny mules.

Washakie was surprised when he saw how many mules and fine horses had been collected, as he thought, from the Sioux. Casualties in Longley's party were one killed and two wounded.

Longley expected the cavalry to track them down and attack the village. But autumn passed, turning the bluejoint grass into a glorious reddish-brown. Life was peaceful. He spent his time hunting buffalo and deer, learning the Indian sign-language which overcame language barriers (the plains Indians had at least twenty different languages), baited pit traps to catch eagles and began to appreciate the timeless qualities of Indian life; eating when he was hungry, drinking when he was thirsty, sleeping when he was tired and adjusting his life to the seasons. But old habits and desires were too strong to abandon. He longed for the company of white women and he longed, too, for whisky.

When the tribe moved on to Vintah Valley in Utah he told the chief that he had a sister in the territory he was anxious to visit and promised to rejoin the tribe at its winter camp. It was late October when he said farewell to the Snakes, who gave him enough jerky (dried meat) to last for four or five days. Leaving on the pretext of visiting a relative with the intention of returning was a wise precaution. The Snakes, who trusted him, might have forced him to stay if they though he was deserting them with the possibility of his bringing the army to the camp. Out of sight of the village, he turned south-west, toward New Mexico, his intention being to return to Texas. On the Western Plains, the verdant charms of Texas had a magnetic pull for him. He doubted if he could ever feel at home anywhere but Texas, even as a hunted man.

His long journey was just beginning. First he would have to cross Sioux country. Every mile or so he would stop to scan the skyline and sometimes he would come across signs that Sioux parties were ahead of him or to the side. To be safe from ambush he rode mostly at night and tried to sleep in the daytime. Sleep was difficult. Every few moments he woke to make sure no one was creeping up on him.

Reaching a pleasant valley that seemed secure from intrusion, he unsaddled his horse, spread his blanket on the ground and fell asleep. He had been asleep for four hours or more when rain lashed his face and wakened him. A north wind had blown up - 'a blue norther' - and the rain brought sleet. Cold and drenched, he saddled his horse and journeyed on to a mountain range. To keep warm he walked, leading his horse. What made him turn he did not know. Instinct, perhaps. The horsemen he saw were too far away to be heard, but they had seen him and were galloping toward him. It was impossible to make out at the distance whether they were Indians or white men. It would have been foolish to stay and find out. Mounting his horse, he dug his heels into its flanks and rode furiously, hoping to find a ravine and cover. What appeared to be one led instead to a deep gulley. A hundred yards ahead the gulley stretched ominously across his path. There was no way round. Pulling on the reins, he brought his horse to a halt on the very edge and looked down. There was a drop of more than 70 feet. The gap was ten feet across. He was trapped. His pursuers were getting close. Turning in his saddle, he could now see them. They were not Indians, but Mexicans - bandits who had roamed up the course of the Pecos River or Rio Grande.

They had him where they wanted him. At least, he did not intend to go down without a fight. Drawing his Colt, he spurred his horse around and rode straight at his pursuers, firing as he went. His sudden counter-attack was unexpected. The bandits, taken by surprise, failed to take direct aim and their shots passed over him As he rode at them, they scattered to bring him down with their rifles as he went past. A hundred yards from them, he reined his horse, turned and galloped back to the edge of the gulley. With a good run-up and luck, his horse might be able to leap across. Urged on, the horse did not falter and a few yards from the brink Longley loosened the reins. The leap took the creature's forelegs to the opposite edge, but it failed to find a foothold for its rear legs. Man and horse crashed over the jagged rocks into the gulley. Longley was thrown out of the saddle and hurled into some mesquite bushes down the bank. Bruised, gashed and knocked almost senseless, he remained there, out of sight from above. The bandits, looking down, saw the horse was dead and must have assumed its rider was also killed. They rode away and Longley lost consciousness. When he came to, some hours later, he was lying on a rough bed in a jacal, (a small house), dimly lit by a single candle. Looking around the whitewashed room, he saw a crucifix on the wall above his bed and knew he was in a Mexican home. After a while a young woman brought him some soup and spoke to him in Spanish. He had learned rudimentary Spanish in Texas and understood that some of her father's workers had found him in the gulley and brought him to the house. Her father was a herder, who spent part of the year with friends hunting in the valleys. Her name was Dolores Gomez and their home was in Santa Fe.

She said there were bandits in the area, but he would be safe in the house. Her father was away for two weeks on a hunting trip. He could stay until her father was due back. It did not take long for his strength to return. No bones had been broken in the fall and apart from severe bruises and cuts, he was unharmed.

Longley was fascinated by the dark-haired senorita. They walked together in the twilight, not for its romantic associations but to make sure he was not observed. She, too, was fascinated by this black-eyed Texan and was sorry when the time came for him to go. If her father returned and found him there he would turn him over to the military authorities, as all strangers were suspect. Reluctantly, he took his leave, promising to return when he had found work on a farm and could settle down. Her servant, a free pueblo, would accompany him part of the way south-west and help him on his journey to Texas.

Saying farewell, Longley assured her he would return the following year. This brief idyll was tinged with false sentiment and appears to have passed from his mind within a few days of setting out again.

The girl was generous enough to provide him with a horse, food and blankets, which might not have been so freely given had he not promised to return.

After several days' travelling, his guide took him to a Mexican habitation for fresh provisions and then set him on the trail for Morris County, Kansas.

In Parkersville, a small village often used as a temporary hideout for cattle thieves, he set eyes on the first white men he had met peacefully since leaving Miners' Delight. . It was like old times when he joined them in a card game. He had not lost his touch and soon there were only two players left in the game - Longley and a youth named Charlie Stuart. It was Stuart's misfortune that he happened to get into a game with a man who had no scruples about killing when it served his immediate purpose, the gratification of an impulse. According to custom, both men placed their pistols on the card table. The game went on for a long time and looked like a stalemate until Longley, who had introduced himself as Tom Jones, accused Stuart of cheating. What happened after this is confused. It may well be that Stuart reacted like a prototype of all those Hollywood Western bit-players who reach for their pistols the moment they are challenged. If he did so, it can only be said that Longley reached his pistol first. Two bullets, one in the head and the other in the heart, left Stuart dead on the sawdust-covered floor of the saloon, his cards scattered around him. No one was rash enough to try to seize the killer. Had anyone tried, there would have been more than one dead man on the floor.

Longley went into hiding not far from the village. A day or so later he met up with two outlaws and from them discovered that Stuart's father, a wealthy cattleman, had offered a reward of 1,500 dollars for his capture. An audacious scheme flashed into his agile mind. When he explained it to the two outlaws they laughed and took it to be a joke. But when he persuaded them that he was not joking and described how it could be put into practice, they agreed to co-operate. All that was required was some daring.

The two men, unknown in that part of the country, rode into the village posing as lawmen and made the acquaintance of Stuart's father, who confirmed he had offered a reward for the killer of his son. They told him they were on the trail of cattle thieves, but if he placed the reward money in the bank at Council Grove, the county seat, they would help him find the killer.

Stuart agreed to do this and when the legal formalities had been completed; they went through the procedure of getting a detailed description of Tom Jones (Longley) and said they would do their best to track him down. A week later, when sufficient time had elapsed to make plausible the success of their mission, the two bogus lawmen arrived in town with their 'prisoner'. Longley was promptly put in jail and identified as the killer of Charlie Stuart. Stuart's father said this was the man he had seen playing cards with his son when he had called briefly at the saloon during the game.

The reward money was paid and the 'captors' spent the rest of the day idling around the village. Toward dusk, they told the sheriff they would be on their way, but first they would like to say goodbye to the man they had brought in. The sheriff, pleased they had done his job for him, took them to the cell and felt a pistol in his ribs. 'What the hell's this about?' he demanded. Disarmed, bound and gagged, he was left in the cell now vacated by Longley, to work out for himself what was happening.

Instead of dividing the reward money three ways, which meant 500 dollars each, the two outlaws could have made off with it once their accomplice was behind bars. Was it honour among thieves or did they fear that if he were freed after a trial plea of self-defence, he would track them down?

Whatever the reasons for keeping the bargain, they carried through the scheme Longley had proposed and afterwards separated to continue their own journeys.

Longley still had a long distance to cover. Passing through what in 1907 became the state of Oklahoma, he met another fugitive, a counterfeiter, named Rogers, who was glad to have someone share his home-made fortune. Rogers had left a trail of counterfeit dollar bills from one county to another. Longley joined him in a 'spending' spree, getting through a large amount of whisky, until they reached the small depot town of Boggy, where they were apprehended by a Federal marshal and arrested for 'passing currency prohibited by the Government'. The marshal told them they would be taken as his prisoners to Fort Smith, Arkansas.

Longley argued that their arrest was an infringement on their franchise as American citizens.' He talked glibly about the rights of citizens under the law and confused the marshal with protestations involving civil rights. When he and Rogers produced all the genuine money they had between them, two thousand dollars, (some of it Longley's 'reward' money and what he had won at cards) and threw in a few counterfeit bills too, they hit on the price of their freedom. The marshal took the money and let them go.

Rogers said he was going to St. Louis. 'Where you making for?' he asked Longley.

'There's only one place for me,' Longley said, 'Evergreen.'

7

'I am a friend to anyone who will allow me to be,'- Bill Longley.

Much had changed in Texas while Longley had been away. The final act of reconstruction had been carried out and a proclamation issued remitting all civil authority to the officers elected by the people. Nine years of political and social violence had culminated in the return of Texas to the Union, if not with absolute equality, at least with freedom to sort out internal problems without a military dictatorship. Governor Davis was now fully-fledged under the civil administration and intended to use his power to deal with what he called 'a slow civil war still going on in Texas'.

Radical senators had been kept under arrest for two or three weeks while administrative measures were rushed through the Lower House. Davis had set up a state police force of 250 men and his Militia Bill required the enrolment of all able-bodied men aged eighteen to forty-five, with the exception of those who could pay a privilege tax.

As Commander-in-Chief, Davis had the power of appointment and could call into active service the state's military force 'in time of war, rebellion, insurrection, invasion, resistance to civil process, breach of the peace or imminent danger thereof whenever in his opinion the enforcement of the law is obstructed within any county or counties, by combinations of lawless men too strong for the control of the civil authorities, to declare such county or counties under martial law and to suspend the laws therein until the legislature shall convene and take such action as it may deem necessary.'

Through a chain of authorised newspapers, which monopolised public notices and were given rights of public printing,

Davis sought to 'radiate civilization into the darkest corners of the state'.

In effect, Texas was a one-man power state, in its way as militaristic as it had been under the command of the Fifth Military District.

It was not 'a dark corner' of the state Longley sought, but work on his father's land. On his way through Grayson County he met an old friend, Dan Sawyer, who informed him that the Longleys had left Evergreen and were now living in Bell County.

There were mixed feelings in the Longley home when he arrived. His parents, brothers and sister Elizabeth were overjoyed to see him. The youngest boy, named after the son killed in the Civil War, was now six years' old, Jim, who idolised his older brother, was fifteen and wanted to hear of Bill' s adventures.

'I'm putting away my pistol,' Longley told his father. 'I just want to settle down and work the farm.' It was not possible, his father regretted. The reward for his capture, offered by the previous military authorities, was still operative. Even so, Longley was in no mood to take up his travels again and said he would take his chance in Bell County.

For three months he showed no sign of restlessness and worked on the farm from daybreak to dusk, chopping cotton, ploughing furrows, with a mongrel dog for a companion in the fields.

On these occasions, marking odd periods in his life, his mood was calm and he appeared to be no different from other sons of toil in the fields. He worked thoroughly and appears not to have grumbled about doing routine chores around the farm. At these times, he was the son Campbell Longley wanted him to be. They were, however, remissions in a malady that had no cure but the ultimate one made from hemp. It was as if the turbulent, and predominant part of his nature needed rest before another surge of violence, lulls before further stormy outbursts.

Campbell Longley knew it could not last. Sooner or later the law officers who had harassed the family in Lee County, would learn of his son's return and come after him. The inevitable day arrived.

While he was working in the fields, Longley looked up to see a friend riding hard toward him and shouting that a posse was on its way from Lee County to get him and claim the reward.

Edmund J. Davis. He was governor of Texas at the close of the civil war and early reconstruction period when Longley began his reign of terror.

There was no time to lose if he wanted to evade capture. No time to get his belongings and six-shooter from the farmhouse. He went straight to the woods and hid there until friends could bring him a Colt and provisions. After the posse had searched the farm and surrounding district, Campbell Longley waited until dark and, guided by the friend who had given the warning, took a horse to his son in the woods.

Surely Billy now realised how impossible it was to stay in Bell County or any other part of Texas?

In six months the state police had made a thousand arrests and the militia movement, in which 100,000 citizens had been enrolled, was making life more difficult for lawbreakers and fugitives. Yet Longley was reluctant to leave Texas.

It is strange that in the state which constituted the greatest threat against his life and liberty, he felt the greatest emotional security. It was impossible for him to shake off the one enduring feeling imparted to him during his childhood, that he belonged to Texas. Beneath the bluster and bravado, the to-hell-with-everyone truculence and unbalanced temperament, was his pride of place; a sense of identity with the surroundings of his boyhood. This may account for the streak of sentimentalism he sometimes displayed, particularly when writing to women after his trial and in his interviews with journalists.

On a deeper level it might be argued that his refusal to stray for long beyond the boundaries of Texas and his compunction to revisit his home, in spite of the obvious dangers, were prompted by the thrill of exposing himself to disaster and defying Nemesis. Vanity too played its part. His reputation usually preceded whatever route he took in Texas and the border areas and must have had a stimulating effect on a young outlaw of his disposition.*

At some stage in his wanderings, Longley became involved in the notorious Taylor-Sutton feud, a Western equivalent of the Capulets and Montagues. He took the Taylors' side only because he happened to be working for them as a hired hand after arriving in DeWitt County when the feud was at its height.:

The feud had begun when Longley was seven years old. Its origin is said to have been in Alabama, though North and South Carolina were attributed as its starting point at various times, and it had spread into Texas when the two families moved there.

* see appendix three

What touched it off, according to the Suttons, was cattle rustling, for which Charley Taylor received his just desserts at the hands of outraged citizens led by William Sutton, in 1868. The Taylors denied that Charley Taylor was one of their family and accused William Sutton of ambushing Buck Taylor. It wasn't like that at all, countered the Sutton, who maintained that Buck began the fracas and everyone started shooting at the same time.

Wherever it started, the feud certainly reached its fury and finale in Texas, in DeWitt County, where the Taylors and Suttons were neighbours.

'Who sheds a Taylor's blood, by a Taylor's hand must fall,' became a Taylor motto.

Among the 200 or so protagonists supporting the Taylors was John Wesley Hardin, outlaw son of a Methodist preacher; a fugitive from the age of fifteen when he killed a Negro named Mage after a quarrel following a wrestling bout.

Years later, explaining the killing and his decision not to face a court with the plea of self-defence, he claimed the Negro had threatened to kill him or die himself. All the courts, in Hardin's view, were conducted by bureau agents and renegades, inveterate enemies of the South, administering a code of justice to suit every case that came before them 'and which invariably ended in gross injustice to Southern people'. Realising that to be tried at that time for the killing of a Negro meant certain death, he had gone into hiding - a fugitive, he contended, not from justice, but from injustice. Not long afterwards he had killed two white soldiers and a Negro soldier when they tried to seize him. By the time he joined the Taylors, a dozen or more men had fallen victim to his Colt ·44 six-shooter.

His contribution to the feud was the killing of J.B. Morgan, a deputy, who tried to apprehend him in a Cuero saloon and got a ball of lead in his forehead for his pains, which killed him instantly.

Pitkin Taylor, one of five brothers, was shot down when taken off his guard by the tinkling of an oxen bell. Thinking an ox had got loose, he went outside to investigate and the Suttons shot him. His son, Jim, did his best to even the score, but managed only to wound William Sutton in a shoot-out at a saloon and billiard parlour. A month later two Sutton men were killed when a peace conference between the two sides ended in a riot.

John Wesley Hardin, second only to Bill Longley in the list of Texas desperadoes. He was sentenced to 25 years in the State penitentiary. Longley, comparing his sentence to his own, was outraged.

All that can be established about Longley's involvement is that he rode for the Taylors. In effect, the feud, often revolving around the Gulf Hotel in Cuero, forshadowed the gang warfare of Chicago in the l920s, and Longley, in gangster terms, would have been 'a hood'.

In March, 1874, Jim Taylor shot William Sutton through the head on a steamer about to leave for New Orleans. Sutton was taken by surprise at the moment he thought he was safe on board the steamer. His wife and young child were with him and watched horrified as he fell to the deck, dying almost at once.

Wes Hardin had told the Taylors about Sutton's impending departure from Indianola and has been held responsible for helping to set up the killing. After this he moved on to Comanche Town.

Even the English press of the time reported the mayhem of the Sutton-Taylor feud. A Midlands evening newspaper published an editorial about it.*

Longley's trail peters out in DeWitt County and re-emerges some months later in another county where he took work as a cattle herder for one Willis Johnson. He lived in a bunkhouse with the cowhands. If cowhands were curious about a newcomer's background, it was customary to keep one's curiosity to oneself. Questions were rarely asked about a man's past. He was taken at his own evaluation. All that mattered was his willingness to work and share the communal life of the bunkhouse, which invariably reeked of sweat, cow dung from the cowhands' boots, tobacco and lamp oil; a combination which has to be smelled to appreciate its effects on a sensitive stomach.

Evenings were spent playing poker or dominoes. Days drifted by and fate again took a hand, as if inextricably bound to Longley's violent nature. An errand Johnson asked him to undertake at a ranch in Brown County led him to stop at the ranch of a Mr. Forsythe to get water. He found Mrs. Forsythe in a distressed state. She said that a burly Negro had barged into the house while her husband was away and had forced her to give him a meal and feed his horse. The man, she said, was probably still in the district.

Later in the day Longley was in a country store when a Negro, drunk and belligerent, came in. Whether he was the same man

*see appendix 4

Texas Ranger Captain Lee Hall (photographed in 1898). He was a U.S. Army Officer instrumental in ridding Texas of its worst desperadoes and was prominent during the Taylor-Sutton feud.

Captain Creed Taylor, frontiersman, who also figured in the Taylor-Sutton feud.

who terrified Mrs. Forsythe was never determined. Longley, through no sense of gallantry toward the poor woman but rather driven by his own prejudice, decided he was the same man and obstructed him.

'Who the devil are you?' the Negro asked, taking hold of Longley's hat and pushing it back over his head.

Longley's reply was two shots from his pistol into the man's head.

It is difficult now, as it was in his day, to keep pace with his killings. Noticeably, many of them followed periods of quiet, industrious work on the land.

Having killed the Negro in Brown County, it would have been imprudent for him to have returned to the ranch. A troop of Negro soldiers was stationed in the district. Longley's next stopping point was Coleman County, where ranchers and farmers had a system for aiding anyone in trouble with the authorities. They had no liking for, or trust in, the state government which had come into power in 1869 and they were not inclined to assist the state police, especially when there was every indication that Davis would be defeated in the forthcoming election.

A relay system of warnings operated in some areas. Messages were taken on horseback from one ranch to another or conveyed by a series of bonfires, informing outlaws and persons in hiding from the authorities of police and military movements.

By this means, Longley was kept informed of the search for him while he camped with two men, Mitchell and Martin, near the Santa Anna mountains. When one of the search parties began moving in his direction, he packed his few belongings and saddled his horse. His companions were slower off the mark and while he was waiting for them, they were approached by five men on horseback. It does not follow they were from a search party. It is more likely they were on a hunting expedition. Longley was not prepared to see if they challenged him and his companions. The moment they came into view he ordered them to drop their pistols. Either they refused or were too slow in obeying his command. Longley fired and one of the riders slumped from his saddle.

Realising that a gunfight was breaking out, Martin drew his pistol and fired at another of the riders but hit the man's horse.

Further shots stampeded the horses and the two parties broke off the engagement, leaving one dead man and one dead horse.

'To this day,' Longley admitted, when he was in prison, 'I do not know who those men were.' Nor did he know much about his companions, Mitchell and Martin. He seems to have taken up with them to share the facilities of their camp. They did not stay together after the incident and Longley drifted on, toward the frontier which he knew was practically ruled by Comanche and Kiowa Indians. The Kiowa (Ka-i-gaw, meaning Principal People) had been driven by their enemies, the Arapahos, from the Yellowstone district of what is now Wyoming and Montana, across the plains down to the south-western desert. Settlers confused them with Comanches, who roamed over Texas, Kansas and Colorado. Because of their ferocity and nomadic ways, they were known as the Lords of the South Plains. The Kiowas were said to have killed more white people than any other south-western tribe. Longley was as anxious to avoid them as he was the police, who by now had replaced the Texas Rangers.

On his way to the frontier he chanced to arrive in Mason County when horse races were in progress. He was fond of horse races and would have competed in them himself if his horse had not been so tired. He decided to watch the races while his horse was being fed and rested. In any crowd Longley was conspicuous.. His dark complexion, lean frame and height gave him an air of self-composure. So it was not surprising that the local sheriff, Finley, should have paid particular attention to him. What Finley observed caused him to hurry back to his office to check a description which had been circulated to all sheriff's offices in the area:

> 'Sinewy, six ft. tall, dark hair and eyes, soft moustache, going heavily armed. Must be approached with caution. . . a very dangerous man, always ready to fight.'

There was little doubt in the sheriff's mind that the description of Bill Longley fitted the young man now watching the races. 'A very dangerous man.' He mulled over the phrase and decided to play a cool hand. Returning to the races, he approached him casually, like someone simply trying to be friendly, and asked him if he was enjoying the races, Longley nodded.

'You staying in the county?' Finley asked.

Longley said he was just passing through but might stay a few days.

'Mind telling me your name?'

'William Henry,' came the reply, another alias Longley made up on the spur of the moment. They talked about horses, about the possibility of Davis being defeated at the polls, the need for greater protection from the Indians along the frontier and how long it might be before Texas had the sort of rights other states enjoyed.

Finley wanted to keep him in conversation and break down any suspicion Longley might have that he was under surveillance.

After the races he invited him to a saloon for a few drinks and a game of cards. Evidently, the sheriff was excited and nervous. A desperado was almost in his grasp but he was conscious of Longley's reputation and did not intend to make a move until he was absolutely sure he would get a prisoner and not a bullet in his own brain. Besides, he was not yet 100 per cent sure that William Henry was Bill Longley. Why he waited two or three days, putting the stranger at ease, can only be explained by assuming that Finley was an ultra-cautious sheriff afraid of making a mistake.

Longley was not the sort to be put off his guard by the blandishments of a lawman and one can imagine a game of cat-and-mouse between them, though who played which role is conjectural.

Finley needed assistance to make an arrest and found two men to be sworn as special deputies. He introduced them to Longley as his friends and said they would like to play cards with him. The four arranged to meet that night for a poker session.

This confirmed for Longley that he was being set up. Pretending to go along with the arrangement, he returned to his hotel, packed his travelling bags and rode away before Finley realised his plan had come unstuck. The arrest was to have been made at the poker table. By the time he discovered his quarry had fled, Longley was in Fredericksburg. Even so, Finley was not to be defeated. He guessed correctly where his man had gone and set out with one of his deputies to get him. They came face to face in a saloon. Still, the pretence was maintained. Finley faked surprise at seeing him and Longley apologised for having missed the poker game, explaining that a business matter had come up and he did not have time to let the sheriff know he was leaving.

Finley offered to buy him a drink and the three moved to the bar. Longley had his wits about him. He sensed that an attempt was about to be made to seize him and if he resisted there would be shooting. The reward notice stipulated 'dead or alive.' Finley and the deputy were trying to position themselves either side of him to prevent his drawing a pistol. Quickly, he moved to the end of the bar counter and faced them, ready to draw his Colt if they tried to grab him. After a few glasses of rye, another arrangement was made for a card game later in the evening. Finley was not at this stage aware that Longley had guessed they were seeking to arrest him. On the pretext that he wanted to have a bath at his hotel, Longley left saying he would be pleased to meet them later in the saloon.

Having nearly lost his man once, the sheriff might have been expected to keep him under scrutiny. Incredibly, he let him out of his sight, which must testify to Longley's bluff manner. While the sheriff and his deputy were waiting for him to return to the saloon, he was riding hard to Kerrville.

Furious when he discovered how easily he had been duped, Finley mustered a posse and the chase was on. This time there would be no cat-and-mouse game, but a direct confrontation. It was easy to get a posse together. Frank Eastwood, a desperado of Kerr County, had recently been shot and killed and the citizens were determined that no other outlaw should come and go with impunity. The shooting of Eastwood had renewed their confidence in dealing with renegades. Finley was eagerly joined by vigilantes as the posse rode through Kerrville. Meanwhile, Longley had turned west and was heading toward Edwards County. Unaware of the large posse after him, he dismounted to camp for the night on the High Divide. As in the past, he ate in one spot and moved on to another to bed down for the night. On this occasion he did not move far enough. The posse saw the smoke from his camp fire and tracked him down. Before he could rise from his blanket, he was surrounded by a hundred men. Pistols and rifles were levelled at him.

Finley announced that he had papers authorising his arrest and there was a reward of one thousand dollars for his capture.

Longley surrendered his six-shooters and was taken back to Fredericksburg, where a mob gathered and threatened to lynch him. Finley stood his ground and, supported by the posse, held back the mob. The prisoner, he declared, would be returned to his home county.

For safe keeping he decided to take him to Austin, the state capital, and claim the reward.

The governor, nominated by the Republicans for re-election in their state convention at Dallas the previous August, was involved in a bitter political fight with the Democrats, who had nominated Judge Richard Coke for governor.

Anxious to avoid any distractions while he concentrated on the election, he curtly informed the Mason County sheriff that no reward could be collected. Finley was given no reason for the rebuff. No one, least of all a minor sheriff, argued with a governor noted for his self-willed, obstinate temperament. Possibly the reward was withheld under a technicality, having been issued under military jurisdiction and no longer considered valid.

As Longley had not committed any known offence in Mason County and Finley had been acting only on the information of a reward notice, he was not sure what to do with his prisoner. The arrival of Longley's cousin, William Patterson, with 563 dollars in gold, resolved the situation. Patterson had got word of his cousin's arrest and hurried to the jail hoping to bail him out. Having been denied the state's reward, Finley accepted Patterson's offer of the gold for his release.

'Remind me to write to the governor and thank him,' Longley said to his cousin, who found him a horse and two new six-shooters. 'I never thought I'd get anything from him.'

Back in Bell County his father disillusioned him of the idea that because the state's reward was no longer payable, he was safe.

County warrants still existed for his arrest on charges of murdering Negroes and there were plenty of people, his father said, who would be glad to turn him in, with or without a reward.

They discussed the possibility of a short prison sentence if he gave himself up and answered the charges. 'It would do no good,' his father said. 'It would bankrupt me to try to clear you.

Campbell and Sarah Longley despaired of trying to reform their wayward son and were worried about his influence on the rest of the family.

Their daughter, Martha, had died at the age of 29, while Bill was in Wyoming. Frances, whose first husband had been killed in the Civil War, had died two years earlier and their boy, Joseph, had died young. Mary, married for twenty years, was living with her husband in Arizona. George had married a widow, Mattie Baker, who already had three children. This left at home Elizabeth aged 20, Jim and Alexander.

Campbell Longley forbade Bill to talk to the boys of his exploits and said it would be better for everyone if he left and never returned. In spite of an underlying paternal affection, he wanted to shut him out of his mind and try to live down the shame of having a desperado for a son. Jim, impressionable and often showing indications that he would like to accompany his elder brother across country, was given long, serious lectures on the folly of living against the law. 'Those who live by the gun will die by the gun,' His father intoned in the manner of his lay preaching.

When the outlaw son left and was told not to set foot in the house again, Democrats throughout Texas were celebrating the end of Davis's regime and the new administration of Governor Coke.

It did not mean an amnesty for outlaws. The best any outlaw could hope for was obscurity in another county or another state, under an assumed name. Longley's new destination was Frio County. On the way he traded his horse for the sturdier mount of a Mexican. It was a good deal, which convinced him that the other man did not appreciate equine quality. Later, he found out why the Mexican had been so willing to exchange horses. He was stopped by a man who claimed the horse was his and he had a bill of sale to prove it. Longley did not argue. He turned over the horse and set off on foot to catch up with the Mexican. Eventually, he found him and demanded the return of his own horse and some money that had been part of the deal. The Mexican refused and the two stood arguing for a while until Longley decided he would get no satisfaction from argument alone. He had been cheated and was in a rage. Drawing his pistol he fired at point blank range at the Mexican, who was hurled back by the force of the shot and was left dying, as Longley collected his horse and the money and rode away.

Longley's journeyings most of the time were aimless, apart from the aim of avoiding the clutches of the law. He would wander until a place took his fancy and there he would look around for work, until circumstances or restlessness caused him to move on again. He was in Madison County when he met another outlaw, Bill McKiver. They roamed about together and one day got into conversation with a girl. Longley was attracted to her from the start and asked if she would like to go with him to pick blackberries. She agreed. Blackberry picking, however, was not on Longley's mind. While she was busy filling a small basket with the fruit, he took hold of her and tried to kiss her. His sudden approach alarmed her. She struggled free and ran away, calling for help. Her home was not far away and she ran there, calling her brother, who rushed out of the house to see what was happening.

She shouted to him that Longley had assaulted her. Longley was close behind, wanting to reassure her that he intended no harm.

The girl's brother did not grapple with him. Instead, he challenged him to a duel. This was not the way Longley liked to settle a quarrel, but to avoid a further scene in front of the girl he accepted the challenge, without having any intention of keeping it. After a time and place for the duel had been set he left what he called 'that neck of the woods' and went on to Fort Ewell. It was not long before he became involved in another quarrel. The details of his quarrel with a gambler, Dave Clark, are not known. What is known is that Clark was left seriously injured, with two bullet wounds.

It was inevitable, wherever Longley went, that violence, death or injury would be left in his wake. The pattern continued at Logansport, after he had passed again through Madison County and journeyed east to the Sabine River. Once more, the details are sketchy, but he is known to have killed there a Negro who was said to have insulted an old friend of Longley's.

This pathological attitude toward Negroes was demonstrated yet again on the road to Homer, in Angelina County, where he encountered a white man and a Negro pounding one another with their fists.

Their wagons had collided and a wheel of the Negro's wagon had broken off. The Negro was getting the upper hand, which was something Longley could not allow. Though he had nothing to do with the quarrel he put an abrupt end to it by shooting the Negro in the neck.

Evidently in the mood for another bout of terrorism, he 'celebrated' his arrival at Lovelady, in Houston County, by cracking a coloured man on the head with his pistol butt.

By this time he was short of provisions and money. Had he been like other outlaws, this would have presented no particular problem. He would have resorted to armed robbery. This was not Longley's way of providing for himself, whether due to some virtue in the recesses of his mind or to a conviction that such ventures were too risky, in a matter of conjecture. In any case, there was an easier method, putting his horse into a raffle. All he had to do was make out a set of numbers and sell them at a dollar each. Soon he had collected several dollars. Someone was entrusted to keep the stubs and at an appointed time to draw the lucky number. Longley did not wait for the draw. He had the dollars in his money belt and he still had his horse. He was galloping off when those who had bought raffle tickets discovered they had been duped.

Longley's next stop was Bastrop County, where he tethered his horse at the farm of William Baker on Walnut Creek and introduced himself as Baker.

'Why, that's my name too,' said the farmer.

'Could be we're kinfolk,' said Longley, who had probably found out his name and wanted to ingratiate himself by pretending some affinity. 'I'd like to work for you.'

Baker gave him odd jobs around the farm, jobs that he knew well, such as mending fences, feeding and watering the stock, ploughing firebreaks. For some weeks he got along well and appears to have been popular with the other farm workers, none of whom suspected his real identity. They were together in the bunkhouse one night when mention was made of a new sheriff, appointed in Lee County, whose name was Jim Brown. Longley tried not to show his shock when one of the hands said he had heard the sheriff had Bill Longley high on his list of wanted outlaws. Lee County was close to Bastrop County, too close for comfort. It was time for Longley to move on again.

On the point of departure, having said farewell to Baker, he learned that one of his cousins, Caleb Longley, son of Campbell

Longley's younger brother, Caleb, had been killed by Wilson Anderson.

There were different versions of what had happened. One story was that the two men, both in their early twenties, were out riding when Caleb's horse stumbled and threw him, causing fatal head injuries.

Another account and the one that Longley took to be accurate, was that Anderson had murdered him over some grievance.

Longley and Anderson had been childhood friends, but an old friendship had no value to an outlaw bent on revenging his cousin's death. Without trying to find out if Anderson was being questioned by the law and what sort of investigation was being conducted into the death of Caleb Longley, he set out for Anderson' s farm.

On the outskirts of the farm, he stopped and from the cover of a clump of trees, surveyed the land. He saw Anderson in the middle distance, ploughing furrows. There was no one working with him and it was unlikely, while ploughing, that he had a gun handy. On the way to the farm Longley had spoken to a number of relatives and had told them he was going to 'hunt up Anderson', an indiscretion that was to weigh heavily on him in the future.

Intent on ploughing, Anderson did not see Longley approach and became aware of his presence only when he was nearing the end of a furrow. Longley was standing with a shotgun aimed at him.

If any conversation ensued, it was not recorded in Longley's recollections.

No source has been attributed to the two sentences said to have been uttered after a blast from the shotgun had cut Anderson down.

'Oh, God,' the dying Lee County farmer is said to have moaned. 'What did you shoot me for?' Longley's reputed reply was : 'Just for luck.'

If Anderson, in his dying breath, did demand an explanation of his assailant, Longley's reply was at least in character.

A fanciful story which later circulated is that Anderson was singing Longley's favourite hymn while he was ploughing and Longley waited for him to finish it before shooting him.

Instead of remaining silent about the killing, Longley enthused over it. He had, in his own estimation, exacted appropriate justice. He had avenged a relative's death. If he expected to earn the approval of his family, his hopes were confounded. Whatever lingering sympathy his parents had for him was now lost. They despised him and wanted only to forget he had ever been part of the household. Never again would they welcome him. Their shame was that such a son had ever been born.

The Longleys were no longer living at the farm a mile south of Evergreen. They had sold it to Sheriff Brown and it was Brown to whom Longley wrote a surprising letter in which he confessed, without regret, to killing Anderson.*

The letter, which recently came to light, displays his self- righteousness and unctuous attempt to ingratiate himself with the sheriff, as if Brown would be sympathetic toward him because he was living in the Longleys' old home. He had the gall to address the sheriff as 'kind friend' and in a flowery opening to his letter, pictured himself floating through 'the gentle breezes of misery' and in the same metaphorical spirit, as a sunflower bowing and bending in the breeze. He described riding past the house and stopping near the old yard fence, thinking of his childhood. He told Brown how hurt he had been on discovering that an old boyhood friend, Johnson McKowan, had been hunting for him.

The letter goes on expressing sorrow and indignation over his family's attitude toward him. He had been told never to set foot in the house again and even his brother, Jim, had turned against him. This, to Longley, was no cause for self-reproach. His reaction was that his family were 'goddam cowardly'.

A clue to the imbalance between extrovert and introvert in his nature comes in his plaintive cry about 'treading alone the living land, destitute of friends'. Here is the self-dramatising Longley, feeling sorry for himself, looking for a shoulder to cry on, posing as a lost soul in an alien world. In the same sentence he is rebuking the world around him, Figuratively shaking his fist, brandishing his pistol, defying everyone, 'every son of a bitch that don't like me,' representing himself as a wolf howling in the night. There is also a strong touch of fatalism, as when he says he expects to be killed sometime.

*See Appendix five.

It is not until the end of his letter that he gets round to the business of Wilson Anderson. You all know, he tells the sheriff, that Anderson killed little Caleb 'and why in the hell does outsiders want to take a hand in it for?' It was a simple case of dog eating dog.

When, eventually, Longley was arrested and tried for the murder of Anderson, his brother, Jim, was also arrested as an accomplice and later discharged. The suggestion is that Jim accompanied Bill to Anderson's farm. In his letter Longley emphasises that Jim had nothing to do with the killing. 'He did not know that I was going to do it until it was done.' He asked the sheriff to use his influence, if Jim were arrested, to get him released. If Brown agreed to do so, Longley 'would be his bosom friend.'

8

'Ten years ago I launched my boat on the mighty river that leads to destruction.' -Bill Longley.

Governor Coke and his Lieutenant Governor, R. B. Hubbard, had promised that the state government would be administered in the interests of every citizen regardless of colour, station or politics. The Negro reconstruction troops had been disbanded and replaced by the Texas Rangers, who were active in every county. To show they meant business, the Rangers had taken every man in the county at the head of Liano River, near Junction, to a 'bull pen' for screening and released all but forty on the wanted list. The same procedure had proved effective near the Nueces River. Thousands of warrants were being issued for wanted men, and there was to be no respite.

Six months after the killing of Anderson, Longley turned up north of Waco and found work on the farm of Captain Sedbury. He was using the name of Jim Patterson. Sedbury was impressed by his hard work, ten hours a day, and allowed him to board in his home instead of the bunkhouse.

On Saturday nights Longley and another farmhand liked to go to Frank Jones's store on the Dallas-Waco road, two miles from the farm, to play cards and 'chew fat'. There are two versions of what happened in the store when they got into a card game with George Thomas.

One is that when the storekeeper went to his room above the store an argument broke out between Longley and Thomas, who banged on the store door and shouted for Jones to come down and sell or lend him a pistol. Before the storekeeper came down, Longley walked over to Thomas and shot him dead on the doorstep.

The other version is that Sedbury, who kept a pack of fifteen foxhounds, organised a moonlight foxhunt. There was a big following and after a while the hunt was abandoned in favour of a horse race. Money was staked, jugs filled with gin and fights broke out. Thomas picked a quarrel with Longley, who drew his pistol. Someone grabbed the pistol and there was a brawl. Longley then challenged Thomas to a duel next day, with pistols, from a distance of ten paces. Later, Thomas returned and said he wanted to settle the matter the next time they chanced to meet. Retrieving his pistol, which had been handed to Sedbury, Longley went after him and found him at the store, where he had awakened the storekeeper and was talking to him on the step. 'This is our first meeting and I'm ready to settle the argument,' Longley is reputed to have said. Thomas drew, but Longley beat him to the draw and put a bullet through his heart, then fired three more at him.

Whatever version is nearest the truth, Longley shot and killed Thomas and had to leave the Sedbury farm.

Twenty miles from San Antonio he came across a Mexican ranch on the Medina. It was a tumbledown place, dirty and rough. Dogs and chickens appeared to have the run of it. But he needed somewhere to stay for the night and asked if he could bunk there. Four Mexicans and their womenfolk were living in the shack and had no objection to his staying the night. They did not talk much and accepted his presence without wanting to know anything about him.

During the night he felt uneasy and rested without going to sleep. After midnight his unease was justified. One of the Mexicans crept out of the shack and it was near daybreak before he returned. In the morning Longley discovered that his horse was missing. The Mexicans said it must have been stolen by Indians and shrugged aside the complaint as they ate breakfast.

Longley strode over to the table, grabbed the man who had gone out in the night and brought the butt of his pistol down on his head. Turning to the other three, he threatened to shoot them if they did not return his horse. His fury left them in no doubt that he meant what he threatened. They urged their companion, staggering about the room semi-conscious from the wound on his head, to return the horse. 'Si, si. . .' he muttered. After his wound had been bathed and he had regained his senses, he led the way seven miles downriver to the place where he had tethered the horse to a tree.

Longley showed no mercy. Though he had safely recovered his horse and already inflicted a head wound on the Mexican, it was not the end of the matter. He shot the hapless man dead in a way that can only be described as 'an execution' and rode back to dispense similar 'justice' to the other three. They saw him coming and seeing no sign of their companion, realised what had happened and fled for safety into the chaparral. Longley could not be bothered to pursue them and decided to make tracks for Frio Canyon in Bandera County, which had appealed to him when he passed through it once before. 'One of the prettiest localities I had ever seen,' he said.

For a few weeks he worked at the Wadkins ranch, mending farm equipment, and in the district met a less notorious desperado named Will Scrier, who told him his real name was Lon Sawyer. They became friends, but Longley's instinct told him not to trust the fellow.

In a magazine article some years ago, Bill Longley's nephew, Dewey Byron Longley, wrote: Bill had that keen intuition that seems to run in our family. It happened that he and Sawyer used the same mail box. Bill later explained to my grandfather:

'Something inside my head kept telling me to watch that mail box. I had a feeling I had to examine every letter Sawyer placed in that box. I did. And one day I found he had written one to the sheriff. I opened it and read it. Sawyer told who I was and promised to split the reward with the sheriff.'

This was enough to decide Sawyer's immediate fate. Longley's first impulse was to put a bullet through him. But an idea occurred to him and he smiled wryly to himself. Sawyer had tried to betray him. There was a price on Sawyer's head. Why not betray him?

Without delay, he rode to Uvalde, the county seat, and told Justice of the Peace Herman Rice he had reason to believe that Will Scrier, working on a farm next to the Wadkins ranch, was Lon Sawyer. Rice thanked him for the information and deputized him to make the arrest. He also deputized a man named Hays to help him. The most notorious outlaw in Texas now left Uvalde with a deputy sheriff's badge pinned to his shirt.'

As a ruse, he introduced Hays as a friend and to get Sawyer into the open told him they had killed a cow a mile or so away and needed help to cut it up. Sawyer was promised a good quarter of beef if he would help.

There were plenty of caballos and longhorned cattle roaming the area and Sawyer suspected nothing out of the ordinary. He instructed a farmhand to hitch a wagon for carting the beef and the three set off together.

In open country, Longley produced the warrant he had been given by the sheriff and said he was arresting him. Sawyer looked at the piece of paper, taking it to be a joke. It was official-looking and Longley's expression confirmed it was not a joke. 'I'll see you in hell,' Sawyer roared and, brandishing his pistol, broke away into the brush. A bullet from Longley's Colt struck him under the right shoulder. Sawyer lurched in his saddle and fired wildly in Longley's direction. Hays was nowhere in sight. His horse had bolted into a cedar brake. The fight was between Longley and Sawyer. With their horses rearing and stumbling as they plunged into the brush, accurate firing was impossible, but more by chance than aim four of Longley's bullets found their way into Sawyer's back and one struck his saddle, disabling his horse. In a glade Sawyer fell but managed to grab hold of his shotgun and bring down Longley's horse with a point blank blast.

Finding he had forgotten to bring extra ammunition for his Colt, Longley tried to use a cap-and-ball pistol, but the caps were wet and would not ignite. Sawyer was crawling into the undergrowth and if he got far enough into it, there were hundreds of places where he could hide. Quickly, Longley ran back to the wagon to see if Sawyer had left a gun. There was a cowboy rifle with three cartridges. Taking one of the horses from the wagon team, he rushed back into the brush and was searching for Sawyer when he heard hounds in full cry.

Hearing the shots and suspecting that his father was in trouble, Sawyer's son had turned them loose. While Longley's attention was distracted by the sound of the hounds, Sawyer seized his chance and from behind a clump of bushes, fired his shotgun. He missed. Longley jumped from the horse and fired at Sawyer with the cowboy rifle, then turned to fire at the hounds which were almost on him. Two of the hounds were killed and the rest, described by Longley as 'a sorry lot', ran off into the brush.

Pushing his way slowly through the undergrowth, Longley worked his way round to the back of the spot where Sawyer had fired at him and found him lying dead, a rifle bullet between his eyes.

'Bill told my grandfather that Sawyer was the bravest man he ever fought, ' said Dewey Longley.

Sawyer's body was strapped to a horse and taken to Uvalde, where Longley, unrecognised by the sheriff, collected the 500 dollars reward and surrendered his commission, taken out in the name of James Webb. Impressed by his success, the sheriff gave him a number of other warrants for such outlaws as Jack Bolt and King Fisher, in case he happened to come across them.

King Fisher, three years younger than Longley, was high on the list of desperadoes wanted by the Texas Rangers, whose Book of Knaves (also called Crime Book and Bible Two) gave the names, aliases and descriptions of more than three thousand men, most of them drifters from outside the state who lived by gambling and theft.*

Fisher was a product of the 'terrible seventies', the head of a well-organised gang of renegades who operated close to the Mexican border where they made their own laws.

For four years, during the Civil War, the border had been unprotected and Mexican bandidos had a free run, stealing cattle and raiding settlements. When Fisher arrived at the Nueces Strip in 1871 to ride the ranges and help protect settlers, he threw himself wholeheartedly into the task of waylaying Mexican bandits, retrieving stolen cattle and breaking in horses. Left to use his initiative and finding plenty of stray horses and cattle he could sell for ten dollars a head to the drovers preparing for the big drives to the cattle towns, the dream of an empire began to take shape in his mind. As he rode around the settlements on a mustang, Yaller Lightnin, his reputation grew. He was a natural leader of men, especially desperadoes; he attacked the Mexican bandits with relish and earned the gratitude of the settlers in protecting their livestock. The criminal element were attracted to his camp because he gave them the same kind of protection. His empire in south-west Texas expanded and his confidence was reflected in the warning

*See Appendix six.

King Fisher, top gun in the border country along the Rio Grande.

outside his ranch in Dimmit County: 'This is King Fisher's road. Take the other.'

What would have happened had Longley, armed with the warrant, tried to serve it on Fisher when Fisher was at the height of his power and influence, can be readily imagined. The two did not have much in common, While Fisher was a forceful leader whose men never hesitated to obey his commands, Longley was a lone rider without any desire to lead a gang or control his own territory. What they did have in common was marksmanship, self-determination and, until overtaken by fate, a capacity for survival in a violent society. Few gunslingers - there were at least 250 in the south-west in the 1870s - reached middle age. The average life span was thirty years. Ben Thompson reached the ripe age of forty-two, Fisher thirty.

Violence was a normal, everyday fact of life to these men. They had grown up in a period when sudden death was a common occurrence, especially in the frontier areas where marauding bandits and hostile Indians took a heavy toll of life.

> These were frontier towns, ol' pardner;
> Twas a game & take an' give
> And the one who could draw the fastest
> Was the only one who'd live.

After the Civil War young men who had been trained to kill returned home ready and willing to make use of their skill with firearms at a time when proper law enforcement was impossible under the reconstruction government's preference for political lackey in high office.

The Texas Rangers, formed in the 1830s, represented the state's underlying social conscience and desire to free itself of anarchy, lawlessness and bloodshed. *

Where the likes of Longley, Fisher and other outlaws gained in popular notoriety was in their defiance of the much-hated state police, mostly comprised of Negroes, formed by Governor Davis. A curious syllogism operated. The state police were feared and loathed, as instruments of carpetbagger and scalawag rule.

*The first task of a Texas Ranger was to patrol the Rio Grande. If he survived this initiation test, being shot at by Mexican bandits, he was called 'a good man to ride the river with', a phrase which has continued in Texas to denote a reliable, endurable companion.

Ben Thompson, another noted Texas gunslinger. He outlived most of his contemporaries by surviving until he was aged 42.

Outlaws such as Longley and Fisher were on the state police wanted list. Therefore, the outlaws, while condemned, enjoyed a certain fame as enemies of the state police. In the circumstances it was fairly easy for writers of pulp-fiction to romanticise these outlaws, concentrating on their prowess with pistols, their horsemanship and their independence. Unattractive aspects of their characters were suppressed for the sake of romantic appeal.

They lived and died according to prevailing conditions and the insecurity which governed livelihood beyond the collective forms of civilised restraint.

Towns such as Abilene were 'wide open,' filled with gamblers, cowboys hot and dusty from the cattle trail, outlaws and opportunists. In these communities, there were no traditions, no established ethics, and few civilizing influences to control behaviour.

Fisher tried, and for a while succeeded, to establishing his own empire, medieval in its self-jurisdiction. Longley was caught between the devil inside himself and the Evergreen trees of home. Bouts of homesickness punctuated his roaming, but his foremost emotional response was not to homely virtues; it was to the social upheavals and the implicit convictions that arguments could most effectively be resolved with a six-shooter.

He had faith, even when in jail, that fortune would smile on him and in this respect he was usually willing to let destiny guide him. Meanwhile, he was an opportunist.

Outside Castroville, on the road to San Antonio, he encountered two men who told him that their brother was in the town jail. They offered him 250 dollars if he would help to get him out.

'What's he in jail for?' Longley asked.

'Killing a dago'.

'If he was in jail for robbery I would not help, Longley said.

The strategy was first to put the sheriff off his guard. This proved fairly easy over whisky and cards in the saloon.

'What brings you to these parts?' the sheriff asked.

Longley explained he had been a lawman in Uvalde and was looking for Jack Bolt and another man, whose description he had jotted down. He showed the sheriff the description, roughly written on a piece of paper, and, of course, it fitted the prisoner in jail.

'Better come and see him,' said the sheriff. 'He may be your man.'

The sheriff got poor return for his generosity in first inviting Longley to his house for supper. Once inside the jailhouse the convivial mood of the bogus lawman changed abruptly and became threatening, reinforced with a Colt prodded into the sheriff's back.

'Just a little joke,' said Longley. 'You won't be hurt. Just stay quiet and unlock the door. There's a friend in there I want.'

The sheriff infuriated by the trick played on him, asked Longley not to turn loose all the other prisoners.

'It's just one I want,' Longley said.

Prisoner and sheriff exchanged places and outside the town Longley was paid his reward.

Near Lockhart it was Longley's turn to be held up at pistol point. A local ordnance forbade the carrying of weapons. A lawman noticed his Colt and asked him why he was carrying it. Longley showed him the warrants he had been given in Uvalde and asked to see proof of his questioner's identity. The man said he had no badge or papers with him, so Longley 'relieved him of his pistol' and continued his journey.

His wanderings led, in February 1876, to the northern section of Delta County, where he stopped for a night at a farmhouse. He had been roaming through east Texas and Arkansas and was again looking for a farm where he could settle down to work. He was hungry after living for weeks on ground corn, mixed with water and rolled in hot ashes, and he needed rest.

No one, provided he looked respectable - and Longley was fastidious about his appearance - was turned away from a farmhouse without food and lodging. To the farmer, Herman Jack, he introduced himself as William Black. The moment he set eyes on Jack's sixteen year old daughter, Livina (or Louvena) he was infatuated. She had polite manners and considerable poise and over supper Longley decided he had to find an excuse for staying longer than one night, in order to get to know her.

During the night he slipped quietly out of the house and drove a nail into his horse's hoof. In the morning, after going through the motions of taking his leave, he mounted his horse, went a few yards and turned back to say it was lame and would need time to recover.

Jack said he could stay as long as he needed and if he wanted work, he could arrange it with the Reverend Roland Lay, who had a farm nearby. The two rode over in Jack's buggy. Lay, a circuit-riding preacher, said he needed someone to attend to his farm while he was away and was glad to hire Longley.

He worked hard on the farm to make a good impression on Livina. He did not know that the Reverend Lay's nephew was in love with her and hoped to marry her. Livina, however, responded to Longley's attention. When the Lay family noticed that she was spending time with him and that her interest was more than casual friendship, they decided to intervene. Lay's sister told him that Livina was too young and too good for him. She came from a very respectable family and he, a hired hand, had no business thinking of marrying into such a family, if that was his intention. Her son would soon be running his own farm, with a brace of mares and a rig, and would be able to provide a proper home.

Longley was not put off. In a letter home he wrote 'I have met the first girl I ever loved and never on earth will forget the feeling in my heart the moment I laid eyes on her.'

The Reverend Lay agreed that William Black would have to go. He had no complaint about his work. In fact, his hired hand was far more industrious than any other worker he had employed and did more work about the farm than he had to.

Intimidating tactics were tried. Longley found a note tied to his plough handle: 'Do you know that danger is all around you? This is to tell you that if you don't get out of this country at once your hide won't be worth shucks.'

The ruse did not work. Longley wrapped the note around a rock, flung it into the air and blasted it with his six-shooter.

One of the Lay family was watching from the bushes to make sure he read the note. Soon the story was known throughout the community and instead of being driven away, Longley found himself something of a hero. Three days later he found another note attached to his plough handle, with a similar threat. He ignored it.

The following Sunday, after attending a morning church service at White Rock, he saw a letter nailed to a tree 'Bill Black - Did you know that hell had tore loose in Georgia? Well, it has. You have been asked to leave this community and now you are going to have to go and that pretty quick.'

Longley went straight to the Reverend Lay and accused him of being responsible for the notes or of approving them. Lay denied it, but said it would be best if he left before there was any trouble.

Given his pay, Longley went off in search of work on another farm and found employment at fifteen dollars a week, plus beans, on a farm ten miles away. Then he rode back to see Livina. They were sitting on her veranda when one of the Lay clan rode up in a violent temper, shouting at Longley to go away. As the argument became more heated, Livina's dog ran from inside the house barking and the horseman shot it dead. Screaming and in tears, Livina tried to fling herself at him, but he turned and rode off. Longley jumped on his horse and went after him. The chase continued for two miles. Finally, Longley got alongside and pulled him from his horse. For once he did not use his six-shooter to settle an argument. He used a riding whip, slashing him across the face, chest and arms and after smashing his pistol against a tree, whipped him on his way.

The Lays were influential in Delta County and if Longley expected to avoid arrest he was mistaken. He was on a cotton wagon when lawmen arrested him on a charge of assault and battery. The Lays had sworn out a warrant, accusing him of threatening the life of Lay. A bond of two thousand dollars was imposed, normally the sum set when a killing was involved.

For six days Longley languished in jail, fearful that his real identity would be discovered. There was no hope of his raising the bond money for his release, as he had no friends in the county.

On the night of June 12 he made a pile of his bed clothes, wood shavings and paper in the plank jail and set it alight.

In the panic and confusion that followed he escaped and 'borrowed' a horse to ride to the Lay farm. It was the middle of the night when he arrived. At daybreak the Reverend Lay would be first out of the house to milk the cow. Longley decided to rest in the barn and wait.

Lay's daughter, who at the time was six weeks' old, described in later years, when she was Mrs. Will C. Havens, what happened that fateful morning, as told to her by her grandparents

'Father rose about daylight on the morning of June 13, 1876, and went out to the cow lot to milk the cow. He, Black, shot father while he was milking the cow and made his escape. Father lived until late in the afternoon. Black said, after killing father, that he had killed fifteen other men before he killed father.'

Longley shot him with buckshot from a shotgun he had collected from the Jacks' farm after his jail escape. It was one of the rare occasions on which Longley killed an unarmed man. Lay's shotgun was propped against the side of the barn.

Longley's own account of the shooting claimed that he asked the preacher why he did not let him alone when he was at peace with him and his family. Lay gave no answer, so he (Longley) dropped his gun level with his body and fired. 'He fell backwards and I left him.'

A hue-and-cry broke out as Longley rode toward the Red River.

The community was outraged by the killing and a large posse was formed. But the posse was unable to catch up with him before he crossed into Indian territory. None of them was willing to go that far after him and risk a skirmish with border Indians.

9

'You had better tie me and tie me hard and fast.'- Bill Longley

For nine days Longley wandered in the border country without seeing any Indians, living on what he could shoot or trap and longing for a bowl of sonofabitch stew, a staple Bunkhouse diet.

On the tenth day he met a lone Indian who spoke a little English and they agreed to trade horses. The Indian had a far fitter horse and so Longley threw in a shotgun. Later, the Indian caught up with him, complained that the horse he had been given was no good and demanded the return of his own horse. Longley refused. The Indian drew a knife and lunged at him. Longley jumped back and before the Indian could lunge again, shot him with his Colt at point-blank range.

Three squaws on a ridge a hundred yards away screamed at him and shouted. They turned and began making signals. Correctly, Longley guessed they were calling their braves. Several of them appeared as he rode off. His horse, the Indian's horse, was fresh and he had no trouble drawing away from his pursuers.

For the next two days he kept as much as possible to the woods and when on open ground, covered his tracks by trailing brushwood. Feeling, as he put it, 'like a wild and hunted animal,' he reached the Arkansas River and paused for a while on a bluff. His rest was shattered by the cries of the Indians. They had seen him from a distant hill and were riding toward him. In his hurry to get away he dropped his saddlebags and hat. There was no time to collect them. The river was four miles away and the country between was open, giving no protection. It was a race between him and the Indians. He had gone only a few hundred yards when one of the Indians, who appeared to be a chief, drew level. Longley felt a stab of pain in his ribs, but stayed on his horse without slackening his pace.

His speed took him on and he did not look round until he had reached the river. The Indians were still some way behind, but catching up fast. Only then did he realise that a bullet had broken one of his ribs. He was losing blood and felt weak.

Summoning all his strength, he dropped from his horse and plunged into the river. It was the only possible way of escaping from the oncoming Indians. His gamble was that they would not follow against the strong current. Had he been any weaker, he would surely have been borne away by the current and dashed on the rocks in the rapids downstream. In spite of his leanness and his wound, Longley had tremendous reserves of strength and they served him now, against the current. When he reached the opposite bank, he saw the Indians had stopped and were watching him, making no attempt to follow. On foot, he stumbled through thickets, dazed and in pain until finally he fell, exhausted.

How long he had been unconscious he did not know. When he came to, a half-breed Cherokee girl was bathing his head. She had found him on her way to get water from a spring.

It is one of the romantic ironies of Longley's life that twice when he was in a desperate position and in danger of losing his life, a young woman was at hand to help him, unaware of the reasons for his plight and apparently attracted by his looks. He was, in these circumstances, the epitome of the tall, dark stranger.

Speaking English, the Indian girl said it would be dangerous for him to move until he could walk properly. It was safer for him to remain and rest in the thickets. For nine days she came every day to tend to him. She dressed his wound, brought him food and water and must have felt a strong attraction toward him to risk the punishment that would have been meted out to her if the Indians had discovered her charity.

The bullet had not lodged in his body and thanks to the special care he received, he was soon well enough to travel on. The Cherokee girl brought him a pair of moccasins and told him how to get to the railroad, by walking east toward Fort Gibson. He thanked her, but if he seized the chance to express his gratitude more amorously, he did not recount it.

Outside Fort Gibson he managed to scramble on to a slow-moving freight wagon, without knowing where it was going. Any destination, he thought, would do in the circumstances.

Along the line, he remembered he had a friend in Sebastian County, which he estimated to be about ninety miles away. Leaving the freight wagon, he set out to finish the journey on foot. It must have been an ordeal. Apart from the constant danger of walking into an Indian hunting party, there was a risk of exhaustion in the sun by day and attack from wild nocturnal animals when he slept in the woods. Without a horse, he was particularly vulnerable, but he kept going and completed the journey in six days.

His friend was pleased to see him and invited him to stay as long as he liked, provided him with a horse, new clothes and bullets for his Colt. For three months he made the most of his friend's generous hospitality.

Then homesickness once more got the better of him. No matter how far he roamed and whatever befell him, Evergreen beckoned. He had long since run foul of his parents, who now preferred to blot him out of their lives as if he had never been born and did not speak of him, even among themselves. But in his wishful thinking he imagined they would be glad to see him at their home in Bell County and would forget the past.

On his way to Evergreen he was unaware that Governor Coke had revoked a 250 dollar reward for the killer of Wilson Anderson and increased it under a new proclamation dated June 23, 1876, concerning the killing of the Reverend Roland Lay. The earlier proclamation (August 24, 1875) read :

> 'To all to whom these presents shall come : Whereas it has been made known to me that on the 31 day of March, 1875, in the County of Lee, State of Texas, William Longley did murder Wilson Anderson and that the said William Longley is still at large and a fugitive from justice. Now, therefore, I, Richard Coke, Governor of Texas, do hereby offer a reward of two hundred and fifty dollars for the arrest and delivery of the said William Longley to the sheriff of Lee County inside the jail door of said County and revoke and annul all proclamations heretofore issued by the Governor of Texas offering a reward for the arrest of the said William Longley.'

The new proclamation read:

> 'Whereas, it has been made known to me, that on the 13th day of June 1876, in the County of Delta, State of Texas, William Black, alias William Longley, did murder Roland Lay and that said murderer is now at large and a fugitive from justice. Now therefore, I, Richard Coke, Governor of Texas, do, by virtue of the authority vested in me by the Constitution and laws of this state, hereby offer a reward of five hundred dollars for the arrest and delivery of the said William Black, alias William Longley, the sheriff of Delta County inside the jail door of said County and hereby revoke and annul all rewards heretofore offered for the arrest of William Longley.'

What distinguished Longley as an outlaw was his detachment and indifference to rewards on his head. Had he known when he crossed the Red River into Texas and carried on to Denison, that his price had doubled, he would not have changed directions. Experience and fortuitous events in the past had given him an inert conviction that whatever the circumstances, he would survive.

The homeward road was strewn with whisky bottles. In need of stronger drink than he carried in his canteen, he stopped at a shack on the road into Denison and drank himself into a boisterous and belligerent condition.

The bar-tender sent someone into Denison to get law officers to arrest him. When they approached and tried to quieten him, he shouted defiance, pushed past them and got on his horse to go cantering down the Bonham Road. As he was heading away from town they did not bother to chase him. As far as they were concerned, he was just another drunken saddlebum who could not hold his whisky.

Eight miles from Denison, when he had sobered up a little, he ran into a deputy sheriff who had arrested two brothers, Dick and Jim Saunders and was taking them to jail. Longley recognised them as old acquaintances and stopped to pass the time of day with the sheriff. With a sly wink at the brothers, he offered the lawman a drink of whisky from the bottle he had bought at the store. The moment the bottle touched his lips, the deputy felt Longley's Colt in his ribs.

'Drop your belt and release them,' Longley commanded.

'You'd better do it, Bryant,' said one of the brothers. 'This is Bill Longley and he'll kill you sure if you don't act quick.'

Bryant needed no further persuasion. He dropped his gun belt and released the prisoners. Longley ordered him to move away and kept him covered with his six-shooter as he picked up the officer's pistols and gave them to the brothers.

The scene was witnessed by some farmers on three wagons which had pulled up, and by people at a nearby farmhouse, none of whom intervened.

The brothers and Longley celebrated with whisky and then rode off, leaving the deputy standing.

Next night Longley appeared at the Jack farm in Delta County. In spite of the search for him and the risk he was taking returning so close to the scene of his crime, he wanted to see Livina. She told him that lawmen had found a picture of him at the Reverend Lay's house and from this had discovered his real identity. Copies of the picture had been circulated all over the state.

The Saunders waited for him while he spoke with the girl. She urged him to get far away from the county and not to make contact with her again. She appears to have had sympathy for him, even after the murder.

In the morning Longley and the brothers left the area, but realised they could not ride together without arousing suspicion. Posses would be after them. Again, Longley's simple ingenuity asserted itself. He would pose as a sheriff, with Jim Saunders as his deputy and Dick as their prisoner, his feet tied under his horse and his hands bound to his saddle horn.

If anyone stopped them they would say they were taking in a desperado named Bill Taylor, for whom they had a warrant from Gonzales County.

This way, they rode through several small towns and villages and went on to Milam County to visit the brothers' home. After supper, Longley said he wanted to be on the trail to his home county. Jim offered to ride with him, if Longley did not mind waiting until morning. Longley said he would be glad of the company and next morning they set off. On the road to Milano deputy sheriff Matt Shelton stopped them and began questioning them, wanting to know where they had been and where they were going.

By this time Longley had discarded his fake warrants and tried to bluff his way out. He pretended to be an officer from Bell County on the trail of a horse thief. Shelton said he did not believe him and when he persisted with his questions, Longley drew his pistol and disarmed him. (The pistol he took from the deputy, a Smith and Wesson, was later found in Longley's possession in Louisiana). The officer's horse was turned loose into the oak woods and like the other deputy, Shelton was left standing to watch the desperadoes ride away.

Longley's homecoming must have been fraught with tension and displeasure. His parents had forbidden him to set foot in the house, but must have relented, possibly because he was with a companion. He and Saunders were allowed to stay the night, provided they left in the morning. Longley learned of the latest proclamation against him and was told that the Texas Rangers were anxious to seize him. Furthermore, local bitterness and resentment against him had increased after the killing of Wilson Anderson. Even those who would have helped him in the past were now his sworn enemies. Although the Longleys believed that Anderson had killed Caleb by a blow on the head, consensus in the county favoured Anderson's story that it was an accident.

Saunders returned home and Longley was once more on a wandering trail to nowhere in particular while the Texas Rangers intensified their hunt for outlaws. Deciding that retreat was the better part of valour, he went to Louisiana and on the farm of W. T. Gamble, near Keatchie, on Cypress bayou, he made a sharecropping deal that gave him a cotton patch living. Gamble knew him as Will Jackson and had to concede he had never known such an ardent worker. From dawn to dusk Longley worked his cotton patch and at weekends went coon-hunting with his employer. On one of the hunts around Cypress Creek, Gamble introduced him to a friend, Junius Courtney, a young farmer who had been elected town constable.

There was an immediate rapport and Courtney, being new to law enforcement, asked him to help him when arrests had to be made. All he needed, he explained, was a little physical assistance and moral support. Longley said he would be pleased to oblige and was true to his word. He helped Courtney make several arrests, mainly of petty criminals and drunks. On these occasions Longley must have over-played his hand, for Courtney became suspicious. For a farm worker and share cropper, 'Jackson' was surprisingly good at making arrests, resolute and confident. He was deadly accurate with a six-shooter and rifle on coon and fox hunts, more than an ordinary farm worker was likely to be. And why did he carry his six-shooters when he was working his crop when they could only be a hindrance to him?

To confirm or allay his suspicions, Courtney wrote to Sheriff Milton Mast in Nacogdoches, across the state line in Texas. He gave a description of 'Jackson' and asked if it tallied with anyone on the wanted list.

Mast had been studying a letter sent to him by a Lee County official, describing Longley as 'the worst man in Texas' and asking him to be on the look-out for the desperado:

> 'He is about six ft high, weighs 150 lbs. tolerable spare built, black hair, eyes and whiskers, slightly stooped in shoulders. . .. can be recognised in a crowd by the keenness and blackness of his eyes several rewards offered for him by citizens, one from this county for 250 dollars. . . You will have to take advantage of him. He will fight and is a good shot.'

Courtney's description of Jackson resembled that of Longley. Without delay, Mast set off with his deputy, William Burrows, for Keatchie. First, they consulted Courtney and showed him a picture of Longley. 'That's him,' Courtney said. 'No doubt about it.'

Mast was excited. He was close to capturing an outlaw who had managed to evade, or escape from, law officers over a sizeable area of Texas. But he knew it would be fatal, for him and his deputy, to approach without the utmost caution and without a plan. They decided to wait until Longley was hoeing and act on the presumption that he would be wearing his six-shooters.

Gamble had to be informed and his assistance sought in the plan. He was astonished and when he was convinced there was no mistake, said it was a terrible shame, for 'Jackson' was a good worker and was bringing the crop on well. He did not know of Bill Longley, and if he were a dangerous desperado, he would help to capture him. All he had to do, Mast told him, was keep out of the way while he, Mast, and his deputy sat on the porch of his house, in the shadows. If everything went according to plan there would be no shooting.

The officers placed seats on the porch and signaled Courtney to make the first move. This was for him to go to the corn patch and tell Longley that he needed his help in making another arrest.

Two lawmen from another parish, he said, had also come to help arrest a desperate criminal and were waiting at Gamble's house. Longley agreed, put down his hoe and in his overalls and brogans, left the field and strode with Courtney to the house. The moment he stepped on the porch, Mast and Burrows moved from the shadows to seize his arms before he could get a hand to the six shooter in his overalls hip pocket. Quickly, they bound his hands behind his back and told him he was under arrest.

Struggling and protesting, he was bundled on to a wagon and no time was wasted in getting over the Texas border, ten miles away.

The arrest was made on Wednesday, May 13, 1877. Two days later he was under close guard in Henderson, fifty miles away. Mast stayed with his prisoner throughout the night and kept him bound.

In the morning, Longley was taken by train to Overton and put on another train first to Palestine, then to Houston. Full circle. Eleven years ago he had been to Houston to buy his first single action Dance six-shooter. Now he was back in Houston, but his six-shooters were in the possession of Sheriff Mast.

From Houston he was taken to Giddings, where, on May 18, he was delivered to the jail. Various rewards for his capture amounted to 1,050 dollars.

Bill Longley (centre) immediately after his capture flanked by officers Bill Burrows and Sheriff Mast.

10

Well the blow is over, the die is cast and I am condemned without the sympathy of a single person.' - Bill Longley

The *Galveston News* was pithy and succinct in its report of Longley's capture: 'The veritable Bill Longley, notorious Texas desperado after being captured in Louisiana a few days ago, was brought to this place and confined in Lee County jail today to await trial in one of his thirty-two murders.'

'Abundance of rain. Crops very promising.'

The 'one murder' was that of Wilson Anderson, for which his brother, Jim, aged seventeen, was indicted as an accomplice.

Reporters were allowed to visit Longley in jail. He was pleased to see them. They found him composed, cocky in his belief that somehow he would get out of jail and boasting that no jail had ever kept him for long. He was voluble during the interviews and enjoyed the attention he was receiving from the press. Most of his time awaiting trial was spent giving interviews and writing long, self-justifying letters to newspapers.

A 'sketch of the man and his history' appeared in the *Galveston News* on July 7 under the title of 'The Arch Desperado of the West,' by a special correspondent, who reported that the jail was a good one of the iron cage kind, kept clean and tidy by the sheriff, 'who watches William like a hawk'.

Longley was described by the correspondent as 'a tall, well-made young man of very pleasing address, not a repulsive feature in his face, eyes sharp but not savage'. The prisoner, he continued, had no hesitation in speech, laughed and talked freely.

'The listener would not, if ignorant of his history, dream that he was talking with perhaps the most desperate and bravest man in the West. His personal controversies of an exciting and aggravating nature began when he was a mere boy and up to this time he has killed about thirty-two men.'

He had not travelled about, like Wesley Hardin and King Fisher, with 'a crowd of murdering followers,' but had usually operated on his own, 'asserting his rights to liberty and freedom under magna charta through the prowess of his own right arm'.

The cell in which he was incarcerated was also occupied by two thieves and a Negro, who had killed his own nephew, a young boy.

> 'Longley and the thieves tried the Negro upon being caught and condemned him to a hundred lashes which one of them, the most athletic, administered with a boot and subsequently stripped him of his clothes, which they burned to smoke off the mosquitoes. When visitors come in the jail Longley orders out the naked Negro murderer and indulges in various satirical and jocular remarks at his expense'.*

This he did for the edification of the News reporter.

According to the reporter, Longley had spent nine months in the guard-house at one of the frontier posts, and:

> ' . . .was sentenced to be shot by court-martial, then to 30 years' imprisonment in the penitentiary. These troubles he escaped, having a charmed life, like Washington at Braddock's defeat'.

A gross exaggeration of the facts.

The military archives division of the United States' National Archives and Records Service shows conclusively that Longley's court-martial sentence was two years' hard labour for desertion.

A fabricated story that he shot and killed a quarter-master, while sentenced to be shot and escaped by sawing off his leg-irons after the sentence had been commuted to thirty years in the Idaho penitentiary, was recalled by Corporal Henry Cross, of the 17th Infantry, Standing Rock, Dakota Territory, former sergeant of B Company, Second Cavalry:

> He was an excellent shot as all of us had already discovered at the weekly company target practice. He excelled with the pistol or revolver and none in camp were his equal with that weapon. I knew him personally. No murder was committed by Longley at Camp Brown, nor did he send the post commissary to the happy hunting grounds.'

* It was common practice by jailers to allow prisoners to strip and flog newcomers who did not have money enough to buy tobacco and various luxuries for other inmates.

Longley, said Cross, who read of the impending trial in the *Chicago Tribune,* was considered by the whole company a man of low instincts and habits, but tolerated on account of his good nature, gift of the gab and excellent marksmanship.

This 'good nature' was not visible to a writer in the *Galveston News,* alarmed by lawlessness in Lee County, where there had been fourteen victims of mob law. in the paper's July 10th edition he wrote

> 'I heard it said that Longley, the champion mankiller of the Lone Star State, in jail here, would try to get a continuance and that if he did he would be taken out of jail and hanged. The people of the county have been sorely tried by the depredations of thieves and murderers and if anywhere lynch law is justifiable it has been here and if any case I have ever heard of could be singled out as one of greater enormity of turpitude than Longley's, it. does not occur to me now, and it may be that in the absence of proof in the particular case he is now charged with in this county he may escape punishment and lynch law be provoked. But until the court fails the mob should desist. If the sheriff can protect his prisoner he should do it.

The Galveston News declared on August 1st, a month before the trial.

> The extent to which Longley was pre-judged before his trial was plain to all who read the newspapers. He will doubtless expect to play the hero if not the Christian under the gallows,

So many reporters and visitors were anxious to see Longley in jail and talk to him, that Sheriff Brown was worried a rescue attempt might be made under cover of a visit or press interview. After a file had been thrown through the bars, he announced that no further visits would be permitted and Longley would be heavily and securely ironed and perpetually guarded.

The *News* commented

> 'It may save the country future expense if a few of his confederates would attempt a rescue and are shot in the meantime,

The trial began in the Giddings courthouse before Judge E. B. Turner, on September 3, 1877. A motion for continuance was overruled, Counsel for the defence having failed to allege the facts to be proved by absent witness.'

The courthouse was packed, many women were among the spectators when Longley was brought in and his shackles removed. Sheriff Brown had summoned a large guard of 'resolute men' armed with shotguns and six-shooters. The atmosphere was tense as fifty men were called to select a jury among them.

Longley was charged with the murder of Wilson Anderson in Lee County.*

His day of reckoning had come. It has been asked why, when he had openly admitted killing several men, he did not face other murder charges. It is conceivable that the authorities, confident that he would be convicted on this single charge and sentenced to hang, saw no point in going to the expense of assembling witnesses and prolonging the proceedings on charges that could exact no greater penalty than the one anticipated for the killing of Wilson Anderson.

'Anyone can kill, but there's no excuse for lying and stealing.' Wife of 'South-West governor, quoted at a cocktail party in Texas, June 1974.

The indictment against Longley's brother, charged with being present at the time and encouraging him in the act, was withdrawn because there was no specific evidence against him.

Longley pleaded not guilty. A reporter noted 'He exhibits or affects exuberant spirits.'

The trial, which had been expected to last for several days, was over in under two days. The jury was out for one hour and thirty minutes, returning to pronounce him guilty of murder in the first degree. The verdict was written on a piece of paper and handed by the foreman to the district clerk, who read it aloud. Judge Turner approved the verdict by pronouncing sentence of death by hanging.

Longley showed no reaction, but back in his cell he felt bitter about the way his lawyer, S. R. Kenada, had represented him. He wrote to the Judge, saying he wished to appeal. But being unfamiliar with civil trials, instead of asking for a new trial, he appealed only against the sentence - a technical detail he had cause to regret.

* See Appendix Seven.

To make sure he was well represented in the appeal he began a correspondence with an eminent criminal lawyer in Richmond, Texas, to secure his services before the Appellate Court. His letter giving an account of the trial was forwarded by the lawyer to the *Galveston News* which published it in full :

'S. R. Kenada, of Burton, Texas, defended me, He is about thirty-five years of age and has been practising law two or three years. He has been in Texas over twenty years and may have been raised here. I think he was. The reason I employed him was this My father was threatened with death if he assisted me in the least and I was not allowed to receive letters or forward any and Sam Kenada came to the jail to see a man that he was defending and I employed him for the pitiful sum of fifty dollars which was all I could raise from my own resources. I was not allowed to talk to him privately. He came back to the jail the second time and the jailer insulted him and he came no more. I saw him no more until inside the bar. They carried me to the courthouse chained hand and foot. They had 30 armed men with shotguns inside the bar all the time with their guns pointed toward me, almost in the act of firing.

The judge ordered the irons taken off when they brought the blacksmith inside the bar and cut them. When the court would adjourn at noon or night, they would rivet the irons on me again right in the bar. I believe if I had raised up on my feet they would have shot me into doll rags.

I must say I never saw as many contemptible, dirty cowards in the crowd before in my life - who one of them would happen to get close to me - and me chained, too - he would become so excited his teeth would chatter like he had an ague.'

Well, Kenada made a very short talk to the jury and asked them to not give me more than imprisonment for life and walked off. That was the last I saw of him. Then Seth Sheppard got up and gave me a blast, and demeaned me to the lowest pitch and said that I had committed many dastardly and cowardly murders and he thought that I certainly ought to die. He was a volunteer lawyer against me - he told me himself that he volunteered his services, though he said the citizens told him if he did not do it they would take me in daylight and hang me.

I am not able to tell you hardly what disadvantage it was for Kenada to abandon me when he did, because I am so unacquainted with law and I do not know what harm it did me. No one ever made a motion for a new trial. Sir, I was even ignorant of such a thing as a new trial, for I never was tried before by civil law. When Kenada left me in the bar, he whispered and told me they would hang me in spite of hell - that is his words - if not by law, they would kill me before I got to jail.

> I was not the least excited because I expected to be killed at any minute. I just thought to myself if God has drawed off from me they will certainly kill me, but I thought to myself just let them kill. If I was only guilty of one cowardly trick in my whole life I would not care if they did kill me, but they cannot say that I am, in truth. All in the world they have against me is that they are afraid of me.'

Longley went on to complain that his lawyer never wrote any statement of facts, never had the state's witnesses put under the rules and said that no one ever did swear that they saw him kill Anderson.

> 'Nothing was positive - only a letter that Jim Brown said he received from me and swore to it. There have been ten or twelve letters written to men in that county with my name signed to them and I never wrote one of them; and as to my witnesses, I had three summoned. One of them was impeached without a cause and another came to me and told me that he would be mobbed if he swore the truth in my case - and he was a good friend to me; and I told him I would let him off for his own good; and the third one was not there at all. So I had no witnesses at all.'

Longley claimed that one witness against him swore a lie.

> He swore that I met him and three other men and told him that I killed Anderson and the date had all four of them summoned and three of them swore that they did not hear my say one word about Anderson and these three were all respectable citizens of Lee County and the one that swore that I told them this was a man by the name of - who had been indicted in Caldwell County for cattle stealing in twenty or thirty cases and they wrote down his evidence and never noticed the three others and was a relative of Anderson's.

Longley maintained in his letter that the testimony against him was not positive. He did not know how the jury was impanelled, whether fair or not.

> The jury was just as prejudiced as they could be. One of them was a Dutchman by the name of - , that my father and several other citizens had whipped about 25 years ago for hog stealing and I am satisfied that all of them were concerned in a mob that came to the jail about one month before court and tried to get the jailer to give them the keys. The only way he could get rid of them was to tell them if I was not convicted that they might have me after court. I heard the conversations and knew nearly all of them. It was about one o'clock

at night. Jim Brown was not there and then they found that I knew them they were determined to kill me then. The man that summoned the jury was an enemy of mine. I don't know whether the jury separated during the trial or not. I never thought of that even. And I don't know of any misconduct of the jury, only they were very unconcerned while Kenada was speaking and would laugh very heartily at him. Sometimes some of them were reading papers and others were engaged in conversation with some of the guards in a low tone. One of them looked at me and gritted his teeth at me while Sheppard was speaking.'

Kenada, said Longley, was not in court when the jury brought in the verdict. One of the jurymen was heard to say 'Boys was not that done up all right? Let us have something to drink on that.'

Everyone in court, except the prisoner, seemed pleased with the verdict.

> 'One fellow by the name of - - - - - came to the jail after the sentence was pronounced and began tantalizing me and I told him he had the advantage of me and he said, 'Yes, you goddam son of a bitch, I have a notion to blow your damn brains out right now,' and drew his pistol and put it through the grates where I was chained to the wall. I pulled open my bosom and told him, 'You cowardly scoundrel, shoot.' Well, it is no use to tell you this. I could tell you a great deal more, but I will not do it now. My lawyer did not try to move the trial at all. I do not know who fixed up the appeal, nor what evidence was written down - they had it all to themselves. When I went back to the jail I sat down and wrote to the judge and told him how I felt about it and that I wanted to appeal and that I hoped his honour would consider my fix and grant it to me. The men that gave him the letter said he cried when he read it. . . I told him I did not believe I had a fair trial and that I wanted to appeal the case.'

When he wrote this letter to the lawyer in Richmond, Longley had been moved for safety to another jail at Galveston after mobs had tried to break into the Giddings jail.

Almost everyone in Galveston turned out to see him arrive on the noon train. The depot platform was crowded to see what one newspaper called 'the champion man-killer'. The authorities however were taking no chances, either of a lynch mob grabbing him or of confederates rescuing him. They took him to Galveston by another route.

The *Daily News* wrote:

'After the cars had arrived, everybody began to retrace his steps to his place of business, thoroughly disgusted with the disappointment he had encountered. The streets were full of boys of all ages, sizes, colours and conditions of precocity. Bootblacks and newsboys were fraternizing with boys whose mamas didn't know they were out and all seemed to be chuck full of the fact that the immortal Bill Longley was about to stand upon these shores and shake his grey locks at whoever felt disposed to gaze upon them.'

Longley was glad to be in the Galveston jail.

I am treated like a man here, not like a dog

Continuing the correspondence with the lawyer, he told him that if he must hang he would hang like a man.

'If I don't get a new trial, that jury has murdered me in colder blood than ever I did a man If they had given me a fair trial it would not have been so bad but I had no showing on earth. They had just as well went and killed me in jail.'

The letter, in the *Galveston Daily News,* infuriated Sheriff Brown, who was at pains to refute most of it and on Oct 24 1877 wrote to put the record straight from his own point of view:

It is absolutely false that Longley's counsel was insulted when he visited the jail. There were not thirty armed men with shotguns inside the bar of the court pointing toward him, but a guard of fifteen men organised, after consultation with the judge, for Longley's protection. There had been intimations that if Longley secured a continuance, an outraged community would try to prevent it. No gun was pointing at Longley at any time and the prisoner was treated with all due consideration, not only in the courtroom but in jail.

The jury was composed of the very best men in the country, selected by Longley and his counsel, both of whom were personally acquainted with every member of the jury. They were perfectly satisfied with the jury, as was evident from the fact that they exercised only twelve of the twenty peremptory challenges allowed by law to the defendant.

Had any of the jurors belonged to a mob, as Longley claimed, he would surely have excluded them from the jury. Nor was it true that the jury had been chosen specifically to try him and were biased in favour of conviction. They were drawn by the Jury Commissioners of the February term before Longley had been arrested and did not know which trial they were to be allocated. Longley's claim that one man summoned the jury to go against him was untrue because the jurors were summoned by different deputies in different parts of the county. Nor did any of the guards speak to the jurors during the trial.

His trial was in every respect fair and impartial. His own statement admits that the judge was fair to him and even sympathetic.

The sheriff pointed out that Longley had repeatedly, both verbally and in writing, admitted his guilt.

'Immediately after committing the murder for which he was tried he rode to the home of his aunt in Burleson County and told both his aunt and uncle that he had that day killed Wilson Anderson. Unwilling witnesses though they were, yet under oath they had to testify to that fact.

The three respectable witnesses he refers to did not say he did not say a word about Anderson but said they did not remember whether he said in express words that he had killed Anderson, but that they knew he left that impression on their minds. The other witness who swore directly that Longley admitted in words that he had killed Anderson is not a bad character, as Longley asserts, but is a respectable citizen and no relation to Anderson.

Brown recalled a letter written to him by Longley soon after the killing, giving his motives for the deed and stated that Longley had never denied authorship of the letter.

It was not true, went on the sheriff, that Longley was not allowed to forward or receive letters in jail. He was allowed to do both:

He wrote to his father not to employ counsel for him, as the state was bound to furnish him with counsel, that he would not give a nickel for any counsel except to put off his trial for six months and that if he could not escape in that time he deserved to be hung. I furnished ink, pen and paper and he was allowed to write to any one he desired, the only limitations being I should see his letters. He is a ready writer and employed much of his time in writing a romance which he called "his life". His father is a respectable citizen and was never prevented from assisting his son.

But the truth is, the father feared the son and stood in great terror of him as did every one in the community. As to his being ironed inside the bar, the fact is that his irons were taken off when he was first brought into the court-room and not put on again until after he was sentenced.'

There was nothing before during or after the trial, insisted the sheriff, that even the most morbid philanthropist could find to condemn.

Longley must have anticipated the sheriff's reaction to his letter forwarded by the lawyer to the Galveston paper.

On the eve of its publication he wrote to him an explanation:

> 'You need not tax it to yourself at all. I done it to try to change public opinion a little, though it is nothing against you, not at all.'

The sheriff regretted that the name of the eminent criminal lawyer of Richmond, Texas, who caused Longley's letter to be published, was not given in the newspaper. 'I feel some anxiety to know,' the sheriff said:

> . . .if he be the same eminent lawyer of Richmond who paid Longley (according to Longley's statement) 250 dollars to kill a Negro for him.'

Commenting on the sheriff's letter, the *Daily News* commended its 'excellent temper and taste' and suggested it was so forceful and masterly that it would no doubt strike impartial readers as conclusive against all the material allegations of Longley:

> At any rate, intelligent and right-minded citizens who are earnestly desirous of purging the state of a pest of murderers and desperadoes by the infallible inflictions of penal justice, are equally solicitous for adhering strictly to due process of law in dealing with all grades of criminals. Consequently it will be their wish to see the Court of Appeals order the rectification of anything that may have been seriously amiss in the trial and the conviction of Longley however firmly they may be persuaded of his guilt.

Public interest in the case led to a suggestion that the *Comanche Chief* newspaper should publish Longley's life story. This the paper declined to do, explaining in a mordant editorial :

> 'Without forestalling public opinion or expressing any view as to the guilt or innocence of that individual, we are inclined to think there is the slightest shadow of a possibility that his death would be of more interest to the readers of this journal than his life.'

The *Daily Democratic Statesman* in Austin pondered the qualities of hemp:

> Hemp, planted in alternate rows with cotton, will destroy, it is said, the cotton worm. It is good, too, we opine, for those worms of the dust who shoot people out west. The courts propose to test its virtues even here in Austin at an early day and Bill Longley, because of his virtues of hemp, is not long for this world. In fact, hemp supplies the hasheesh of oblivion for knaves here and for howling dervishes of Arabian deserts and if it will destroy pests it becomes, in all its aspects, the choicest gift of Providence.

As he waited for the appeal to be heard, Longley turned for comfort to the religion he had forsaken at home. Hypocritically, he told the *Democratic Statesman* that there had always been a spark of Christianity in his bosom and it had kept him from doing many bad things

'My first sin, he said, 'was disobedience toward my parents, next whisky, next carrying pistols, next gambling and then murder.' His five cardinal sins.

The *Texas News* published what was said to be a communication from Longley confessing to the murder of Wilson Anderson and charging that he was incited and urged to the deed by his uncle, Caleb Longley:

> He warns young men to avoid his career and beware of his fate, assuring them that justice will overtake evil-doers, of whom himself is the chief and the most successful desperado of all Texas. He is penitent and thankful that time remains to seek spiritual welfare.

His 'spiritual welfare' was shattered when he heard that John Wesley Hardin* regarded as second only to Longley in the State's list of notorious desperadoes - had been captured and sentenced to twenty-five years in the penitentiary, while he (Longley) had been sentenced to hang. Hardin said he had never had anything to do with Longley, nor other such characters, only with men of honour!

Longley wrote to the *Nacogdoches News*:

> Now I would like to know where those honourable pards of his are. They certainly are not in jail where the Hon. John Wesley is. I wonder if it is King Fisher, Brown Bowen, Bill Taylor, Gladen Ringe, Scott Cooley, Grisson and two or three dozen more such honourable (?)

*See Appendix Eight.

> characters that I could name. I guess Hardin considers it brave and honourable take fifteen or twenty men of the same stripe that I have mentioned in the above and go into Cuero and shoot to death one Rube Brown, the town marshall, because he arrested one of these honourable pards of his for 500 dollars reward.
>
> And also, when him and Jim Taylor and Dickson killed poor Charley Webb in Comanche, one of the best and bravest of young men that the state of Texas afforded.

On October 5 Longley wrote a long, friendly letter to Captain Mast, the sheriff of Nacogdoches County, who had captured him, saying he was broke and asking for fifteen or twenty dollars as part of the reward Mast had received for the capture. There is no record of Mast sending the money.

His letter read:

> I suppose you heard about my trial. I am under sentence of death. They gave it to me at Giddings, you bet they did. They swore bushels of lies on me and I did not have a friend nor a witness. My own father and brothers never came near me. I have not seen one of my kinfolks since I was captured and was flat broke and I am compelled to make this call on you, not that I consider you under any obligations to me at all, but as a friend I would ask you and Bill* to send me 15 or 20 dollars. I am out of tobacco and as the county does not furnish coffee, if I had money I could get it made for me and if you will, I shall appreciate it as a very great kindness from you.
>
> You remember you said you would give me a few dollars but I hope you will not think that I consider you under any obligations that you ought to pay me any of it, for I know that you hardly made expenses and if you should be so kind as to send me a few dollars I should regard it as a kindness in you and not a duty.
>
> 'You know I told you when you left me that I had no hard feelings toward you and Bill for capturing me and would always be a friend to you though you may not believe me, but you ought to know enough about me to know I am neither treacherous nor cowardly and it would be no use to tell you this no how. But you know I told everybody publicly that you and Bill Burrows deserved great credits for the capture of me and you do, too. And I must say that I never was treated better by any one than I was by you and Bill. Tell old Bill I would like to help him crack a big bottle of whisky once more.
>
> 'I will be here until next March and if you or Bill have any business in Galveston I want you to come and see me at my office and you will be apt to find me in my office for I am so busy that I seldom walk out in town. Sheriff Jordan will be apt to know where I am at most any time, for he and I are very intimate. He takes a great interest in my

* William Burrows, Mast's deputy.

welfare. I have been thinking of emigrating to parts unknown, but the sheriff insists on my staying here. I had collected some transportation material in the shape of a few old case-knives, files etc, but the sheriff conceived the idea that I wanted to abscond and made application for my tools the other day on very short notice and succeeded in getting a very good supply out of my office; and, owing to such luck, I guess I shall have to spend the winter in the city. But the sheriff and all his guards are good, jovial fellows. They never get angry at me but they are wide-awake and full of fleas. Well, I must stop my foolishness. You and Bill must write to me sure and tell me what you heard in Delta County.'

Longley's felicity with the Press was the delight of some newspapers and the bane of others. The Dallas Weekly Herald remarked:

> It is astonishing how large a space in the local history of the times in Texas is filled by John Wesley Hardin and Bill Longley. The papers have been filled with them for a month or so. Eminence has its drawbacks in crime as in all other human pursuits.'

The *Galveston News* took Longley under its editorial wing, which, in another edition, caused the *Herald* to comment sourly:

> Whatever fate overtakes sweet William in the future the *News* and the *Giddings Tribune* have provided for the immortality of his name. Ah! William, you little knew to what lofty heights you were about to ascend when the shrieks of your murdered victims first saluted your ears. So the world goes.

Between fifty and sixty letters were sent by Longley to the newspapers. 'Dry up, William,' snapped the *Herald,* which before Longley's trial had summed up the situation in Texas:

> 'Ever since the war Texas to some extent has be almost helpless in the hands of lawlessness and crime. Whole districts of the country have been terrorised, jails ravished, good people murdered. There has been a vast change within the last few months. Some of the most renowned of the desperadoes have been killed, captured or driven off. The Hardin gang about Comanche i scattered and its leading spirit languishes in jail. Longley, who boasts that the blood of thirty-two men stain his hands, is now on trial for his crime. King Fisher, the Taylors and Suttons, are at peace. The Harrell and Higgins feud, which kept the Lampass valleys in a turmoil and which rendered even her mountain fastnesses but an insecure resting place, have made peace. The courts all over the state are in regular operation and juries no longer fear to record a righteous verdict.'

Longley was indignant when the *Brenham Banner* appeared to associate him with the Irvin gang and implicated him in a store robbery at Gay Hill. Replying to his demand for an apology, the Banner replied that it denied that it said he was either connected with the gang or implicated in the robbery. It did say, however, that he was connected with a gang of Yegua Bottom desperadoes, and was 'said to have been' implicated in the Gay Hill robbery:

> These were current reports. The *Banner* has no disposition to do Mr. William Longley an injury, and would not intentionally say anything derogatory to the character of the gentleman. It is good to learn from so reliable a source as Mr. Longley himself that he is innocent of the charges made and cheerfully gives him the benefit of this correction. It also feels perfectly satisfied that he has an abundance of crimes that he really did commit to answer for without accusing him of those in which he had no hand.'

Longley, continued the *Banner*, always put himself in the position of being the aggrieved party:

> There is much cowardice displayed in many of his shooting scrapes. To use a familiar expression, he has always managed to place himself in a position to have 'the drop'.

The *Herald*, meanwhile, agreed with Longley's complaint about the inconsistency between his sentence and that imposed on Hardin, but displayed, too, sardonic satisfaction in the fate allocated to him:

> Bill Longley says he did not get a fair trial. He seems to think there should be a loophole somewhere through which he could get out. He will find it at the end of a rope halter.'

There is no surviving record of Longley's appeal. In 1935 the Court of Criminal Appeals, with the consent of the Board of Control, ordered all the papers from 1909 back, to be destroyed through lack of storage space. All that remains is the legal document setting out the nature of the appeal and the court's findings. From this it is clear that Longley, through his counsel, J.H. Catlin, who filed an ingenious and able brief (in the view of the court), was seeking a particular loophole.

A series of adjudications had firmly established the general rule that, without a statement of facts in evidence before the lower court, the appeals court would only consider whether the indictment would sustain the instructions given to the jury and the judgment rendered.

The court was placed in the 'embarrassing situation of having to pass upon his appeal without the transcript of the record disclosing a single bill of exceptions or a statement of the facts adduced upon the trial.'

Catlin's brief contended that the statute conferred on his client the right to have a statement of the facts certified as part of the record and that the court could not affirm a judgment of conviction in a felony case without having the facts before it, upon which the conviction was based.

To do so, he argued, would be a contravention of the constitutional guarantee that 'no citizen of this state shall be deprived of his life, liberty, property, privileges or immunities or in any manner disfranchised, except by due course of the law of the land'.

The statute conferring this right read:

> 'If a new trial be refused, a statement of facts may be drawn up and certified and placed in the record, as in civil suits. When the defendant has failed to move for a new trial, he is nevertheless entitled, if he appeals, to have a statement of the facts certified and sent up with the record.'

But who was to make out the statement of facts? The parties themselves in the first instance and if they could not agree, then the judge, from their respective statements and his own knowledge. There was no law requiring a district judge, of his own motion, to make out a statement of facts when the parties themselves had expressed no wish and made no effort to have such a statement made and incorporated in the record.

In its adjudication the appeals court said:

> As to who is to blame for the failure to have a statement of the facts made out in the present case, it would be perhaps unprofitable for us to inquire. In a case involving the life of a defendant, and especially after a verdict of conviction imposing the death penalty, and notice of appeal given, it would hardly be presumed that the condemned criminal would quietly suffer the punishment without having first availed himself of every remedy afforded by the law. And yet he himself alone may be to blame; or his attorneys, conversant with the law and the facts, may have been willing to assume the responsibility, honestly believing that a statement of facts could and would admit of but one conclusion - the undisputed establishment of his guilt.

Left without a statement of facts, the court's inquiry into the case was limited to determining the sufficiency of the indictment and the correctness of the charge of the court in its presentation of the law.

In this respect the court found there had been 'a clear, able, full and complete exposition of the law, so far as it is possible for us to determine in the absence of a statement of the facts'.

In conclusion, the court announced that it had investigated the case with all the care which the solemn issues involved demanded and was compelled to believe that the appellant had had a fair and impartial trial, according to the forms of law. A jury of his countrymen, after hearing and patiently weighing all the evidence, had declared, by their verdict, that the violated law in his case could only be satisfied by the forfeiture of his life.

'Believing as we do that no error has been committed requiring a reversal of the case, it only remains for us to declare that the judgment of the lower court is in all things affirmed.'

As a side comment, the court regretted that the record of the case failed to disclose the facts of the homicide, 'which probably includes the career of one of the most noted malefactors of the state, whose imputed exploits have contributed largely to the most sanguinary chapters of her annals'.

Longley accepted the rejection of his appeal, in April, 1878, with fatalistic composure.

He consoled himself with the thought not only that everyone had to die, sooner or later, but that everyone living had previously been dead. Dying, he said, was just a matter of returning to the place you were in before being born.

To Captain Mast, his captor, he wrote :

> 'About eleven years ago I launched my boat upon that mighty river that leads to distraction and without the least idea where it would land me. Of course, you are aware that when one gets under good headway going down this mighty channel it is very hard to check up.
>
> 'I have found that this great river has but one landing place, from its head to its mouth, and the name of that place is Reformation town, and after one passes Reformation town there is no stopping place between him and eternity. No, none. But Oh, how few there are who get off this landing The reason of it is, the country looks beautiful on either side and still more promising ahead, and on we go until finally we begin to strike our boats against the terrible boulders and snags. Then it is we begin to see our companions wrecked and lost on either

side of us; then it is that we see whither we are going. But, alas, too late, for we are then beyond the hope of human hands. Then we cast a look or a thought back to our once happy home and mother.'

It is remarkable how sections of this letter, published in the *Daily Democratic Statesman* on the 7 April 1878, foreshadowed the closing words of Scott Fitzgerald's novel, *The Great Gatsby*:

> Gatsby believed in the green light, the orgiastic future that year by year recedes before us. It eluded us then, but that's no matter - tomorrow we will run faster, stretch out our arms farther. . . And one fine morning - 'So we beat on, boats against the current, borne back ceaselessly into the past'.

Longley was borne back into the past by a sympathetic letter from a young woman named Bettie Southern who had been one of his school friends at Evergreen. His reply is preserved in the Western History Collections of the University of Oklahoma Library. It is a tenderly written letter, recalling their school days, 'happy days long ago', and an incident involving her pony Charlie, on which she rode to school.

> 'Don't you remember how all of us boys used to have a race when school would turn out and see which would get to saddle your pony for you?'

(The letter here is torn, but remaining words indicate that he threw his hat at the pony, which jumped and pitched her off).

> 'I was scaired nearly to death when you fell and when I found that you was not hurt I told you I just done it to get to help you upon your pony. Well, I could write a great deal but I hope you will come and see me soon and when you come don't be sad, be lively. I am lively yet and expect to be as long as I live. It is no use to be sad and then I can not be sad when I know that I am soon to be released from all trouble for I well know that I will be better off. Hanging is my favourite way of dieing, if I have to die I would rather die that way than any other way on earth, that is except a natural death.
>
> 'And I would be glad if every body would forgive me before I die but I will forgive all my enemies whether they do me or not.'

Asking her to give his love to a mutual friend, he tells her to keep 'a good shair' for herself. The letter was signed 'from your true friend until death, W. P. Longley'.

In one of his last letters to the *Galveston News* Longley recalled the Civil War period and aftermath when he was a boy:

Giddings Jail
September the 13th 1878

Miss Bettie Southern

[illegible] Esteemed [illegible] Friend.

[illegible] received [illegible] sympathy [illegible]

me to hear you talk as [illegible] yes Bettie. It [illegible] remember our happy days, long ago passed [illegible] with you.

that it on this [illegible] yes Bettie. I am happy to say to you that I am ready to die, and I look forward to the day of my execution as being the end of all trouble. It is the gate, dark as it may seem, to endless happiness. and oh, how true it is, that I have been a wild and [illegible] Boy since our old school days. that you well know yourself but as you say Bettie, God is more merciful than man. [illegible] is willing to save all who come to him with a penitent and contrite heart, and though I may be chief of sinners, I have no right to doubt God's mercy if I ask it from my heart, and if I will freely confess my sins both of which I have done and am daily trying to do. My Dear little Friend Bettie, I have underwent a very great change since [illegible] last saw your [illegible] you said you would try and come to see me, and I want you to be shure and do so and tell Melinissa to come with you. [illegible] that seen me, he [illegible] this letter with the [illegible]. you asked me if I remembered you. why Bettie how could I forget one that I went with almost every day during my childhood. [illegible] remember the [illegible] pony you and Melinissa used to ride to school. his name was Charlie. don't you remember how all of us Boys used to have a race when [illegible] would turn out to see which would get to saddle your pony for you.

This and the following page: A photograph of the actual letter written by Longley to a lady friend, Bettie Southern, just before his execution.

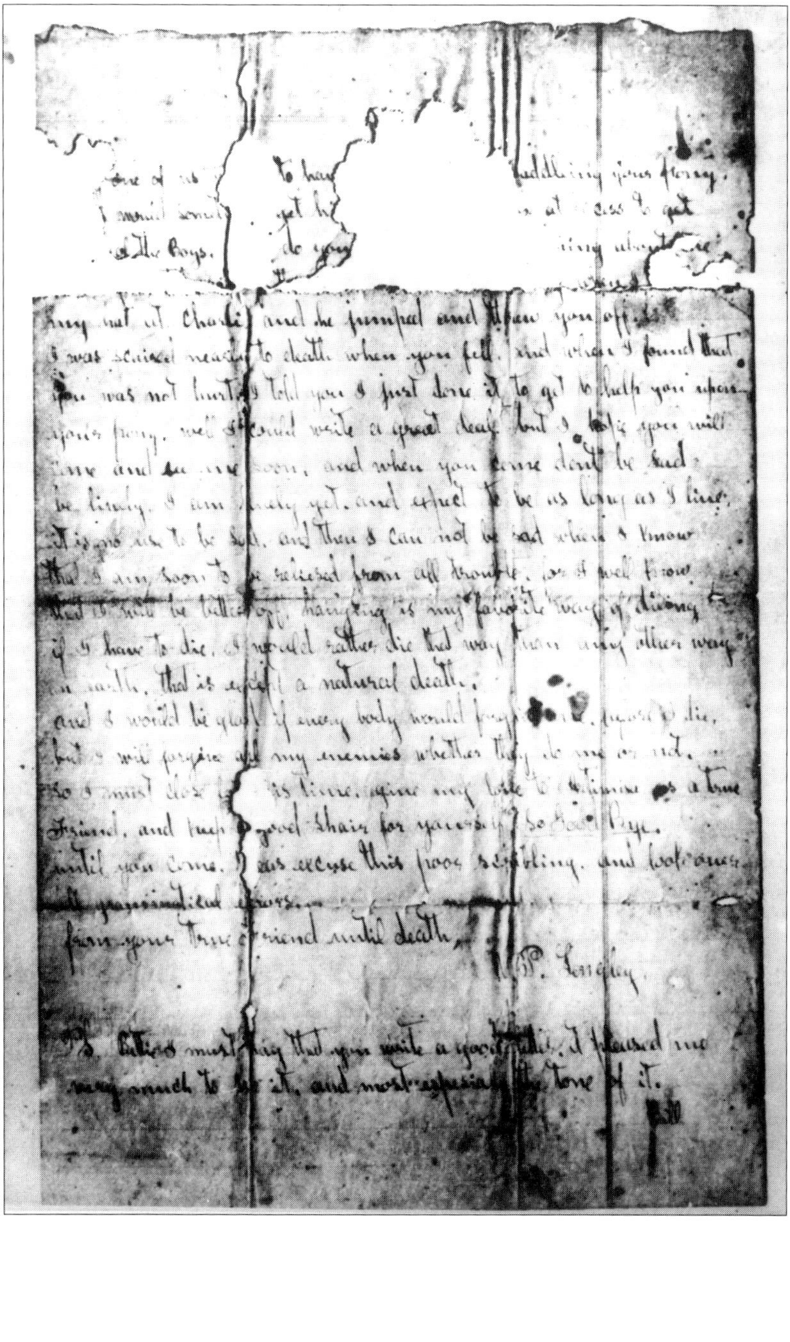

... one of us ... to hav ... peddling your pony.
I would sorry ... get ... at a cess to get
... the Boys. ... to you ... ing about ...

him out at Charlie and he jumped and threw you off.
I was scared nearly to death when you fell, and when I found that
you was not hurt I told you I just done it to get to help you upon
your pony. well I could write a great deal but I hope you will
come and see me soon, and when you come don't be sad.
be lively. I am lively yet. and expect to be as long as I live,
it is no use to be sad. and then I can not be sad when I know
that I am soon to be released from all trouble. for I well know
that I will be better off. hanging is my favorite way of dieing
if I have to die. I would rather die that way than any other way
on earth. that is except a natural death.
and I would be glad if every body would forgive me before I die,
but I will forgive all my enemies whether they do me or not.
So I must close for this time. give my love to [illegible] as a true
Friend, and keep a good chair for yourself. So Good bye.
until you come. Please excuse this poor scribling. and look over
all grammatical errors.

from your true friend until death,
W. P. Longley

P.S. Mattie I must say that you write a good letter. it pleased me
very much to get it. and most especially the tone of it.
Bill

> I well remember the heart sickening murders committed by the secession party upon as good men as the sun ever shone on, simply because they remained true to the Star Spangled Banner and the cause of the union. If all the bloody deeds that were done in Texas during the war could be written down on paper without exaggeration it would chill and freeze the blood of every human being and would shame and shock the civilized world. It was nothing uncommon in those bloody times to see from two to seven men hanging on one live oaktree with cards - one pinned on the back of each man with these words written on the cards, 'Thus to Traitors'. The meaning of that was that they had simply voted for the Union. I have known mobs to go to houses and pull the very best men out of their beds while on their knees praying to God, while their wives and helpless children begged their leaders to have mercy and spare the lives of their husbands and fathers. But mercy was unknown and the poor men were ruthlessly butchered and murdered in presence of their heart stricken wives and innocent children. My father voted a Union ticket and came near being murdered on the spot. All that saved him was being one of the oldest settlers in Texas, had served in the Mexican war between the United States and Mexico.' (In fact, it was a War of Independence between Texans and the Mexicans, 1835-36, Texas was not admitted to the union until 1846).
>
> Soon after the Civil War, the sons of murdered men grew to manhood and wanted revenge for their murdered relatives.
>
> I sympathised with them and befriended them on numerous occasions. Because I did so the people became embittered against me and I was waylaid and shot at and the boys who I had helped were getting killed on every side. It was the old law of tooth and fang and I made up my mind to live up to that law and to do so I had to fight and kill in self-defence when it became necessary.

Here, once more, is the killer who sees himself as victim, the criminal whose good intentions have been thwarted by others, the creature of circumstance forced into a situation not of his making. Whether Longley read the pulp fiction being written about Western desperadoes of the time by Eastern writers is not on record. Certainly he showed a propensity, in the months after his arrest to portray himself as a romantic figure with a soulful disposition, as if to soften the focus on his homicidal crimes. His vanity was given its head by the hordes of reporters who jotted down his reminiscences and went away to transcribe them, to some extent overawed by his reputation.

In his wilful self-romanticism, Longley convinced himself that he was on the side of the angels of mercy against the devils who had wreaked havoc on his homeland after the war, in which his brother had been killed. He played to the columns that were being devoted to him in the press.

Longley's execution was set for Friday October 11, 1878, on a gallows in an open field six hundred yards north-west of the Giddings railway ticket office.

A *Galveston* reporter, who visited him in his cell on the eve of the scheduled execution, found him calm, collected and in good spirits. 'Though not as jocular as formerly, he has not gotten over his habit of speaking lightly of killing. In answer to the question if he had prepared any statement, he said 'No, sir. I have none written and don't think I will write any.' Answering the question, 'Will you make a speech?,' he said 'I don't see what good it will do. Let others learn by experience as I have.'

Longley spoke kindly of his treatment in jail. 'It is notable,' remarked the reporter, 'that he has left off using profane language entirely.'

A Catholic priest from Austin spent some time with the condemned man in the evening and offered him absolution.

11

I am in good health and good spirits- as good as a man can be under the circumstances. - Bill Longley.

'This is the first judicial hanging we have had in Lee County,' declared Sheriff Brown,* addressing a silent crowd pressing against the ranks of scaffold guards. He added : 'I trust there will never be another.'

Brown felt a pang of sorrow. Privately, he had hoped the sentence would be commuted to life imprisonment, if only for the sake of Longley's respected parents, whom he counted among his close friends. There was no doubt in his mind that another judge, especially the one who had given a prison sentence to Wesley Hardin, every bit as much a killer as Longley, would have sentenced him to hard labour instead of hanging.

Turning to his prisoner, who had been allowed to smoke a last cigar, he asked: 'Have you anything to say?'

This was the opportunity for a condemned man to purge his soul or say farewell to relatives and friends.

Longley had made his spiritual peace in jail, converted to the Roman Catholic Church and been baptised by Father Chambudot. Two priests, Father Spillard, of Austin, and Father Querat, of Houston, stood close to him on the scaffold.

Taking the cigar from his mouth, Longley spoke in a calm, steady voice

'Well, I haven't got much to say. . .'

Crowds tried to move closer, to catch every word. Reporters took them down in shorthand.

*Later shot and killed in Chicago after he had shot two policemen who wanted to question him about an unpaid hotel bill.

I see a good many enemies around me and only a mighty few friends. I hope to God you will forgive me. I will you. I hate to die, of course. Any man hates to die. But I have learned this by taking the lives of men who loved life as well as I do.'

If I have any friends here I hope they will do nothing to avenge my death. If they want to avenge my death let them pray for me.

I understand my brother, Jim,* was in here to kill the man who cuts the rope to hang me. If you are in this crowd, Jim, don't kill anybody on my account. I knew that if I was ever caught I would have to pay the penalty which I am now paying. I deserve this fate. It is a debt I owe for my wild, reckless life. When it is paid it will all be over. I hope you will forgive me. I will forgive you. Whether you do or not may God forgive me. I have nothing more to say.'

It was a contrite speech, humble by comparison to his previous jauntiness.

Father Querat offered a short prayer. Longley knelt and the two priests each placed a hand on his head.

After the prayer there was a stir in the crowd at the foot of the gallows, where a young woman was struggling to get past the guards.

'It's all right, let her through,' ordered the sheriff.

The woman hurried up the scaffold steps, walked over to Longley and placed a flower in the button-hole of his suit. She was Bettie, the friend from schooldays, to whom he had written in jail. He thanked her, gave her a light kiss on the cheek and, with tears in her eyes, she returned to the crowd.

Longley then shook hands with everyone on the platform.

Facing the crowd once more, he raised his right hand and waved to the onlookers as he bid them : 'Goodbye, everybody.'

There was intense curiosity in the crowd. People familiar with his reputation and his record of killings wanted to see how he would face and accept his own death. Sheriff Brown was now certain there would be no rescue attempt. His prisoner, who has cheated fate so often in the past, through cunning and luck, had bowed to the inevitable and was, at least, taking his leave of life with a kind of grace he had not displayed to those who ran foul of him.

A black hood was drawn over his head and his hands were tied behind his back. The rope was adjusted and a signal given for the

* He later moved to California.

trapdoor to be released. The drop was 12 feet - twice Longley's height. But the rope slipped on the top beam and instead of dislocating his neck in a sudden jerk, it stretched so much that it took his 150 lbs weight to the ground. Longley's legs buckled as they touched the earth. Writhing and half conscious, he groaned. Sheriff Brown and a deputy leaped down the steps, grabbed hold of his legs and raised his body while others on the scaffold took up the rope's slack. Someone had adjusted the rope carelessly.

While the sheriff and his deputy held on to his legs, the rope was made secure to take up the body. For eleven minutes the doomed man dangled by his neck three feet above ground. Some spectators laughed and shouted ribald remarks. Others, such as a seventeen-year-old girl* visiting relatives in Giddings that day, could not bear to watch the hanging and turned away in disgust.

Three doctors were in attendance. When they were satisfied he had been hanging for long enough, one of them, without the stethoscope that R. T. Laennec had invented fifty-nine years earlier, called for the body to be cut down. Taking hold of Longley's head, he twisted it round, 180 degrees. The head turned easily as an ox being road on a spit. A deputy sheriff from a neighbouring county applied the same test.

William Preston Longley, born at Mill Creek, Austin County, Texas, on October 6, 1851, was at 2p.m. on October 11, 1878, pronounced dead.

Recalling the scene, Sgt. W. J. L. Sullivan, a Texas Ranger, of Co. 'B' Frontier Battalion, wrote in his memoirs, *Twelve Years in the Saddle,* in 1909, that Mrs. Anderson, widow of the murdered Wilson Anderson, was present with her children and when the doctors pronounced him dead she said she was satisfied.

Describing Longley, he remembered him on the gallows as

> 'young and fine-looking, with dark hair and a long black moustache and with a complexion as fair as a lady's, he looked so handsome before his death that it seemed a pity for him to die in such a terrible and unnatural manner.'

The body was placed in a coffin and the hemp rope used for the hanging was coiled and laid on his breast. The coffin was taken on a hack-cart to the cemetery outside the town, near the railway tracks, where Longley was buried beside a blackjack tree in what

* Her son, Roy Whiteker, became secretary of the Giddings Cemetery Association.

Bill Longley's grave marked with a petrified log which has since been replaced with an official marker by the Texas State Historical Commission.

was then known as the San Antonio prairie. Flint rocks were used to mark the outline of the grave. Years later some of his friends made a headstone out of a petrified hollow log, but no name or date recorded the interment.

Visitors of a future generation found a violet growing beside a three-lobed cactus on the grave. Wistfully, one of them saw the flower and cactus as a symbol of Longley's contradictory nature, the violet representing sweet innocence and the cactus his prickly toughness. As it to compound the symbolism, the cactus overshadowed the violet.

At the time of the burial care was taken that such a reprobate should not be buried anywhere near the graves of law-abiding citizens. Death might be the great leveller, but not where Longley was concerned. His grave was set far apart.

Over the years the cemetery expanded and eventually overtook the grave. In the cemetery's revised layout it was in a lane which had to be crossed to get from one set of plots to another. To avoid embarrassing relatives of the newly deceased who might have resented their loved ones sharing ground with an infamous outlaw, the authorities moved the petrified marker six feet, subsequent visitors seeking Longley's grave did not realise they were standing by a marker below which there was no grave.

In the burial plot adjacent to Longley's, lies a prominent Lee County judge, Judge Tate. The 'worst man in Texas' next to one of its leading citizens.

Descendants of the Longley family are scattered about the United States. Inevitably, they emphasise the contribution made to the foundation of Texas by Campbell Longley and his religious work in the pioneering community. They acknowledge Bill Longley as a violent desperado, but feel the dishonour he brought to the family is best forgotten. Yet Texas, more than any other state in the union, produces psychopathic killers for whom the old frontier code still applies. The state's murder rate is alarming and one does not have to juggle with statistics to follow Bill Longley's trail from the 1870s to the present day. It is a trail spattered with blood and sudden violence, accompanying the ease with which firearms can be bought and used. Longley epitomised the ruthless activist without a cause. He extolled the belief that an argument is best settled by violence, an attitude all too prevalent over one hundred years after his death, when, significantly, desperadoes of his ilk are still romanticised as adventurous cavaliers.

Epilogue

As mentioned in the foreword Dick spent considerable time in locating Longley's grave. He knew of course that it was likely to be in or around Giddings Cemetery. He also knew it was in the form of a log driven into the ground since in the course of his research he was sent a picture of it anonymously. (See page 167).

Together with a family descendant and attended by the Sherriff of Lee County, not to mention a few bemused on-lookers, they finally found the by now petrified marker. It was overgrown and lying outside the original cemetery boundary. Presumably the marker was placed there by a family member or friend of Longley's at the time of his burial.

Although Longley deserved no special favours Dick knew that the Texas State Historical Commission permanently marked the graves of such men – both good and bad – who played a part in the growth of the state of Texas.

Dick made an application to the Commission with the backing of several local residents and in due course an official Historical Marker was placed at Longley's grave. It was dedicated in a ceremony held on Saturday, October 16th, 1976.

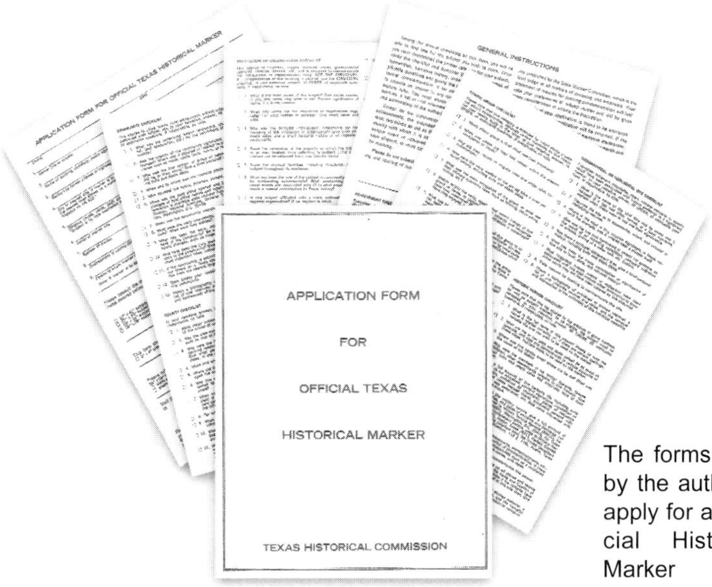

The forms used by the author to apply for an official Historical Marker

Left:
The author photographed with a Longley descendant (right) who helped him locate Bill's grave. Giddings Cemetery, Texas, April 1974.

Right:
Dick Brownson having located Longley's grave in Giddings Cemetery, Texas, April 1974. A petrified log as marker.

DEDICATION OF AN OFFICIAL
Texas
HISTORICAL MARKER

BY THE

LEE COUNTY
HISTORICAL COMMISSION

AND

TEXAS STATE
HISTORICAL COMMISSION

FOR

WILLIAM PRESTON (Bill) LONGLEY

(October 6, 1851 - October 11, 1878)

SATURDAY, OCTOBER 16, 1976

GIDDINGS CEMETERY

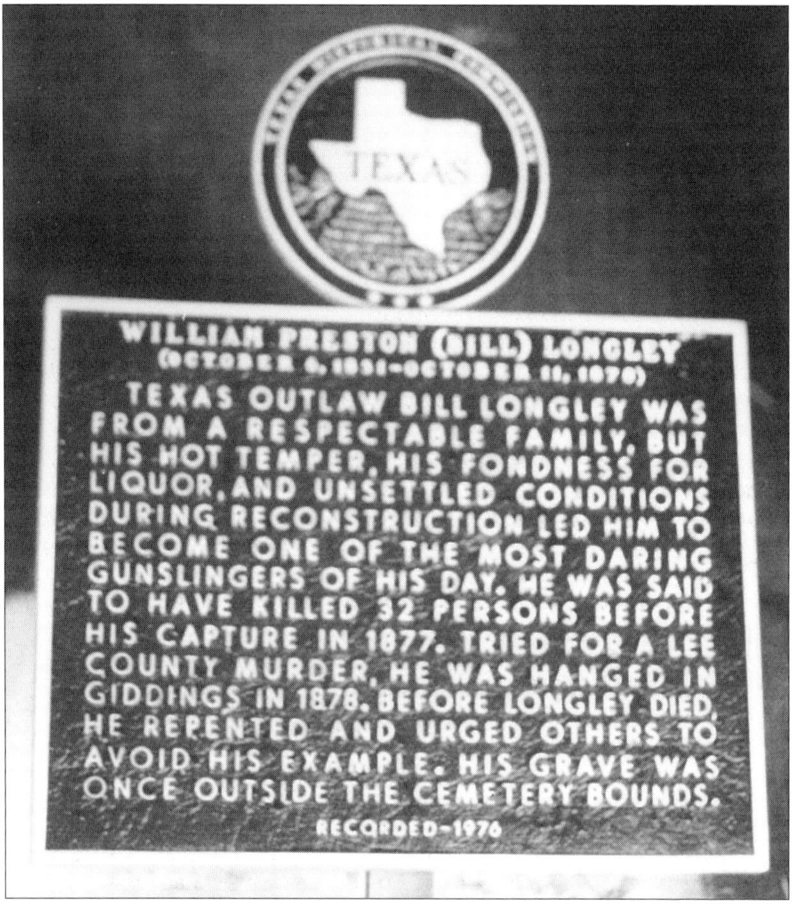

Inscription on Marker

WILLIAM PRESTON (BILL) LONGLEY

(OCTOBER 6, 1851 – OCTOBER 11, 1878)

Texas Outlaw Bill Longley was from a respectable family, but his hot temper, his fondness for liquor, and unsettled conditions during reconstruction led him to become one of the most daring gunslingers of his day. He was said to have killed 32 persons before his capture in 1877. Tried for a Lee County murder, he was hanged in Giddings in 1878. Before Longley died, he repented and urged others to avoid his example. His grave was once outside the cemetery bounds.

RECORDED – 1976

Appendix One

Evans 1.

Letter from Alfred Evans to Governor E. M. Pease, December 30, 1868

This is a truthful narative of a most brutal murder and robery which was perpetrated about 8 miles below the town of Evergreen on Sunday evening, the 20th December,

'Two Freedmen named Green Evans and his brother, Pryor, a lad of about 18, together with an old black man named Ned, who had been one of Evans' slaves, set out from Bell County to visit friends and relatives, intending to return after Christmas.

'They traveled on peaceably and quietly until they arrived at Evergreen, all three riding good horses, Pryor Evans an extra horse, upwards of 15 hands high, young and in good condition.

'They were accosted by three young white men in the town of Evergreen and a swap proposed to Pryor. He told them he did not desire to trade his horse and the Freedmen rode on about 3 or 4 miles from Evergreen. At a branch the boys got down to take some dinner which they had with them. On starting again Pryor and Green changed horses, as Pryor said to rest each other. Green was then riding Pryor's horse. They had travelled about 3 or 4 miles further on, bordering toward Nail Creek, when all of a sudden, the same three young men, who proposed the swap in Evergreen. rode up behind them, with six-shooters cocked and presented.

They were ordered to halt and stop their horses. The white men said 'Gentlemen, where are you from?' The boys answered from Bell County and were going down to Mill Creek in Austin County to see there friends. 'Well, god dam you, give up your six-shooters.' The boys informed them that they had but one in the crowd and they could have that, Green Evans taking it off and presenting it to one of them. After searching the other two for arms and finding none, they ordered the boys to mount their horses and follow them. God dam them, they intended to learn them manners, one of the white men leading the other two in the rear with six-shooters cocked and presented.

The Freedmen were taken one hundred yards from the road in the direction of Nails Creek Bottom when Green said he had committed no offence and he saw no reason for being marched out there. He was ordered to march on, when the poor boy, seeing no alternative, broke and ran. The one in the rear and the one in front dashed there horses in pursuit. The remaining one in the rear imediately dismounted but the other two boys were already under headway and he hallowed to them in pursuit of Green, dont Johns, dont Johns, twice distinctly and loud. At that one of them fired on Green, the ball entering the back of his head and scattering his brains. Seeing Green fall, the one on foot quickly shot at Pryor who at that time was about 80 yards off, missing him.

'The old man Ned at the same time made his escape, when he hollered at Johns not to shoot. He evedently saw that some of them would get aways and he did not want any killed unless he could have got them all,'

'Pryor run till he reached a house in the neighbourhood and there he found two Freedmen and a young white man named McDaniel who was armed and he volunteered his services together with the two Freedmen to go with him to the place where his Brother fell. They found his pockets turned and what money he had taken, which Pryor says was but four dollars, 30 cents, he had five dollars when he started but had spent 70 cents on the road. Pryor succeeded with the aid of the Freedmen In question to get his brother on a horse and by the time he got him to the Freedmen's house it was then dark or near dark. After getting the Freedmen to bury his brother he paying them for it, he left next morning and arived home in two days and informed me of the circumstances and gave all the details. I felt mortafied haveing raised the boys, purchasing them from Wm. J. Hutchens of Houston when they were quite small together, with his mother and older brother.'

Evans set out to track down the murderers.

'I armed his brother Burrill and his step father Henry Evans and the boy Pryor with double barell shotguns for our mutual protection on the highway and started for Evergreen the next morning with the intention to investigate the matter and try and find out the perpetrators of the outrage. We arrived at Evergreen Friday evening Christmas Day. In going through Lexington I had the boys to go around the town. I did not want our business made public for fear of defeating the end in view. I met a gentleman on the road between Lexington and Evergreen. He informed me he lived in Dallas and had been down to Evergreen transacting some business.'

I ventured to communicate with him. He informed me that he was close to the place where the murder was committed at the time and said suspicion rested on some of the neighbours boys in this town, from the discription the boys gave who got away. I asked if he knew their name. He said he did not know any but Longly, the son of a very respectable family. I told him that was the boy that was along, pointing to Pryor and he had him to give the discription of them and said that suited exactly Longly. He did not know his christian name, the other two he did not know. Gaining no further information we resumed our journey, arriving in sight of Evergreen about dusk, made a circuitous rout to the left of the town crossing the prong of the creek on which the town is situated about one mile below, directed the Freedmen to go down the road and stay all night at the Freedmens where Green was intered while I rode up into town, put up the tavern and endeavoured to elicit all the information I could, without letting them know me or my business. I could learn nothing definite in regard to it, was informed by some that it was supposed from the discription to be some boys living about town, but would not give names.

I got the description of the Longley boys and found that one answered the description Pryor had given me. I left next morning and arrived at the Freedmens where the boys was directed to stay. They had the horse that Green was shot from. He was taken up in the neighbourhood of where the murder was committed.

I then started with the three Freedmen for Brenham with the intention of getting a warrant for the arrest of the Longly boys and if I could, some troops to see it executed.'

On the road to Brenham he discovered that Squire Maxwell and deputy sheriff Nunn had gone to Evergreen to investigate the killings, so he turned back to overtake them. He met them at Evergreen and found that Maxwell and the deputy were making no efforts. They said they could not arrest anyone on suspicion. Evans then fetched Pryor and asked him to walk around the town to see if he could identify the guilty party. Pryor looked at 50 or 60 men and then spotted a young man who appeared to recognise him.

The letter continues

As quick as he recognised Pryor he wheeled short and stepped into a store, came out again as quick as he could turn and walked fast up town. I asked the crowd the name of that man. Pryor did not know his name. Some of them responded and said his name was William Longly. I had the magistrate to find and then he wrote the warrant and it was sworn to by Pryor and placed in the hands of Deputy Sheriff Nunn. He read it and summoned a bystander to go with him and started in the direction of Longly's home.

While the sheriff was gone some friend to justice, I suppose, placed in the hands of Henry the stepfather, the following note with no name signed to it and directed him to give it to me. The purport of it was 'You have a Jim Gilmore and Johnson McQueen arrested with Bill Longly and make them prove where they were on last Sunday evening'. I gave the note to the magistrate. He told me he would have their names inserted as soon as the sheriff returned. By that time we saw the sheriff coming without the prisoner. I asked him what success and he said they were all gone, taken the bresh. I said I suppose

Longly is gone. Oh, he said, the rest have gone with him. We know now who they are. I said give their names James Gilmore and Johnson McQueen or McKowen.

Maxwell advised him to go to Brenham and get some soldiers. Evans said that would not do any good if Longley had already gone and was keeping friends on the look-out.

'Thus ended the farce. Now it was near dark. The Squire and Sheriff left for home. Three diferent men who I supposed friendly to justice and law came to me and said it would not be safe to keep them Freedmen, anywhere in that vicinity, said he dont you see those men yonder waching you like hawks. They are the brothers of the accused and will take any advantage after dark. Believing I could do no more at that time I concluded to return home.

'Governor, I found the better portion of the citizens in that vicinity that I conversed with, opposed to these murderers and cut throats and appeared to be desirous of having them brought to justice but they are affraid to express there honest sentiments for fear of being injured in some way by these desperate scoundrels and outlaws.'

The letter goes on to describe how

. . .lightly and indiferently they attempted to cover up these crimes while I was in Evergreen on Christmas night, trying to get at the desired information and when they did not know me or my business I heard many different statements about this transaction.

Some said a Negro was found killed, with a rope at one end of his neck and a log tied to the other end. Some said they were fellows that had stolen horses up in Bell County and was followed from that county and one of the party killed, while others contended it was done by some of the boys in that vicinity but would not give names. But that was all disipated when I told them I raised the boys and that they were honest, industrious, sober, peaceable and inofensive and had come by there horses and what they had honestly by the sweat of there brow and I made full inquiry of there conduct all the way and it was that they were quiet, peaceful and courteous to all they met and particularly so at Evergreen.

'Meeting many on the road comeing from church they invariably gave the road to them. It was their deliberate intention to take those three Freedmen to Nails Creek Bottom and there murder them just for what little money they had and their horses but two of them escaping and there plan hence they left the horses unmolested from fear of being identified.

‘I do think that if these men loiter around Evergreen they ought to be taken and brought to justice and that the usual reward should be offered for their apprehension for if these guilty parties should be suffered to go unpunished I shudder for the safety of society, Squire Maxwell informed me that he intended to take up the body on Monday and hold an inquest over it. It was on Saturday evening near dark I left Evergreen

There is no record of the governor’s reply.

Appendix Two.

Letter written by 1st Lieutenant J. Whitney from the District Post of Burnham, Texas, on 19th February 1870 to the Secretary of Civil Affairs Headquarters District, Fifth Military District, Austin, Texas

Sir,
I have the honour to report that several complaints having been made by different individuals and a petition having been received from citizens from Evergreen appealing for assistance and protection from John Wilson and Bill Longley who were murdering freedmen and stealing horses with impunity, that I started early Sunday morning with a guide and a mounted detachment of Co. A, 11th Infantry, and proceeded to the head of Wimberley Lake, Burleson County, where I succeeded in placing my men without being discovered. From that vicinity I operated in conjunction with a large body of citizens from Washington, Brazos, Burleson, and Robertson counties and endeavoured by patrolling the timber, scouting through the bottoms, guarding the roads and visiting infrequented places by day and night for six days to accomplish the arrest of these two men but without success.

Finding the citizens too much aroused and excited to act secretly and in harmony and my presence having been discovered I decided to return and wait for a more favourable opportunity to act, leaving instructions with certain men who were honest and reliable to watch over and communicate with me as circumstances might require. The country is so favourable, particularly the bottoms, for concealment that it is almost impossible to find anyone desirous of avoiding arrest or discovery and besides there are very many men who although they pretend to be good and law abiding citizens and anxious to have the laws enforced and criminals brought to justice, will take sides with them, watch for them and inform them of every movement made to secure their arrest.

I did my best to discover the whereabouts of these men but I might as well looked for a needle in a hay-stack particularly when there was so much interest felt for and against them. I returned last evening I remained on Monday night at Captain Shaw' s about 1 mile from Lexington at Evergreen on Tuesday at Parks on Wednesday night at Wilson's stand on Thursday night. The whole country is aroused, too much so, to accomplish anything now.

Parties came into Lexington from Caldwell, Calvert and from Bryan for these men who had stolen valuable horses from these points. I communicated with all of them and gave such instructions to them as would enable them and myself to act together and with some degree of success. The men John Wilson and Bill Longley should be treated simply as outlaws and shot on sight. They openly boast, particularly Wilson, of shooting some 18 freedmen and that they intend to kill more and to take the county with their own hands and defy arrest. They have threatened the lives of several white citizens good and law abiding men and also threatened to burn certain houses. The statements made by Pinir Green to Lieutenant Irwin and referred to this post on the 13th inst. from your headquarters is substantially correct and the number of horses stolen by them, even within the last 10 days, I would not presume to state. The several acts of lawlessness and crime committed by them can be substantiated beyond peradventure. They unquestionnably belong to and are connected with the Ben Brown clan. A man by the name of Brace or Braice who is in authority with that class of men, has been seen with them. They were run out of Caldwell Burleson County Sunday night by some of the citizens but there was no organisation and because their guns were loaded with bird shot only, they gave up the chase permitting them to get away with two horses which they were leading. Campbell Longley living near Evergreen and the father of Bill Longley is a very good man and has endeavoured to prevent his son from associating with John Wilson. Wilson married Bill Longley's sister. Stephen E. Wilson, father of John, is known as Dog Wilson. He is a very doubtfull character in my opinion, particularly when drunk. I would not assent that he assists his son and upholds him in his lawlessness but there are many suspicious circumstances surrounding him. At the time the circus was in Evergreen on or about the 3rd inst. Dog Wilson, as he is named by citizens, was there very drunk and publicly announced that he believed in John Wilson, that John was all right and that no Yankee or anyone else would take him except by cutting or shooting old Steve and further said they (Wilson and Longley) would be in town soon and there would be heel soon after this. They did come into town, robbed a negro of a six-shooter before everybody forced themselves into the circus and afterwards shot and murdered the freedwoman referred to by Pinir Green in his statement. I called old Wilson to account and fined him 100 dollars for drunkenness and disorderly conduct and made him give a bond for 15 hundred dollars to keep the peace. His plea was that he was drunk and was not aware of what he said and done. Proceedings in this case forwarded by same mail. These men are so thoroughly beyond the pale of civilisation that I particularly request for authority to offer a reward of 500 dollars for each to be paid upon their arrest, dead or alive. Wilson is the worst of the two and when cornered will probably resist unto death knowing as he does if arrested and the laws are properly enforced, that he will be hung. They are both nothing more or less than murderers and horse thieves and should be publicly punished as such. I have laid a trap for them and by working secretly feel assured of succeeding in dispos-

ing of them and if the Commanding General will grant the authority requested am satisfied it will result favourably. The free state or republic of Evergreen, as it is called, is really a most wretched place and in miserable condition. It never has been properly organized, not even before the late war. Life and property are not safe there. Some of the citizens are preparing to leave and go elsewhere for fear of their lives. By taking strong measures and by putting out of the way such men as Wilson and Longley the state of affairs can be materially improved. I have promised to visit the town and neighbourhood if possible once a month and bring all offenders to justice before a military court. This I intend to do with the permission of the Commanding General provided my other duties will allow it.
Evergreen Precinct is really the only spot in the District Post that is troublesome, but even it is curable provided the proper remedies are properly applied.

Headquarters District Post of Brenham, Civil Bureau, Burnham, Texas, March 1, 1870 - Special Orders No. 20;

By authority of the Commanding General of the 5th Military District State of Texas, a reward of one thousand dollars is offered and will be paid for the apprehension and delivery at this military post, dead or alive of John Wilson and Bill Longley, murderers and horse thieves or five hundred dollars for either one.

By order of Bvt. Lieutenant Col. James Biddle;
J. Whitney, 1st Lieutenant 11 Infty. Bvt. Capt., USA, Post Adjutant.

Letter to Captain Charles E. Morse, ADC, at the Bureau of Civil Affairs, Austin, Texas, from a Bastrop magistrate, James E. Brady dated 5 February 1870, now in the National Archives of records of US Army Continential Commands, 5th Military District:

Two whitemen and a Negro recognised by the name of Cook rode up to the residence of Alfred - of the name of Paul Brice, 10 miles north east of Bastrop, shot the freedmen and drove off his horses Feb 4. A circus company showed 23 miles Sheriff W. Miller was present. Four men entered the circus supported by a body of armed men, shotguns and six-shooters, presented their pistols at him ordering him to leave on sight. Miller left at the double quick step. They then charged on the freedmen taking their six-shooters and money. A man of the name of John Wilson, well known as a desperado, and a fellow of the name of Long (Longley), seemed to be the leaders. Wilson and Long (Longley) boasted that they were the men that took Paul Brice's horses on the 2nd and shot him. This said John Wilson murdered a freedmen at Bastrop County some two years past for which he has not yet been arrested or tried. He is a citizen of Burleson County. They boast they will be here tonight at the circus. If so, I will if possible house them.

Letter from the same magistrate to General Reynolds, 9 February 1870:

Dear Sir,
Complaints are hourly coming to me of rape, rapine and murders, robbery from the borders of Burleson and Bastrop countys. I am helping to give them protection or to enforce the law. A band of armed men headed by one John Wilson and William Longwell [Longley] are murdering, robbing and ravishing, especially all people of colour on whom they can lay hands. These desperadoes are generally citizens of Burleson county. They, the coloured people, are driven to desperation and even my life is not safe an hour as they know that I am the only magistrate they dread here. In haste,
Respectfully.

Appendix 3.

On 28 February 1873, Sgt. of State Police J.M. Redman sent this letter to Attorney General Frank L. Britton* Chief of State Police at Austin, reporting on affairs in Lampasas County:

'When I reached that place my first object was to see Justice Pratt, which I did. I asked him if there was any warrants out for the arrest of those parties who have been shooting upon the streets of Lampasas. When he told me there was none, I then asked him if we could not get someone who had seen them violating the law to swear out warrants for the parties, when he told me then the people was afraid to make complaints against them.

My only chance then was to watch in the streets of night which I did sometimes until 3 o'clock at night, but detected none of them in their shooting though some of them did shoot a few times on the streets of night when my men were absent. When the proclamation of the governor came out and was posted up, all of the men laid down their arms, but it was only because the police force was there to watch over them and I have no doubt but what as soon as all the police leave there they will go to carrying their pistols again.

At least, that is the opinion of most of the law abiding men of the county and they say they want a police force stationed there all the time.

A company of minute men was organised on the 22nd inst. He told me they was all good men and it seemed to me the same as I seen nothing to the contrary. All of the state arms were turned over to Mr. Geo. E. Haynie, except one gun that was lost to which affect you now have B.C. Turner's affidavit and one that Ben Horrell has which if not returned his brothers agree to pay for as soon as they learn the state price.

I started Pvt. Happe on the 20th inst. with two men, Ray and Evans out went to investigate the murder of Geo. .W. Hughes and Robt. T. Payne, also the murder of Price, a coloured man who was most brutally murdered for his money in Brown Co. at Bakers Ranch on or near the 2nd day of February 1973, by Bill Longley, John Jones, Geo. G. Alberta - Hammond and two other men, names not known.

Mr. Happe took a full statement of a coloured man who was an eye witness to the affair which affidavit accompanies this letter. Longley

* Adjutant General of Texas from 15th November, 1872, to 15th, January 1874. At one time served as city attorney of Austin.

and his gang is 15 miles above Camp Colorado on Hordes Creek on some ranch where they stay most of their time.

Richard Doublin and Ge. Lankford Jr, the murderers of Hughes and Payne, was two miles from Camp Colorado at Sam Gaiston's ranch. They are all together at times and go well armed having a Winchester or other guns equally as good and two six shooting revolvers each. Pvts Happe, Ray and Evans arrested in Lampasas County A. Wilkenson and Bill Hoffman for killing cattle for the hides. The former was fined in all sixty two dollars and the latter twenty some odd dollars, fine and costs. . .'

Appendix Four.

The Taylor and Sutton Feud

Midland Counties Evening Express,
4, November, 1874 :

The lawlessness of Western Texas has long been notorious.

The last story respecting it relates to two families named Taylor and Sutton who 18 years ago lived and quarrelled in Alabama. A series of faction fights took place, in one of which one of the combatants was killed. . . His friends left the state for Texas. Soon afterwards they were followed by their enemies and hostilities were renewed, the land of their adoption being kept in perpetual hot water by their feuds. Curiously enough, settlers in no way related either to the Suttons or the Taylors were drawn into the war, until at length over 1, 000 people were involved in it. The representatives of the law were powerless to suppress the rival clans. If a man was arrested it was difficult to find a jury with sufficient courage to convict.

Indeed, it was but seldom that it was necessary to trouble a jury about the matter for as a rule no sooner was one of the ruffians lodged in gaol than the building was attacked and the prisoner either restored to liberty or summarily lynched.

So matters have been going on for years and altogether, we are told, 19 murders have been committed by the two bands. At last, the length to which things have gone has been too much even for society in Texas, and there is said to be some talk of proclaiming martial law with a view of putting a stop to the continued ruffianism.'

Appendix Five.

Longley's letter to Sheriff Jim Brown, exactly as written (without spelling corrections and the editorial 'tidying up' of his later letters to newspapers)

Letter 1.

> Kind friend, this lieves me still floating through the gentle breeses of misirie and feel just as hapy as a big sun flour that bows and bends in the breeses will. I understand that I have threatened your life and if I done it it must have been when I was a-sleeping. . . know nothing about it, myself I killed only one in that county that I had any thing against at that time. Now Jim Brown if I ever kill any man in that county it will be eather for killing some of my kinfoiks or els it wil be in resisting capture for if the court knowes its self I will not be captured in that county alive tho I will come there just when I please. I wrode by your house the first Monday night in August 1875. I stoped near the old yard fence and stood for an hour and my mind run back over my whole childhood and the happy hours that I had passed in the old cabin home. Oh what dreadful thoughts pierced my breasts intermost for a little while but I cussed my weekminded soul and treated myself to a drink of good old brandy and wrode on with a bold heart. It hurt me very bad when I heard that Johnson McKowan* had bin hunting me with the intention of betraying me and getting me into a snair to be killed for I loved him like a brother.

Letter 2.

> 'Oh, the hapy hours that I have passed with Johnson but now they are over. Two nights before I passed your house I was at home and my own dear father told me never to put my foot in his house again and brother Jim quit me and said I was too bad for him and my kinfolk is all so goddam cowardly they don't want me to come about them so I still alone tread the living land destitute of friends but goddam the world and every sons of a bitch that dont like me for I am a wolf and it is my night to howl. I expect to get killed sometime but you may bet your life. . . (indecipherable) will keep the. . . off the son of a bitch that does it while he is at it.'

Longley goes on to say that he has nothing against the sheriff, who was not to blame for hunting him, if he thought he had threatened him:

* an old boyhood friend, sometimes known as McQueen, thought to be responsible, with Longley, for the murder of Green Evans.

But if you will all let me alone I will not bother none of you nor your property. I understand that some fellow in that county intends to get in with me and help me do mischief a while and then kill or capture me but you soon tell the son of a bitch that I am a lone hand or I would like very much to fall in with him. Tell old Anderson he will find me somewhere between the Rio Grand and the Rocky mountains and if he ever hires any one to kill Uncle Cale he might find me some where near his yard fence some dark night. You all know that Wils Anderson did kill little Cale and why in the hell does outsiders want to take a hand in it for? Why not just say it is dog eat dog and all of you go on about your business and let the bigest dog eat the most dog if he can and I will bet old Bill will get his shir of dog. Brother Jim did not have any thing to do with killing Wils Anderson. He did not know that I was going to do it until it was done and if they arrest and you wil use your influence in giting him out I will be your busom friend and wil do anything for you that I can.

Letter 3.

I will be back through there in two weeks and I will come and see you. So no more at present. I remain ever your true friend until further. Do not doubt me Jim for I am true. W.P. Longley.'

Appendix Six.

King Fisher is said to have controlled a region of five thousand square miles along the Mexican border, enforcing his own laws and dealing ruthlessly with trespassers who tried to bite into his domain. Asked, near the end of his life, how many men he had killed, he answered with bravura : 'Seven - but I don't count Mexicans.'

So great was Fisher's popularity that in spite of his record of lawlessness, he was elected deputy sheriff of Uvalde County. Evidently, it was thought that his skill with firearms and his criminal experience could best be put to effective use with a law officer's badge. Not long after his appointment, in company with Ben Thompson, a former city marshal of Austin, he was shot and killed in the Vaudeville Variety Theatre at San Antonio. Thompson, who two years earlier had shot Jack Harris, owner of the Vaudeville, was also killed in the shooting. Fisher was hit thirteen times by bullets from Winchester rifles and Colt revolvers, while Thompson was hit nine times. Fisher, apparently, was the victim of an ambush intended solely for Thompson.

A Texas Ranger, George Durham, said that Fisher was assassinated by killers who were paid to get Thompson. 'They didn't want King, but King stuck by Ben as he always stuck by a friend and King was killed.'

Appendix Seven

The indictment of Bill Longley, signed by Robert H. Flanniken, foreman of the Grand Jury, read:

> In the name and by the authority of the State of Texas, the Grand Jurors and lawful men of this State of Texas County of Lee, duly tried upon oath by the Judge of the District Court of said County, touching their legal qualifications as Grand Jurors selected, empannelled. sworn and charged to inquire into and true presentments make of all offences against the penal laws of the said State committed within the body of the County aforesaid, upon their oaths present in the District Court of said County, that one William Longley whose full name is to the said Grand Jurors unknown and one James Longley, whose full name is to the Grand Jury unknown, late of the County of Lee, laborers, on the - day of March, in the year of our Lord one thousand, eight hundred and seventy five (AD 1875) with force and arms in the said County of Lee and State of Texas, did then and there willfully, knowingly together and with each other, well knowing the unlawful intentions of each other feloniously and of their malice aforethought in and upon the body of one Wilson Anderson, a reasonable creature in being, make an assault and that he, the said William Longley, acertain gun in his hands then and there had and held - which said gun was then and there loaded and charged with gun powder and certain leaden bullets which said gun was then and there of the value of fifteen dollars in money, which said gun was then and there a deadly weapon at toward and upon the said Wilson Anderson did then and there - the aforesaid gun draw and present - shoot off and discharge - and that he, the said William Longley - with the leaden bullets aforesaid out of this gun aforesaid, so as aforesaid shot off and discharged, did then and there strike, shoot penetrate and wound him, the said Wilson Anderson, in and upon the body of him, the said Wilson Anderson, giving to him the said Wilson Anderson, one mortal wound of the depth of six inches and of the breadth of one inch of which said wound he, the said Wilson Anderson, then and there instantly died and that he, the said James Longley, well knowing the unlawful intention of the said William Longley, was then and there present and did then and there by the utterance of encouraging words and by the use of threatening gestures - and assist, encourage and comfort him, the said William Longley, while the said William Longley shot - killed - and murder the said Wilson Anderson. That in the manner aforesaid and by use of the mear aforesaid that they, the said William Longley and James Longley, did then and there, the said Wilson Anderson willfully, knowingly, feloniously and of their malice aforethought kill and murder - and - did - thereby commit the offence of murder - contrary to the form of the Statute to such case made and provided and against the peace and dignity of the State.

Appendix Eight

John Wesley Hardin was barely seventeen when he first met Bill Longley. He was working on his uncle's farm as a ploughboy, spending his spare time and his money gambling in the saloons at Brenham, when friends advised him to get away to avoid the state police. First, he went to Evergreen and won twenty dollars playing seven-up. That evening 'a dark-looking man' came to him and said : 'My name is Bill Longley and I believe you are a spy. . . If you don't watch out, you will be shot all to pieces before you know it.' Later, realising he had made a mistake, Longley invited him to see the races next day. They played poker and Hardin won 300 dollars.

With a score of killings on his record, Hardin lost his appeal against a sentence of twenty-five years hard labour for the killing of Charles Webb, a deputy sheriff from Brown County, who had ridden to Comanche with fifteen men to capture him and Jim Taylor. Hardin claimed that Webb intended to assassinate him. In his biography, published after his death in 1895, he alleged that Webb wanted to kill him to enhance his reputation. 'He fired the first shot at my vitals when I was unprepared and who blames a man for shooting under such conditions?'

During his imprisonment he studied theology and law. After a full pardon in 1894 he passed an examination to practice law and opened an office at Junction, Texas. Three months later he was arrested and accused of holding up a faro game.

Released on payment of a fine of twenty- five dollars, he lived at a lodging house. On August 19 he was shot through the head while standing at a saloon bar, by John Selman, a fifty-eight year old constable, who had previously arrested Hardin's mistress, Mrs. Helen McRose. Less than a year later Selman was slain by ex-sheriff George Scarborough, with whom he had quarrelled over a card game.

BIBLIOGRAPHY

'Bill Longley, A Texas Hardcase', Ed Bartholomew Texas 1953
'Adventures of Bill Longley', Henry C. Fuller, Nacadoches Texas 1878
'Reconstruction of Texas', Charles William Ramsdell, Texas Press 1910
'Bill Longley and his Wild Career', T.U. Taylor, University of Oklahoma.
'Triggernometry, A Gallery of Gunfighters', Eugene Cunningham, Caldwell Idaho 1952
'Swamp Fox of the Sulphur', T.U. Taylor, University of Oklahoma.
'A Gallery of Western Badmen', William Walters, Kentucky, 1954
'Frontier Days', Judge WL Kuykendall 1917
'Cullen Baker Texas Gunfighter', Ed Bartholomew Houston Texas.
'The Handbook of Texas', Vol. 11, The Texas State Historical Society 1952
'Golden West', Vol. 1 6 Sept. 1965
'Bill Longley with Cullen Baker', T.U. Taylor from a file on Baker in the *Giddings Tribune* 1877
'Real West', Vol.X111 No. 80 March 1970
'True West' Vol. 19 No. 3 Jan. 1972
'Scribbling Bill The Outlaw', Vivian Richardson from a file on Longley in the Barker State History Centre Texas
'Twelve Years in the Saddle', Sgt. W.J.L. Sullivan Texas Rangers, Austin Texas 1909
'The History of Bell County', San Antonio Texas, George W. Taylor 1936
'The Bad Man of the West', San Antonio Texas, George D. Hendricks 1941
'The Album of Gunfighters', J. Marvin Hunter and. Noah H. Rose, Bandera Texas
'They Die But Once, The History of a Tejan', James Bradas O'Neal, New York 1935

NEWSPAPERS

Houston Post Dispatch October 25th 1931
Galveston News, various dates 1877 & 1878
Brenham Daily Banner 1877-1878
Dallas Weekly Herald 1877-1878
Chicago Tribune Sept. 29th 1877
Houston Post Sept. 5th 1937
Daily Democratic Statesman, Austin Texas June 1877-October 1878
Texas Weekly State Gazette October 19th 1878
Frontier Echo, Jacksboro Texas Sept. 21st 1877
The Texas Star, June 25th 1972
Giddings Tribune 1877-1878

PHOTO CREDITS

The ROSE collection in the Western History Collections, University of Oklahoma Library:

Bill Longley. (Head & shoulders).
Bill Longley - Bill Burrows - Sheriff Mast
Campbell Longley.
Ben Thompson
King Fisher
John Wesley Hardin
Captain Lee Hall.
Governor Edmund J. Davis.
Capt. Creed Taylor
Bill Longley's grave marker, petrified log, at Giddings.
Letter written by Bill Longley to a lady friend just before his execution
A herd of Texas cattle at Dodge City Kansas
Judge Henry Clay Plesants.

The SMITHSONIAN Institution National Anthropological Archives:

Washakie or Shoots the Buffalo Running.
Washakie's lodge & encampment.

The CAMPBELL Collection in the Western History Collections, University of Oklahoma Library:

Front Street, Dodge City.

The Original. ROBERT E. EAGAN Collection, Dodge City, Kansas.

The Long Branch Saloon on Front Street.

The KANSAS State Historical Society, Topeka, Kansas.

Merchants Hotel, Abiliene, Kansas.

WYOMING State Archives and Historical Department.

Rollins House, Court House in the Territory.

The WALTER BARNES STUDIO, Austin, Texas

The gun that killed Cullen Baker

INDEX

K

L

M

S

T

Edward Gaskell *publishers*
DEVON
UK